The Letters of

Anton Pavlovitch Tchehov

To

Olga Leonardovna Knipper

Tchehov and his wife in 1901, the year of their marriage.

The Letters of

Anton Pavlovitch Tchehov

To

Olga Leonardovna Knipper

Translated and edited by Constance Garnett

New Edition, with index

Benjamin Blom, Inc.
New York

NOTE

THIS translation is the only complete
authorised version in English of
*The Letters of A. P. Tchehov to O. L.
Knipper*; it was made by arrangement from the original copyright
text first published in Berlin
1924

First published 1925
Reissued 1966
by Benjamin Blom, Inc., Bronx, N.Y. 10452
New index © copyright 1966
by Benjamin Blom, Inc.

L.C. Cat. Card No. 65-16232

Printed in U.S.A. by
NOBLE OFFSET PRINTERS, INC.
NEW YORK 3, N. Y.

A Few Words

about Tchehov

by

Olga Knipper-Tchehov

A Few Words about Tchehov

Tchehov as I knew him was the Tchehov of the last six years of his life—growing weaker in body and stronger in spirit, taking a marvellously simple, wise and beautiful attitude to his bodily dissolution, because ' God has put a bacillus into me.'

The impression that those six years have left is one of anxiety, of rushing from place to place—like a sea-gull over the ocean, not knowing where to alight : the death of his father ; the sale of Melihovo ; the sale of his works to Marks ; the purchase of land near Yalta, building a house, and laying out a garden, and at the same time an intense attraction to Moscow, to the fresh, novel theatrical movement there ; the continual rushing between Moscow and Yalta, which already seemed like a prison to him ; marriage ; efforts to find a piece of land near Moscow, which he loved so touchingly ; the partial fulfilment of his dream—he was permitted by the doctors to spend the winter in Central Russia ; dreams of travelling along the northern rivers, to Solovki, to Sweden and Norway, to Switzerland ; and last dream of all, cherished at Badenweiler in the Black Forest just before his death—of returning to Russia through Italy, which allured him with its colours, its pulsing life and, above all, its music and flowers—and all this turmoil, these dreams, ending on July 2nd, 1904, in his own words, ' *Ich sterbe* ' (' I am dying').

His inner life throughout those six years was extraordinarily full, crowded, interesting and complex, so that its external disorganisation and discomfort lost their sting. We had no luck in finding lodgings, no luck with our summer holidays— for example, in 1902 Tchehov was forced, owing to my illness, to be content with a fortnight's trip on the Volga, as far as Perm, instead of the tour he dreamed of, and to spend the rest of the summer on the Stanislavskys' estate, where the family

3

so kindly lent us a little lodge during their absence abroad ; and in 1903, when we had decided to go to Switzerland, intense heat in Moscow made him reluctant to face a stifling train-journey, and after a delightful driving excursion to the Zveni-gorod and New Jerusalem Monasteries, and a stay on the Yakuntchikovs' lovely estate, we went back to Yalta.

Life had already exhausted him, but his spirit was not quenched, his genius did not flag.   During those years he wrote ' In the Ravine,' ' Three Sisters,' ' The Bishop,' ' Betrothed ' and ' The Cherry Orchard.'

We met first in 1898.   On September 9th Anton Pavlovitch came to one of the first rehearsals of ' The Sea-Gull ' by the Moscow Art Theatre Company.   It is hard to describe the immense excitement with which we actors were thrilled at our first meeting with our beloved writer, when we felt all the extraordinary subtle fascination of his personality, his sim-plicity, his incapacity, one may say, for ' teaching, directing.' We did not know what to say to him or how to address him. . . . And he looked at us, sometimes smiling, and sometimes with extraordinary gravity, with a sort of embarrassment, pinching his beard and flinging up his pince-nez.   He was puzzled how to answer some questions—while we had been thinking that the author would come and reveal all the mysteries of acting ' The Sea-Gull.'

When he was questioned he would answer in a strangely unexpected way, as it were, generally, irrelevantly, and we did not know how to take his remarks—in jest or in earnest.   But this was only for the first minute, and after a moment's thought one felt at once that this apparently casual utterance was making its way to one's brain and one's heart, and the whole essence of a character seemed to grow out of some scarcely perceptible trait.

For instance, some one asked what one was to make of a certain part.   ' The best you can,' answered Tchehov.   Another one asked him to define the character of the author in ' The Sea-Gull,' and the answer followed : ' Why, he wears check trousers.'   It took us some time to get used to the author's way of communicating with us.

The second time I saw Anton Pavlovitch he came to the rehearsal of ' Tsar Fyodor ' at the Hermitage, where we were intending to play that season. We were rehearsing in the evening in a damp, cold building, which was far from being finished, without a floor, with candle-ends stuck in bottles by way of lighting, and the actors wrapped up in great-coats. We rehearsed the scene of the reconciliation between Shuisky and Godunov, and it was agitating and thrilling to hear the sound of our own voices in that cold, damp, dark emptiness, filled with immense, gloomy, creeping shadows, and no walls or ceiling visible . . . and it was joyful to feel that in the dark, empty stalls he who was our ' soul,' beloved by all of us, was sitting listening to us.

Next day, in damp, rainy weather, Anton Pavlovitch went away to the south, to the warmth.

In the winter we played ' The Sea-Gull ' with great success, and in the spring of 1899 we performed the play before its author, who had come to Moscow again. It was a delightful, exquisite spring, full of thrilling experiences—the creation of our new theatre, which was unlike anything else, the achievements of our first season, the successes and failures of different performances, our extraordinary solidarity, and the anxiety and excitement we all felt before every performance. The great and exceptional success of ' The Sea-Gull,' the joyful sense of having our own special author whom we all loved tenderly—all this filled us with joy and enthusiasm. A group of the actors who took part in ' The Sea-Gull ' was photographed with Anton Pavlovitch in the middle apparently reading the play to them. There was already talk of producing ' Uncle Vanya ' the following season.

That spring I came to know Anton Pavlovitch better, and at once loved the whole atmosphere of his family. I had made his sister's acquaintance during the winter. I remember Vishnevsky brought her to my dressing-room at one of the performances of ' The Sea-Gull.' That spring I stayed for three days with the Tchehovs on their little estate, Melihovo, and everything there completely fascinated me : the house, the lodge where ' The Sea-Gull ' was written, the garden, the pond with the carp, the fruit-trees all in blossom, the calves and the ducks, and the village schoolmistress walking along the path with the schoolmaster—I could fancy it was Masha walking with Medvedenko ; I was fascinated by the kindness, the friendliness, the snugness, the witty, amusing talk. . . .

When the theatrical season was over I went for my holiday to the Caucasus, where my brother and his family were spending the summer. Our first letters date from this period. Before leaving Moscow I promised to come from the Caucasus to the Crimea, where Anton Pavlovitch had bought a piece of land and was building a house. We agreed by letter to meet on the steamer at Novorossiisk about July 20th, and travelled together to Yalta, where I stayed with the Sredins, who were intimate friends of all my family, while he stayed at the Hotel Marino on the sea-front. He went every day to superintend the building of his house at Autka, and did not get proper meals, for he never thought about food, tired himself out, and however much the Sredins and I tried on various pretexts to invite him so as to see that he was properly fed, we were rarely successful : Anton Pavlovitch disliked paying visits, and avoided dining away from home, though he liked the Sredins. They were always so informal and hospitable, and all the musical, artistic and literary people visited the Sredins (Gorky, Naidyonov, Arensky, Vasnetsov, Madame Yermolov).

The place which Anton Pavlovitch had bought for his house was far from the sea, from the pier, from the town, and was in the fullest sense of the word a wilderness, with a few old pear-trees.

But through his efforts, through his great love for everything that the earth brings forth, this wilderness was gradually transformed into an exquisite, luxuriant, varied garden.

He superintended the building of the house himself, drove out and watched the progress of the work. In town he might often be seen at Sinani's, the bookshop on the sea-front. He had a great liking for Isaac Abramovitch Sinani and his family, and the bookseller was particularly devoted to him, and almost with reverence helped him in negotiations for the

purchase of land, supervising, giving good counsel, and carrying out every commission with touching readiness.

Near the shop was a seat—the famous seat at which all the
celebrities that visited Yalta met together, sat and chatted—
literary men, singers, artists and musicians. . . . In the
shop there was a book in which all these celebrities signed
their names (and Sinani was proud that all these distinguished
persons gathered there) ; in the shop or on the seat one learned
all the news, everything that happened both in little Yalta
and in the great world. And for some reason one was always
drawn to the dazzlingly white, sun-bathed sea-front, to breathe
there the warm, stimulating fragrance of the sea, to gaze,
screwing up one's eyes, and smiling at the blue glitter of the
water ; one was drawn to greet the bookseller and to exchange
a few sentences with him, to look at the shelves, to see whether
there were any new books, to learn whether there were any
new arrivals, to listen to innocent gossip.

In August, Anton Pavlovitch and I set out for Moscow
together and drove as far as Bakhchisaray over the mountain
Ai-Petri. . . . It was delightful being borne along on soft
springs, breathing the air laden with the fragrance of pines,
chatting in the charming, amusing Tchehov style, and dozing
when the southern sun was scorching and overwhelmed one
with sultry heat. . . . It was delightful to drive through the
picturesque Kokkoz valley, which is full of peculiar fascination
and charm. . . .

The highroad passed at a little distance from the district
hospital. On the verandah there stood a group of people who
waved their hands frantically at us, and seemed to be shouting
to us. . . . We passed them, deep in some conversation, and,
though we looked and saw the people gesticulating, we did not
imagine it could have anything to do with us and decided that
they were lunatics. Later on it appeared that they were not
lunatics but a party of Yalta doctors of our acquaintance,
who were at the hospital for some consultation and did their
utmost to stop us. . . . This incident became the subject of
endless anecdotes and chaff.

Anton Pavlovitch did not stay long in Moscow, but returned

to Yalta at the end of August.   On September 3rd we began
an interchange of letters, which continued till the end of
March 1900, when the Art Theatre Company decided to go
to the Crimea to act ' The Sea-Gull,' ' Uncle Vanya,' Hauptmann's ' Lonely Lives ' and Ibsen's ' Hedda Gabler.'

I arrived in Holy Week with Tchehov's sister, and how snug
and warm it seemed in the new house which was being built
in the summer ! . . . Everything interested me, every trifle :
Anton Pavlovitch loved walking about showing things and
describing what he had not yet but would have in time ; he
was particularly eager about the garden, the planting of fruit-
trees. . . .

With the help of his sister, Mariya Pavlovna, he drew a plan
of the garden, marking where every tree, every seat was to go,
ordering trees and bushes from all parts of Russia, making
espalier fences of pear- and apple-trees, and in the end he had
magnificent crops of peaches, apricots, cherries, apples and
pears.   With tender care he watched over a birch-tree, which
reminded him of Northern Russia, pruned his standard roses,
and was very proud of them, and tended the eucalyptus
planted by his favourite seat.   Unluckily, however, neither
the eucalyptus nor the birch-tree did well—there was a storm,
a squall of wind broke the fragile white tree which, of course,
could not develop its natural strength and power of resistance
in an alien soil.   The avenue of acacias grew up incredibly fast ;
tall and supple, at the slightest breeze they seemed to hesitate,
bowed their heads and drew themselves up again, and there
was something weird, restless and disconsolate about their
movements. . . . Tchehov could always see them from the
big French window of his study.   There were Japanese trees,
too, a spreading plum-tree with red leaves, huge currants, vines
and almond-trees, and pyramidal poplars—all these did well and
grew with amazing rapidity, thanks to Anton Pavlovitch's
loving eye.   The only trouble was the continual shortage of
water, until Autka was joined to Yalta and it was possible
to have water laid on.

In the mornings Anton Pavlovitch usually sat in the garden,

and with him his adjutants—two stray mongrels who had very quickly made themselves at home, thanks to his friendliness, and two cranes with clipped wings who always followed people about but never allowed themselves to be touched. These cranes were particularly devoted to Arseny, who was both porter and gardener, and were much depressed when he went out. Every one in the house knew when Arseny came back from the town by the shrieks of those grey birds and the strange antics, something like a waltz, with which they expressed their joy.

Gorky, who was in those days soaring into fame with the speed and brilliance of a rocket, was also staying in Yalta. He used to visit Tchehov and to give us wonderful enthralling and vivid descriptions of his wanderings. He himself and all that he told us seemed so fresh and original, and we would sit silent in the study and listen and listen.

That Holy Week—my week of holiday—in those quiet, cosy surroundings passed rapidly, and I had to go to Sevastopol, where the Art Theatre Company was staying. I remember the feeling of loneliness that came over me when I found myself alone in a hotel room, on Easter-night too, and after the warmth and friendliness of the Tchehov household. . . . But we had to get to work again at once ; Anton Pavlovitch arrived, and life was full of movement once more. . . . It was a kind of spring festival.

We went on to Yalta, and there the festival was even more brilliant, we were almost smothered in flowers. . . . And the festival was crowned with a gorgeous entertainment on the roof of the hospitable Madame Tatarinov, who took so warm an interest in our youthful theatre, and did not know how to express her admiration for Stanislavsky and Nemirovitch-Dantchenko, who had founded it. The actors and actresses were frequently at Tchehov's house, dined there, sauntered about the garden, sat in his cosy study—and how Anton Pavlovitch enjoyed it all ! He so loved a life of gaiety and movement, and we were at that time all so full of hope, so brimming over, so joyful !

I was sad to leave the south, the sun and Tchehov, and the

festive atmosphere . . . but I had to go to Moscow for rehearsals. Soon Anton Pavlovitch, too, came to Moscow ;
Yalta seemed to him empty after the life and movement
brought into it by the visit of our company, but in Moscow he
felt ill and quickly returned to the south.

At the end of May I went with my mother to the Caucasus,
and what was my surprise and joy when in the Tiflis-Batum
train I met Tchehov, Gorky, Vasnetsov and Dr. Alexin on
their way to Batum.   We travelled together for six hours, as
far as the station Mihailovo, where my mother and I had to
change.

In July I stayed with the Tchehovs at Yalta.

Our correspondence was renewed after my departure to
Moscow at the end of August, and continued until Anton
Pavlovitch arrived in Moscow on October 23rd with the play
' Three Sisters.'   In the middle of December he went to Nice,
where he stayed for about three months.   All this time he
was much concerned about the progress of the rehearsals of
' Three Sisters.'

In Moscow he had seen the performance of ' When We Dead
Awaken ' ; Tchehov looked somewhat critically and ironically
at Ibsen's work—he thought it involved, artificial and intel-
lectualised.   He was rather against our acting Ostrovsky's
' The Snow-Maiden,' too ; he used to say that we ought not as
yet to produce such plays, but to confine ourselves to plays of
the class of ' Lonely Lives.'   At the beginning of April I went
for a brief visit to Yalta.

In the middle of May, Anton Pavlovitch came to Moscow.
On May 25th we were married and went by the Volga, the Kama
and the White River to Ufa, which is six hours by rail from
the Sanatorium at Axyonovo.   On the way we stopped at
Nizhni-Novgorod to visit Gorky, who was forbidden by police
order to leave that town.   By the advice of Dr. Dolgopolov
we changed to another steamer at the landing-stage *Pyany
Bor* (Drunken Market) on the Kama—this was a mistake ; we
had to wait for twenty-four hours, and to sleep on the floor in
a peasant's hut some miles from the landing-stage ; and we
could not sleep because there was no telling when the steamer

for Ufa would come. Several times in the night and early
morning I went out and watched for a steamer. That night,
remote from all civilisation, the grand, silent night, full of
serene gravity, weird beauty and significance, and the quiet
daybreak, made a great impression upon Anton Pavlovitch ;
and in the note-book in which he jotted down his ideas ' Pyany
Bor ' is mentioned.

At Axyonovo Tchehov was delighted with the scenery, the
long shadows in the steppes after six o'clock in the evening, the
snorting of the horses in the drove ; he liked the flowers and
the river Dyoma (familiar to readers of Aksakov), where we
once went fishing. The Sanatorium stood in a beautiful oak
forest, but was arranged in a primitive fashion, and he could
not live comfortably there. We even had to go to Ufa for
pillows. Anton Pavlovitch at first thought the koumiss very
nice, but was soon tired of it, and, without staying to the end
of our six weeks, we went home to Yalta by way of Samara,
down the Volga to Tsaritsyn and then to Novorossiisk.

From that time his life was divided between Moscow and
Yalta, and we were constantly parting and seeing each other
off at the Kursk station in Moscow, and at Sevastopol. He
had to live in Yalta, while his heart was drawn to Moscow.
He wanted to be nearer to life, to watch it and feel it and take
part in it ; he longed to see people, for, though they sometimes
tired him with their conversation, he could not live without
them, and he could never bring himself to refuse to see a man
who had come to talk to him.

What had attracted him at first in Yalta was the building
of his house, the laying out of his garden, the organisation of
his life, and later on he got used to the place, although he
called it his ' warm Siberia.' He was always yearning to be in
Moscow, yearning to be nearer the theatre, to be among the
actors, to be present at the rehearsals, to talk and jest, to look
at the performances ; he was fond of walking along Petrovka
and Kuznitsky, looking at the shops and the crowd. But just
at the time of year when life in Moscow is at its height he had
to be away from it. Only in 1903 the doctors allowed him
to spend the winter in Moscow, and how rejoiced and delighted

he was at the real Moscow winter with its snow, at being able
to come to the rehearsals ; he was as pleased as a child with his
new fur-coat and beaver-cap !

That winter we were looking for a little house with a piece
of land near Moscow, so that he might be able to spend future
winters, too, near his beloved Moscow (no one thought that
the end was so near). And one sunny February day we went
to Tsaritsyno to look at a little house and garden which was
for sale. Either because we missed the train, or because there
was no train, we had to drive back to Moscow—a distance of
about twenty miles. In spite of the sharp frost, Anton Pavlovitch greatly enjoyed watching the white plain sparkling in
the sun, and listening to the scrunch of the sledge-runners on
the hard, trodden snow. It was as though fate were gracious
to him, and resolved to bestow upon him during the last year
of his life the joys he prized most : Moscow, winter, the production of ' The Cherry Orchard,' and the people he so
loved. . . .

The production of ' The Cherry Orchard ' was difficult,
agonising, I might say. The producers and the author could
not understand each other, could not agree.

The first performance of ' The Cherry Orchard ' was the
occasion of an ovation to Tchehov on the part of his friends
and other literary men. Such things tired him ; he did not
like public ceremonies, and even refused to be present. He
was very anxious about the production of ' The Cherry Orchard,'
and did not arrive till the Third Act, and only came then after
we had sent to fetch him.

The first performance of ' The Sea-Gull ' was a triumph for
the theatre, and the first performance of his last play was also
a triumphant occasion, but how unlike were those two triumphs !
There was a feeling of anxiety, a sense of something ominous
in the air. I do not know, perhaps it is all coloured in this
way because of what followed—but that there was no moment
of unclouded joy that evening of January 17th is true. Tchehov
listened very gravely, very attentively to all the addresses read
in his honour, but from time to time he threw up his head with
his characteristic movement, and it seemed as though he were

taking a bird's-eye view of all that was going on, as though he
had no part in it; his face was lit up by a soft, twinkling
smile, and characteristic lines appeared round his mouth—he
must have heard something amusing which he would recall
afterwards, and at which he would invariably laugh.

Tchehov was always extremely fond of everything comic,
humorous; he liked listening to funny stories, and sitting in a
corner, his head propped on his hand, pinching his beard, he
would go off into such infectious laughter that I often left off
listening to the story and enjoyed it second-hand through him.
He was very fond of conjurors and clowns. I remember our
standing once a long time in Yalta watching the tricks of the
performing fleas, unable to tear ourselves away. He was fond
of making up all sorts of amusing fancies, and did so easily,
artistically and very funnily—it was a characteristic trait of
the whole Tchehov family. Thus, at the beginning of our
acquaintance, a great part was played by ' Nadenka '—Anton
Pavlovitch's imaginary wife or betrothed, and she figured in
everything, she came in at every moment, she even appears
in his letters.

Even a few hours before his death he made me laugh, in-
venting a story. It was at Badenweiler. After three painful
and anxious days he felt better towards evening. He sent me
to have a run about the park, as I had not left his side all those
days, and when I came in he was worried at my not going
down to supper, to which I answered that the gong had not
sounded yet. It appeared afterwards that we had simply
missed the gong, and he began making up a story describing
a very fashionable health-resort where there are a number of
fat, well-fed bankers and healthy, red-cheeked English and
American tourists, fond of good fare. Some have been for a
drive, some for a long walk or excursion into the neighbourhood,
and all meet together on their return, dreaming of a good and
satisfying meal after the fatigue of the day, and it suddenly
appears that the cook has run away and there is no dinner at
all! And he described how this stomach-felt blow finds expression in all these spoiled people. . . . I sat curled up on the
sofa, after the anxiety of the previous days, and laughed

heartily. I could not imagine that in a few hours I should be standing by his lifeless body !

During the last year of his life Tchehov had it in his mind to write a play. It was still indistinct, but he told me that the hero of the play was a scientific man, in love with a woman who either does not love him or is unfaithful to him, and he goes off to the far north. He conceived the third act like this : an ice-bound steamer, Aurora Borealis, the hero standing solitary on deck, complete stillness, peace and the grandeur of the night. And against the background of the northern lights he sees floating the shadow of the woman he loves. . . .

Tchehov passed quietly and peacefully into the other world. Early in the night he woke up, and for the first time in his life asked for a doctor to be fetched. The sense of something immense swooping down upon me gave to everything I did an extraordinary calm and precision, as though some one were guiding me with a sure hand. I only remember one awful moment of being overwhelmed : the sense of masses of people near me asleep in a great hotel and at the same time my complete isolation and helplessness. I remembered that two brothers, Russian students, with whom we were acquainted, were staying at the hotel, and I asked one of them to run for a doctor, and I went myself to break up ice to lay on the dying man's heart. I can hear now the sound of retreating footsteps on the crunching sand in the midst of the oppressive stillness of the unbearably sultry July night. . . .

The doctor came, and ordered champagne. Tchehov sat up and said aloud, significantly, to the doctor, ' *Ich sterbe* . . . ' (he knew very little German). Then he took the glass, turned to me, and with his wonderful smile said, ' It 's a long while since I have drunk champagne.' He calmly drank it to the last drop, quietly lay down on his left side, and soon afterwards sank into silence for ever. . . . And the fearful stillness of the night was only broken by a black moth of huge proportions which burst in like a whirlwind and dashed itself in terror against the electric light and fluttered about the room. . . .

The doctor went away ; in the midst of the stillness and sultriness of the night the cork shot out of the unfinished champagne bottle with a terrible noise. . . . It began to get light, and together with awakening nature I heard like the first requiem the tender, lovely singing of the birds and the strains of the organ floating in from the church hard by. No sound of human voice was heard, there was none of the bustle of daily life, nothing but peace, beauty and the grandeur of death. . . .

And to me, the consciousness of my sorrow, of the loss of a man like Tchehov, came only with the first sound of awakening life, with the coming of people, but what I felt and went through as I stood alone on the balcony and looked now at the rising sun and the melodious awakening of nature, now at the lovely, serene face of Anton Pavlovitch, smiling as though with the comprehension of something—this, I repeat, still remains an inscrutable mystery to me. . . .

There had been no such moment in my life, nor will be, I imagine.

OLGA KNIPPER-TCHEHOV.

The Letters

The Letters of

Anton Pavlovitch Tchehov

To Olga Leonardovna Knipper

*T*chehov saw Olga Leonardovna Knipper first on September 9, 1898, at a rehearsal of 'The Sea-Gull' at the Moscow Art Theatre, and shortly afterwards again in the part of Irina at a rehearsal of 'Tsar Fyodor.' He wrote to Suvorin: 'Irina, to my mind, was magnificent. Voice, dignity, earnestness—it was so good that it actually brought a lump into my throat. . . . Best of all was Irina. If I had stayed in Moscow, I should have fallen in love with that Irina.' During the following winter O. L. Knipper made friends with Tchehov's sister. Tchehov, who was in an advanced stage of consumption, was compelled by the doctors' orders to spend the winters in Yalta, but in the spring of 1899 he visited Moscow again, and a special performance of 'The Sea-Gull' was arranged that he might see it. Later in the spring the actress spent three days with the Tchehovs on their estate at Melihovo. When the summer holidays came, she went to stay with her brother in the Caucasus.*

1

June 16 (1899. *Melihovo*).

What does this mean ? Where are you ? You so persist-ently send me no news of yourself that we are lost in conjecture and are already beginning to think that you have forgotten us and have got married in the Caucasus. If you really have got married, to whom is it ? Have you made up your mind to leave the stage ?

The author is forgotten,—oh, how awful that is, how cruel, how treacherous !

All send you greeting. There is no news. And no flies even. There is nothing here. Even the calves are not biting.

I meant that day to see you off at the station, but luckily the rain prevented me.

I have been in Petersburg, I have had two photographs taken.   I was almost frozen there.   I shall not go to Yalta before the beginning of July.

With your permission I press your hand warmly and wish you all things good.

Yours A. TCHEHOV.

2

July 1 (1899.   *Moscow*).

Yes, you are right ; the author Tchehov has not forgotten the actress Knipper.   What is more, your suggestion of a journey together from Batum to Yalta seems to him enchanting.[1]   I will come, but on condition, first, that, on getting this letter, without a moment's delay you telegraph approximately which day you intend to leave Mtshet,[2] you will keep to this form : ' Moscow, Little Dmitrovka, Sheshkov's, Tchehov, Twentieth.'   That means that you will leave Mtshet for Batum on the 20th of July.   Secondly, on condition that I go straight to Batum and meet you there without going to Tiflis.   Thirdly, that you will not turn my head.   Vishnevsky regards me as a very sober-minded man and I should not like to let him see me as weak as every one else.

When I get a telegram from you, I 'll write to you, and everything will be excellent ; meanwhile I send you a thousand sincere good wishes and warmly press your hand.   Thanks for your letter.

Yours A. TCHEHOV.

We are selling Melihovo.   My Crimean estate Kutchukoy [3] is

[1] O. L. wrote, June 22: ' I thought that the author Tchehov had forgotten the actress Knipper—it seems then that you think of me sometimes. . . . You ought to come here, Anton Pavlovitch, it really is nice, and from here we might travel together to Batum and Yalta ; what do you say ? '

[2] The ancient capital of Georgia, near which O. L. was staying with her brother.

[3] Tchehov had bought very cheaply six acres of land and a little Tatar cottage near Kekeneiz.

wonderful now in the summer, so they write to me. You must come and stay there.

I have been in Petersburg, and there had two photographs taken. They have turned out pretty well. I am selling copies at a rouble each. I have already sent Vishnevsky five on credit.

It would suit me best of all if you would telegraph 'Fifteenth,' and in any case not later than the twentieth.

3

TELEGRAM

Moscow, July 8 (1899).

Going to Taganrog important business will be Novorossiisk Sunday seventeenth will there meet on steamer.

4

July 8 (1899. *Moscow*).

I write this to explain my telegram. About the 15th of July I have to be in Taganrog on important business. I shall not have time to be in Batum by the 17th. I will leave Taganrog on the 17th and be at Novorossiisk on the 18th, there we will meet on the steamer. If anything detains you at Mtshet or Batum even for a day, and you do not set off from Batum on the 17th, telegraph to me : Taganrog, Tchehov.

On Saturday, the 17th, a good steamer leaves Batum.

I have no luck. My proofs [1] are not sent regularly from Petersburg, I am staying in Moscow, there's nowhere to dine, it's dull at the Aquarium,[2] and so on and so on.

I escape from Moscow on the 12th. I shall be in Taganrog on the 14th.

And so, in case you change your plans, telegraph to Taganrog.

Till the 18th ! We will have some wine on the steamer.

Yours A. TCHEHOV.

[1] Tchehov was correcting the proofs of the complete edition of his works to be published by Marks.
[2] The summer garden.

Nobody could live worse, more piggishly than Moscow people do in the summer. There are no entertainments but the Aquarium and the Farce Theatre, and in the streets every one is gasping from the asphalt. They are boiling asphalt just under my window; I can hardly breathe for the fumes from it and N.'s conversation.

Tchehov and O. L. Knipper met at Novorossiisk on July 18, *as arranged, and went by steamer to the Crimea; the latter then stayed with her friends the Sredins in Yalta, where she saw a great deal of Tchehov, and with him early in August travelled to Moscow.*

5

ON A VISITING CARD

(*Aug.* 1899.   *Moscow.*)

I have a business interview at 2 o'clock. I will be with you to dinner after 3, say between 3.30 and 4 o'clock.

A. TCHEHOV.

6

ON A VISITING CARD

(*Aug.* 1899.   *Moscow.*)

To-day I am not going out, but shall come at 7 o'clock nevertheless.

Tchehov spent about three weeks in Moscow, and returned to Yalta towards the end of August 1899. *He did not see O. L. Knipper again till the end of March, or beginning of April,* 1900.

7

Sept. 3 (1899.   *Yalta*).

Dear actress, I answer all your questions.[1] I had a good journey. My fellow-travellers let me have a lower seat, after-

---

[1] O. L. wrote, Aug. 29: ' In my thoughts I went with you. Were you all right ? You weren't frozen ? And were your fellow-travellers boring or tolerable ? You see what a lot of questions I ask you. Shall

wards it came about that there were only two of us left in the compartment—a young Armenian and I. Several times in the day I had tea, three glasses each time, with lemon, and drank it sedately, without hurrying over it. I ate up everything in the basket. But I think that carrying on with a basket and racing about the station after boiling water is not quite dignified, it's undermining the prestige of the Art Theatre. As far as Kursk it was cold, then it began to get warm, and by Sevastopol it was quite hot. In Yalta I am staying in my own house, guarded by the faithful Mustafa.[1] I don't dine every day, because it's a long way [2] to go into the town and cooking over an oil-stove is lowering our prestige again. I have bread and cheese in the evening. I see Sinani. I have already been twice to the Sredins; they looked with feeling at your photograph, they have eaten the sweets. Leonid Valentinovitch [3] is feeling tolerably well. I am not drinking Narzan. What else? I scarcely go into the garden at all, but sit indoors and think of you. And as I passed Bakhchisaray I thought of you and remembered our journey together. Dear, marvellous actress, wonderful woman, if only you knew how delighted I was with your letter. I bow down very low to you, so low that my forehead touches the bottom of my well, which is forty feet deep now. I have grown used to being with you, and now I cannot reconcile myself to the thought that I shall not see you again till the spring; I am raging—in fact, if Nadenka found out what is going on in my heart there would be a to-do.

I have an answer? And did the neat little basket of provisions come in useful and did you eat the sweets? There, I won't go on, I'm boring you. No doubt you have revived in the south; after our damp, and cold, and leaden skies—to see the kindly southern sun and the sparkling sea—why, it would make one's spirits rise at once. You are superintending the building, going to Sinani's on the sea-front, drinking Narzan, all as before, only without the actress Knipper. . . . Give my love to the Sredins, you do go to see them, don't you? And do you dine every day? Mind you feed properly.'

[1] A Turk, at that time caretaker of the house that was being built for Tchehov.

[2] It was about a mile and a half from Tchehov's house at Autka to the sea-front of Yalta.

[3] Dr. Sredin, who was in consumption.

It is glorious weather in Yalta, only for the last two days, for no rhyme or reason, it has been raining, it 's muddy and one has to wear goloshes. It is so damp that centipedes are crawling over the walls and toads and young crocodiles hopping about the garden. The green monster [1] in the flower-pot that you gave me and I brought here successfully is sitting in the garden now basking in the sun.

A squadron has arrived. I look at it through my field-glasses.

There is an operetta at the theatre. The performing fleas continue to serve the sacred cause of art : I have no money. Visitors come often. On the whole it 's dull, and an idle, aimless dulness.

Well, I warmly press and kiss your hand. Be well, merry, happy, work, skip about, be enthusiastic, sing and, if possible, don't forget the retired author, your devout admirer.

A. TCHEHOV.

8

Sept. 9 (1899. Yalta).

I have received the note, the scent and the sweets.[2] Greetings, dear, splendid, precious actress ! Greetings, my faithful fellow-traveller to Ai-Petri and to Bakhchisaray ! Greetings, my joy !

Masha tells me that you haven't had my letter. How 's that ? Why ? I sent you a letter long ago, immediately after reading yours.

How are you ? How is your work ? How are the rehearsals going ? Is there no news ?

My mother and sister have come. We are gradually settling into the big house. It begins to be tolerable.

There 's a telephone. I am so bored that I ring somebody

---

[1] A cactus—the Queen of the Night—which flowers once in four years —at night.

[2] O. L. wrote, Sept. 3 : ' I am cross and offended with you—you don't care to write to me, you have forgotten your actress ; well, so be it, then. All the same I am sending you some nice scent, perhaps you may remember me.'

up every hour. Bored without Moscow, bored without you,
dear actress. When shall we meet again ?

I have had a telegram from the Alexandrinsky Theatre.
They ask for ' Uncle Vanya.'

I am just off to the town and the bazaar. Be well, happy,
joyous ! Don't forget your author, don't forget me, or I 'll
drown myself here or marry a centipede.

I kiss your hand warmly, very warmly !!

Entirely yours A. TCHEHOV.

' Parshak ' [1] has just gone.

9

Sept. 29 (1899. *Yalta*).

I have received your sensible letter with a kiss on my right
temple and the other letter with the photographs. Thank you,
dear actress, thank you awfully. To-day your performance
begins, and so in gratitude for your letter, for your remembering me, I send you my congratulations on the beginning of the
season. I send you a million good wishes. I meant to send a
telegram to the directors with good wishes to all, but since they
don't write to me, since they have evidently forgotten me and
don't send me the report (which has appeared recently judging
from the newspapers), and as that Roxanova is still playing in
' The Sea-Gull '—I thought it better to make a show of being
offended—and so I send my good wishes only to you.

We have had rain, but now it is bright, cool weather. There
was a fire in the night, I got up and looked at the flames from
the verandah and felt terribly solitary. We are living in the
house now, we have dinner in the dining-room, there 's a
piano.

I have no money, absolutely none, and I do nothing but
hide from my creditors. And it will be so till the middle
of December when Marks will send.

I meant to write you something sensible, but I can't manage
to think of anything. You see my season has not begun, I
have nothing new or interesting to tell you, everything is just

---

[1] The nickname they gave to the dredging steamer.

as it was.   And there 's nothing I 'm looking forward to except bad weather, which is already close upon us.

They are producing ' Ivanov ' and ' Uncle Vanya ' at the Alexandrinsky.

Well, take care of yourself, dear actress, glorious woman, and God keep you.   I kiss both your hands and bow down to your little feet.   Don't forget.

Yours A. TCHEHOV.

10

Sept. 30 (1899.   Yalta).

At your command I hasten to answer your letter in which you ask me about Astrov's last scene with Yelena.[1]   You write that Astrov behaves to Yelena as a man passionately in love, ' clutches at his feeling like a drowning man at a straw.' But that 's not right, not right at all !   Astrov likes Yelena, she attracts him by her beauty, but in the last act already he knows that nothing will come of it, that Yelena is disappearing for ever, and he talks to her in that scene in the same tone as of the heat in Africa and kisses her quite casually, to pass the time.   If Astrov takes that scene violently, the whole mood of the fourth act—quiet and despondent—is lost.

I sent the Japanese massage to Vishnevsky by Prince Shahovskoy.   Let him (Vishnevsky) show it to his Swede.

It has suddenly turned cold in Yalta, there 's a wind blowing from Moscow.   Ah, how I long to come to Moscow, dear actress !   Your head is turned, though, you have caught the infection, you are in a fever—you have no thoughts now for me.   You can write to me now : ' We are making a noise in the world, my friend, we are ! '

As I write to you, I keep looking out of my huge window :

[1] O. L. wrote, Sept. 26, apropos of the rehearsals of ' Uncle Vanya ': ' I am disturbed by a remark of Stanislavsky's about Astrov's last scene with Yelena ; according to him, Astrov behaves to her like a man passionately in love, catches at his feeling like a drowning man at a straw.   I think that if that were so, Yelena would have gone to him and would not have had the spirit to answer : " How absurd you are ! " . . . On the contrary, he talks to her extremely cynically and even seems to be jeering at his own cynicism.   Is that right or not ?   Tell me, author, tell me at once.'

there 's an immense view, such a view that one simply can't describe it.   I shan't send you my photograph till I receive yours, O serpent !   I have never called you a ' little snake,' as you write.[1]

You are a serpent, a huge serpent, not a little snake.   Isn't that flattering ?

Well, I press your hand and bow low to you, tapping my forehead on the floor, honoured lady.

I am going to send you another present soon.

Yours A. TCHEHOV.

11

Oct. 4 (1899.   *Yalta*).

Dear actress, you have exaggerated everything dreadfully in your letter, that 's evident, as the newspapers are quite good-natured about your first performance.   In any case, two or three unsuccessful productions are not reason enough for being dismal and not sleeping all night.[2]   Art—and particularly the stage—is not a field in which you can go straight on without ever having a stumble.   You have many more unsuccessful days—and whole unsuccessful seasons—before you, there will be great mistakes and immense disappointments—you must be prepared for all that, you have to expect it and in spite of everything to plough on obstinately, fanatically, and of course you are right. . . .

For the last three or four days I have been ill, now I am kept indoors.   There are insufferable crowds of visitors.   Their idle, provincial tongues wag and I am bored.   I rage and rage, and envy the rat that lives under the floor of your theatre.

[1] O. L. wrote, Sept. 26 : ' Aren't you ashamed, you bad man, to call me a little snake ? '

[2] O. L. wrote at 4 o'clock in the morning, Sept. 29 : ' I can't sleep. The " Terrible " has been performed, and . . . all, most likely, are sick at heart.   I can't see anything clearly yet, but I am conscious that it ought to have been different on the opening day of the second season of the Art Theatre. . . . We were received coldly, feeling behind the scenes was gloomy. . . . I feel so sore, so heavy-hearted, I can't tell you.   Now it 's all chaos, and to-morrow it will be worse still. . . . I can imagine how all the papers will begin tearing us to pieces to-morrow—many of them have been waiting ever so long for a chance to fall upon us.'

Your last letter you wrote at four o'clock in the morning. If it seems to you when ' Uncle Vanya ' is acted that it is not as successful as you would wish, please go to bed and sleep soundly. Success has spoiled you all and now you can't put up with ordinary working days.

I believe Davydov is to play Uncle Vanya in Petersburg and he 'll act it well, but the play is certain to be a failure.

How are you ? Write a little more. You see I write nearly every day.

The author writes so often to the actress — perhaps my pride may begin to suffer. Actresses have to be kept strictly in order and not written to. I am always forgetting that I am inspector of actresses.[1] Keep well, my angel.

Yours A. Tchehov.

12

Oct. 7 (1899. *Yalta*).

Dear, illustrious, wonderful actress, I send you a case to keep jewels and gold things in. Accept it !

In your last letter you complain that I don't write, though I send you letters very often, not every day, it 's true, but oftener than I get them from you.

This letter will be given you by **Dr. P. I. Kurkin,** the author of the map which appears in ' Uncle Vanya.' He has been staying with us, and if you like will tell you about our new house and our old life.

Be well, merry, happy, sleep sound, and God keep you.

Yours A. Tchehov.

13

Oct. 30 (1899. *Yalta*).

Dear actress, splendid little creature ! You ask whether I shall be excited.[2] But you see I only heard properly that

---

[1] He had been called in jest ' the inspector of the actresses of the Art Theatre.'

[2] O. L. wrote, Oct. 23 : ' We have had our first dress rehearsal of " Uncle Vanya," to-morrow there 'll be the second, on the 25th the third, and on the 26th we play it. I have not seen the scenery of the third act

'Uncle Vanya' was to be given on the 26th from your letter which I got on the 27th. The telegrams began coming on the evening of the 27th when I was in bed. They send them on to me by telephone. I woke up every time and ran in the dark with bare feet to the telephone and got very much chilled; then I had scarcely dozed off when the bell rang again and again. It's the first time that my own fame has kept me awake. The next evening when I went to bed I put my slippers and dressing-gown beside my bed, but there were no more telegrams.

The telegrams were full of nothing but the number of calls and the brilliant success, but there was a subtle, almost elusive something in them from which I could conclude that the state of mind of all of you was not exactly of the very best. The newspapers I have received to-day confirm my conjectures.

Yes, dear actress, ordinary, medium success is not enough now for all you artistic players; you want an uproar, big guns, dynamite. You have been thoroughly spoiled, deafened by constant talk about successes, full and not full houses: you are already poisoned with that drug and in another two or three years you will all be good for nothing! So much for you!

How are you getting on? How are you feeling? I am still in the same place and am still the same: I am working and planting trees.

But visitors have come, I can't go on writing. Visitors have been here for more than an hour. They have asked for tea. They have sent for the samovar. Oh, how dreary!

Don't forget me and don't let your friendship for me die away, so that we may go away together somewhere this summer. Good-bye for the present. We shall most likely not meet before April. If you would all come in the spring to Yalta, you could

yet, it's not ready. We are tremendously excited. All the tickets are sold. The programmes will be very interesting—the scenery of the first act, Uncle Vanya's reckoning-frame and the portrait of Tchehov; they say Simov has done it well, I haven't seen it yet. In the second act there will be real trees rustling behind the scenes, the thunder and lightning is wonderful. I 'm afraid to speak of the acting before the first night; I feel that everything will go well and the audience will be pleased. You will be excited, of course? So you ought to be; do share our excitement. I shall go straight from the theatre to send you a telegram.'

act here and also take a rest. That would be wonderfully artistic.

A visitor will take this letter and drop it into the post-box.

I press your hand warmly. My greetings to Anna Ivanovna [1] and your uncle [2] the officer.

Yours A. TCHEHOV.

Actress, write for the sake of all that's holy, I'm so dull. I might be in prison and I rage and rage.

14

Nov. 1 (1899. Yalta).

I understand your mood,[3] dear actress, I understand it very well, but yet in your place I would not be so desperately upset. Both the part of Anna [4] and the play itself are not worth wasting so much feeling and nerves over. It is an old play. It is already out of date, and there are a great many defects in it ; if more than half the performers have not fallen into the right tone, then it is naturally the fault of the play. That's one thing, and the second is, you must once and for all give up being worried over successes and failures. Don't let that concern you. It's your duty to go on working steadily day by day, quite quietly, to be prepared for mistakes which are inevitable, for failures—in short, to do your job as actress and let other people count the calls before the curtain. To write or to act, and to be conscious at the time that one is not doing

[1] O. L.'s mother.

[2] Alexandr Ivanovitch Zalts—an army captain, O. L.'s maternal uncle.

[3] O. L. wrote, Oct. 27 : 'I ought not to write to you to-day, dear Anton Pavlovitch. There is such gloom, such horror in my soul that I can't describe it. Yesterday we played "Uncle Vanya"! The play was a tremendous success, it captured the whole house, there can be no two opinions about that. I haven't closed my eyes all night and to-day I keep crying. I acted inconceivably badly—why? A great deal I understand, a great deal I don't. So many thoughts are racing through my head at this minute that I can hardly tell you clearly. They say I acted well at the dress-rehearsal—now I don't believe that. My God, how wretched I am! Everything is shattered.'

[4] A slip of the pen for Yelena. Anna was O. L.'s part in Hauptmann's 'Lonely Lives,' which was being rehearsed at the same time as 'Uncle Vanya.' The whole letter refers only to 'Uncle Vanya.'

the right thing—that is so usual, and for beginners so profitable ! The third thing is that the director has telegraphed that the second performance went magnificently, that every one played splendidly and that he was completely satisfied.

Masha [1] writes that it is not nice in Moscow, that I must not come, and I so long to get away from Yalta where I am already bored by my solitude. I am a Johannes [2] without a wife, not a learned Johannes and not a virtuous one.

Remember me to Nikolay Nikolayevitch [3] of whom you write in your letter. Keep well ! Write and tell me that you have quite recovered and that all is going capitally. I press your hand.

Yours A. TCHEHOV.

15

Nov. 19 (1899. *Yalta*).

Dear actress, Vishnevsky writes that you would give no more than three kopecks to see me now—so you told him. Thank you, you are very lavish. But a little time will pass, another month or two—and you will not give even two kopecks !

How people change !

And meanwhile I would give seventy-five roubles to see you.

But fancy ! I can't write : they are ringing the alarm bell, there's a fire here in Autka. There's a high wind.

Keep well ! I am off to the fire.

Yours A. TCHEHOV.

16

Dec. 8 (1899. *Yalta*).

We are cut off from the world ; the telegraph wire is broken everywhere, the post has not come. For three days there has been a storm raging—such as has never been known, so they say.

---

[1] His sister, Mariya Pavlovna Tchehov.

[2] The hero of Hauptmann's ' Lonely Lives.'

[3] N. N. Sokolovsky, a professor of the Moscow Conservatoire and a great friend of the Knippers.

Dear actress, enchanting woman, I don't write to you because I have set myself to work [1] and don't allow myself to be distracted.

I shall have a breathing-space in the holidays and then I shall write longer letters.

Do write and tell me seriously, in earnest : is the company coming to Yalta or not ?   Is it definitely settled or not ?

You like to keep cuttings from the papers ; I send you two. There is a furious wind.

Do you see Prince Shahovskoy ?   In his life there is an up-heaval going on that is rather interesting.

Well, may you live and keep well, desperate actress, I wish you health and wealth and gaiety—everything that your little heart desires.   I warmly press your hand and bow down to your little feet.

Yours A. TCHEHOV.

17

Jan. 2, 1900 (*Yalta*).

Greetings, dear actress ! Are you angry that I haven't written for so long ?   I have written often, but you didn't get my letters because our mutual friend intercepted them in the post.

I wish you a happy New Year.   I really do wish you happiness and bow down to your little feet.   Be happy, wealthy, healthy and gay.

We are getting on pretty well ; we eat a great deal, chatter a great deal, laugh a great deal and often talk of you.   Masha will tell you when she goes back how we spent Christmas.

I have not congratulated you on the success of ' Lonely Lives.'   I still dream that you will all come to Yalta, that I shall see ' Lonely Lives ' on the stage and congratulate you really from my heart.   I wrote to Meierhold and urged him not to be too violent in the part of a nervous man.   The immense majority of people are nervous, you know ; the greater number suffer and a small proportion feel acute pain ; but

---

[1] Tchehov was at work on the story ' In the Ravine.'

where—in streets and in houses—do you see people tearing about, leaping up and clutching at their heads ? Suffering ought to be expressed as it is expressed in life—that is, not by the arms and legs, but by the tone and expression ; not by gesticulation, but by grace. The subtle emotions of the soul natural to educated people must be expressed subtly too. You will say—stage conditions. No conditions justify falsity.

My sister tells me that you played Anna exquisitely. Ah, if only the Art Theatre would come to Yalta !

' Novoye Vremya ' praised your company highly. There is a change of tactics in that quarter, evidently they are going to praise you all in Lent.

My story, a very terrible one, will be in the February number of ' Zhizn.' There are a great many characters, there is scenery too, there 's a crescent moon, there 's a bittern that cries far, far away : ' Boo-oo ! boo-oo ! ' like a cow shut up in a shed. There 's everything.

Levitan [1] is with us. Over my fireplace he has painted a moonlight night in the hayfield, cocks of hay, forest in the distance, a moon reigning on high above it all.

Well, good health, dear, wonderful actress, I am pining for you.

Yours A. Tchehov.

And when are you going to send me your photograph ? What barbarity !

18

Jan. 22 (1900.   Yalta).

Dear actress, on Jan. 17th I received telegrams from your mother and your brother, from your uncle Alexandr Ivanitch (signed Uncle Sasha) and from N. N. Sokolovsky. Be so good as to give them my warm thanks and the expression of my sincere feeling for them.

Why don't you write ? What has happened ? Or are you already so fascinated by the moiré silk lining on the revers ? Well, there is no help for it. God be with you !

I am told that in May you 'll be in Yalta. If that is settled,

----

[1] A well-known artist, an intimate friend of Tchehov's.

why shouldn't you make inquiries beforehand about the theatre ? The theatre here is let on lease and you could not get hold of it without negotiating with the tenant Novikov, the actor. If you commission me to do so, I would perhaps talk to him about it.

The 17th, my name-day and the day of my election to the Academy, passed dingily and gloomily, as I was unwell. Now I am better, but my mother is ailing. And these little troubles completely took away all taste for a name-day or election to the Academy, and they, too, have hindered me from writing to you and answering your telegram at the proper time.

Mother is getting better now.

I see the Sredins at times. They come to see us and I go to them very, very rarely, but still I do go. Doctor Rozanov (one of those lunatics we saw at Kokkoz) will soon be in Moscow and will go to see Masha ; arrange that he should go to the theatre.

So then you are not writing to me and not intending to write very soon, either. The moiré silk revers on that coat are to blame for all that. I understand you !

I kiss your hand.

Yours A. TCHEHOV.

19

Feb. 10 (1900. *Yalta*).

Dear actress, the winter is very long, I am not well, no one has written to me for nearly a whole month—and I had made up my mind that there was nothing left for me but to go abroad [1] where it is not so dull ; but now it has begun to be warmer and it 's better, and I have decided that I shall go abroad only at the end of the summer to the exhibition.[2]

And you, why are you depressed ? What are you depressed about ? You are living, working, hoping, drinking ; you

[1] O. L. wrote, Feb. 5 : ' What does this mean, dear author ? Yesterday I heard from Mariya Pavlovna that you are going abroad for the whole summer. That cannot be, that must not be, do you hear ? You only wrote that and have already forgotten it, haven't you ? It 's incredibly cruel to write such things. Answer me this very second that it 's not so, that we shall be together in the summer.'

[2] The International Exhibition in Paris.

laugh when your uncle reads aloud to you ; what more do you want ?   I am a different matter, I am torn up by the roots, I am not living a full life ; I don't drink, though I 'm fond of drinking ; I love excitement and don't get it—in fact, I 'm in the condition of a transplanted tree which is hesitating whether to take root or to begin to wither.   If I sometimes allow myself to complain of boredom, I have some grounds for doing so —but you ?   And Meierhold is complaining of the dulness of his life too.   Fie !   Fie !

By the way, about Meierhold, he ought to spend the whole summer in the Crimea.   His health needs it.   Only it must be for the whole summer.

Well, now I am all right again.   I am doing nothing because I intend to set to work.   I dig in the garden.   You write that for you little people the future is wrapped in mystery.   I had a letter from your chief, Nemirovitch, not long ago.   He writes that the company is going to be in Sevastopol, then in Yalta at the beginning of May.   In Yalta there will be five performances, then evening rehearsals.   Only the precious members of the company will remain for the rehearsals, the others can have a holiday when they please.   I trust that you are precious.   To the director you are precious, to the author you are priceless.   There 's a pun for a tit-bit for you.   I won't write another word to you till you send me your portrait.

I kiss your hand.

Yours ANTONIO ACADEMICUS.

In the spring the company will be in Harkov, too.   I will come and meet you there, only don't talk of that to any one. Nadyezhda Ivanovna [1] has gone to Moscow.

Thank you for your good wishes in regard to my marriage. I have informed my *fiancée* of your design of coming to Yalta in order to cut her out a little.   She said that if ' that horrid woman ' comes to Yalta, she will hold me tight in her embrace. I observed that to be embraced for so long in hot weather was not hygienic.   She was offended and grew thoughtful as though she were trying to guess in what surroundings I had picked up

---

[1] The mother of Dr. Sredin.

this *façon de parler,* and after a little while said that the theatre was an evil and that my intention of writing no more plays was extremely laudable, and asked me to kiss her. To this I replied that it was not proper for me to be so free with my kisses now that I am an academician. She burst into tears and I went away.

20

Feb. 14 (1900. *Yalta*).

Dear actress, the photographs are very, very good, especially the one in which you are leaning in dejection with your elbows on the back of a chair, which gives your discreetly mournful expression under which there lies hidden a little imp. The other is good too, but in it you are a little like a Jewess, a very musical person who attends a conservatoire, but at the same time is studying dentistry on the sly as a second string, and is engaged to be married to a young man in Mogilev and whose *fiancé* is a person like N. Are you angry? Really, really angry? [1] It's my revenge for your not signing them.

Of the seventy roses I planted in the autumn only three have not taken root. Lilies, irises, tulips, tuberoses, hyacinths are all pushing out of the ground. The willow is already green; the grass is luxuriant by the little seat in the corner. The almond-tree is in blossom. I have put little seats all about the garden, not grand ones with iron legs, but wooden ones which I shall paint green. I have made three bridges over the stream. I am planting palms. In fact, there are all sorts of novelties, so much so that you won't know the house or the garden or the street. Only the owner has not changed, he is just the same moping creature and devoted worshipper of the talents that reside by the Nikitsky Gate. I have heard no music nor singing since the autumn, I have not seen one interesting woman. How can I help being melancholy?

I had made up my mind not to write to you, but since you have sent the photographs I have taken off the ban and, here you see, I am writing. I will even come to Sevastopol, only, I repeat, don't tell that to any one, especially not to

_____

[1] This is in mimicry of a sentence in O. L.'s letter.

Vishnevsky. I shall be there *incognito*. I shall put myself down in the hotel-book Count Blackphiz.

I was joking when I said that you were like a Jewess in your photograph. Don't be angry, precious one. Well, herewith I kiss your little hand and remain unalterably

Yours A. TCHEHOV.

What is Ivan Tsinger [1] doing in your theatre ?

21

TELEGRAM

(Feb. 19, 1900.)   *Yalta.*

Sweets pocketbook [2] received thanks dear actress God give you health gladness you are kind jolly and clever spring birds singing in my garden camellia in flower.

22

March 26 (1900.   *Yalta*).

There is a feeling of black melancholy about your letter,[3] dear actress ; you are gloomy, you are fearfully unhappy—but not for long, one may imagine, as soon, very soon, you will be sitting in the train, eating your lunch with a very good appetite. It is very nice that you are coming first with Masha before all the others ; we shall at least have time to talk a little, walk a little, see things, drink and eat : only please don't bring Vishnevsky with you, or he will follow you and me about and not let us say one word to each other ; and he will bore us to death, reciting from ' Uncle Vanya ' all the time.

I haven't a new play, it 's a lie of the newspapers. They

---

[1] A Tolstoyan, brother of Prof. A. V. Tsinger, who was for a time a workman at the Moscow Art Theatre.

[2] O. L. wrote, Feb. 16 : ' Has Altschuller's wife given you a pocket-book ? I had quite forgotten that she was leaving to-day, and I wanted to send you something. I hadn't much time to consider, but I decided that for a man who is intending to buy up all the south coast of the Crimea the most suitable thing was a pocket-book, or you 'd have no-where to put your money. Was that right ? '

[3] O. L. wrote, March 22 : ' Oh, how dull life is, and duller than ever when one knows that the dulness comes from oneself.'

never do tell the truth about me. If I did begin a new play, of course the first thing I should do would be to inform you of the fact.

It 's windy here. The spring has not begun properly yet, but we go about without our goloshes and fur-caps. The tulips will be out soon, in a day or two. I have a nice garden, though it 's still untidy and full of rubbish—a dilettante garden.

Gorky is here. He is warm in his praises of you and your company. I will introduce him to you.

Oh dear ! Some one has arrived. A visitor. Good-bye for now, actress.

Yours A. TCHEHOV.

The Art Theatre Company came in April for Easter to Yalta to give a performance of ' Uncle Vanya.' O. L. arrived with Tchehov's sister a few days before the rest of the troupe and stayed with the Tchehovs. Then the company moved on to Sevastopol— returning to Moscow at the end of the month. Ten days later Tchehov went to Moscow for a fortnight.

23

May 20, 1900. (*Yalta.*)

Dear enchanting actress, greetings ! How are you ? How are you feeling ? I was very unwell on the way back to Yalta. I had a bad headache and temperature before I left Moscow. I confess I concealed it from you ; now I 'm all right.

How is Levitan ? I feel dreadfully worried at not knowing. If you have heard, please write to me.

Keep well and be happy. I heard Masha was sending you a letter and so I hasten to write these few lines.

Yours A. TCHEHOV.[1]

O. L. spent part of the summer with the Tchehovs. From this time a tone of intimate tenderness is given to the letters by the

[1] This is the last of the letters published in the edition of Tchehov's Collected Letters, of which a selection was published in English in 1920. The following letters have only been published this year (1924) in Berlin. —(*Translator's Note.*)

transition from the formal plural to the 2nd person singular throughout.

24

Aug. 9 (1900. Yalta).

My dear Olya, my joy, greetings ! I received a letter from you to-day, the first since you went away. I read it through, then read it over again and here I am writing to you, my actress. After seeing you off [1] I went to Kist's Hotel, and there I stayed the night ; next day, being bored and having nothing to do, I went to Balaclava. There I kept hiding from ladies who recognised me and wanted to get up an ovation to me, there I stayed the night and went on in the morning to Yalta in the Tavel.[2] The sea was fiendishly rough. Now I am settled in Yalta, I am dreary, cross and pining. Stanislavsky [3] was here yesterday. We talked of the play,[4] I promised it to him and undertook to finish it not later than September. You see how sensible I am.

I keep fancying that in a minute the door will open and you will come in. But you will not come in, you are now at rehearsals, or in Merzlyakovsky Place,[5] far from Yalta and from me.

Farewell, and may the heavenly powers and guardian angels keep you. Farewell, good little girl.

Your ANTONIO.

25

(Aug. 13, 1900. Yalta.)

My dear, glorious, magnificent actress, I am alive and well, I think of you, I dream and pine because you are not here. Yesterday and the day before I was at Gurzuf,[6] now I am again

[1] Tchehov had accompanied Olga Leonardovna in the train as far as Sevastopol.

[2] A small steamer.

[3] The stage name of Alexeyev, a founder, director, manager and actor of the Moscow Art Theatre.

[4] 'Three Sisters.'   [5] Where O. L. lived.

[6] At Gurzuf, about twelve miles from Yalta, Tchehov bought a small piece of land with a little house on the sea-shore. This little place now belongs to O. L. Knipper-Tchehov.

in Yalta, in my prison. A most cruel wind is blowing, the cutter is not going, the sea is tossing savagely, people are being drowned, there is still no rain and no rain, everything is dried up, everything is withering, in fact since you went away it has been perfectly horrible here. Without you I shall hang myself.

Be well and happy, my good little German. Don't be depressed, sleep soundly and write to me more often.

I kiss you warmly, warmly, four hundred times.

Your ANTONIO.

26

(*Aug.* 14, 1900. *Yalta.*)

My darling, I don't know when I am coming to Moscow,[1]— I don't know because, only fancy, I am actually writing a play[2] now. It is not a play, but a sort of tangle. There are a great many characters,—perhaps I shall get in a muddle and give it up.

The brown boots about which you ask haven't been brushed since the day I saw you off. And no one brushes me. I go about all covered with dust, fluff and feathers.[3]

Sonya and Volodya are still with us.[4] It is nasty, dry weather, the wind never stops. I am not in good spirits because I am bored.

Keep well, dear little German, don't be angry with me and don't be faithless to me. I kiss you warmly.

Your ANTONIO.

[1] O. L. wrote, Aug. 7 : ' Every one greeted me warmly (in the Moscow Art Theatre), every one asked about you, when you would be coming.' And Aug. 10 : ' I have kept the most important question till the last : when are you coming ?   Of course you must come.'

[2] ' Three Sisters.'

[3] O. L. wrote, Aug. 10 : ' How are you spending your days ? Are you bored by crowds of people ?   Do you go to the town in the evenings ? Do you have heart-to-heart talks with Madame Bonnier ?   How is your study getting on ?   Is it dusted ?   Do you get your coat brushed and your brown boots, or not ?   Are the cranes all right ?   So many questions— will you answer them ? '

[4] Sonya, short for Sofya Vladimirovna, the wife of Tchehov's brother Ivan ; Volodya, short for Vladimir, their son.

27

Aug. 17 (1900. *Yalta*).

Greetings, my dear, good little actress. I am writing my play, but visitors hinder me fiendishly. Yesterday from nine o'clock in the morning till evening, and to-day ever since dinner. Everything is in a muddle in my head, my mood is made petty, I am cross and every day I have to make a fresh start. The head-mistress of the Girls' High School has just come and with her two young ladies, relatives of hers. These came and sat in my study, but now they have gone down to tea.

Ekaterina Nikolayevna [1] is staying at the ' Russia.' They are expecting Nemirovitch.

It 's windy. The sea is rough. I have come out of my study into my bedroom and now I am writing at the window. If visitors don't spoil my mood, if I don't get cross, I shall finish the play between the 1st and 5th of September, that is, I shall write it and make a fair copy. And then I shall come to Moscow, most likely.

I have not had a line from you for ages.[2] It 's too bad, dear.

Take care of yourself and don't be depressed.

Your ANTON.

28

Aug. 18 (1900. *Yalta*).

My precious, I answer the questions that pop up out of your letter.[3] I am not working at Gurzuf but in Yalta, and I am cruelly hindered, horribly and meanly hindered. The play is in my head, is already coming out, has got into shape and is clamouring to be on paper, but no sooner do I sit down to write than the door opens and some ugly face pokes in. I don't

---

[1] Madame Nemirovitch-Dantchenko, the wife of a director of the Moscow Art Theatre.

[2] There had been no letter from O. L. on Aug. 11, 12 and 13.

[3] O. L. wrote, Aug. 14 : ' You are working now, then. In Gurzuf ? Write to me how the play is getting on and how you 're working— with energy, with ease ? Don't rage, don't be dull, don't fret. When we see each other we shall forget it all. . . . But when shall we see each other ? '

know how it will be, but the beginning has turned out fairly well, pretty smooth, I fancy.

Shall we see each other ? Yes, we shall see each other. When ? Early in September, in all probability. I am bored and cross. Money is going at a devilish rate, I am being ruined, I shall go broke. To-day there is the most cruel wind, a regular hurricane, the trees are parched.

One crane has flown away.

Yes, my dear actress, I could be as happy as a frisky foal now running about in the fields, by a wood, a stream, a herd of cattle. You know it sounds absurd, but it is two years since I have seen grass.[1] My darling, it is dreary.

Masha is going away to-morrow.

Well, take care of yourself. I don't see the Stanislavskys nor Madame Nemirovitch.

Your ANTONIO.

Vishnevsky does not write to me. I suppose he is angry. I will write him a horrid part to pay him out.

29

Aug. 20 (1900. *Yalta*).

My dear, what next ! ! ! You write that you have had only one letter from me as yet, while I write to you every day or almost every day ! What is the meaning of it ? My letters have never been lost.

Yesterday I went into the garden to rest a little, and all at once—oh horror !—there comes up to me a lady in grey, N. N. She talked all manner of twaddle to me and among other things gave me to understand that she could only be found at home between one and three o'clock. Only ! She said good-bye to me, then a little later came back again and said she was only at home from one to three. Poor dear, she is afraid I may bore her.

The play has begun well, I think, but I have cooled off to the

---

[1] O. L. wrote, Aug. 14 : ' Anton, my own, let us spend the coming summer somewhere here in the country—would you like it ? I keep thinking how wonderfully in keeping you are with that purely Russian nature, the breadth, the fields and meadows, the ravines and the snug shady little streams.'

beginning, it has all grown cheap to me—and now I don't know what to do. A play ought to be written, you know, without taking breath, and this is the first morning that I have been alone, that I have not been interrupted. But there, it's no matter.

You ought to find a wife for Uncle Sasha.[1]

When I come, let us go to Petrovskoye-Razumovskoye, only it must be for the whole day, and it must be very fine autumn weather, and you must not be depressed and must not repeat every minute that you must get back to a rehearsal. Madame Nemirovitch told me as a secret that her husband is coming here for a fortnight to work. At the end of the month. I shall cut away to Gurzuf so as not to hinder him.

It is autumn in Yalta already. Well, my darling, take care of yourself and write, write as long as it doesn't bore you. Good-bye, my precious, my angel, my lovely little German, I am hellishly dull without you.

Your ANTONIO.

30

Aug. 23 (1900. Yalta).

Greetings, my sweet! In your letter you are cross at my writing such short letters to you. But then I write so often! Stanislavsky was here yesterday. He stayed till 9 o'clock in the evening, then we went (or to be more correct I took him) to the Girls' High School, to the head-mistress's. In the High School there is a pretty Hungarian girl,[2] who speaks Russian

---

[1] O. L. wrote, Aug. 16: '. . . I feel depressed—I have just heard Uncle Sasha's confession—dissatisfaction, consciousness of a life foolishly misspent, descriptions of his drinking-bouts and debaucheries, painful seeking for a little bit of something pure and humane in himself, remorse, a desire to reform, and all this in a hollow monotonous voice by the light of a single candle. On the table, sausage and a plate of gooseberries which I ate as I listened to him. I am awfully sorry for him, he talks of his revolver. . . . He kept asking whether I believed in him. . . . I am wretched at not having been gentler with him. . . . He blurted out that he would like to tell you all about it, that perhaps you were the only person who would understand him better than I do.'

[2] M. B. Toiman, afterwards teacher of the harp in the Petersburg Conservatoire.

very funnily ; she played on the harp and made us laugh.   We stayed till 12 o'clock.

To-day I went to the town on business, met Verotchka there and brought her home to dine with us.   This Verotchka has come from Harkov.   She is an heiress.   You see what a Don Juan I am !

I am writing a play, but I am afraid it will be dull.   I shall write it and if I don't like it I shall lay it aside and put it away till next year or till I feel inclined to write it again.   One season will pass without a play from me—there 's no harm in that. However, we will talk about that when I am in Moscow.

There is still no rain.   We are having a barn built in the yard.   The crane is depressed.   I love you.

Will you come to the station to meet me ?   And where am I to stay ?   In what hotel—comfortable and close to you and not too dear ?   Think about that, and write to me, my darling.

It is quiet and peaceful in our house, I abide in lovingkindness with my mother, I don't quarrel.

You go to an operetta with Vishnevsky ?   H'm. . . .

Write to me a little oftener, don't be stingy.   I will reward you for it, I will love you as fiercely as an Arab.   Farewell, Olya, keep well and happy.   Don't forget me, write and think a little oftener of your

ANTOINE.

31

Aug. 30 (1900.   *Yalta*).

My dear Olya, I am alive and well and wish the same to you, actress.   I don't write to you because you must wait a bit, I am writing my play.[1]   Although it 's rather tedious I think it is all right, it is intellectual.   I write slowly ; that is something unexpected.   If the play won't come out as it ought I shall put

---

[1] O. L. wrote, Aug. 20 : ' How you grieve me when you write that visitors keep hindering you from working !   Only think—day after day is wasted in empty gossip while you say yourself the play is clamouring to take shape and are yourself indignant at being hindered.   Darling, dear one, do get rid of them, do arrange somehow that it shouldn't happen, so that you may be able to work quietly without being interrupted.'

it away till next year. But I will finish it now, one way or another.

Oh, how I am interrupted, if only you knew ! ! I can't refuse to see people, I am not equal to it.

It is cold in Moscow, is it ? Oy ! Oy ! that 's bad.

Well, take care of yourself. You are offended at my not calling you by your name in some of my letters.[1] Honour bright, it was not intentional.

Your Anto—.

I kiss you twenty times.

I have been a little unwell and grumpy, but now I am all right and better-humoured again.

32

Sept. 5 (1900. Yalta).

My sweet, my angel, I don't write to you, but don't be cross, be indulgent to human weakness. All the time, I have been sitting over my play, more thinking than writing, but yet I fancied that I was busy and that I had no time now for letters. I am writing the play, but I am not hurrying over it, and it is very possible that I shall even come to Moscow without finishing it ; there are a very great many characters, it 's crowded, I am afraid it may come out indistinct or pale, and so it would be better to put it off till next season. By the way, ' Ivanov ' I did produce at Korsh's [2] immediately after writing it, but all the other plays I had by me for a long time waiting for Nemirovitch to ask for them, and so I had time to put in all sorts of corrections.

There are visitors here, the head-mistress of the High School with two young ladies. I am writing at odd minutes. To-day I escorted to the steamer two young ladies of our acquaintance and, alas !—I saw N. N. setting off for Moscow. With me she was cold as a tombstone on an autumn day ! And I, too, in all probability, was not particularly warm.

Of course I shall send a telegram, you must come and meet

---

[1] In the same letter (Aug. 20) O. L. wrote : ' You have never called me by my name, except in the first letter. Don't you like it ? '

[2] ' Ivanov ' was first performed at Korsh's theatre in 1887.

me, you must ! I shall come by the morning express, I shall come and the very same day sit down to my play. And where am I to stay ? At Little Dmitrovka[1] there is neither bed nor writing-table for me, I shall have to put up at a hotel. I shall not stay long in Moscow.

There is no rain in Yalta, the trees are being parched, the grass has been parched up long ago ; it is windy every day. It 's cold.

Write to me a little oftener, your letters rejoice me every time and raise my spirits, which are almost every day as dry and arid as the Crimean soil. Don't be cross with me, my sweet.

The visitors are going, I am going to see them off.

Your ANTOINE.

33

Sept. 6 (1900. *Yalta*).

My sweet Olya, my angel, I am very, very, very dreary without you. I shall come when your rehearsals are over [2] and the performances begin, by which time it will be cold in Moscow, that is after the 20th of September. Now I sit at home and fancy that I am writing. Well, take care of yourself, granny.

Your ANTOINE.

Write !

I say ' fancy ' because some days one will sit and sit at the table and walk and walk about and think and think and then sit down in an easy-chair and pick up the newspaper or begin musing over one thing or another, sweet granny.

34

Sept. 8 (1900. *Yalta*).

You write : ' Oh, to me everything seems so bewildering.' It is a good thing it does, my dear little actress, it is a very good thing ! It shows that you are a philosopher, an intellectual woman.

---

[1] His sister's lodgings.
[2] The rehearsals of Ibsen's play ' When We Dead Awaken,' and Ostrovsky's ' Snow-Maiden.'

I fancy it is a little warmer ? Whatever happens, I shall come to Moscow on the 20th of September and stay there till the 1st of October. Every day I shall sit in the hotel and write my play. Write or make a fair copy ? I don't know, dear granny. One of my heroines has gone a bit lame, I can do nothing with her and I am cross.

I had a letter to-day from Marks : he writes that my plays [1] will come out in ten days.

I am afraid you will be disappointed in me. My hair is coming out frightfully, coming out so that, behold, in a week I shall be a bald old grandad. Apparently it is due to the barber ; as soon as I had my hair cut, I began growing bald.

Is Gorky writing a play or isn't he ? Where did that paragraph in the ' News of the Day ' about the title ' Three Sisters ' not being suitable come from ? What tosh ! Perhaps it isn't suitable, but I have no thought of changing it.

I am fearfully depressed. Do you understand ? Fearfully ! I live on nothing but soup. In the evenings it 's cold, I stay at home. There are no beautiful young ladies. My money is growing less and less, my beard is turning grey.

My darling, I kiss your little hand, the right one and the left one too. Keep well and don't be depressed, don't think that everything seems bewildering to you.

Good-bye, my splendid Olya, crocodile of my soul !

Your Ant—.

35

Sept. 14 (1900. *Yalta*).

My sweet, my nice Olya, wonderful little actress, your last letter in which you describe your excursion to the Sparrow Hills touched me, it 's enchanting like yourself.[2] And here I have

---

[1] The volume of Marks's edition containing the plays ' Ivanov,' ' The Sea-Gull,' ' Uncle Vanya,' ' The Anniversary,' ' The Wedding,' ' The Bear ' and ' The Proposal.'

[2] O. L. wrote, Sept. 10 : ' It is soft, warm weather, breathing is easy, walking is easy, everything is smiling so pensively, so caressingly. I had such a craving to rest, " to listen to the silence," as my Maia says (" When We Dead Awaken "). For several days past as I walked along the Tverskoy boulevard I greedily sniffed the fragrance of the autumn leaves,

been kept indoors for six or seven days, for I am unwell. Fever, cough, a cold in the head. To-day I fancy I am a little better and on the way to recovery, but still the same weakness and emptiness and it's nasty to feel that I have done nothing, written nothing, for a whole week. My play looks dejectedly at me, it lies on the table and I think of it dejectedly. You do not advise me to come to Moscow ? [1] Early in October Mother is going to Moscow. I must get her off, so that obviously I shall not be able to come to you. That means that in the winter you will forget what sort of man I am, while I shall fall in love with some one else if I meet another woman like you—and everything will go on in the old way, as it was before.

To-morrow I will write more to you, and meanwhile keep well, my sweet. Altschuller has just come. Be well and happy.

Your ANT—.

and it fretted me and drew me to the country. We took the tram as far as the Novo-Dyevitchy Convent, then walked a mile and a half among kitchen gardens—there was a smell of fennel and cabbage ; then we crossed the river Moskva, and found ourselves at Vorovyovka. There, happily, there was not a soul, the silence was extraordinary, the air was still, so still, not one leaf quivered ; and I longed to be alone, quite alone, or to sit with you in that autumn softness saying nothing and feeling nothing but nature around us. You would have understood it all. I picture at once so vividly sharing that mood with you. In the copse we could see already golden maples, birches, aspens turning red, while the little oaks are still green. The damp earth smells of mushrooms, here and there one finds the belated little flowers I love, there are spiders' webs in the air, in fact such beauty everywhere that I could not tear myself away. The sunlight was so tender and dreamy and there was such softness in the outlines of the clouds. We spent a long time admiring Mother Moscow with her golden domes veiled in smoke ; the sun seemed to light it up in patches. I have loved this since I was a child. We drank tea on the terrace, laughed and were foolish, ran about and went off to wander in the wood and among the ravines. Uncle Sasha and I were in a lyrical mood and gathered big nosegays of all possible sorts of autumn leaves, grasses and flowers. I brought Masha a huge bunch, she liked it. We rowed back in a boat as far as Dragomilovsky Bridge. It was downright hot on the water. We rowed and sang, then sank into thought. Geese were promenading on the banks, we saw two wild geese flying in the air. We came home joyful and excited and had a noisy dinner.'

[1] O. L. wrote, Sept. 10 : ' I have just received your letter, my own. I want to see you dreadfully, but how can you come in the cold ? It worries me terribly ; think it over well, my dear. How will it be ? '

I am driving with Altschuller into the town.

I did not go with Altschuller, for we had no sooner walked out of the house than the head-mistress of the High School came into the yard. I had to stay at home.

Forgive me, dear, for this dreary letter. To-morrow I will write a more lively one.

36

Sept. 15 (1900.   *Yalta*).

Do you know, dear ?   The very theatre in which you acted in Yalta has been burnt.   It caught fire in the night a few days ago, but I haven't seen the ruins, as I have been ill and haven't been in the town.   And what else is there to tell you ?   Nothing else.

I have learned from the newspapers that your performances are beginning on September 20th, and that Gorky has written a play. Mind now you must write how ' The Snow-Maiden ' goes, and what Gorky's play is like, if he really has written it. I like the man very, very much, and I am delighted and interested by what they write of him in the papers, even if it is twaddle. As for my play, it will be sooner or later, in September or October, or even November, but whether I shall make up my mind to produce it this season—that is uncertain, my sweet granny. I hesitate, because in the first place the play is not quite ready—let it lie on the table a bit, and in the second I must be present at the rehearsals, absolutely must ! Four important female parts, four young women of the educated class I can't leave to Stanislavsky, for all my respect for his gifts and understanding. I must at least have a peep at the rehearsals.

Illness delayed it first and now I am too lazy to set to work on the play. But there, never mind.

Yesterday, after the head-mistress, Madame Bonnier arrived and stayed to supper.

Write me another interesting letter.   Go again¡ to the Sparrow Hills and write about it. You are my clever girl. Only write a longer one, enough to need two stamps on the envelope. You are in no mood for writing now, though ; first, you have a great deal to do, and secondly, you are already

drifting away from me.   It 's true, isn't it ?   You are devilishly
cold, as an actress ought to be, indeed.   Don't be cross, pet,
I just mention it in passing.

There is no rain, no water, the plants are perishing.   It is
warm again.   I shall most likely go into the town to-day.
You write me nothing about your health.   Are you all right ?
Have you grown fatter or thinner ?   Write about everything.

I kiss you hard till you faint, till you 're dizzy.   Don't
forget your

ANT—.

37

TELEGRAM

Sept. 20 (1900.   *Yalta*).

Saturday Mother goes Moscow play not ready coming later
greetings kiss hands ANTONIUS.

38

Sept. 22, 1900.   (*Yalta.*)

My pet, Olya darling, greetings !   How are you getting on ?
It 's a long time since I have written to you, quite a long time.
My conscience pricks me a little for it, though I am not so much
to blame as might appear.   I don't want to write, besides
what have I to write about ?   About my life in the Crimea ?
I long not to write but to talk to you, to talk on, even to be
silent, only with you.   To-morrow Mother 's going to Moscow,
perhaps I shall soon go too, though it passes my understanding
why I should go.   What for ?   To see you and go away again ?
How interesting that is !   To come, look at the theatrical hurly-
burly and go away again.

I shall go to Paris, then probably to Nice, and from Nice to
Africa if there isn't the plague there.   I shall have to live through,
or rather to drag through, this winter one way or another.

There has been no letter from Masha for over a month.
Why doesn't she write ?   Tell her she ought to write at least
once a week.   If I go abroad letters will be forwarded to me
by the post-office here.

Madame Bonnier comes to see me almost every day. Aren't you jealous ?

So I must congratulate you on the beginning of the season. You have already played at least in ' Lonely Lives.' I congratulate you, dear love, I wish you the fullest success, I hope you may do good work so that you may be tired and enjoy it. Above all, that you may have decent plays so that it will be interesting to act in them.

Are you angry with me, darling ? What 's to be done ! It 's dark for me to write, my candles give a poor light. My dear, I kiss you warmly, good-bye, keep well and merry ! Think of me a little oftener. You rarely write to me [1] ; I put that down to your being tired of me and having other people making love to you. Oh, well ! Bravo, granny !

I kiss your little hand.

Your ANT—.

39

Sept. 27, 1900. *Yalta.*

My pet Olya, my nice little actress, why this tone, this plaintive doleful mood ? [2] Am I really so much to blame ? Well, forgive me, my good sweet one, don't be cross, I am not so much to blame as your suspiciousness makes you think. I haven't managed to get off to Moscow yet because I have been unwell ; there have been no other reasons, I assure you, dear, on my word of honour. Word of honour ! Don't you believe me ?

I shall stay on in Yalta till the 10th of October, I shall work, then I shall go to Moscow or abroad, according to the state of my health. In any case I shall write to you.

No letters either from brother Ivan or sister Masha. Evidently they are cross, but what for I don't know.

I was yesterday at Sredin's. I found a lot of visitors with

---

[1] There are letters from O. L. dated Sept. 1, 4, 10, 12, 16, 19.

[2] O. L. wrote, Sept. 24 : ' Why don't you come, Anton ? I can't understand it. I don't write because I am expecting you, because I want dreadfully to see you. What 's preventing you ? What 's troubling you ? I don't know what to think, I am dreadfully uneasy. . . . Every day I want to cry.'

him, all people I didn't know.   His little daughter is suffering
from chlorosis, but she goes to the High School.   He suffers
from rheumatism.

Mind you write me exactly how ' The Snow-Maiden ' went
off and how the performances have begun, how you are all
feeling, how the audience is behaving and everything else.
You are not like me, you see, you have plenty of material for
letters, plenty and to spare, while I have nothing to say except
perhaps one thing : I caught two mice to-day.

There is still no rain in Yalta.   This is a dry place, it is dry !
The poor trees, especially those on this side of the mountains,
have had not one single drop of water all this summer and now
are yellow ; so it happens that men have not one drop of
happiness in their whole lives.   I suppose that is how it must be.

You write : ' You have a loving, tender heart, you know, why
do you make it hard ? '   And when did I make it hard ?   In
what precisely did I show that hardness ?   My heart has
always loved you and been tender to you, and I have never
hidden that from you, never, never, and you accuse me of
hardness for no reason at all, just to say something.

Judging from your letter in general,[1] you want and expect
some sort of explanation, some sort of long conversation—
with grave faces, with grave consequences ; and I don't know
what to say to you except one thing, which I have told you
ten thousand times already and shall probably go on telling
you for years, that is that I love you and nothing more.   That
we are not together now is not my fault or yours, it's the
devil who has put the bacillus in me and the love of art
in you.

Good-bye, good-bye, sweet granny, and the holy angels keep
you.   Don't be angry with me, darling, don't be depressed, be
a good girl.

What news of the theatre ?   Please write.

Your ANTOINE.

---

[1] O. L. wrote, Sept. 24 : ' Write me everything openly, everything
ought to be clear and open between us, we are not children.   Tell me
everything that is in your heart, ask me any question, I will answer
everything.'

40

Sept. 28 (1900. *Yalta*).

Letter sent yesterday everything all right probably coming October ANTONIO.

41

Oct. 4, 1900. (*Yalta.*)

My dear, if I come, it will be the 12th of October, not sooner. I will telegraph, that 's certain. There has been a little hitch with the play. I haven't worked at it for ten days or more as I have been ill and am a little sick of it, so that I don't know what to write to you about it. I have had influenza, a sore throat and incessant cough; I had hardly begun to go out when I began having headaches, but now things are mending, I am already able to go out. The play will come off in any case, but it can't be played this season.

Think what hotel or what furnished rooms I am to stay at. Think about it ! I want a room where it won't be depressing to walk along the passage, where there won't be a bad smell. In Moscow I shall make a fair copy of my new play, most likely. From Moscow I shall go to Paris.

Well, take care of yourself, my lovely golden girl. Go on acting steadily, but sometimes think of me.

There is no news. I repeat, take care of yourself, don't be depressed.

Your ANTO—.

42

Oct. 8 (1900. *Yalta*).

Twenty-one without fail.

43 [1]

Oct. 14 (1900. *Yalta*).

Dear, I will come to Moscow on October 23rd, at half-past five in the evening—you see the express trains are not running now. If you are playing that evening, don't meet me.

The weather in Yalta is wonderful, such as it was not once while you were here. Everything is in flower, the trees are green, the sun shines and it is as warm as though it were summer and not too hot. Yesterday and the day before it rained, rained furiously, but to-day it is sunny again. You see what a nice time I am having. Don't ask about my play, it won't be acted this year, anyway.

From Moscow I shall go abroad. You write that you are tired of ' The Snow-Maiden ' and ask : ' Are you triumphant ? ' [2] Why should I be triumphant ? I wrote that the play was not for your theatre, that it is not your job to act such plays, and if the play had an immense success I should still be against its being produced in your theatre. Your line is ' Lonely Lives,' that 's the type of play you ought to keep to, even if they—I mean plays like ' Lonely Lives '—are a failure. Keep well, darling ! Till we meet ! I am eating meat again. I have left off fasting. My stomach protests, but still I eat it obstinately, and don't see much use in it.

I shall be at the theatre on the 23rd for certain.

Your ANTO—.

44

TELEGRAM

Oct. 17 (1900. *Yalta*).

Coming Monday for certain.

[1] Enclosed in this letter is a cutting from a newspaper : ' During the last public performance, at the end of the third act of Tchehov's play " Ivanov," the audience was startled by shouts in the stalls. A very well-dressed woman was so overcome by what was taking place on the stage that she completely forgot herself and began screaming : " Sarka, you Jewess, serve you right ! " '

[2] O. L. wrote, Oct. 11 : ' Your plays have the greatest success now (' The Sea-Gull ' and ' Uncle Vanya '). The audience loves them, the actors

Tchehov arrived in Moscow on Monday, October 23, and stayed at the ' Dresden Hotel,' where O. L. Knipper paid him brief visits in the intervals between rehearsals and performances. On December 11 he left Moscow to go abroad.

45

Dec. 11, 4 o'clock in the afternoon, 1900.   Brest.

I am approaching Brest.   All is going well.   There is no sun yet.   I wish you health and everything, everything, everything good !

A. TCHEHOV.

Greetings to all.

46

Dec. 12, 1900.   Hotel Bristol, Vienna.

My dear, what a fool I 've been !   I 've arrived here and all the shops are shut, it appears it is the German Christmas ! And I am sitting now in the hotel room feeling awfully sold and positively don't know what to do—what 's known as a perfect fool, in fact.   There is nowhere I can buy straps for my luggage. Only the restaurants are open and they are packed full of swells beside whom I should look simply a sweep.   Well, there is no help for it !

To-morrow I shall go on to Nice, but meanwhile I keep looking with ardent longing at two beds standing in my room : I am going to sleep, I am going to think !   Only it 's a shame that I am here alone without you, my spoilt darling, it 's an awful shame.   Well, how are you getting on in Moscow ? How are you feeling ?   Are the rehearsals going on ? [1]   Have they gone far ?   Dear, write me all about it, all, in the fullest detail, every day !   The devil only knows what a state I shall be in if you don't.

From Brest to Vienna there was no snow.   The earth looks

play them better than in previous seasons, we play them with enjoyment, with delight. " The Snow-Maiden " is hard labour, a torture for all of us. Are you triumphant ?   You know you predicted that, do you remember ? '
[1] Of the play ' Three Sisters.'

as dismal to-day as in March.   It is not like winter.   My fellow-
travellers were bores.

I am going downstairs, darling, to dinner or supper, I don't
know which to call it, then I shall tumble into bed.   I kiss you
warmly, I press your little hands, my exquisite little girl.
Don't forget me, don't !   As soon as I reach Nice, the very
same day, I shall go to the post—perhaps your letter 's there
already.

Write, child.

Your ANT—.

47

Dec. 14 (1900.   *Nice*).

My exquisite little actress, angel, little Jewess, greetings !   I
have only just arrived in Nice and had dinner, and here first
thing I write to you.   This is my address :

Rue Gounod, Pension Russe, Nice,

and for telegrams : Pension Russe, Nice.   My head 's going
round with exhaustion from the journey, to-day I am not going
to write anything.   I shall write to-morrow, but to-day only
allow me to kiss you ten thousand times, my little one.   It 's
raining a little, but it 's warm, wonderfully warm.   Roses are
in bloom and flowers of all sorts, in fact one can't believe one's
eyes.   The young men are in summer overcoats.   Not a single
fur-cap to be seen.   There 's an araucaria before my window
just like yours, only the size of a big fir-tree and growing in
the ground.

It was boring in Vienna ; the shops were shut, and besides
you told me to put up at the Hotel Bristol.   That hotel, it
appears, is the best in Vienna, they fleece you damnably, don't
allow you to read newspapers in the restaurant, and are all
dressed up such swells that I was ashamed among them, I felt
a clumsy old Kruger.   I came from Vienna first-class in the
express, they stripped me fiendishly like birds on a tree.   I had
a compartment to myself.

Well, take care of yourself, my darling, and God and the

heavenly angels keep you. Don't be false to me even in your thoughts. Write how the rehearsals are going. In fact, write as much as ever you can, I beseech you.

Your ANT—.

I kiss you, understand that. I bow down to your little feet.

48

Dec. 15, *next day* (1900. *Nice*).

Strange as it may seem, my dear, I feel as though I had got into the moon. It 's warm, the sun shines everywhere, it 's too hot in an overcoat, every one is going about in summer clothes. The windows in my room are wide open, and it seems as though my soul were wide open too. I am copying my play out and wondering how I could write the thing, what I wrote it for. Oh, my good darling, why aren't you here ? You could look about you and rest, you could listen to the strolling singers and musicians who keep coming into the yard, and, best of all, you could bask in the darling sunshine.

I am going at once to the sea. I shall sit there and read the newspapers and then, when I come back, I shall copy my play— and to-morrow I shall send Nemirovitch Act III., and the day after it Act IV., or both together. In Act III. I have made some alterations and additions, but very little.

My darling, send me your photograph. Be a dear and send it.

There are a great many flies here.

I meet Russians. They seem somehow flattened out here as though weighed down by something or ashamed of their idleness, and their idleness is flagrant. I embrace you warmly, I kiss you a thousand times. I am waiting with impatience for a letter, a long letter. I bow down at your little feet.

Your ANT—.

I went to the post-office to-day and found nothing. Keep well, my child. I love you very much.

49

Sunday, I don't remember the day of the month.
(Dec. 17, 1900. Nice.)

This is my third night in Nice and not a single line from you. What means this dream ? How do you wish me to interpret it ? My sweet Olya, don't be lazy, my angel, write a little oftener to your old man. It's glorious here in Nice, the weather's amazing. After Yalta the scenery and weather here seem simply like paradise. I bought myself a summer over-coat and am a dandy. Yesterday I sent Act III. to Moscow and to-morrow I will send Act IV. In Act III. I have altered scarcely anything, but in Act IV. I have made startling changes. I have given you many more words. (You ought to say thank you . . .) So for that, write to me how the rehearsals are going, what's happening and how. Write all about it. Since you don't write to me I won't write to you. Basta ! This is my last letter.

The artist, Yakobi, was with me to-day. The day before yesterday I saw Maxim Kovalyevsky—a Moscow celebrity. I received an invitation from him and I am going soon to dine with him at his villa in Beaulieu. I shall soon go to Monte Carlo to play roulette.

Write to me, darling, don't be lazy. You have a heap of my letters while I haven't one. What have I done to provoke your wrath ?

Has Masha gone ?

Give Vishnevsky my address if he wants it : 9 rue Gounod, Nice (or Pension Russe, Nice).

They give us a great deal to eat here. After dinner one has to doze and do nothing and that's not good. I shall have to change my way of living and eat less. The people in our *pension* are Russian and also awfully dull, awfully. And mostly ladies.

I kiss you warmly and embrace my sweet granny. Don't forget me, think of me at least once a week. I embrace you once again, and again.

Your ANTOINE.

When you see Sulerzhitsky [1] tell him I am not going to Africa
now but am going to work. Tell him I have put off Egypt and
Algiers till next year.

50

Dec. 21, 1900. (*Nice.*)

I have just received your letter, my dear little actress. Masha
ought to have telegraphed to Marks [2] that I had written at the
proper time, but that she had forgotten to post my letter.
Besides the letter there were two registered parcels. It 's more
than careless, it is simply beastly. It has suddenly turned cold
in Nice, I am aching all over—that 's why I am abusive in my
letter. My back aches. But I am still wearing my summer
overcoat. The play is finished and sent off. I have given you
a great deal more, especially in Act iv. You see I grudge you
nothing, only do your best.

Write what happens at the rehearsals and how they go,
whether there are any misunderstandings, whether it is all
intelligible. Is Nemirovitch coming to Nice ? If so, when ?

I lunch and dine in a large company, almost all women—and
all awful frights. And all Russians. I have not yet been to
Monte Carlo.

Have Mother and Masha gone to Yalta ? From them not a
single line all this time.

My little ballerina, I am very dreary without you, and if
you begin going to Omon's [3] and forget me I shall go into a
monastery. Don't go to Omon's, child.

[1] One of the stage-managers of the Art Theatre.
[2] O. L. wrote, Dec. 15 : ' Yesterday Masha had a telegram from
Marks with a prepaid reply ; he was anxious to know if you had received
a cheque from him. Masha answered that you were in Nice and that she
thought you had received it.'
[3] O. L. wrote in the same letter : 'Do you know where we were
yesterday ? you 'll be horrified—at Omon's.[1] Well, and it is nasty.
Such coarseness and vulgarity. We saw a revue of Moscow. The only
interesting turn was Shilling, who sang topical couplets on the water
supply, mimicked Zimin, dressed up as Homyakov the house-owner,
Moscow in the form of a fat peasant woman pushing in a go-cart a small
baby, the Moscow Town Council.'

[1] Omon's was a theatre of varieties into which the Art Theatre moved in 1902.

I have two rooms here, one big, the other rather smaller. My bed is such that when one gets into it one can't help smiling; it's wonderfully soft and wide. I speak French a little, I am by degrees remembering what I used to know and have forgotten. I often dream of you, and when I shut my eyes I see you though I'm awake. To me you are a wonderful woman.

Take care of yourself, darling. And God keep you. Be a good girl, work hard and come here in the spring. I want to say something in your ear. I kiss you warmly and hug you and kiss you again.

Your ANTOINE.

Do describe at least one rehearsal.

A happy New Year to you. Here it is New Year already, it is the 3rd of January. It will soon be spring here.

51

Dec. 26 (1900. *Nice*).

Sweet actress, this letter will reach you on New Year's Day; so may the New Year bring you happiness! I kiss you, if you like, a thousand times and hope that every wish you have may come to pass. And that you may remain as kind and nice as you have been till now.

But how are you, though? Your last two letters, written in pencil, frightened me, and though I have not sounded your spleen I am a little afraid that you have a slight attack of typhoid, and that would mean that they wouldn't let you go to the theatre for at least a month, that plays wouldn't come on and I should be forced to play roulette. But are you quite well? Yes? Well, that's all right then, my wonderful darling. I rely upon you.

No sign of life from Masha. I shall write to Sredin, let him write me a couple of words how Mother is.

Only fancy, it has turned suddenly cold here as never before. A real frost. There are perfect mountains of snow at Marseilles, and the flowers here have withered in a single night, and I go about in my autumn overcoat. There are complaints in the newspapers of the extraordinary cold. It 's disgusting, I am afraid I shall sink into the dismal dumps. Yesterday I went to Mentone to see Nemirovitch's sister; she is consumptive and will soon die. They are expecting him. Dear little actress, I embrace you and kiss you ; but if you are tired of me and leave off writing, then I shall go to Australia or somewhere far away. No one writes to me except you. I am forgotten. My greetings to Uncle Sasha and Nikolay Nikolaitch. I kiss you tenderly.

Your ANT—.

52

TELEGRAM

Dec. 26, 1900. *Monte Carlo.*

Salue ma belle ANTOINE.

53

Dec. 26, 1900. (*Nice.*)

My actress, why are you anxious ? I received your telegram [1] to-day and for a long time could not decide what to answer. Strong as an ox—should I answer that ? But I was ashamed to. And how are you ? Are you still staying indoors or are you going to the theatre ? My good darling, of course one can't avoid being ill, but it is better not to be ill. When you are so far from me the devil knows what thoughts come into my head and I am positively terrified. Don't be ill, dear, while I am away, be a good girl.

I was at Monte Carlo to-day and won 295 francs. I had a telegram from Nemirovitch from Mentone, we shall meet to-morrow. I have bought a new hat. What else ? Have you received your part in its new form ? [2]

You write you have forwarded me two letters—apparently addressed to me in Moscow. If you did send them, I can only say I haven't received them. Judging from the newspapers, it

[1] Telegram from O. L. : ' Télégraphié santé inquiète OLGA.'
[2] The part of Masha in the play ' Three Sisters.'

is cold, stormy, frosty weather now ; it will seem very dreary and depressing to Mother there.

Your last letter touches me very much, it is written so poetically. My clever girl, if only we could spend five years together, and then let old age catch us ; anyway we should really have something to remember. You are in a good mood, that is as it should be, only don't let yourself be swallowed up by trivialities, my child.

I kiss you warmly, though apparently you are already tired of that. Or aren't you tired of it ? In that case I embrace you warmly, hold you twenty minutes in my arms and kiss you in the most fervent way. Write how the rehearsals are going.[1] Which act is being done and so on. In fact, how things go in general and whether it wouldn't be better to put the play off till next season.

How should I address telegrams ? Mechtcherinoff—*c'est long et incommode.* Won't it do simply : ' Olga Knipper Merslia-kovsky Moscou'? The postman knows where you live, you see. Well, good-bye for now ! Write or I 'll smash you.

Your ANTOINE.

---

[1] O. L. wrote, Dec. 13 : ' To-day, dear, there was a splendid rehearsal of " Three Sisters "—the tones begin to come out—in Solyony, Tchebuty-kin, Natasha, Irina and in me. Marya Petrovna (*i.e.* the actress Lilina, wife of K. S. Stanislavsky) has decided that I am the image of the papa, Irina of the mamma, while Andrey is his father in face and his mother in character. I have found the right walk for myself, I speak in a low voice. Only don't be afraid I shall overdo the roughness. To-morrow we shall go into the second act, on the 23rd we want to have the first dress rehearsal, in the rough. Marya Petrovna is delighted with her part, she makes her both bashful and free and easy. I don't see Tusenbach, Olga or Vershinin (Sudbinin) quite clearly.'

Dec. 16 : ' To-day we blocked out the second act. To-morrow we go through it with Stanislavsky. I think it will be very interesting. He put in something of his own, of course—a mouse scratches in Masha's scene with Vershinin and there is a droning sound in the stove—but that, of course, is by the stage direction. Tusenbach pounces upon Andrey, sings : " My porch, oh my new porch ! " all begin dancing, even Irina and Tchebutykin. Afterwards when Tusenbach is playing the waltz, Masha flies out and begins dancing alone, then Fedotik seizes her, but she pushes him away (he can't dance), while Irina dances with Roddey, and it is this uproar that brings Natasha in.'

Dec. 23 : ' I can tell you nothing about the rehearsals—for the last six days I haven't been to the theatre.'

54

Dec. 28, 1900. (*Nice.*)

Fancy, my sweet dog, how awful ! To-day I was informed
that a gentleman was below asking for me. I go down and
behold an old man ; he introduces himself as Tchertkov, he has
in his hands a pile of letters, and it appears that all these letters,
addressed to me, were received by him because his surname is
like mine. One letter of yours (and there were three altogether
—your three first letters) had been opened. What do you say
to that ? For the future it is clear that you must write on the
envelopes : Monsieur Antoine Tchekhoff, 9 rue Gounod, Nice.
But be sure to put Antoine, or I shall not get your letters till
ten or fifteen days after you have sent them.

Your lecture about Vienna in which you call me a limp
Slav jelly [1] has come very late ; fifteen years ago I did, it is
true, feel lost abroad and didn't go where I should, but this
time I went everywhere in Vienna where one could go. I went
even to the theatre, but the tickets had all been sold, though
afterwards, as I was going out of Vienna, I remembered that I
had forgotten to look at the *affiche*—that was like a Russian. In
Vienna I bought a splendid purse at Klein's ; he opened his shop,
as it turned out, the second day. I bought straps for my luggage
there too. You see, my darling, how business-like I am.

You scold me, too, for not writing to my mother. Dear, I
have written both to Mother and to Masha many times, but
have had no answer and most likely shall not have. And I have
given them up in despair ! I haven't had a single line from
them up to now, yet I have always, according to you, been a
jelly and always shall be—I shall always be to blame, though
I don't know what for.

[1] O. L. wrote, Dec. 16 : ' At home I found your letter from Vienna
which I was expecting to-day. It is true, dear, we didn't think about the
New Style, but of course the whole world lives by it except us Asiatics.
But that 's no matter. Well, you should have hustled about the streets
and have looked at the holiday crowd, and you can always buy things
as well in Nice and probably no dearer. Surely you didn't spend the whole
day in your hotel room ? You should have walked about the Rings.
And didn't you go to the theatre ? Ah, you limp Slav jelly.'

Thanks for what you tell me about Tolstoy.[1] Shehtel[2] has arrived here from Moscow. He has won a devilish lot at roulette and is going away to-morrow. Nemirovitch is here with his wife. He is, as always, a nice fellow and one is not bored in his company.

It has been cold, but now it is warm and we go about in summer overcoats. I have won five hundred francs at roulette. May I play, darling ?

I was in such a hurry with the last act, I thought you needed it. It appears that you won't begin rehearsing it before Nemirovitch returns. And if I had kept that act another two or three days it might have been much richer, perhaps. ' Three of Us ' is a good thing, but written in an old-fashioned style, and so it is not easily read by people who are used to literature. I, too, could hardly finish it.

Have you quite recovered ? I should hope so ! Though you are a good little girl when you are ill and write good letters, don't dare to be ill again.

A great many ladies dine with me, there are some from Moscow too, but I never utter a word. I sit sulky, hold my tongue and eat persistently, or think about you. The Moscow ladies keep turning the conversation on the theatre, apparently wishing to draw me into conversation, but I sit mute and eat. I am very much pleased when they praise you. And, would you believe it, they praise you very much. They say you are a good actress. Well, little one, be well and happy. I am yours. You may take me and eat me with oil and vinegar. I kiss you warmly.

Your ANTOINE.

[1] O. L. wrote, Dec. 13 : ' Oh, Lyov Antonovitch (Sulerzhitsky) asked me to write to you that Tolstoy was very sorry that he had not seen you, that he would have come but was afraid of being in your way, as last time he noticed that he had come at the wrong moment. He said that he did not quite understand your enthusiasm over Gorky, that he could not finish reading his ' Three of Us '; he said of you that it had never happened yet that he could not read any work of yours to the end—in short, that he loves you as a writer, that he always reads everything you write, though he may sometimes not agree with it.'

[2] An architect and artist, a friend of the Tchehov family.

55

Dec. 30, 1900. (*Nice.*)

Dear little actress, it is an enchanting day, quite like summer, and I begin it by sitting down to write this letter. Your last letters were somewhat gloomy, but that 's nothing, it won't last long. Above all, don't be ill, my joy. Yesterday Nemirovitch and I dined at Kovalyevsky's at Beaulieu ; he, that is Nemirovitch, apparently feels quite well and is a swell in a red tie with white stripes. I got a letter from Vishnevsky yesterday. He writes that he was magnificent in a dress rehearsal of the first two acts. No letters from Masha or Mother, so far, and of course there won't be any. I have written to a doctor in Yalta and begged him to write me how my family is getting on. They don't spoil me at home, my dear, and don't imagine in any case that I am an ungrateful beast. Are you by now going out and are you present at the rehearsals ? Do you know of the changes I have introduced in Acts III. and IV. ? And are you well up in Act II. ? Have they re-copied your parts or do you still read them from the old manuscript ? Vishnevsky writes that Sanin is playing Solyony and Katchalov Vershinin ; the latter will not be bad, and if Sanin does not overdo it he will be exactly right.

I am already longing to be in Russia. Couldn't I come home in February ? What do you think, my angel ?

I kiss you warmly, intensely. I embrace you.

Your ANTOINE.

Here the apricots will soon be in flower.

56

TELEGRAM

Jan. 1, 1901. (*Nice.*)

Félicite maman oncle Nicolasha actrissa souhaite bonheur argent gloire TCHEKHOFF.

57

Jan. 2, 1901. (*Nice.*)

My sweet love, good splendid little girl, wonderful one, your letter which you sent off on the 11th of December has just been brought me. It is an exquisite glorious letter, and thank heaven it was not lost. Your letters have most likely all been received, and now do not be anxious, my little beetle—everything is all right. I have not yet had a single letter from Mother or Masha, though they have had my address since the 20th of December.

Life here is restless, there are more people I know than in Yalta, there's no hiding oneself anywhere. I simply don't know what to do. I had a long letter from Stanislavsky. He wrote it before the 23rd of December, but I only received it yesterday. He writes about the play and praises the actors, among them you. Nemirovitch is under arrest; . . . and for that reason I am not seeing him. On Friday I took him to Kovalyevsky's to dine. . . . Yesterday I ate pancakes at Yurassov's, he is the Vice-Consul here. I received an enormous bouquet yesterday from an unknown lady; after twisting it about in my hands, I divided it up into little nosegays, which I sent to our Russian ladies of the Pension Russe, thereby touching their hearts.

Here, my darling, it is wonderful weather. I go about in summer clothes. It's so nice that one is positively ashamed. Twice already I have been to Monte Carlo, I sent you a telegram and a letter from there. My sweet darling, you are angry that I don't write, and threaten that you won't write to me. But you know without your letters I shall pine away. Write often and long letters. Your long letters are very good, I love them, I read them over several times. In fact, I had no idea that you were so clever. Write, child, write, I beseech you by all that's holy.

Did you tell Sulerzhitsky that I am not going to Egypt? Do tell him, dear. I am writing now and am going to write, so as to do nothing in the summer. Besides it is so warm here that one doesn't want to go elsewhere. I love you, but that you don't understand, though. You need a husband, or, to be more accurate, a spouse, with side-whiskers and a cockade, and what am I ? I 'm no great shakes. But, anyway, I kiss you warmly, hug you furiously, and once more thank you for your letter, and bless you, my joy. Write to me, write, I entreat you ! ! !

Your Toto, titular councillor and cavalier.

58

Jan. 2, 1901. (*Nice.*)

Are you depressed now, my darling, or merry ? Don't be depressed, sweetheart, live and work and write more often to your hermit Antony. I have had no letters from you for a long time.[1] I do not count the letter of the 12th of December which I received to-day, in which you described how you cried when I went away. What an exquisite letter it is, by the way ! You couldn't have written it, you must have asked some one else to write it for you. A wonderful letter.

Nemirovitch does not come to see me. The day before yesterday I sent him a telegram asking him to come to see me ' seul.' So that 's the reason. And meanwhile I must see him to talk about the letter I have had from Stanislavsky. To-day I am staying in all day as I did yesterday. I am not going out. The reason : I have been invited to dinner by a great personage and have said I am ill. No dress-coat, no inclination. A Moscow man, Maklakov, came to see me to-day. What else ? Well, nothing else.

Do describe at least one rehearsal of ' Three Sisters.' Ought anything to be put in or taken out ? Are you acting well, my darling ? Oy, mind now ! Don't make a mournful face in a single act. Angry, yes, but not mournful. People who have borne a grief in their hearts for a long time and are used to it only whistle and often sink into thought. So you may often be thoughtful on the stage during conversations. Do you understand ? Of course you understand, because you are clever. Did I send you greetings for the New Year ? Surely

[1] O. L. wrote letters on Dec. 23 and 24, and sent telegrams on Dec. 26 and 27.

I did ?   I kiss both your hands, all your ten fingers and your
forehead, and I wish you happiness and peace and more love,
and that it may last a long time, say fifteen years.   What do
you think, can there be such love ?   In me there could, but
not in you.   I embrace you, in any case.

Your Toto.

From time to time you might send me a newspaper of some
sort (not the ' Russian News '), stick a two-kopeck stamp on.

59

Jan. 6, 1901.   (*Nice.*)

My dear skittish little girl, I have not had a letter from you
for a long time ; evidently you have chucked me.   By the way,
I have received all the letters you sent, you can rely entirely
on those which were fully addressed ; those without an address
were terribly late, as they went to Tchertkov, but still I have
received every one of them.

My precious, I have now completed my observations in the
Pension Russe, and now I want to move into another hotel,
which must be lively and full of people too.   I will telegraph
at once as soon as I move.   Here in the Pension Russe I have
been studying Kiev professors—one might write a farce !   And
such worthless women, oh, darling, such worthless women !
One has forty-five lottery tickets, she lives here because she
has nothing to do, she does nothing but eat and drink, she
often goes to Monte Carlo where she plays timidly, but does
not go to play on the 5th of January because it 's the eve of
a holiday !   What a lot of Russian money is wasted here,
particularly at Monte Carlo !

At last I have a letter from Masha.   Now I shall write to
Mother every three days, that she may not be dull.   Yesterday
I wrote to Vishnevsky and called him in my letter Alexandr
Leontyevitch—the name of a Russian doctor here, who hap-
pened to be with me just as I was writing the letter.

How are ' Three Sisters ' going ?   Not a damned soul writes
to me about it.   You don't write either, and I will beat you for
it.   Nemirovitch has been at Mentone, lived in grand style at

the Hotel Prince de Galles, and in grand style saw no one and nothing, and is going away to-day ; . . . I rarely saw them.

You don't write to me. If you have fallen in love with some-body else, write that I mustn't dare to kiss you in imagination and even hug you as I am doing now. Well, darling, good-bye for now. Live, silly girl, and trust in God. Don't have doubts.

Your ANTOINE.

60

Jan. 7, 1901. (Nice.)

Dear tippler, I have just received your letter with the de-scription of the evening at Luzhsky's.[1] You ask about a letter, or rather three letters enclosed in one envelope. Don't be anxious, darling, I have received it. Thanks.

I have just read Boborykin's story ' Fellow-Students ' in the ' Vyestnik Yevropý.' It 's a wretched dull story, but interest-ing. The Art Theatre is described in it, and Marya Petrovna is praised up to the skies. Read it. ' The Sea-Gull ' and ' Uncle Vanya ' are discussed in it.

I am already cruelly bored here. Keep well, grow younger and be more and more charming, so that your old man may not be disappointed.

You write nothing of how the play is going, what is happen-ing and whether one can reckon upon it and so on and so on. It 's very possible that on the 15th of January I shall go to Algiers. Write to me all the same at the old address, *i.e.* to Nice, and they will forward it from here to Algiers. I want to have a look at the Sahara.

Well, take care of yourself. I embrace you warmly, my darling.

Your TOTO, hereditary honorary academician.

61

Jan. 11, 1901. (Nice.)

Cruel savage woman, a hundred years have passed and no letter from you.[2] What is the meaning of it ? Letters reach

[1] An actor at the Moscow Art Theatre.
[2] Between Dec. 11 and Jan. 9, eighteen letters had been sent.

me punctually now, and if I do not get them no one is to blame
for it but you, my faithless one.

In a few days if the sea is not as stormy as it is now I shall
go to Africa. My address will remain the same, *i.e.* Nice, 9 rue
Gounod, they will know here where I am. I shall only stay a
short time in Africa, a fortnight.

It 's exquisite summer weather here all the time, warm and
lovely, flowers, ladies, bicycles, but alas ! ! it 's all only an
oleograph, and not a picture, for me anyway.

Write, dog ! Ginger-haired dog ! not to write to me—it 's
so base of you ! You might at least write what is being done
with ' Three Sisters.' You have written me nothing about
the play, absolutely nothing, except that you have been at a
rehearsal or that there wasn't a rehearsal. I will certainly give
you a beating, damn it all. Has Masha arrived in Moscow ?

The days are growing longer, soon it will be spring, my good
splendid actress, soon we shall see each other. Write, darling,
I beseech you.

Your Toto.

62

Jan. 14 (1901. *Nice*).

Dear actress, I am anxious. In the first place you write that
you are ill, and in the second I read in the ' Russian News ' that
' Uncle Vanya ' is being taken off. Why are you ill, little silly,
if you really are ill ? Why don't you take care of yourself,
instead of skipping about and not going to bed till seven o'clock
in the morning ? Oh, I ought to take you in hand. I receive
your letters punctually, I read them over two or three times.
Why do you write nothing about ' Three Sisters ' ? How is
the play going ? You have only written about Sanin and
Meierhold, but nothing about the play in general, and I suspect
my play will be a failure, and when I saw Nemirovitch-Dantchenko here and talked to him I felt very dreary and fancied
that the play will certainly be a failure and that I shall write
no more for the Art Theatre.

I have been a little out of sorts, but now am all right, everything is going well. I am meaning to go with Kovalyevsky to Algiers and shall most likely set off on the 21st. Now the sea is rough, we must wait. My address will still be the same, 9 rue Gounod, Nice. I shall write to you, my darling, from the steamer and Algiers almost every day. And you read my letters and then think about me just now and then. If you will be ill, on my word of honour, I 'll divorce you, and before the divorce, I will beat you so that you will go about with a black eye for a week.

The secretary from the Consulate has paid me a call and prevented my writing. I received your letter while he was here. I get all your letters quite punctually now, only you don't write every two days, but rather less often, my darling. But there, God bless you ! I didn't send the flowers to Marya Fyodorovna.[1] But I would have sent them with pleasure if I had been certain that they would not be withered. And I would have sent you some too. There is a blight upon my soul. My precious, keep well, work hard, don't be depressed, don't spend too much time paying visits, write to me oftener and more fully.

I kiss you warmly.

Your Toto, retired doctor and dramatist.

63

Jan. 17 (1901. *Nice*).

My darling, don't be anxious. I get your letters regularly and am ready to bet that not one has been lost. Thank you, dear dog, and if in these later days, as you write, I am going to receive short letters from you and not to receive them so often, so be it. You really have a great deal of work, though one must suppose that the play will not appear this season, but will only appear in Petersburg.

Why do you ask me about the photograph of Lel ?[2] You should have sent it straight off. And when am I to have your real photograph ?

---

[1] M. F. Andreyev was at that time an actress at the Art Theatre, afterwards Gorky's second wife.

[2] O. L. played the part of Lel in Ostrovsky's ' Snow-Maiden.'

Now I am perfectly well. We are going to Algiers, but I doubt whether we shall go very soon, as the sea is rough. To-day, for instance, there is a storm. Yes, quite enough people come and see me, and quite enough they hinder and irritate me ; and to-day they sat on from five o'clock in the evening till half-past eleven. I can't work, and chiefly from fury. After Algiers I want to go straight to Yalta.

Darling, do you know that to-day is my name-day ? No one knows about it here, luckily. When Masha[1] comes, tell her that Marks will send a sum of money from Petersburg addressed to her which she is to receive.

I bow down to your little feet. I kiss you and hug you and bow down again to your feet.

Your hermit ANTONY.

What am I to bring you ? Or shall I send you something ? Of course the third act must be taken slowly on the stage, that it may be felt that they are exhausted and sleepy. . . . How could a noise come in ? There are stage directions where there should be ringing.

64

TELEGRAM

Jan. 20, 1901. Nice.

Santé merveilleuse ANTOINE.

65

Jan. 20, 1901. (Nice.)

Dear actress, exploitress of my soul, why did you send me a telegram ? You had better have telegraphed about yourself than for such a silly reason. Well, how are ' Three Sisters ' ? Judging from your letters, you are all talking unconscionable nonsense. In Act III. there is noise, why noise ? There should only be noise in the distance behind the scenes, a confused hollow noise, but here on the stage all are exhausted, almost asleep. If you spoil the third act, the whole play is done for, and I shall be hissed in my old age. Stanislavsky in his letters

---

[1] Tchehov's sister had gone to Yalta for the Christmas holidays.

praises you very much and Vishnevsky also. And though I don't see you I praise you too. Vershinin pronounces ' tram-tram-tram ' by way of a question and you by way of an answer, and that seems to you such an original joke that you utter your ' tram-tram ' with a little laugh, you call out ' tram-tram,' and laugh not loudly, but just audibly. You must not make the sort of face you do in ' Uncle Vanya,' but look younger and more full of life. Remember that you are given to laughing and being cross. But there, I rely upon you, my darling, you are a good actress.

I said at the time that it was unsuitable to carry Tusenbach's dead body across your stage, but Stanislavsky insisted that they couldn't do without the dead body. I wrote to him not to carry the dead body across, but I don't know whether he had my letter. If the play 's a failure, I will go to Monte Carlo and lose till I can't see straight.

I am already eager to get out of Nice and longing to be off, but where ? I can't go to Africa for the time being because the sea is rough, and I don't want to go to Yalta. I suppose in any case I shall be in Yalta in February, and in April in Moscow. And then from Moscow we will go away together somewhere.

I have absolutely no news. Keep well, my darling, my desperate actress, don't forget me and keep a little love for me, just a ha'porth. I kiss you and hug you ! I wish you happiness. Keep well.

Your hermit ANTONY.

66

Jan. 24, 1901. (Nice.)

My darling, remarkable woman, I have still not gone to Algiers because the sea is rough and my companions refuse to go. It will end in my giving it up and going home to Yalta.

By the way, they write that the weather 's fine there, and by the way, Mother 's all alone there now.

I send you my photograph.

I have received a letter from Marya Fyodorovna to thank me for the flowers I did not send her. I hear from you that in the third act two of you lead Irina in supported on each arm. What 's that for ? Is that in your mood ? You ought not to leave your sofa. And can't Irina come in by herself ? Why these innovations ? The Colonel [1] has sent me a long letter, he complains of Fedotik, Roddey and Solyony. He complains of Vershinin, his immorality, upon my soul he seduces another man's wife ! I think, though, that that Colonel has done what I asked him, that is, the soldiers will be dressed like soldiers. The three sisters and Natasha he praises highly, by the way. He praises Tusenbach too.

I kiss you warmly and hug you tight. They are calling me to dinner. The Consul has come and advises me not to go to Algiers. He says that it is the time of the mistral now. I am perfectly well and don't cough, but I am fearfully bored. I am bored without Moscow, without you, you sly doggy.

And so I kiss you.

Your holy man ANTONY.

67

Jan. 26, 1901. (*Nice.*)

Well, my good darling, to-day in all probability I shall set off for Algiers. Go on writing to Nice ; from here they will send everything on. Or write one or two letters to the Poste Restante, Algiers. From Algiers I shall go to Yalta. There stay a month and then go off somewhere with my dog. Judging from the rumours that reach me from my fellow-travellers I shall spend a fortnight in Algiers, including the time I shall take on a visit to the Sahara. From the Sahara I shall return tropically ardent, hellishly fiery.

How have the ' Three Sisters ' gone ? Telegraph to me : ' Algiers, Poste Restante.' Telegraph the exact truth without sparing my life. It has turned cold here the last few days. As cold as in Yalta, and I am glad I am going away. If the

[1] Colonel, afterwards General, V. A. Petrov had kindly consented to revise the correctness of the uniforms of the military men in the play.

sea begins to be choppy in the evening, my precious, I shall in obedience to my fellow-travellers not go to Algiers, but to Italy, to Naples, and I will write to you about that not later than this evening. I shall be travelling to Marseilles all night . . . brrr!

But my spirits have risen, anyway. I love travelling. My dream of the last few days is a visit to Spitzbergen in the summer or to Solovki.

Are you worn out with visitors and rehearsals, my splendid, my illustrious actress? Never mind, have a little patience! Whatever happens, we will spend the summer together, anyway. Won't we? Mind now, yes, or I will punish you. I am going to get things ready before setting off. It's dull and I believe the wind is rising. I am going to buy myself new— saving your presence—trousers, and the old ones I shall cast off here in France.

I kiss you warmly and I hug you desperately hard. Don't be cross, don't be depressed, don't make a very grave face, and write a little oftener to the man who loves you in spite of your defects. No, no, darling, I was joking, you have no defects, you are perfect.

I hug you once more.

Your holy man ANTONY.

68

Sunday (Jan. 28, 1901. Pisa).

I write you this from Pisa, my darling. I go from here to Florence, then to Rome, then to Naples, where I shall get your letters sent on from Nice. My address for letters and telegrams is Naples, Poste Restante.

Has my play been acted or not? I know nothing.

I will write you a longer letter from Florence, but, for now, be happy. I kiss you warmly, warmly, and hug you. Write when you will be going to Petersburg. I shall be at home in Yalta in Lent. I shall probably go home from Italy by sea, by Corfu.

My splendid darling, I kiss you once more.

Your ANTONIO.

69

Sunday (Jan. 28, 1901).

My precious, Masha's repentance in Act III. isn't repentance at all, but only frank conversation. Take it nervously, but not desperately, don't scream, smile just occasionally, and the great thing is to do it so that the exhaustion of night may be felt. And that it may be felt that you are cleverer than your sisters, think yourself cleverer, anyway. As for tram-tram-tram, do as you think best. You are my sensible girl.

I sent you a telegram yesterday, did you get it ?

I am writing, of course, but without any eagerness. I think ' Three Sisters ' must have exhausted me, or simply I am sick of writing, I have grown old. I don't know. I should like not to write for five years, but to travel for five years and then go home and settle down.

And so ' Three Sisters ' will not be produced in Moscow this season ? You 'll produce them for the first time in Petersburg ?

By the way, don't lose sight of the fact that you will have no success in Petersburg. That 's lucky, of course, as you won't go on tour after Petersburg, but will settle down in Moscow. You know going on tour is not at all the right line for the Art Theatre. In Petersburg there will be good houses, but not a grain of success, please excuse my saying so.

Keep well, sweet spouse. I remain your loving

Academician Toto.

70

Monday (Jan. 29, 1901. Florence).

My darling, I write you this from Florence, where I shall probably stay two days. One thing I must say, it is wonderful here. Who has not been in Italy has not lived. But it is so cold in my room that I would put on my fur-coat if only I had it.

Has ' Three Sisters ' appeared yet ? You are not in good spirits ? My darling, it 's all of no consequence, not worth thinking about.[1]

[1] The first performance of ' Three Sisters ' was on Jan. 31.

I would write to Masha if I had her address. You write me
that she has changed her lodging. I hope that in from five to
seven days I shall find your letters Poste Restante in Naples ;
without them, that is without your letters, I am very dreary.

I went to the theatre yesterday to see a new play, very, very
boring. A Madame Orlov, a Russian Nihilist, is one of the
characters and a young man is in love with her, but I did not
wait for her entrance, I went out of the theatre. To-day they
are giving ' Dr. Stockman.' I shall certainly go, and then write
to you about it.

My hotel room, a very good one, costs three francs here ;
food is cheap too, and they give you wine at dinner for nothing.
The theatre is conventional, but the actors are not bad. The
audience keep their hats on.

Well, take care of yourself, my angel, my good wonderful
darling. I kiss you and embrace you warmly.

Your ANTOINE.

71

Feb. 2, 1901. (Rome.)

My good little girl, I am now in Rome. To-day your letter
has come here, the only one after a whole week. I imagine
that 's the fault of my play, which must have been a failure.
Not a word, not a breath about it—evidently it has missed fire.

Oh, what a glorious country this Italy is ! A wonderful
country ! There 's not a corner here, not an inch of land
which would not seem intensely interesting.

And so I am in Rome. From here I shall go to Naples, where
I shall spend five days (so your letter will find me there if you
send one), then to Brindisi, and from Brindisi by sea to Yalta,
by the Island of Corfu, of course. You see, darling, what a
good traveller I am ! Going from place to place like this and
looking at everything is far more agreeable than staying at
home and writing even for the theatre. We, that is you and I,
will go together to Sweden and Norway, shall we ? We shall
have something to remember in our old age.

I am now perfectly well, perfectly, my treasure. Don't be
anxious but keep well yourself.

I heard to-day that Mirolyubov, the editor of the ' Journal for All,' is at Nervi and I have written to him.   If he will go to Corfu I will stay there a week perhaps.

Two friends are travelling with me, Maxim Kovalyevsky and Professor Korotnev.

I kiss you warmly, my darling.   Forgive me for writing little.   On the other hand I love my dog very much.   Have you been in Italy ?   I believe you have, so you will understand my state of mind.   This is the fourth time, by the way, that I have been in Italy.

I am eating immensely.   I have had a letter from Nemirovitch ; he praises you.

Your hermit ANTONY.

Masha asks me to bring her a parasol and some kerchiefs, and what am I to bring you ?   It 's a pity I am not in Paris, for parasols are not good in Italy, I think.

72

Feb. 4, 1901.   (Rome.)

My sweet darling, I am still in Rome.   From here I shall go to Naples, from Naples to the Island of Corfu, if only it appears, on inquiry, that the plague is not in Constantinople ; if it is, I shall go to Russia by Vienna.

It 's horrid writing, there 's a bad light and a great shadow lying on my paper.   Yesterday I had a telegram sent on from Naples from Nemirovitch with the news that ' Three Sisters ' has appeared.   According to him the women's parts were superbly played.   Now I shall expect a letter from you.   To-day I had a letter from Lyons from Sulerzhitsky, and a telegram from Nervi from Mirolyubov.   To-day I have been viewing ancient Rome with a Russian family and two young ladies. Professor Modestov gave us explanations and the young ladies were very charming.   I bought Masha a parasol, but I think it is not nice.   I have bought some kerchiefs too, but they are not good for much either.   Rome is not Paris.   It is cold weather here.   I am going to Naples to-morrow and shall stay there four or five days.   Your letters are sent on to me from Nice, my dear girl, not one has been lost. And so I shall be in Yalta before the end of February ; there I am going to write, write a lot before I see you, and then we will go off together somewhere. Shall we ?

I kiss you warmly, keep well, don't be depressed.

Your ANT—.

73

Feb. 20 (*Feb.* 7), 1901. (*Rome.*)

My dear, within two hours I am setting off for the North to Russia. It 's very cold here, snowing, so that I have no inclination to go on to Naples, and so write to me now to Yalta.

Not one letter from you about the performance of ' Three Sisters,' [1] and meanwhile in the telegram in ' Novoye Vremya ' it says that you acted better than any one, that you distinguished yourself. Write to me fully to Yalta. Write, my darling, I implore you.

It 's hard to write, there 's a scurvy electric light. Well, I embrace you and kiss you warmly. Don't forget me. No one loves you as I do.

Your ANTONIO.

Write now to Yalta.

74

TELEGRAM

Feb. 11, 1901. *Volotchisk.*

Telegraph Odessa London [2] going Yalta greetings TCHEHOV.

75

TELEGRAM

Feb. 19, 1901. (*Yalta.*)

Await full telegram well in love dull without dog I send letters how are things health spirits TCHEHOV.

---

[1] O. L.'s telegram : ' Grand succès embrasse mon bien-aimé OLGA,' sent to Algiers, Poste Restante, was received by Tchehov only in Yalta.

[2] The Hotel London.

76

Feb. 20, 1901. (*Yalta.*)

My treasure, my divine precious, I embrace and kiss you ardently. I have been a fortnight on the way. I got no letters and thought that you were tired of me, and now all at once there is a heap from Moscow, from Petersburg and abroad. I left Italy so soon because it is cold and snowy there now, and because I felt suddenly wretched, without your letters, from uncertainty. You know I only heard about 'Three Sisters' here in Yalta. Hardly anything, the merest scrap reached me in Italy. It looks like failure because every one who has read the newspapers says nothing, and because Masha is very free with her praise in her letters, but, there, it doesn't matter.

You ask when we shall see each other ? At Easter. Where ? In Moscow. Where shall we go ? I don't know ; we will decide together. My remarkable, clever girl, my splendid little Jewess.

It 's warm in Yalta, the weather is nice, the rooms are cosy, but on the whole it 's dreary. Bunin [1] is here and I think he comes to see me every day. Mirolyubov, too, is here. Nadyezhda Ivanovna has been. She has grown more deaf. Sredin looks a thoroughly healthy person. Altschuller is stouter.

Well, darling, they are calling me to supper. I will write again to-morrow or else after supper. And God keep you. Write exactly how things go in Petersburg. Why doesn't Visnevsky write to me ?

Once more I kiss my darling.

Your holy man ANTONY.

77

Feb. 22, 1901. (*Yalta.*)

My sweet darling, how are you getting on in Petersburg ? [2] I fancy that that town will soon tire and disgust you all by its coldness and its hollowness, and you, poor dear, will begin to

[1] I. A. Bunin, the well-known writer.
[2] The Moscow Art Theatre was on tour in Petersburg.

be bored. Yesterday I had a telegram from Nemirovitch that ' Lonely Lives ' has had no success.

So the tiresome business is beginning already. Anyway I fancy you will never go again to Petersburg.

Here the weather isn't cold, but grey, dirty and dull. The people are grey and spiritless, the dinners at home are not nice. ' Russkaya Mysl ' has printed ' Three Sisters ' without my correcting the proofs, and Lavrov, the editor, says in self-defence that Nemirovitch ' corrected ' the play. So, my darling, everything is uninteresting for the time and, if it were not for the thought of you, I should go abroad again.

When the sun shines, I shall begin working in the garden. Now it is damp and cloudy. The trees will do very well this year as they have lived through one summer and have settled now.

Why don't you write to me ? So far I have had only one letter and one telegram from you here. You are in good spirits and I thank God, my darling. You mustn't be depressed.

Apparently your season tickets [1] go on to the fourth week in Lent [2]; and what after that ? Will you go back to Moscow ? Write, dear.

I kiss and hug you hard, frightfully hard ; I long to speak to you, or rather to have a talk with you. Well, good-bye till we meet. Write to me, don't be lazy.

Your holy man ANTONY.

78

Feb. 23 (1901. *Yalta*).

My dear actress, my remarkable dog, why are you cross with me, why don't you write to me ? [3] Why don't you telegraph ? Do you grudge the money for the telegrams ? Send me a telegram costing twenty-five roubles ; honour bright, I 'd pay it back and bind myself to love you for twenty-five years besides.

I have been ill for three days. Now it seems to be all right,

---

[1] The season tickets for the performances of the Moscow Art Theatre.

[2] At that time the theatres were closed during the first and fourth weeks of Lent.

[3] O. L. had sent letters on Feb. 2, 5, 8, 10, 12, 15, 21 (letters and telegrams, 24).

I am a little easier.   I have been ill and lonely.   Of the Petersburg papers I get only 'Novoye Vremya' and so I know nothing
at all of your triumphs.   So you might send me the newspapers, for instance the ' Financial News ' and ' Novosti,' that
is, the cuttings of them in which your theatre is mentioned, but
if that will be a bore for you, don't bother.

You have not written how long you will stay in Petersburg,
whom you are seeing there, what you are doing.   Will there be
a supper (or a dinner) at ' Zhizn ' ? [1]   If so, be sure to describe
it.   I envy you, it is a long time since I have had a good dinner.

I have a bottle of scent waiting for you, a big bottle.

Bunin has been here, but now he has gone away and I am
alone.   Lavrov, the editor of ' Russkaya Mysl,' comes in now
and then, though ; he saw you in ' Three Sisters ' and speaks
very highly of you.

There is no news and so I am expecting a letter from you,
my splendid, splendid actress ; don't be lazy, for God's sake,
and don't be too conceited.   Remember that the wife is in
subjection to her husband.

Your holy man.

79

TELEGRAM

Feb. 25 (1901.   *Yalta*).

Sent three letters all going well [2] expect telegram more precise
how feeling.

80

(*Feb.* 26, 1901.   *Yalta.*)

Darling, to-day is already the 26th of February and no letters
from you, none.   Why is it ?   Have you nothing to write
about, or has Petersburg, with its newspapers, brought you so
low that you have given me up ?   Never mind, darling, it is
all nonsense.   I read nothing but the ' Novoye Vremya ' and
the ' Petersburg Gazette ' and I am not indignant, because I

---

[1] That is, at the office of ' Zhizn,' a monthly review.
[2] O. L. telegraphed, Feb. 25 : ' Telegraph get no letters strange.'

knew long ago that it would be so. Of the ' Novoye Vremya '
I expected, and expect, nothing but nastiness ; and for the
' Petersburg Gazette,' Kugel writes who will never forgive . . .[1]
I had a telegram from Posse [2] that you are all sad. Despise
them, my dearest, despise all these reviews, and don't be sad.

Won't you come to Yalta with Masha in Holy Week and
afterwards you could go back together to Moscow ? What do
you say ? Think of it, my joy.

I have been ill, coughing and so on. Now I am better,
to-day I have been out for a walk and have been on the sea-
front.

The 28th of February is the ' Novoye Vremya's ' jubilee. I
am afraid they will get up some demonstration against Suvorin.
I shouldn't be sorry for ' Novoye Vremya,' but for those who
get it up.

How much longer will it be before you write to me ? A
month ? A year ?

I kiss you warmly, warmly, my own. God bless you.

Your holy man ANTONY.

81

March 1 (1901. *Yalta*).

My dear, don't read the newspapers, don't read them at all,
or you will pine away altogether. It 's a lesson to you for the
future : listen to your old hermit. I have told you, you know,
I assured you that things would go badly in Petersburg, you
ought to have listened. In any case your theatre will never
go again to Petersburg, thank God !

I personally am giving up the theatre altogether, I am never
going to write for the stage again. Writing for the stage is
possible in Germany, in Sweden, even in Spain, but not in
Russia, because dramatic authors are not respected, they are
kicked and not forgiven their successes and their failures. You
are being abused now for the first time in your life. That is
why you are so sensitive, in time it will come easy, you will
get used to it. But I can imagine how glorious, how divine

---

[1] A. R. Kugel, dramatic critic.   [2] V. A. Posse, the journalist.

Sanin [1] is feeling. I expect he carries about all the notices in his pockets and raises his eyebrows very high. Here it is extraordinary weather, warm and sunny, the apricots and the almonds are in flower. In Holy Week I expect you, my poor, reviled actress, I am waiting, waiting for you, keep that in mind.

I sent you between the 20th and 28th of February five letters and three telegrams ; I asked you to telegraph to me, but not a word in answer.

I have had a telegram from Madame Yavorsky about ' Uncle Vanya.'

Write till which day you will all be in Petersburg. Write, actress.

I am well, honour bright. I embrace you.

Your holy man.

82

March 7, 1901. (*Yalta.*)

I have received an anonymous letter telling me that you have been fascinated by somebody in Petersburg and are head over ears in love. And, indeed, I have suspected it myself for a long time past, you miserly little Jewess. You have most likely left off caring for me because I am not economical and asked you to ruin yourself over one or two telegrams. Well, well ! so be it, but I still love you from old habit, and you see what fine paper I write to you on.

Little miser, why didn't you write and tell me that you are staying for a fourth week in Petersburg and not going to Moscow ? I have put off writing to you all this time expecting that you were going home.

I am alive and I believe well, though I still go on coughing furiously. I work in the garden, where the trees are now in blossom ; the weather is exquisite, as exquisite as your letters which are coming now from abroad. The latest ones are from Naples. Ah, what a splendid, clever thing you are, my darling! I read every letter over three times—that is the minimum.

---

[1] A. A. Sanin, who acted the old father in Hauptmann's ' Lonely Lives,' was the only one of the company praised by the newspapers.

And so I work in my garden, in my study there is precious little work done ; I do not want to do anything, I read proofs and am glad they take up my time.   I am not often in Yalta, I have no inclination to go there ; on the other hand, the Yalta folk sit for hours with me, so that I grow dejected every time and begin swearing to go away again, or to get married so that my wife might drive them away, I mean my visitors.   So I will get a divorce from Ekaterinoslav province and get married again.   Allow me to make you an offer.

I have brought you some scent from abroad, a very nice sort, come and fetch it in Holy Week.   You really must come, my sweet, kind, splendid darling ; if you don't come, you will wound me dreadfully, you 'll poison my existence.   I have already begun looking forward to it, I am counting the days and the hours.   It doesn't matter that you have fallen in love with some one else and already been false to me, I will forgive you, only do come, please.   Do you hear, dog ?   You know I love you, understand that.   It is hard for me to live without you.   If they are making plans at the theatre for rehearsals at Easter, tell Nemirovitch that it is mean and piggish.

I have just been downstairs and have had tea there with bread rings.   I have had a letter from Petersburg from Kondakov, the Academician.   He has been to see ' Three Sisters ' and is unutterably enthusiastic.   You haven't written a word to me about the banquets which have been given in your honour ; you might write to me now anyway, if only for the sake of our friendship.   I am a friend of yours, a great friend, you sly doggy.

I had a long telegram to-day from Solovtsov, from Kiev, telling me that they have performed ' Three Sisters ' in Kiev and had a tremendous desperate success, and so on.   The next play I write will certainly be amusing, very amusing, anyway in conception.

Well, sweet granny, keep well, be merry, don't grieve, don't be despondent.   I, too, have been honoured by Madame Yavorsky ; I have had a telegram about ' Uncle Vanya ' ! You see, she went to see you at the theatre with the feeling of a Sarah Bernhardt, no less, with a sincere desire to rejoice the

whole company by her attention. And you almost picked a
quarrel with her ! [1]

I kiss you eighty times and embrace you warmly. Remember, I shall be expecting you. Remember that !

Your holy man ANTONY.

83

March 11, 1901. (*Yalta.*)

En découpant ce morceau d'une vieille gazette je pensais à
vous ; (ce n'est pas une allusion croyez-le bien) mais je me rappelais alors.[2]

You don't want to come to Yalta,[3] precious—well, do as you
like, I am not going to force you. Only I am awfully disinclined to leave Yalta ! I don't want a railway carriage, I
don't want a hotel. That is all nonsense though, I 'll come to
Moscow and—basta !

You are merry, you are not depressed, and that shows you
are a good, splendid little girl. You write that I don't like
Petersburg. Who told you that ? I like Petersburg, I have
a weakness for it. And what memories I have, connected with
that city ! As for the Petersburg theatre—except Savina and
Davydov to some extent—I think nothing of it and, like your
Uncle Karl, disbelieve in it utterly and dislike it. I have had
a letter to-day from Flyorov, who is ill ; he asks me to take
lodgings for him in Yalta for the whole summer. To-day I
read of the attempt on Pobyedonostsev.[4]

Your dear delightful letters give me extraordinary pleasure,
only why don't you like me to sign myself your holy man ?
You see I live now exactly like a monk and my name is monastic
too. Very well, I won't be a holy man any more. Write to
me, my good, my remarkable darling. Your letters affect me

[1] O. L. wrote, Feb. 21 : ' Yesterday after the first act Madame Yavorsky
burst into my dressing-room to make my acquaintance. What ever for ? '
[2] These lines were printed on the notepaper on which the letter was
written.
[3] O. L. wrote, March 3 : ' All the same I am not coming to Yalta for
Easter ; think a little and you will understand why.'
[4] An attempt had been made to assassinate the Procurator of the
Synod, K. P. Pobyedonostsev.

like the song of a nightingale, I love them very much. And I love your handwriting.

We shall soon see each other, I suppose; that is so splendid! We shall see each other and then go off somewhere together.

Well, darling, good-night! Keep well and merry, don't forget.

Your ANTOINE.

84

March 16 (1901. *Yalta*).

Greetings, my little sweet! I am certainly coming to Moscow, but whether I shall go to Sweden this year I don't know. I am so sick of gadding about and it seems I am growing quite like an old man in my health, so that you will acquire in my person, by the way, a grandfather not a husband. I dig in my garden now for whole days together, the weather is warm and exquisite, everything's in flower, the birds are singing, there are no visitors, in fact it is not life but raspberries and cream. I have quite given up literature. And when I marry you, I shall order you to give up the stage and we'll live together like planters. You don't want to? Oh, very well, act another five years and then we shall see.

To-day I received the 'Russian Veteran,' a special army paper, and behold, I saw in it a notice of 'Three Sisters.' It is No. 56, of the 11th of March. It is all right, it praises and finds no blunders on the military side.

Write to me, my good darling. Your letters give me joy. You are false to me, because you are a human being as well as a woman as you write.[1] Oh very well, be faithless, only be the good, splendid creature that you are. I am an old gentleman, it is impossible not to be false to me, I understand that very well, and if I am false to you myself by some accident you must excuse it. As you will understand, though my beard is grey my heart is gay. That is right, isn't it?

Do you see Madame Avilov?[2] Have you made friends with

[1] Quoted from a jesting letter from O. L. on March 2.
[2] L. A. Avilov, the authoress.

Madame Tchyumin ? [1]   I expect you have already begun writing stories and novels on the sly.   If I find out you have, then good-bye, I shall get a divorce.

I read of the appointment of Pchelnikov [2] in the newspapers and marvelled, marvelled at Pchelnikov's not being ashamed to accept these strange duties.   But they will hardly take 'Dr. Stockman' off your list, you see it is a conservative play.

Though I have given up literature, still from old habit I write something from time to time.   Just now I am writing a story called 'The Bishop,' on a subject which has been haunting me for fifteen years.

I embrace you, traitress, a hundred times.   I kiss you warmly. Write, write, my joy, or when we are married I 'll beat you.

Your hermit ANT—.

85

March 18 (1901.   *Yalta*).

And so, actress, you are going back to Moscow in a day or two ; then I won't write to Petersburg any more.   Well, but the Moscow address ?   Am I to write as before ?   Or to wait till you send the new one ?

We are having simply extraordinary marvellous weather, a most exquisite spring such as we have not had for years.   I should be enjoying it, but the trouble is that I am alone, utterly alone !   I sit in my study or in the garden, and that is all.

Why have they taken off 'Hedda Gabler' ?   What plays are put down for next season ?   Have they decided at last to build a new theatre ?   Write, precious, more fully, more minutely, you know you are my clever girl, so practical and sensible.

Here everything is as of old, there is nothing new.   Yesterday, though, I unexpectedly received a thousand roubles that was owing to me.   I get letters from Petersburg and from

[1] A poetess and translator and a very good friend of the Art Theatre and its founders.

[2] O. L. wrote, March 2 : 'We read the other day that Pchelnikov has been appointed censor of private theatres, of their repertoire, and is to watch over the influence these theatres have on the public and the younger generation.'

Moscow, rather ominous ones; I read the newspapers with loathing.

My nice little actress, don't play in ' Michael Kramer,' [1] or for the sake of that rubbishy part you will be kept in Moscow all May and June, and besides, the part is not interesting. Do as I say, my dear; you know if we are alive and well, you have time yet to play a thousand parts. Ah ! what enchanting weather ! The barometer has gone up tremendously.

Well, darling, my splendid little actress, till we meet ! I kiss you warmly. Write, don't abandon me.

Your poor little man ?

86

TELEGRAM

March 20 (1901. *Yalta*).

Well coming after Easter greetings awaiting letters ANTONIO.

87

TELEGRAM

March 27 (1901. *Yalta*).

Delighted expect arrival spring weather steamer Friday Sunday.[2]

O. L. spent the Easter holidays in Yalta with the Tchehovs and returned to Moscow with Tchehov's sister the week after Easter.

88

(*April* 16, 1901. *Yalta*.)

Knipshits dear, in the last number of the ' Niva ' [3] there is a picture of your company—among others, Marya Fyodorovna and Savitskaya and you. You have come out better

[1] Hauptmann's play, which they were intending to produce at the Moscow Art Theatre.

[2] In answer to O. L.'s letter of March 22 saying that she was coming to Yalta.

[3] The periodical the ' Niva,' published by A. F. Marks.

than in any other portrait. The number is worth buying and keeping as a souvenir. Among other things you will find the Academicians there too ; me with a very thick nose.

I am miserably dull without you. To-day I received the postcard in which you complain of toothache. My poor little girl. Write how it is now, what you are doing and how you feel altogether.

I send you a letter I received to-day. I had meant to drop it into the post-box, but I changed my mind and send it with this letter. Oh, my darling, my good darling ! I was reckoning I should sit down to my table when you had gone and begin working,[1] but, as before, I do nothing and feel not quite up to the mark. Don't forget that I am coming soon. Behave well. I kiss you warmly.

Your ANTONIO.

89

April 17 (1901. *Yalta*).

I have just received a great *affiche*, my ' Uncle Vanya ' has made a great hit in Prague. My darling, it is raining and damp every day in Yalta. It is getting like Vologda. It must be from excess of moisture that my tulips have grown so huge.

What are you doing in Moscow ? Write, little one, don't be lazy. I am depressed without you and your letters.

To-day I have taken C.O.[2]

Soon, soon we shall see each other, we will go to Petrovsko-Razumovskoye,[3] we will go to a restaurant, in short we will be in bliss. Your portrait in the ' Niva ' is very good, you look so good-natured in it.

The roses are not yet in flower, but they will be soon. After the rains my vegetation has grown at a furious pace. And the sky is cloudy to-day too.

Till we meet, dog ! Farewell, dog ! I stroke you and kiss you.

Your fool who is in love with Knipshits.

[1] At the story, ' The Bishop.'   [2] Castor oil.
[3] The old-world palace of the Razumovskys near Moscow, an agricultural institute with a big park.

90

Thursday (*April* 18, 1901. *Yalta*).

Dog Olka! I am coming early in May. As soon as you get a telegram, go at once to the Hotel Dresden and find out whether room No. 45 is empty; that is, in other words, take the cheapest little room you can find.

I often see Nemirovitch; he is very nice and does not stand on his dignity; I have not seen his wife yet. I am coming to Moscow chiefly to enjoy myself and eat a lot. We will go to Petrovsko-Razumovskoye and to Zvenigorod.[1] We will go everywhere if only the weather is fine. If you will consent to go with me to the Volga we will eat sterlets.

Kuprin is apparently in love, fascinated. He has fallen in love with that enormous buxom female whom you know and whom you advise me to marry.

If you will give me your word that not a single soul in Moscow shall know of our marriage until it is over, I will marry you on the very day of my arrival if you like. For some reason I have a fearful dread of a wedding and congratulations and champagne, which one has to hold in one's hand while smiling vaguely. From church it would be nice to drive off, not home, but straight to Zvenigorod, or be married in Zvenigorod. Think it over, darling, think it over! Why, you are a clever creature, so they say.

The weather in Yalta is rather scurvy. The wind rages unceasingly; the roses are in flower but not much yet; they will flower luxuriantly later. The irises are gorgeous.

Everything is in good order with me, everything except one trifling matter—my health.

Gorky has not been exiled but arrested, he is detained in Nizhni. Posse is arrested too.

I embrace you, Olka.

Your ANTOINE.

[1] A very beautiful, picturesque monastery and town near Moscow.

91

(*April* 19, 1901.   *Yalta.*)

My sweet actress, my darling, think ; couldn't we go together
down the Volga, if only to Astrahan ?   What do you say ?
Think it over and I will come soon and we will go together to
Yaroslavl or to Nizhni or to Rybinsk.   We must spend the
summer as comfortably as possible, that is, as far as possible
from our friends.

Here in Yalta it is raining.   The dog Kashtanka has had
her foot trampled on by a horse and I am taking up medical
practice again.

Mind you don't get thinner in Moscow or I shall drag you
back to Yalta again.

Keep well, light of my eyes.   I kiss you desperately.

Your ANT—.

92

April 22, 1901.   (*Yalta.*)

My sweet, glorious Knipshits, I did not prevent your going
because I hate Yalta and because I had the thought in my
mind that anyway I should soon see you in freedom.   In any
case you have no need to be angry, my darling.   I have no
secret thoughts of any kind, I tell you everything that I
think.

At the beginning of May I am coming to Moscow ; if it 's
possible we will be married and go down the Volga, or first go
down the Volga and then be married—that is, as you think
most convenient.

We will take the steamer at Yaroslavl or Rybinsk and go
down to Astrahan, from there to Baku, from Baku to Batum.
Or don't you care for that ?   We might do this : go by the
Northern Dvina to Archangel, to Solovki ; whichever you
choose there we will go.   After that I will live the whole or the
greater part of the winter in Moscow in the same flat with you.
If only I keep well and don't get seedy.   My cough takes away
all my energy, I think apathetically of the future and write

quite without eagerness. You must think about the future, you manage for me, I 'll do as you tell me, otherwise we shall never live, but go on sipping life a tablespoonful once an hour.

So you are left without a part now ? That is very pleasant. To-day I was sent the notice of ' Three Sisters ' from the ' Revue Blanche.' I was sent Tolstoy's answer to the edict of the Synod.[1] I have been sent the almanac called ' Northern Flowers,' with my story.[2] I have had a letter from my brother Ivan ; he writes that he has been ill. The Olympia Company have sent me a telegram from Petersburg asking permission to perform ' Three Sisters.' To-day it is raining and there is a desperate wind, but it is warm and pleasant out of doors. Kashtanka, the dog you call Ginger in your letter, had her foot trodden on by a horse and now I have to look after her and put on bandages—and I am simply saturated with the smell of iodoform. You left a rouble on my table. Vassilyeva, the young lady you saw, is still melancholy and eats nothing.

I have not written mournful letters to Vishnevsky.[3]

What shall I find at your theatre ? What rehearsals ? Rehearsals of what ? Of ' Michael Kramer,' of ' The Wild Duck ' ? At times I am overcome by a violent desire to write a four-act farce, or comedy, for the Art Theatre. And I shall write it, if nothing prevents me, only I shall not let them have it before the end of 1903.

I shall telegraph to you, don't tell anybody, but come to the station alone. Do you hear ? Well, till we meet, darling, my sweet little girl. Don't be depressed and don't imagine God knows what ; on my word of honour, I have nothing whatever that I would keep secret from you for a single minute. Be kind and good, don't be cross.

I kiss you warmly, dog.

Your ANTOINE.

---

[1] The edict of the Synod excommunicating him from the Church.

[2] The story ' At Night,' called in the complete edition of Tchehov's works ' At Sea.'

[3] In answer to O. L., who wrote, April 17 : ' Vishnevsky says that you have sent him a very mournful letter. Is it true ? '

93

April 24 (1901. *Yalta*).

The weather is perfectly horrible in Yalta, my darling, it is cold, it rains and the winds blow. Yesterday Nemirovitch was with me, gentle but dispirited and, as I fancy, looking older of late. He is very anxious to write.

Kuprin [1] spends the whole day with us, he only sleeps at home. Bunin is in Odessa. Madam Bonnier does not come often.

Have you yet decided where we are going ? To the Volga or to Solovki ? Think about it, darling.

A collection of stories, ' Northern Flowers,' has come out in Moscow ; in it is my story, ' At Night.'

I asked Dr. Borodulin a week ago about Tchaleyeva [2] ; she undoubtedly has tuberculosis, so Borodulin says, but not in a severe form ; she may recover if she will live in the Crimea. I can tell you nothing more about her.

It certainly is nice in Zvenigorod, I was at one time *locum tenens* in a hospital there. We will certainly go there, my excellent spouse.

You write that I must bring with me the necessary papers for our wedding. But I have no papers at all except my passport.

So, farewell, my little Lutheran, keep well and merry and don't get thin, be a plump, rosy-cheeked little German. You want me to call you Olya ? All right, take care of yourself, Olya.

Gorky, so they write, was arrested in Nizhni.

I kiss you warmly.

Your ANT—.

94

April 30 (1901. *Yalta*).

My dear actress, my splendid Olya, I am going to Foros to stay with Ushkov.[3]

Keep well, I kiss you most warmly.

Your ANT—.

[1] A. I. Kuprin, the well-known writer.

[2] V. I. Tchaleyev, at that time an actress at the Moscow Art Theatre, suffering from tuberculosis, was staying in Yalta.

[3] K. K. Ushkov, one of the founders and directors of the Moscow Art Theatre, had an estate called Foros, in the Crimea.

95

May 2 (1901 *Yalta*).

My sweet darling, I only stayed one night at Foros, was bored there and taken ill. And to-day, as ill luck would have it, it is cold and cloudy. I am sitting in my study without going out, and for lack of anything better to do spend my day in thinking and coughing. Don't be angry with me, darling, for behaving like this, don't punish me with cheerless thoughts. Soon we shall see each other, very soon. I shall leave Yalta on the 5th of May, or at the latest the 10th, according to the weather. Then we will go down the Volga, in fact we will do anything, whatever you want. I am in your hands.

If [1] you ever marry Vishnevsky, it won't be a marriage of love, but of prudence. You will reflect that he is not a bad fellow and marry him. Obviously he is reckoning on your soon being a widow, but tell him that to spite him I am leaving a will forbidding you to marry again.

My splendid darling Olya, anyway we shall soon see each other, and we will talk over everything. Now it is evening and I feel better than I did in the morning and in the day. I shall probably arrive in Moscow in the morning, as the express runs again after the 4th of May. I will send a telegram. Behave yourself. If May is cold we will go to the Volga early in June. From Yaroslavl ? And why not from Nizhni ? The good steamers only start from Nizhni—I think that is so. But there, we 'll discuss it all when we see each other. Good-bye till we meet, dog.

Your ANT—.

Kuprin, about whom you ask, sleeps at his lodgings, but lives with us.

Vassilyeva is going away to-morrow. Arseny brushes my coat every day. Kashtanka is recovering. I am eating with a good appetite, but to-day had no appetite—here are answers to your questions. As for the Grand Duchess, tell her that I can't

[1] O. L. in her letter, April 26, referred to Vishnevsky's saying, in jest, that O. L. would soon marry him.

go to see her and that she never will see me.   If anything goes wrong, over my passport, for instance, I shall send you[1] to her.

96

TELEGRAM

May 6 (1901.   *Yalta*).

Probably coming Friday well.

97

TELEGRAM

May 9 (1901.   *Yalta*).

Coming Friday positively certainly Dogman.

On May 10 Tchehov went to Moscow, where the following letter was written referring to their wedding, which took place on May 25.

98

May 1901.   *Moscow.*

I have everything ready, we must meet before one o'clock to talk things over.   We will go away on Friday for certain.

A. TCHEHOV.

On May 25 the Tchehovs left Moscow, went by rail to Nizhni, where they visited Gorky, thence by steamer up the Kama.   They stayed at Axyonovo in the Ufa province, where Tchehov took a koumiss cure.   Some weeks later they went together to Yalta, where they spent the rest of the summer.   In the third week of August O. L. returned to Moscow.

99

Aug. 21, 1901.   (*Sevastopol.*)

My dear, my darling, my good wife.   I have only just got up from my bed, drunk my coffee and with some alarm listened

---

[1] A jesting answer to O. L.'s telling him in her letter, April 26, that the Grand Duchess Elizabeth had made inquiries concerning him.

to the sound of the wind. I shouldn't wonder if there 's a rough sea. My darling, buy me some raffia at some shop, such as Lisitsyn's, and send it me to Yalta. There is none of it here in Sevastopol.[1] Put in with the raffia half a dozen cords for my pince-nez. Put in anything else you like, only be careful the parcel does not weigh more than two pounds.

I am going to Yalta and shall there await a letter from you. Don't be dreary, little one. Don't mope and be depressed. Don't be cross, but be merry and laugh, that suits you so well.

I love you very much and will love you. Give my greetings to all your people. I kiss you a hundred times. I embrace you warmly, and in my imagination I draw all sorts of pictures in which there are you and I only and no one and nothing else. Darling, good-bye !

Your goodman ANTOINE.

100

Aug. 23 (1901. Yalta).

My exquisite wife, my dear friend, yesterday I arrived in Yalta again. I slept well in Sevastopol ; in the morning there was a strong wind and I expected a rough sea, but it was not rough and everything went off very well. And now I am at home, I am sitting at my table and writing this. The weather is glorious. Well, how are you ? What did you find in Moscow ? How did your comrades greet you ? Write to me about everything, my splendid little girl. I think of you continually.

The easy-chair from your room that looks sullen and pensive I have told them to bring into mine. It is so still and lonely in your room downstairs. The portrait of your mother is standing on the table.

Arseny [2] has not come back yet. I am told that Masha [3] will be discharged from the hospital to-day, but Marfusha [3]

---

[1] Tchehov had travelled with O. L. as far as Sevastopol on her way to Moscow.

[2] The manservant, who had gone for a holiday.

[3] The cook and the housemaid, who had both been ill with typhoid.

will have to lie up another three weeks. The Polish Masha [1] is very zealous and, so Sister Masha says, has cooked the dinner in our absence very well from recipes in a Polish book. The police are turning Madame Konovitser [2] out of Yalta and it seems nothing can be done for her. I have put your fan away in my table drawer.

I haven't brushed my clothes to-day—you see your absence is felt already. And my boots have not been cleaned either. But don't be agitated, I'll see about it and Masha will see about it, everything shall be brushed.

I love you, my darling, I love you very much. Give my greetings to your mother, to Uncle Sasha, to Uncle Karl, to Vishnevsky, to Nemirovitch and every one. I kiss you and embrace you warmly, my precious and priceless girl. God keep you. I bless you. Write, write, write every day, or you will be beaten. I am a very stern and strict husband, you know that.   Your ANT—.

It rained yesterday in Yalta. Everything is fresh in the garden.

101

Aug. 23 (1901. Yalta).

My darling, cash the enclosed cheque for eight hundred roubles at the Government Bank, then write to Alexey Alexeyevitch Dolzhenko, Moscow, Antropovy Yamy, Voskressensky Proyezd, Rodionov Buildings, Flat 1—write and tell him when he can find you in, at what time, and then when he comes to you, give him the eight hundred roubles. He is my cousin, the son of my aunt, my mother's sister, and he is a very nice little fellow, so be friendly with him. He is free after dinner on holidays and so you had better tell him to come to you on a holiday.

Arseny has come back at last. The cranes set up a tremendous outcry on the occasion. Masha has come back from the hospital. I believe life will become normal again, though

---

[1] The new cook.

[2] An intimate friend of the Tchehov family. As a Jewess, she was deprived of the right of living in Yalta.

my clothes have not been brushed for three days, however. My boots haven't been cleaned either; I will call Arseny at once and give them to him to clean.

It is fine again to-day. Sasha Sredin and his wife were here yesterday and also Madame Bonnier, with whom I shall obviously have a little affair.

I read that it is cold in Moscow. Is that true?

So, my little one, treat Alyosha like a relation. I repeat he is a good lad. I kiss you warmly. I embrace you and kiss you again. I miss you fearfully, my angel, my extraordinary darling.

This portrait was drawn by Hotyaintsova.[1]

All this time, ever since we parted, I have not received one single letter from you.[2] What means this dream?

I bless you, my better-half. Greetings to your mother and uncles, your brother and every one.

Your ANT—.

102

Aug. 24 (1901. *Yalta*).

My sweet darling, I have received two postcards and one letter from you, thank you! You are a good, kind girl, I love you and love you. But all day long my head has been aching, not aching, but splitting, and meanwhile from morning till evening (just the same as yesterday) there was one visitor after another. I cannot work. Among others, Doroshevitch [3] and one Reformatsky, a doctor from Petersburg, were pleasant ones.

There are rugs now on my floor. It is snug. They will do up the stove. After the watering we gave them, the roses are flowering like mad.

I shall come to Moscow in September when you write to me. I am very dreary without you. I have grown used to you like a little child, and I feel cold and comfortless without you.

[1] An artist and intimate friend of the Tchehovs.
[2] O. L. sent a letter Aug. 21, three postcards on the journey and a letter on the 22nd from Moscow.
[3] V. M. Doroshevitch, a writer.

The head-mistress has come with her niece, Manefa.   It is raining.   The new cook, the Polish Masha, cooks very well. For three days now we have dined quite like human beings. My room is swept and dusted, and to-day Arseny brushed my clothes.   Yesterday Madame Tatarinov [1] came to see us, did I write to you about that ?

You write : ' My heart begins to ache when I think of the quiet misery which seems to be so deeply rooted in your heart.' What nonsense that is, darling !   There is no misery in my heart and never has been, I feel very tolerable and when you are with me quite happy.

Write how they greeted you at the theatre, what plays are being done and what are to be done, and what you will be doing till the 15th of September.   Write longer letters, don't be lazy.   I write you long letters, but my handwriting is so tiny they look short.

It has been cool, but now it is beginning to be warm again. It is still and delightful.   The roses are flowering profusely, in fact it is not life, but raspberries and cream.

I embrace my good wife, I kiss her and bless her and earnestly beg her not to forget me, but to write and think of me a little oftener.   When I come I shall kiss you incessantly for a whole hour, then I shall go to the baths and the barber's, then I shall have dinner, then spend the evening with you and then go to sleep.   Is that all right ?   My darling !   What a vile portrait that is of you in ' Recreation.'   Oy !   Oy !

I kiss both your little paws.

Your ANT—.

103

Aug. 25 (1901.   *Yalta*).

To-day, my sweet, it is just three months since we were married.   I have been happy and thank you, my joy, I kiss you a thousand times.   The Sredins were with us to-day, having just come back from their travels.   He looks better, while

---

[1] At that time a Yalta house-owner, who had in 1899 entertained the Art Theatre company on her roof.   Later on she became teacher of singing at the Moscow Art Theatre.

Sofya Petrovna is thinner, but cheerful and happy. Orlenev, the actor, came in. Doroshevitch and he dined with us.

I am drinking kefeer, apparently with benefit to myself. To-morrow I shall drink three bottles.

Have you taken the place in Spiridonovka? A whole house? And what does that mean?

I am fearfully exhausted, visitors the whole day. Yesterday my head ached, but to-day it's all right, only I feel tired.

I hug you tight, tight. Your husband and your friend for ever and ever.

ANTON.

When shall we see each other?

104

Aug. 27 (1901. *Yalta*).

My dog, I am well, but as before I am doing nothing, since it is now the autumn season and so many people are staying in Yalta. Your friend Karabtchevsky was here twice yesterday. To-day Orlenev turned up, and so on and so on.

There are a great many big spiders in my room. Where they have sprung from the devil only knows. They run very quickly.

In the drawing-room they are pulling the stove to pieces. I am going to wash my head to-day, my hair is still coming out.

To-day I am going into the town on business. Dr. Vitte, an invalid, has come to Yalta. I must go to the post, I must go to see Madame Bonnier (your rival) and so on. To-morrow Madame Konovitser is going away. You see, darling, I write about everything to you most fully, and keep silent or write very briefly only about one thing, how much I love you, how I miss you, my joy, my little German, my child. Your second letter was already shorter and I am afraid you are growing cold to me or, at any rate, getting used to not having me by you.

Well, I won't go into these details. Good-bye, my love. I kiss you. I hug you and do anything I please with you. Greetings to your mother, to Uncle Karl, to Uncle Sasha and your brother.

Your ANTON.

Write more fully ! !

105

(Aug. 28, 1901.   Yalta.)

Doggy, my sweet pup, I have only just received your letter.
I have read it twice and I send you a thousand kisses.   I like
the plan of the flat, I will show it to Masha (she is gone to see
Dunya Konovitser to the steamer).   It is all very nice, only
why have you put ' Anton's study ' next door to a certain
apartment ?   Do you want to be beaten ?

I answer your questions : I am sleeping splendidly, though
it is horribly dull sleeping alone (what habit does !), I eat a
great deal.   I talk the whole day to visitors.   I am drinking
kefeer every day with relish.   My ' innards ' are behaving well
so far.   I don't rub my neck with eau-de-Cologne—I forgot to.
Yesterday I washed my head.

Yesterday I was at Orlenev's and met Leventon [1] ; she is
living in the same flat with him.

Masha will bring almonds from our tree and give them to you.

You see what a good husband I am ; I write to you every
day in the most punctual way.   I do miss you so !   Every
morning I listen, hoping to hear the Hungarian [2] passing with
the pail.   It seems to me I have become a regular bourgeois
and cannot live without my wife.   'ive Aunt Lyolya [3] and
Nikolasha [4] my greetings and a kiss to Nikolasha.

Behave yourself or I shall beat you very hard.   Write,
darling, don't be lazy.

Your ANTON.

106

Aug. 30, 1901.   (Yalta.)

My sweet darling, the city school in Miussky [5] Square is, I
believe, near Sushtchovo,[6] where you are every day now ; so

---

[1] Alla Nazimov, the actress.   [2] Nickname of O. L.
[3] Yelena Ivanovna, the sister of O. L.'s mother.
[4] N. N. Sokolovsky.
[5] Where Tchehov's brother Ivan was at that time living and teaching.
[6] The rehearsals of the Moscow Art Theatre were then being held
there.

go in to brother Ivan's and fetch my coat and the rest of the clothes which I left with him after our wedding. It is the coat in which I was married. See Ivan and Sonya [1] and talk with them as you know so well how.

And last night I had something in the cholerina line ; sickness and the rest of it, most unseemly. And why, I don't know. I ate nothing yesterday but meat. Towards morning I fell asleep and now am all right. Only I have taken castor oil and feel flabby. You write about a cat, but—brrr ! I am afraid of cats. Dogs, now, I respect and think highly of. Do keep a dog ! You can't keep a cat, by the way, because our Moscow flat will be left empty for half a year (almost). However, my love, you know best, keep a crocodile if you like ; I give you free leave and permission for everything and am ready even to sleep with a cat.

Gorky has written to me that he is coming to Yalta. I am sick of the ' Courier '—it writes vulgar things about me in almost every number.

You want to have a piano on the hire system ? Hadn't you better buy it ? It will come very dear on the hire system, you know.

Don't be ill, light of my eyes, don't be depressed, but laugh as often as you can. Soon we shall see each other and I shall be a whole month with you.

I will love you hard.

Good-bye, darling, keep well. I kiss you, my dog, and stroke you.

Your ANTON.

107

Aug. 31 (1901. *Yalta*).

My wife, I get letters from you every day, so the post is punctual and everything is satisfactory. I have taken ' The Bishop ' out of my box. I am coming to Moscow as soon as you move into your new flat and write to me. In any case I ought to come before the beginning of the campaign, as other-

---

[1] Ivan's wife.

wise they won't arrange rehearsals of ' Three Sisters ' for me
—that is, I must come before the 16th of September. Mustn't I ?

I am so dreary without you, just as though I were shut up
in a monastery. And what it will be in the winter I can't
imagine !

The new cook does very well and so far all is satisfactory.
Mother seems pleased and satisfied with her—and I am pleased
too, of course. Only fancy, it is so cool in Yalta I don't go
out now without an overcoat, and I shut the window when
I go to bed. I sleep all alone, like an old bachelor, like an
old fogey. You complain in your letter that I write such
short letters. Dear, it is that my handwriting is so tiny.
Though, indeed, my thoughts are not on a large scale either
now. As soon as I have said two or three words I put a full
stop ; but still I have written to you almost every day and
written about everything that concerns me. Don't be angry
with me, my dear wife, my good helpmate.

Greetings to your mother, Uncle Sasha, Aunt Lyolya, Nikolasha and your brother. Thank Uncle Sasha for reading my
stories, I send him a kiss for that.

Well, God keep you. Don't tire yourself too much. Don't
be depressed, but think a little oftener of your husband. I
embrace you, little one.

Your ANT—.

A squadron is stationed here, for Yalta that is a great event.
Thanks about Alyosha.

Next year the room with a piano in it will be yours. The
subject has been broached already.

108

Sept. 1, 1901. (*Yalta.*)

Dear dog, you write to me every day. I love you for it, and
bless you ; do the same for the future. Be a good girl and ask
Nemirovitch to give me, please, the chance to make the acquaintance of his play.[1] Let him have it copied and send it

---

[1] The play ' In Dreams ' was performed that season at the Moscow
Art Theatre.

me at once, I shall read it with great attention and interest and with immense pleasure—I hope he won't refuse me this request.

Send me your address. Boitsov's House, Spiridonovka, is that right? I am brushed every day, but not as I was when you were here. Arseny does the brushing when he comes back from the town. I have to take off my clothes (jacket) and give it to him; that is not interesting and so it does not happen every day.

I am reading Turgenev. Yesterday I read a very interesting lecture of Metchnikov's, ' The Flora of our Body,' which tells why we don't live hundreds of years. Very interesting. Our descendants will live two hundred years and at seventy or eighty they will be quite young still. I gave back 'Salammbo' to the Sredins. Anything else ? You had a delicious salad, and you describe it with so much relish that I long for some too.

I received the raffia for my trees, thanks. I am wrapping up my trees now for the whole winter. I have ordered some more rose-trees, very nice tall ones. I have ordered two Japanese plums. Tell Vishnevsky that I shall leave Yalta calculating to be in Moscow in time for the rehearsals of ' Three Sisters,' that is, I shall be in your parts, Madam, by the 16th. If there should be no rehearsal, I shan't see ' Three Sisters.' Must I bring a quilt with me to Moscow ? And a pillow ? Write to me what I ought to bring.

Well, I kiss you. Behave yourself.

Your stern husband ANTONIO.

109

Sept. 3 (1901. *Yalta*).

Dear Olga, greetings ! I didn't write to you yesterday, first, because I had a lot of visitors, and second, because I had no time. I sat down and wrote at my story when my visitors had gone.

Thank you, my joy, Mother was highly delighted with your letter ; she read it and then gave it to me to read it aloud to her and spent a long time praising you. What you write about your jealousy is perhaps not without grounds, but you are such a sensible girl and your heart is so good that all that you write of your so-called jealousy does not quite fit in with your character ! [1] You write that Masha will never be used to you and so on and so on. What nonsense it all is ! You exaggerate it all, you imagine silly things, and I am afraid that before we know where we are, you will be quarrelling with Masha. This is what I have to say to you : have patience and keep silent for only one year, only one year, and then everything will come clear for you.

Whatever is said to you, whatever you fancy, you hold your tongue. For all newly married wives and husbands, every comfort in life depends on this non-resistance in early days. Do as I say, darling, be a good girl !

I shall come when you write, but not in any case later than the 15th of September. You may say what you like, but I don't intend to be patient longer. I shall live in Moscow till December, until you turn me out.

Little German, send me Nemirovitch's play ! I shall bring it back safe. I will read it very carefully.

I shall bring very few clothes with me and buy more in Moscow. I shall buy warm under-things, I shall buy a new overcoat, I shall fetch my rug and goloshes (I shall come in my old overcoat), in fact I shall try to travel without luggage.

I am installing an immense wardrobe for clothes for myself and for my spouse. My spouse is very hot-tempered, so I must arrange life as comfortably as possible for her. Yesterday I washed my head with spirit.

I kiss and embrace my old woman. God keep you. Only a little while—and we shall see each other. Write, write, darling, write ! I shall never love any one now but you, not one other woman. Be well and merry !

Your husband ANTON.

110

Sept. 4, 1901. (*Yalta.*)

See what trouble I take about you ! With this passport you can live where you like and as you like, with your husband and

---

[1] O. L. in her letter, Aug. 30, said she would like to carry Tchehov away to keep him for herself.

without him. Only you must : first, sign your name Olga
Tchehov on page 6 of the passport; two, sign your name at the
Yalta Police Station that the passport has been received by
you. This you can do when you are in Yalta again. And so
you see now you are a regular Yalta citizen till the day of your
death. At first I wanted to make you out the wife of ' an
honorary Academician,' but afterwards I decided that it was
a great deal pleasanter to be the wife of a doctor.

Live peacefully and honourably, be kind and friendly and
I 'll kiss you for it every day. ' Three Sisters ' has been performed at Odessa with great success, so they write me. To-
day I have cut my hair, washed my head, clipped my beard,
went for a walk along the sea-front, then dined at home together
with Dr. Reformatsky.

Write every day or I will take away your passport. I am
going to keep a stern hand over you altogether so that you
may fear and obey me. I 'll give it you !

Your severe husband A. TCHEHOV.

I haven't seen our flat yet, but you speak so nicely about it
that I am pleased with it already, very much pleased, my
darling. Thank you for all the trouble you have taken over
it. God keep you, darling.

111

Sept. 5, 1901. (*Yalta.*)

My sweet pup, to-day I have had no letter from you, and
yesterday I had a short and cross one. You are out of humour ?
What for ? I have been unwell now for three days ; my back
aches, my arms ache, altogether I am not good for much. But
yet I am in good spirits. I look forward to the future with hope
and even have two people coming to dinner to-day, Bunin and
a Prosecutor. And in spite of my backache I am furiously busy
over a performance for the benefit of the Benevolent Society.
Orlenev is to act; Varya Panin, the gypsy, who is here now,
is to sing.

I have had a letter from Uncle Sasha, a very nice and amusing one ; I shall write to him when my visitors go. One of

Ostroumov's assistants was here the other day and he told me that Ostroumov now prescribes very readily, almost with enthusiasm, eucalyptus oil mixed with turpentine as a liniment. I sent for some from the chemist's, but it has to be rubbed on for fifteen minutes and it has to be rubbed on by some one else, so nothing has come of it.

The visitors have had dinner, have stayed a little and have gone. I am unwell. I have just heard on the telephone that the gypsy singer is paying me a visit at 6 o'clock, you see what a busy life I have now ! They have just announced that an artist of some sort has arrived.

The artist came to ask a favour. He wants to paint my portrait ; and his throat is bad, he wants to be treated.

Well, good-bye, my wife. God be with you. I love you and I shall go on loving you. I kiss you, I kiss your hands. Write about the flat. I am coming soon.

Your husband A. TCHEHOV.

112

Sept. 6 (1901. *Yalta*).

Darling, I am better to-day, but still pretty bad. I am coming to Moscow on the 15th or the 17th, I have settled that finally.

Yesterday evening a stranger, a Moscow doctor, called upon me and stayed on and on. . . . I almost howled with despair, and to-day I have given Arseny orders to admit no one. Basta ! I thought at first that I might have typhoid, but now I see that it is not that, and that to-morrow, or the day after, I shall be quite all right.

Of course, to wander over the world with a wallet on one's back, to breathe freely and to care about nothing [1] is infinitely pleasanter than to sit in Yalta and read articles about Kondratyev.[2]

I will write to Uncle Sasha. Don't be anxious about my health, sweet pup, all is going well. Soon we shall meet. A

---

[1] O. L. in her letter, Sept. 2, had described how L. Sulerzhitsky had spent the summer wandering about Russia.

[2] A stage-manager of the Imperial Little Theatre in Moscow.

kiss to Uncle Sasha and Nikolasha and Aunt Lyolya and a kiss to you. Marfusha is still in the hospital. Bunin is full of the joy of life. I have not yet been at the Sredins'.

Well, God be with you, keep well.

Your ANTONIO.

113

Sept. 7, 1901. (*Yalta.*)

I shall arrive on the 17th of September, as I am leaving Yalta on the 15th, that is settled and signed. And so that is how it will be. You will have a telegram from me, ' Monday '— that means that I 'll arrive on Monday morning.

I am very much better to-day and should be splendidly well were it not for my cough, which will soon pass off, though. I have received your desperate letter about the flat and don't understand why you are so upset. The flat is probably very nice, and if it is a little cramped, what does it matter ? Don't let it bother you, my darling.

Orlenev has just been to see me. And so we shall soon meet. It 's begun to be magnificent weather in Yalta, but yet I want to get away. I long very much to have a sight of my dog.

I kiss you, my German.

Your ANTONIO.

Don't be upset, darling, whatever happens, don't be upset, for everything in this world is for the best, so I am told. Absolutely everything.

On Monday when I arrive I shall go to the baths, then I shall spend the whole day at home. And on Tuesday I will go with you wherever you take me. I still don't know the name of the house where you moved to, I haven't your address.

114

Sept. 9, 1901. (*Yalta.*)

My wife, what is the meaning of this ? Why have I had no letter from you for two days ? Why don't you tell me your new address ? You write that you 've moved to Spiridonovka, but to what house I don't know.

I shall start on Saturday the 15th (I have taken the ticket already) so as to arrive on the 17th, on Monday. If I have to go by a duplicate train, as Masha did, I will mention that in my telegram.

Now I am quite well. Bunin comes to see me every day. It is inconceivable how my money goes every day, inconceivable ! I must make haste and run away, my darling. One person got a hundred roubles from me yesterday, to-day another came to say good-bye to me and got ten roubles, another was given a hundred roubles, some one else has been promised a hundred roubles and some one else fifty, and all that must be paid to-morrow when the bank opens. My precious, keep well ! ! ! Soon we shall see each other. I kiss you.

Your ANTONIO.

Marfusha has come back from the hospital very thin.

115

TELEGRAM

Sept 9. (*Yalta.*)

Leaving Saturday TCHEHOV.

116

Sept. 10, 1901. (*Yalta.*)

It 's a long while since I have had a letter from you. It is five days till Saturday, when I leave, so I shall be for five days without a letter.

I still don't know your address and so I am sending this letter to Leontyevsky Place.[1] There is no news. I am well, or almost well. Orlenev is still hanging about here. He came to see me to-day.

But enough ! We shall soon meet. Be well, my darling, and God keep you. I bless you with both hands, kiss you and embrace you.

Your ANT—.

[1] Where O. L.'s mother lived.

117

TELEGRAM

Sept. 16, 1901.   *Sevastopol.*

.   .   .   .

118

TELEGRAM

Sept. 20, 1901.   *Lozovaya.*

I am sailing TCHEHOV.

Tchehov went to Moscow on September 16 *and remained there till October* 26.

119

(Oct. 26, 1901.   *Tula.)*

My darling, greetings.   I have just eaten a helping of white sturgeon to your health in Tula, and now to fill up time I am eating *marmelad.*[1]   Stahovitch was in the same compartment all the way from Moscow to Tula and we kept up a conversation.

Don't be depressed, behave yourself and write to your husband.   I didn't say good-bye to every one at the theatre. Make my apologies, my joy.   Tell them it was because I was in such a hurry and ask them not to be cross with me.

I kiss you warmly and press your hand.   My love to Masha.

Your TOTOSHA.

120

Sevastopol, Sunday (Oct. 28, 1901).

There is a violent storm ; they say the steamers will not put in at Yalta.   I am driving with posting-horses.

It is coldish.

Keep well, little one.   Greetings to Masha.   I am quite well. I have had a good journey.   I kiss you warmly and bless you.

Your ANT—.

I shall expect letters from you at home.   Write very fully.

[1] A kind of sweet made by boiling fruit to the consistency of damson cheese.

121

Oct. 29 (1901. *Yalta*).

My sweet, splendid, kind, clever wife, light of my eyes, greetings! I am in Yalta, I am sitting at home and it feels so strange! The Sredins have been here to-day and the head-mistress, and already I have dropped back up to my ears in the old rut which is so empty and boring. Well, I had a very good journey, though I ought not to have taken horses at Sevastopol, for the steamer did put in at Yalta. However, I had a good rapid drive, though it was cold. Here I found it not simply cold, but icy; it was cold driving in my overcoat.

Madame Tatarinov is coming to see me about business immediately and I am writing in a hurry. Mother is well, she says that I might have stayed on a little in Moscow. Sredin is well too, or at any rate he looks well; he was abusing his sister-in-law all the while.

My sweet, my angel, my dog, my darling, I beseech you believe that I love you, love you deeply; don't forget me, write and think about me a little oftener. Whatever were to happen, even if you were suddenly to change into an old woman, I should still love you—for your soul, for your character. Write to me, my pup! Be careful of your health. If you fall ill, which God forbid, throw up everything and come to Yalta, I will look after you here. Don't overtire yourself, little one.

I have received a number of my photographs from Harkov. A photographer came in the summer and took me from every point of view.

They served me a choice dinner to-day—thanks to your letter, most likely. Chicken rissoles and pancakes. The tongue which we bought at Byelov's went bad on the journey, or any-way seems to have gone bad, it smells.

The Lord bless you. Don't forget me, I am your husband, you know. I kiss you warmly, embrace you and kiss you again. My bed seems so lonely, as though I were a niggardly bachelor, old and spiteful.

Write!!

Your ANTOINE.

Don't forget that you are my wife ; write to me every day.
My love to Masha. I am still eating the sweets your mother
gave me. My love to her too.

122

Oct. 30, 1901. (*Yalta.*)

Sweet dog, puppy, Mother bids me thank you for your letter,
sends her love and asks me to write that she will do exactly as
you say.[1] She kisses you.

Balmont [2] was here to-day and dined with us. We had
snipe. Madame Bonnier was here. Tell Vishnevsky that the
subscription list [3] will be sent to him in a day or two.

Tell Nemirovitch that Balmont is writing a play for the
Art Theatre and will certainly finish it by the spring ; I am
delighted, for I expect it will be a good and original play. I
have received a play from Fyodorov,[4] the dark man who came
to see us and whom you didn't like ; I 'll write about it when
I have read it. That 's for the Art Theatre too. All day long
I have been reading the newspapers which had accumulated on
my table in my absence ; in every one of them I find something
about myself. I send you a cutting from the ' Priazovsky
Kray.' If one may judge from the provincial papers, the Art
Theatre has made a complete revolution in the stage. Yes, you
had better produce ' The Wild Duck ' and produce ' Kramer '
whatever happens.

Ah, dog, dear dog . . . well, never mind. We will get
along somehow, we will have patience and then will be together
again. I will not be faithless to you, my darling, set your
mind at rest.

I kiss you warmly. Sleep peacefully, eat with appetite,
work gaily.

Love to Masha.

Your ANTO—.

[1] In regard to Tchehov's diet.
[2] K. D. Balmont, the poet and translator of Shelley.
[3] Tchehov was collecting subscriptions for a sanatorium for consumptives
at Yalta, built by Dr. Altschuller. Vishnevsky had offered to help in
collecting money.
[4] A. M. Fyodorov, the writer.

I kiss you and embrace you ; I have grown so used to your
care of me that now I feel as though I were on a desert island.
Sasha Sredin has been ill, now they say he is all right, he is up
and going out.

123

Nov. 1 (1901.   *Yalta*).

My dear lawful wife, I am alive and well and lonely.   The
weather in Yalta is exquisite, but that does not concern me
much, I sit at home and read proofs which seem to be
endless !   I am going to the town in a minute to have my
hair cut.

I knew you would act in Nemirovitch's play.   I say this not
by way of reproof, just in answer to your letter.   Judging from
the newspapers, 'Kramer' had not the success I expected, and
now I feel hurt.   Our public does not want plays but shows.
But that Stanislavsky should be depressed about it, as you
write, is both foolish and strange ; it shows that he has not
the consciousness that he is doing the right thing.   I kiss
you, my little one, write every detail.   I look forward to it.
I embrace you.

Your ANTO—.

Do seal your letters up better, for they come almost open . . .
and that is your fault, the envelopes are so poor.   Well, darling,
take care of yourself ! !

124

Nov. 2, 1901.   (*Yalta*.)

My sweet dog, greetings !   In your letter you ask about the
weather, about the cranes, about Mogabi.[1]   The weather is
soft and warm but misty.   Mogabi is hidden behind the mist.
About the cranes I have written to you already (there are two
of them) ; the garden is in a good state, chrysanthemums in
flower and roses too, in fact life is a raspberry again.   Yesterday and to-day, all these days in fact, I have been reading

---

[1] The mountain Mogabi at which Tchehov and O. L. used to gaze,
sitting in their favourite spot in the garden on a seat in the corner by the
eucalyptus-tree he had planted.

proofs of which I am sick and I have only just finished them, quite finished them, as they will send no more now.

I am all right, but yesterday and the day before, in fact ever since my arrival here, I have not been quite myself, so that yesterday I had to take castor oil. I am very glad that you are well and in good spirits, my darling. That makes my heart lighter. And I have an awful desire now that you should be the mother of a little half-German who would amuse you and make your life fuller. You ought to be, my darling! What do you think?

Gorky will soon be here on his way to Moscow, he wrote to me that he would leave Nizhni on the 1st of November. He promises to alter your part in his play,[1] that is, to make it broader; in fact, he promises a good deal, of which I am very glad, as I believe that his alterations will make the play not worse but a great deal better, fuller. When that little fellow who eats no meat [2] comes to you, tell him that Popov (who is having a polyp cut out of his nose) sends his greetings to him. I haven't yet been to see Tolstoy. I shall go to-morrow, I am told he feels well.

Olya, wife, congratulate me, I have had my hair cut !! Yesterday my boots were cleaned for the first time since my arrival. My clothes have not yet been brushed. But on the other hand, I change my tie every day and yesterday I washed my head. Yesterday evening Leonid Sredin came to see me. He sat and said nothing and then had supper. With him came Balmont. This morning a consumptive Greek came for treatment. Do I bore you? You told me to write you every detail, so you see I am doing so.

I send you an advertisement from Prague about ' Uncle Vanya.' I keep wondering what I can send you and I can think of nothing. I live like a monk and dream only of you. Though it's a disgrace to be making declarations of love at forty, yet I cannot refrain, dog, from telling you once more that

---

[1] The part of the widow in ' The Petty-Bourgeois.'
[2] L. A. Sulerzhitsky, a Tolstoyan who had taken the Duhobors to America, afterwards a stage-manager of the Art Theatre and the founder of the ' First Studio.' He died in 1916.

I love you deeply and tenderly. I kiss you, embrace you and press you to my heart. Be well, happy, merry !

Your ANTOINE.

125

Nov. 4, 1901. (*Yalta.*)

My darling, I didn't go yesterday to see Tolstoy, the cabman played me false and did not turn up, so I shall go to him to-morrow. It is still fine weather, quiet, warm and sunny, but yet the Moscow winter is better. It is miserable without you. I have to write masses of letters.

My dinners are so far satisfactory. There is no decent milk in Yalta. There is no cream either. No one warms the Ems water in the morning, for there is no one to do it. I take cod-liver oil. My health, by the way, is in a good state again, better than it was three or four days ago. Gorky is expected here. Sofya Petrovna Sredin was looking for lodgings for him yesterday, but could not find any. Most likely Gorky will stay not far from Gaspra, where Tolstoy is. I haven't seen Sasha Sredin yet, I don't go to the town.

My wife must be gentle and very kind as I left her in Moscow and as I picture her now. My sweet dog ! When shall we see each other ?

It should be time to set to work upon ' Dr. Stockman.' The press is evidently in a bad humour, it has indigestion and is sick of everything. It refuses to understand anything, and I am afraid that when Nemirovitch's play appears, our newspaper men will begin hiccoughing again. Your company and Stanislavsky especially ought not to pay attention to them.

Well, my wife, take care of yourself. I kiss both your little paws.

Your Husband ! ! !

126

Nov. 6, 1901. (*Yalta.*)

Well, my joy, I went to see Tolstoy yesterday. I found him in bed. He had hurt himself a little and now he is lying up. He is better in health than he was, but these are only the warm days at the end of October, yet winter is, nevertheless, near, very near. He seemed to be pleased at my coming. And for some reason or other I was particularly glad this time to see him. His expression was friendly and kind, though elderly, or rather aged; he listens with pleasure and speaks readily. He still likes the Crimea.

Balmont was with me to-day. He can't go to Moscow now [1]; he is not allowed, or he would have gone to see you in December and you would have helped to get him tickets for all the plays at your theatre. He is a nice fellow and, above all, I have known him for years and consider myself his friend and he considers himself mine.

How are you getting on, my joy, my charmer? Sredin came to see me to-day and brought a photograph, the one we brought from Axyonovo,[2] only enlarged; and we both come out old with our eyes screwed up in this photograph. Darling, sweet, do write on plainer paper and seal your letters up in plain envelopes, or else your letters come looking as though they had been sealed up in a hurry. It is a trifle, but we provincials, darling, are suspicious people.

Will they build a new theatre? When? Write, my wife, write, for I am bored, bored, and feel as though I had been married for twenty years and this was the first year I had been separated from you. I must come in January. I will wrap up warmly and come. And in Moscow I will stay indoors.

Keep well, my kind little German, my nice, gentle girl. I love you very much and esteem you.

I embrace and kiss you ardently. Be well and merry. Thanks for your letters.

Your ANTONIO.

127

Nov. 7 (1901. Yalta).

You are like a glutton, for in every letter you write about eating, whether I eat much and so on. My darling, I eat a lot!

[1] Balmont had been forbidden by the Ministry of Home Affairs to visit Moscow.

[2] L. V. Sredin had enlarged a photograph of Tchehov and O. L. taken in the porch of a little house in the sanatorium near Axyonovo where they went after their wedding.

Please don't be anxious. I don't drink milk, there is none in Yalta, but at dinner and supper I eat like a crocodile, enough for ten.

You want to give up the stage? So I fancied when I read your letter. You want to? You must think it over thoroughly, darling, thoroughly, and only then decide. All next winter I will spend in Moscow—keep that in mind.

I drove from Sevastopol with posting-horses. It was cold and cheerless, but, worst of all, the driver, when he was un-harnessing the horses, dropped my box with the clock in it. I had to send the clock to be mended and pay three roubles for it, and now when the clock strikes I fancy it is not quite well. It goes all right. My watch is going too.

To-day I caught two mice. So no one can say I do nothing.

Have you been to ' The Irina Sisterhood ' ? [1] How did you like it? Write. I have not had one long letter from you yet, not one letter with reflections. I do love you so when you make generalisations about something.

I am afraid that I bore you; or that little by little you are drifting away from me—I can't say definitely, but I am afraid of something.

The weather is still, but cool and cloudy; evidently it will soon be winter. Have you dined at Luzhsky's? I didn't manage to see him after all. He is good in ' Michael Kramer,' distinctly good; particularly in Act II. In Act III. he is pre-vented from doing well, they baulk him, but still one feels he is a good actor. ' Kramer ' goes splendidly altogether, Stanis-lavsky is very good, and if fresh and broad-minded people were dramatic critics among us the play would have been a brilliant success.

Don't forget that you have a husband. Remember it!

Everything is nice in our garden, there is a great deal of everything, but still it looks pitiful! I despise the natural scenery here. I feel it is cold.

And suppose that all at once you were to come to Yalta for two or three days, you would only need a week to do it. I

[1] A play by A. I. Sumbatov which appeared that season at the Imperial Little Theatre.

would meet you at Sevastopol, I would stay with you at Sevastopol. . . . Yes ? Well, God bless you !

I love you, but you have known that for ages now. I send you 1013212 kisses. Don't forget me.

Your husband ANTONIO.

128

Nov. 9, 1901. (Yalta.)

Greetings, my darling ! It is marvellous weather to-day, warm, clear and dry, and soft as summer. The roses are in flower and the pinks and the chrysanthemums and some sort of yellow flower too. To-day I sat a long time in the garden and thought how magnificent the weather is here, but yet it would be far nicer to be driving in a sledge now. Forgive me this cynicism.

R. acting again in 'The Sea-Gull'! Why, the play was taken off the list till you got a new actress, and now here is R. back again ! How beastly ! In the programme sent me I read, too, that ' Ivanov ' is being rehearsed. To my thinking that is labour thrown away—unnecessary. The play will be a failure because it will seem uninteresting in the limp mood of the audience.

I am beating up all the best authors to write plays for the Art Theatre. Gorky has already written one ; Balmont, Leonid Andreyev, Teleshov and others are writing plays already. It would be suitable to pay me a commission, at least one rouble per man.

My letters to you don't quite satisfy me. After what you and I have lived through together, letters are not enough. We ought to go on living. We are so wrong in not living together ! But there, what is the use of talking of it ! God be with you. I bless you, my little German, and I rejoice that you are in good spirits.

I kiss you warmly, warmly.

Your ANTONIO.

Tell Masha I have had a letter from Roman,[1] he is living at Popovka, and is married. I have also had a letter from

---

[1] Roman was a labourer who worked for the Tchehovs at Melihovo.

Alexandria, from a provincial of some sort. He saw ' Three Sisters ' in Alexandria, could make nothing of it and asks me to explain it. His name is Maloshitchenko.

Arseny has just gone for the things which Sytin [1] has sent (mushrooms, dried fish, a great-coat and so on); the things have arrived.

I am writing, but I can't say I am doing it very eagerly. Tell Masha that Muir and Merrilees have sent our purchases via Novorossiisk.[2] So we shall get them by April, not sooner.

129

Nov. 11, 1901. (Yalta.)

Greetings, dog! To-day I have read the tearful letter in which you describe yourself as utterly worthless.[3] And this is what I say to you. This winter will pass quickly, I will come early in spring if not before, then we will be together all the spring and all the summer, then next winter I will try to spend in Moscow. There is no sense in your giving up the stage for such dreariness as there is now in Yalta.

It is raining, pattering on the roof. It has been raining a long time, pattering monotonously and making one drowsy. Sofya Andreyevna has taken a snapshot of Tolstoy and me together ; I will ask her for a copy of it and send it to you, but don't you let any one copy it. God forbid. Sredin, by the way, copied our photograph at Axyonovo. It is bigger but worse than ever. In that photograph you look such a little German, the good-natured friendly wife of a doctor who has a very poor practice.

I love you so, my dog.

If Gorky is in Moscow give him my love. Tell him that I am expecting him.

I cough very little, but my health was better in Moscow.

---

[1] I. A. Sytin, the publisher, sometimes kindly forwarded things for Tchehov.

[2] Tchehov had bought a writing-table and chairs from the well-known Scotch shop in Moscow, Muir and Merrilees.

[3] O. L. in her letter of Nov. 6 had expressed herself as pining for Tchehov and uneasy about the winter, and reproached herself for weakness of character.

That is, not my health, but my stomach. I eat enough. I am faithful to my wife.

I forgot to write to Masha yesterday about the stoves. Tell her that it is too soon to judge yet, but, to go by the occasions on which they have been heated this autumn, the stoves are no better than they were last year. Our stove-builder, though a God-fearing man, is evidently a person of small ability. The iron stove downstairs has dried the wall and does perceptibly warm both the ground floor and the stairs and even the passage leading to my study. At any rate when one opens the study door it is warm outside. In the vestibule (by the door of the W.C.) it is cold, it is colder than it was last year, but in the W.C. it is warm, even hot. Well, my darling, take care of yourself, and God keep you.

I kiss you, my good little girl. Greetings to every one.

Your ANTONIO.

We have already received the mushrooms Sytin sent us and are eating them. Mother sends her love.

130

Nov. 12 (1901. *Yalta*).

I congratulate you on your move,[1] my joy, only why do neither you nor Masha send your new address ? Masha tells me just in passing that you have looked at a flat in Gonyetsky's Buildings, and whether you have taken it, and where it is, there is no knowing. I shall await the new address, and meanwhile I don't know what to do, how to act, whether to write or not to write.

Madame Elpatyevsky has fibbed a little. She told you that it was warm in my study, while I remember perfectly that she shivered in my study and complained it was cold. Now, my darling, rejoice and be glad, I have had my hair cut, whereof I have informed you already. I clean my teeth with your soap and think of you every time. I eat splendidly.

' In Dreams ' is a good title, soft and pleasant. I would send

---

[1] O. L. and Tchehov's sister moved, Nov. 9, into another flat as the little house in Spiridonovka turned out to be damp and inconvenient.

Nemirovitch a story with great pleasure, but you know everything I write now is long and rather unsuitable for a public reading, and what I am writing just now is hardly suitable, that is, it would not be passed by the Censor for public reading. No, you had better ask him to excuse me.

I have just made a discovery : some one has broken the big round inkpot on my table, evidently they have been tidying up my table.[1]

I kiss my good, splendid wife. I embrace and bless her.

Your ANTONIO.

They have just rung me up to say that Gorky has arrived. I expect him here. Telegraph your address if you have not yet sent it by letter.

131

TELEGRAM

Nov. 14 (1901. *Yalta*).

Congratulations on move all well ANTON.

132

(*Nov.* 14, 1901. *Yalta.*)

To-day I received your address. To-day I telegraphed to you and here I am writing to you. If the flat turns out well, if the heating (by steam ?) does not bring on headache and coughing, I will come in January or February and will stay right up to the summer.

This postcard was sent me as a present and alas ! the portrait [2] is very unlike, very rosy. There is no news and what there is is of no interest. I write in haste as I have to go out. Be well and in God's keeping.

Your ANT—.

So you are nearer the theatre now ? That is good, darling. It has turned cold. Three degrees of frost.

[1] Tchehov greatly disliked having his writing-table tidied by the servants.

[2] A postcard with a portrait of Tolstoy.

133

Nov. 15, 1901. (*Yalta.*)

Yesterday I received your address and yesterday I sent you a telegram, my joy. I congratulate you on the nice flat. You describe the flat and then you suddenly ask, 'You are not angry are you, darling?' Where did you get that idea? What should I be angry at? Set your heart at rest, my precious, I am very much pleased and very glad.

Yes, Tchumikov is translating me. The late A. I. Urussov, who was married to a German and lived for years among Germans, read his translation in my presence and thought that Tchumikov was a good translator. Whoever translates me, Tchumikov or Scholz, anyway it is of little consequence, I received nothing and shall receive nothing. I care little about these translations in general, for I know that we are not wanted in Germany and shall not be wanted, however we are translated.

I haven't read Amfiteatrov, as I don't take 'Russia' and the sale of separate numbers is forbidden. You might try and get me his article about your theatre, just sticking a two-kopeck stamp on it.

I can't drink Ems water in the mornings. The servants are busy and the samovar with hot water is far away. I don't sit on the seat in the garden, because it has turned cold and rains. Indoors it is cold too, by the way, though the stoves are heated every day. I passionately want to see my wife, I miss her and Moscow, but there is no help for it. I dream of you and think of you almost every hour. I love you, my darling.

God bless you, and may you have the sweetest, loveliest dreams. I kiss you warmly and embrace you.

Your husband ANT—.

What part does Butova [1] play in 'Lonely Lives'? My love to Masha.

---

[1] N. S. Butov, an actress of the Art Theatre, took the part of the maid in Hauptmann's 'Lonely Lives.'

134

Nov. 16, 1901.   (Yalta.)

Dear spouse, I send you the photograph about which I have
written to you already.   It is a little too dark, but like.   They
will take some more and I will send you some more.

It is still horrid weather, cold.   Dr. Tihonov, the one who
lives at the Grand Duke's, has been to see me and he told me
that I might live in Moscow now.   How do you like that ?
Why, I 'll just come with Masha after Christmas.

There is no news, everything is stale, of little interest.   I
kiss my good wife.

ANTONIO.

135

Nov. 17 (1901.   Yalta).

My dear spouse, the rumours about Tolstoy that reached you,
about his illness, and even his death, are entirely groundless.
There are no special changes in his health, nor have there been,
and as far as one can see he is a long way yet from death.   It
is true that he is weak and looks decrepit, but he has not a
single symptom which could be alarming, not one except old
age.   Don't believe a word of it ; if—which God forbid—anything should happen, I 'll let you know by telegram.   I 'll call
him ' grandfather ' or perhaps the telegram won't reach you.

Gorky is here ; he is quite well.   He sleeps the night here
and is registered here.[1]   The police-captain came to-day.

I am writing and working, but, my darling, I can't work in
Yalta.   I can't and I can't.   It is far from the world, uninteresting and above all cold.   I have had a letter from
Vishnevsky ; tell him I 'll write a play, but not before the
spring.

The lamp is alight in my study now.   So long as it doesn't
smell of kerosene, it 's all right.

Gorky is not changed, he is just the same nice, intellectual,

---

[1] Gorky was at this time under police supervision and was forbidden
to visit Petersburg or Moscow.

good-natured fellow. There is only one thing in him, or to be more accurate on him, that is not in keeping, that is his shirt. I can't get used to it, any more than I could to a Kammerherr's uniform.

The weather is autumnal and not up to much.

Well, keep alive and well, light of my eyes. Thanks for your letters. Don't get ill, be a good girl. My love to your people. I kiss you warmly and embrace you.

Your husband ANTONIO.

I am very well. Moscow had an amazingly good effect on me. I don't know whether it is Moscow or your doing, but I am coughing very little.

If you see Olga Petrovna Kundasov or any one who will see her soon, tell her that Dr. Vassilyev, the alienist, is in Yalta at the present moment and very seriously ill.

136

Nov. 19, 1901. (*Yalta.*)

Greetings, my good wife! It is a still, sunny day, but cool. I am sitting at home. Yesterday I had an abusive letter from the lady who bought Kutchukoy from us, and to-day an actor-manager turned up who is producing ' Three Sisters ' in Yalta ; he came to invite my co-operation, but, to his great surprise and dissatisfaction, I began begging him not to produce ' Three Sisters.' He is producing the piece only for the sake of a sensation. He stayed with me more than an hour, I am worn out.

I sit at home and am bored as though I were in prison. Your letters are my one consolation, my sweet little girl. I keep wondering whether to go abroad.

The police-captain has just rung me up to know where Gorky is.

My clothes are not brushed, because Arseny is at market in the mornings and Marfa is busy. I don't drink Ems water in the mornings, as I drink coffee, and there is no hot water earlier. There is no cream in Yalta. I have written to you about all that already. I eat a great deal as a rule.

Thanks for your letter, tremendous thanks ! I love you for

it.   I will buy you a purse,[1] and not one but two, but I will buy
them abroad.

I am very glad, darling, that Masha and you are pleased
with your new flat.   There is electric light too.   That is very
nice.   But why have the Obolonskys taken to coming to you ?
They are opponents of the Art Theatre, you know.

Well, good-bye, the Lord save and keep you.   I embrace and
kiss you.   Don't forget me, think of your husband.

Your ANT—.

There is not a word in the papers about the Art Theatre.
Have they cooled off or what ?   If the theatre stays in its old
place it will soon become ordinary, every one will lose interest
in it.

Tolstoy is being attended by Altschuller.   Yesterday the
latter rang me up to say his patient feels well and there is no
cause for alarm.   And, indeed, there never has been.

137

Nov. 21, 1901.   (Yalta.)

Sweet Knippusha, my precious, don't be vexed that I don't
write to you every day.   It just happens so.   Every day something prevents one living and writing ; to-day, for instance,
Lazarevsky (a writer in a naval uniform) turned up in the
morning and he is sitting on and on, sitting on agonisingly,
and there is no telling when the devil will carry him off.

You want to come for Christmas ?   That is a most brilliant
idea, my clever darling, only you must get long enough from
Nemirovitch to spend not less than three days in Yalta.   Not
less !   If you leave Moscow the 20th of December you 'll be in
Yalta on the 22nd, if you leave Yalta on the 25th you 'll be
back in Moscow on the 27th.   My own, my darling, do as I say.
Wring those three days out of your despots.   From the 22nd
to the 26th there are no performances and they can put on
' The Wild Duck,' ' Stockmann,' ' Fyodor Ioannovitch,' ' When
we Dead Awaken ' on the 20th, 21st and 26th.   They have a

---

[1] O. L. had jestingly reproached him with the fact that she had had to
buy a purse herself.

tremendous repertoire for the holidays. Do as I say, Knippusha, be a sensible wife.

I have read your old nurse Pasha's letter [1] and am completely in sympathy with it. It seems to me that you would be very fond of a little half-German, would perhaps love him better than anything on earth, and that is just what is needed. Gorky is just the same nice fellow, even better perhaps. He is a very simple-hearted man. He has been living in Yalta. Now he has moved to Oleiz and has taken a house for the whole winter.

I am all right and everything is going well. The mice are being caught. Now I shall begin dreaming of your coming to Yalta for Christmas. But hold hard! Dr. Rozanov has arrived.

Rozanov has gone, but Lazarevsky is still here. He has filled the drawing-room with tobacco smoke. Now he is dining downstairs.

Madame Bonnier has gone, or is going, to Moscow. She will be sure to come to see you. I kiss you warmly and embrace you still more warmly. Write, don't be lazy. You shall be rewarded for it.

Your ANTONIO.

138

Nov. 22, 1901. (Yalta.)

I sent you a postcard with Tolstoy on it. Did you get it? Tolstoy is all right, his temperature is normal and so far there is nothing particularly alarming, except old age of course.

To-day there is no letter from you, my joy. Consequently I am in low spirits. Also because Lazarevsky has been here again. My health is pretty middling. I can't complain. As I wrote to you, they are giving 'Three Sisters' to-day at the local theatre. The actors are revolting, the staging is even worse. But probably the house will be full. It is warm, still, cloudy weather.

---

[1] The nurse Pasha had congratulated O. L. on her marriage and had begged her to take her into her service as a nurse to her children.

I sent you the photograph, didn't you get it ?   What more do you want ?   You have the one in which we were taken together at Axyonovo.

And so remember, my child, you must be in Yalta in December !   Your coming would be a heaven-sent blessing for me. This winter has been the very dullest of all winters for me.   I should be glad to go away.

To-day Marfusha brushed my jacket and sewed on a button.

Well, I have nothing more to write about.   A kiss to you, Knippusha, don't be bored, work hard, enjoy yourself if you get the chance.

How is Nemirovitch's play going ?   Do you like it ?

Till we meet !   I embrace my Knippusha.

Your ANT—.

If you won't be playing in Petersburg during Lent, let us go to Italy ; what do you say ?

139

Nov. 24, 1901.   (Yalta.)

My child, tell Nemirovitch to send Gorky the fourth act of his play as soon as possible, tell him that it is essential.

It is snowing and raining.   My hands are cold, it is cold and gloomy in the study, it is hard to write, my fingers won't obey me, though the thermometer points to twelve degrees above freezing.   And it will be like this all the winter !   That is till the end of April !

Gorky has settled in Oleiz, he has been to see me ; he seems to be bored.   He would be working at his play, but he has not got it, Nemirovitch does not send it.

' Three Sisters ' was performed here—it was revolting !   The officers had police-stripes on their uniforms, Masha spoke in a hoarse voice.   The house was full, but the audience abused the play dreadfully.

Potapenko abuses your theatre in his story in ' Russkaya Mysl.'

And so get leave not for Sevastopol but for Yalta.   My sweet darling, do me this favour, I entreat you !   Nemirovitch

is an egoist . . . he made you come back for the 20th of
August when there was nothing for you to do, and now you
will be sitting with nothing to do all the holidays. . . . And
I 'll break with the theatre and won't write anything for it.

Tell Aunt Lyolya that I would send her a photograph with
pleasure, but alas ! I have only the Yalta ones and they are
old and not good. When I come in the spring I will get some
from Opitz [1] and present her with one with any inscription
she likes. Meanwhile she must excuse me. Lazarevsky was
here the third time yesterday. To-day I believe he has gone
away. Balmont has gone to-day too. Elpatyevsky has no
doubt been to see you at your theatre.

Let us go to Italy, dog ! Do let us ! Let us go while we
have the money, for in two or three years we may not be able
to travel about !

I embrace you, my wife. Sleep well, and God keep you.

Your ANT—.

When I told Mother you were coming for Christmas she was
highly delighted and said : ' Well, thank God ! ' To-day she
spoke of it again and asked me to write to you that you must
come.

140

Nov. 25, 1901. (*Yalta*.)

My sweet darling, the colonel need not excite himself. The
story—one of many—is not included in the Marks collection,
because it has been changed into a farce, ' An Unwilling
Martyr.'

So my photograph reached you all right, and was not bent ?
Take care of it, it is unique. After my death and yours, it
will have to be sent to the Taganrog town library, where my
archives are being kept.

I am working, but not well. The weather is horrid, it is cold
indoors, Moscow is far away, and everything induces a mood
in which writing seems superfluous.

Are you thinking, dog, of coming to Yalta for Christmas ?
Do you think about it ? Every day I think of how you will

---

[1] A photographer's in Petrovka in Moscow.

come and how we shall spend three days together. The coloured pencils your mother gave me are being cleared away and filched, one by one. Uncle Sasha's holder is still safe.

Have you been to the Malkiels to dine ? You ask whether I have seen Tolstoy since I came back from Moscow. Yes, I went to see him lately with Gorky and Balmont, and I believe I wrote to you about it. If it were better weather, I should go and see him more often.

Keep well, my dear wife. Don't be hard on me because my letters are so empty and so meagre. There is nothing to write about. I cannot even write anything about Scholz, as I have already written to you about him. He promises a fee, but first the stories must be translated and then published and then sold . . . a long affair ! Besides, Russian authors, if they are of use at all, are only of use in Russia, my wise girl.

I kiss your little hands; don't forget me, think of me at least twice in the twenty-four hours.

Your husband ANTONIO.

You ask what Dr. Tihonov it was came to see me. The one who attended the Tsar in Livadia when he had typhoid, the court doctor. He took his degree in my year. Excuse me, I have been for a walk, my hands are frozen, it is hard to write.

The doctors here won't let me go to Moscow.

141

Nov. 26, 1901. (Yalta.)

No letter from you to-day, my good wife. Well, I must wait till to-morrow. You write that you 're thirsting to read my new story. But in my present state of mind, in this scurvy Yalta, I can write nothing that could—to your thinking— quench thirst.

Nemirovitch's play will be a success. Don't be down-hearted. Only you ought at the same time to be rehearsing ' The Petty-Bourgeois,' or after Christmas there will be nothing for you to play but Nemirovitch. Stanislavsky is obviously a little

depressed. He is spoilt by success and so a half-success cuts
him to the heart.

Mother thanks you for your letter. You write to her about
Ems and hot water. But all that, my darling, is not possible.
And don't write about diet, for it's useless. Mother and
Granny [1] are both old, they are very anxious, they both take
a lot of trouble, but you see one is seventy and the other is
eighty.

Your letters are very interesting. I read them two or three
times. There is no bath-house here and nowhere to have a
bath. I only wash my head. I kiss you warmly. Don't
forget your husband. Write me a couple of words about
Luzhsky's health.[2]

Your ANT—.

142

Nov. 28 (1901. Yalta).

' I write dully, monotonously, uninterestingly.' You have forgotten you wrote me those words, my little silly. And I so
love your letters ! Write dully and monotonously, only please
a little oftener and I will send you pictures for it.

What have you decided ? Are you coming to Yalta for
Christmas or not ? I must know that for certain.

It's cold in our house ; the stoves at times are hot but there
is no warmth. The usual temperature in my study is twelve
degrees and it rarely reaches thirteen.[3] It is impossible to light
a fire because the fire makes my eyes bad, and it is hard to work
in a temperature of twelve degrees. I do nothing but rage,
though I know it is stupid.

How delighted I should be now to talk a little with my wife,
to touch her on the brow and the shoulders, to laugh with her !
Ah, darling, darling !

Well, God be with you, live and keep well and merry.
Write !

Your ANT—.

[1] An old servant of the Tchehovs.
[2] V. V. Luzhsky had been ill with pneumonia.
[3] Sixty degrees Fahrenheit.

143

Nov. 30 (1901. *Yalta*).

My sweet Knippusha, my wise girl, I am alive and well and feel not amiss to-day; and the weather is glorious, sunny, though yesterday there was rain and a storm and trees were broken.

The hotels in Sevastopol are loathsome, nasty; let us suppose you would reach Sevastopol on the 21st of December, then you would be in Yalta on the same day. Do come, my sweet, I entreat you! I am very dreary, so dreary that I can't work at all, and only sit and read the newspapers. Next winter I shall live in Moscow whatever happens and whatever the doctors say, or near Moscow somewhere, in a house in Tsaritsyno or Himki.

Tell Masha to bring : (1) Aprons for the servants ; (2) White tape for linen ; (3) Black tape to bind a dress ; (4) Pearl buttons for linen. Mother dictated this to me.

Gorky was with me yesterday, he is quite well and is meaning to write another play; he is living in Oleiz, where he has taken a house.

Did you get a card with a portrait of Tolstoy ?

I like O. O. Sadovsky [1] very much. She is a real genuine artist, very talented.

Well, darling, God be with you. I send you endless kisses and rejoice that I am married to you. Come, my sweet and good kind little German, my actress. Come !

Your ANT—.

144

Dec. 1 (1901. *Yalta*).

Sweet dog, congratulate me, I have had a letter from Varfolomy Smolitch, your friend at Axyonovo. He writes : ' I beg you to give my greetings to Olga Leonardovna and to

---

[1] O. O. Sadovsky was an actress of the Moscow Little Theatre. O. L. wrote, Nov. 25: ' O. O. Sadovsky talked to me a great deal about you, telling me how she likes you and how she divines in you " a real man." '

tell her that the mysterious flower defies my knowledge and remains unknown.' [1]

I have had a letter from Dr. Tchlenov. He is highly delighted with your Moscow flat and with both of you, Masha particularly, and writes, among other things, that you told him that the newspapers are forbidden to print anything about me. He must have misunderstood you.

To-day is dull and horrid. Whatever you may say, Nemirovitch's play will be successful ; he is a Moscow author and everything he writes is just to the taste of the Moscow people. But this winter will be rather flat for you altogether, neither one thing nor the other.

I kiss and embrace my kind, clever, glorious wife. I bless you and kiss you again.

Your ANT—.

I will send a photograph to the cadet corps for Voznitsyn. He does write in a friendly way !

145

Dec. 3 (1901. *Yalta*).

My sweet dog, my precious, two letters have come from you to-day, one pretty middling, the other sad. You write that for two days you have had no letter from me. I have only missed one day, all the other days I have written to you, and yesterday I did not write to you because I had no letter from you, was wretched and did not want to make you melancholy. You complain that my letters have become depressed. Circumstances have been such, my darling, first one thing and then another ; and to-day I am, as it were, muzzy, my head is empty and I feel feeble,—it 's because yesterday they overheated my stove, all night it was hot and stifling, and the heat came from the stove as from an oven. Well, it doesn't matter ! To-day it is very fine weather again, warm and sunny. I have got Turks at work in the garden making a plantation, that is,

[1] When Tchehov and his wife were in the sanatorium at Axyonovo in the Ufa province, O. L. took great interest in the flora of the district and V. Smolitch helped her in identifying the flowers.

digging the earth out three feet deep ; it 's for vines which I have received as a present from one of the staff of the Nikitsky [1] garden.   They are the very best kind which exist in the world.

To-day I received from America ' Foma Gordeyew ' [2] (dedicated to Anton P. Chekhov)—a thick bound volume.

Yesterday Madame Tatarinov was with me.   She stayed two and a half hours.

Go with you to Moscow ! [3]   Oh, my darling !   Come, we will take counsel together and very likely I will go with you.

I write listlessly, without any relish.   Don't expect anything special, anything sensible from me for a time.   I am not speaking of letters but of my writing.   Whatever happens I 'll write a comedy, my darling, and there shall be a part for you.

I love you more and more.   I kiss and stroke you, my dog. Be well and happy, don't forget your husband.   Love him until you get tired of him.

Your . ANT—.

Tell Masha to bring linen for kitchen cloths such as she buys at the Peasant Handicraft shop.   Mother asks for smoked salmon.

146

Dec. 4 (1901.   *Yalta*).

Greetings, my spouse, my darling !   You don't like my letters,[4] I know that and appreciate your taste.

But what 's to be done, dear, since I 've been in poor spirits these last few days ?   You must forgive me, don't be angry with your absurd husband.

Yesterday I was depressed by your letter ;   you wrote that

---

[1] The famous nursery garden on the south coast of the Crimea.
[2] Gorky's novel in the American translation.
[3] O. L. had suggested this in her letter of Nov. 28.
[4] O. L. wrote, Nov. 30 : ' Yesterday I received two of your letters at once.   I had already begun to be uneasy.   Thank you, my dear one; only those letters have made my heart ache, you are dreary, you are in a shocking state of mind, you will grow to hate the theatre because of me, and yet it was that brought us together.'

you wouldn't be coming to Yalta for Christmas.[1]   I don't know
what to do with myself.   Some of the doctors say that I may go
to Moscow, others say that it is utterly out of the question, but
I can't stay here, I can't, I can't !

Well, will you lease Omon's [2] theatre ?   You can't stay in
your old one, for you 'll be burnt down there sooner or
later, and besides it 's not a central position.   I am always
afraid that you 'll have a fire during Act IV. of ' Three Sisters '
—there 's such an awful jostling and nonsense on the stage.

Don't mind what you say, dog, write me everything that strays
through your mind, trifles and nonsense of all sorts ; you can't
imagine how precious your letters are to me ; how they soothe
me.   You see I love you, don't forget that.   To-day I shall go
to see Gorky at Oleiz.   Perhaps I shall go on to Tolstoy's too.

Yesterday a Tatar, a rich one, came and asked me for a loan
at so much per cent.   When I told him I didn't lend money at
interest and thought it a sin, he was surprised and didn't
believe it.   One kind friend has borrowed six hundred roubles
from me till Friday.   They always borrow till Friday.

I kiss and embrace my good wife.   Don't be angry, little one,
if it happens there are no letters from me.   I am guilty, but
there are extenuating circumstances.

Your husband ANTONIO.

Are there no new plays ?   I have had a letter from Fyodorov,
the author of ' The Tempest ' ; he writes that he is sending a
play to Nemirovitch.

147

Dec. 6 (1901.   *Yalta*).

You ask for details, sweet popsey.   Here they are.   I have
drunk Ems for the last two days in the mornings ; it 's not
easy to manage, as I have to get up, put on my boots, ring the

---

[1] From the same letter : ' I doubt if they will release me.   I was
indulging in vain hopes.   Though I shall go on asking for it all the time
. . . before Christmas the public is not very ready to go to the theatre
and so we must give pieces that will be attractive.'

[2] O. L. wrote, Nov. 27 : ' So far nothing is certain about building a
theatre.   It would be a good thing to take Omon's theatre, it 's nice and
in a good position, isn't it ? '

bell, then wait, then take off my boots, then get into bed again. . . . You guessed right about castor oil; I took it this morning, as yesterday I ate pork chops which have set up a regular tempest. I have not seen Sredin for a long time, a fortnight—he has some one seriously ill in his house.[1] I see Altschuller rarely. He is very busy, he is attending Tolstoy. It is warm in Yalta now and so I am not frozen. To act vigorously, as you advise, to give orders and so on is impossible, as they heat the stoves disgracefully; they overheat them, so that there is no sleeping at night afterwards.

Tchlenov did not write to me about the Pirogov Congress and 'Uncle Vanya.'[2] I do go for walks, but not often. In fact, I take very little exercise. Well, here you have a very full answer to your questions.[3] Are you satisfied?

Yesterday I went to see Gorky; his house is in a fine position on the sea-shore, but it 's all at sixes and sevens in his house, children, an old woman, not the surroundings for a writer.

What could thieves [4] have stolen from Vassilyeva?

Let us go abroad, but not to Italy, not to Nice. Let us dash off to Norway to the north and from there to Denmark.

What do you say? Shall we go, my sweet little goose?

You must tell your directors that I won't let you go to Moscow before the 1st of September. They may discharge you if they like. I shall have wonderful apples ripe by the end of August. And pears? You have never eaten such pears.

---

[1] His wife's mother.

[2] The medical congress called after the famous physician Pirogov. The Art Theatre had arranged a matinée for the congress. They performed 'Uncle Vanya.' The assembled doctors brought the company a large framed portrait of Tchehov, a copy of the portrait painted by the artist Braz.

[3] O. L. wrote, Dec. 1 : ' About Ems water, my dear, I am sure you are capricious—it 's all very simple and it 's your duty to say firmly that it must be done and no more talk about it. Write to me more about your health : when you take castor oil and anything else, so that I may know all about it. Do you see the Sredins? Do you see Altschuller, or any one else? I am awfully worried at your being cold—it sends a chill to my heart to think of it. Do for once in your life act vigorously, give orders, insist on your room being warm. Well, Masha will set everything to rights at Christmas. . . . Did Tchlenov write to you about the Pirogov Congress and the performance of " Uncle Vanya " ? '

[4] O. L. wrote, Dec. 1 : ' Do you know Vassilyeva had only just gone away when the porter came to-day with a letter from her landlord to say that burglars had broken into her flat? '

My darling, if I were to throw up literature now and become a gardener it would be nice, it would add ten years to my life.

What am I to do with my stomach ?

Well, as usual, I kiss you, my joy. Keep well and strong. God keep you, may angels stand over you.

Your ANT—.

A Greek came to-day and asked for a loan of six hundred roubles at interest. I have a nice reputation !

148

Dec. 7 (1901. *Yalta*).

My actress, why don't you obey your husband ? Why didn't you tell Nemirovitch to send the last act of ' The Petty-Bourgeois ' ? Do tell him, darling. Ah, how disappointing, how unlucky that you are not coming to Yalta for the holidays ! I feel as though I shan't see you again for many years, not till we are old people.

I have just spoken over the telephone with Tolstoy. I have read the end of Gorky's story ' Three of Us.' There is something wonderfully queer about it. If it hadn't been written by Gorky, nobody would have read it, so I fancy anyway.

I have been unwell the last few days, darling. I have taken castor oil, I feel as though I had grown thin, I cough and do nothing. Now I am a little easier, so that to-morrow I shall most likely set to work.[1] Loneliness apparently has a very bad effect on the stomach. Joking apart, pet, when shall we be together again ? When shall I see you ? If you were to come here at Christmas even for one day it would be infinitely nice. But do what you think best.

I write this letter on the 7th at night ; I shall send it off to-morrow, the 8th. You are always at dinners and jubilees —I am glad, darling, and approve of you. You are a sensible girl, you are a darling.

Well, God bless you, kisses innumerable.

Your ANTO—.

Don't waste much on the play, it won't be a success anyway. Twelve hundred roubles on the dresses, that is beyond any-

---

[1] On the story ' The Bishop.'

thing ! [1] I was reading Leonid Andreyev when I was in Moscow,[2] then I read him on the way to Yalta. Yes, he is a good writer, if he would write more he would have a greater success. There is a lack of sincerity, a lack of simplicity in him, and so it is hard to get used to him, but sooner or later the public will get used to him and he will make a great name.

149

Monday. (Dec. 10, 1901. Yalta.)

Sweet darling, Altschuller came to see me yesterday, listened to me, sounded me, then went away, then I began spitting blood. That is why I did not write to you yesterday.

To-day there's scarcely any blood, but still I have to lie down. Don't be anxious, my dearest. I write to you about it because you told me to.

I will write. There is a furious wind. Write more fully.

Your ANTO—.

150

Dec. 11 (1901. Yalta).

My sweet, good darling, my actress, don't be vexed. To-day I'm much better. The haemorrhage was only in the morning, quite slight, but still I must lie down. I am eating nothing, and I rage, as I can't work. Please God, it will all pass off.

I haven't received 'Russia,' which you promised me in your letter.

I am not expecting you for the holidays, and, indeed, you had better not come here, my darling. Do your work and we shall still have time to be together. I bless you, my little girl, be calm, keep well. I will write to you again to-morrow. I kiss you warmly.

Your ANT—.

[1] O. L. wrote, Dec. 3 : ' For my part in the play " In Dreams " the management sanctions my having three dresses for twelve hundred roubles—Savva (Morozov) told me this. Isn't it gracious ? '

[2] From the same letter : ' Why do you say nothing of what you think of Andreyev, or haven't you read him ? Do you know he is getting married ? —to a student, it seems. I like " Silence " and " Once upon a Time." '

151

Dec. 12, 1901. (*Yalta.*)

Darling, my good dog, I write to you every day or every alternate day and not less often. And so I will write to you in the future, and if you don't get the letters punctually it is not my fault. And in future I will write to you quite as often, be sure of that.[1]

My health through your prayers is much better. There is no haemorrhage now. I am sitting at my table and writing this to you. To-day I had dinner, that is, I had soup.

You ask why I keep you at a distance from me.[2] How silly, child! Who visits me?[3] Altschuller is attending me, Leonid Sredin was here to-day and Arabazhin.[4] No one else has been. I beg your pardon, though; yesterday Anna Vassilyevna Pogozhev came from Moscow. I received her, I am sorry to say, very discourteously, as I was spitting blood and had to be silent the whole time.

Everything I was writing and beginning to write is wasted, as now I shall have to begin over again. . . . I must write without a break, or nothing I do comes off. . . .

My darling, don't be agitated, don't be vexed, don't be indignant, don't be grieved, everything will come straight again, everything will be all right; in fact, what we both want will come to pass, my incomparable wife. Wait and have patience.[5]

[1] O. L. wrote, Dec. 8: ' Your last letter was dated Dec. 1 and to-day is the 8th and nothing all this time. What is the meaning of it? Why do you write so rarely? It is too bad.'

[2] From the same letter: ' How are you feeling, my darling? Why do you say nothing about your health? Why do you keep me at a distance from you? Don't do that, I beseech you. Be open with me in everything—I am not a doll but a human being. You know you wound me a little by treating me so.'

[3] From same letter: ' Who visits you? you don't write.'

[4] A writer.

[5] O. L. wrote, Dec. 8: ' In fact, everything is dreary everywhere. Nothing nice ever comes into one's head. You will all be together at Christmas. Will you think of me? I shall either be jigging about among visitors or shall sit at home like a dummy. I don't know what I 'm going to do. . . . Heavens! when shall we see each other? When am I going to have you near me, to hear your voice? To feel the look in your eyes full of love?'

Tell Nemirovitch not to be too agitated. Everything will be quite all right.

I have received ' Russia.' Thanks.

I hug you hard, improperly so ; I kiss you hard as I have a full right to do, being your lawful husband. Don't forget me, write every day. Your letters are for me a medicine without which I can't exist.

It has been pouring furiously all day.

Well, take care of yourself, be in God's keeping, my little chubby, my actress, my dog.

Your ANT—.

Let Masha bring *hors d'œuvres.* Send your husband some sweets.

152

Dec. 13 (1901. *Yalta*).

Greetings, my actress, I am quite well again now. There is no blood to be seen, all that is left is weakness—it is a long time since I have eaten properly. I think that in two or three days I shall be quite well. I am taking pills, drops, powders.

You write that on the evening of the 8th of December you were half-drunk. Ah, darling, how I envy you, if only you knew ! I envy your vigour, your freshness, your health, your temperament, I envy you because no consideration of haemorrhages and such prevents your drinking. In old days I could drink with any one, as the saying is.

I have read the last act of ' The Petty-Bourgeois.' I read it and didn't understand it. Twice I laughed, for it was funny. I liked the end, only it 's not the right end for the last act, but for the first or the second. He ought to think of something else for the last act. Your part in the last act is insignificant.

I often think about you, very often, as befits a husband. While I was with you you spoilt me, and now without you I feel like an outcast. Emptiness about me, pitiful dinners, no one even rings me up on the telephone ; and as for sleeping, I can't speak of it.

I embrace you warmly, my actress, my fiery dog, and God keep you. Don't forget and don't forsake me. A hundred thousand kisses.

Your ANTON.

153

Dec. 16, 1901.   (*Yalta.*)

Sweet dog, I am alive, and so far as possible for a man in the position of a convalescent, quite well. I am weak and ill-humoured, and doing nothing. Haemorrhoids ! In fact you 've got such a spouse that I can only congratulate you. Anyway things are mending.

Tolstoy has been ill, he was staying in Yalta at his daughter's. Gorky was here yesterday. Now they are both at home.

If I get a telegram after the performance of ' In Dreams,' I shall say ' Thank you, my child ! ' In case of success (of which I am very confident) the telegram should be at the Government expense, that is, a long one.

Why is it ' Stockman ' is performed so rarely ?

There is a fog, every evening the siren howls and we hear the moaning of steamers that have lost their way.

God be with you, keep well and merry, child, don't be depressed, write a little more to your choleric husband. When you are depressed you become old and faded, and when you are gay or ordinary you are an angel. So be always merry.

I kiss you warmly. I hug you tight. Good-bye for now, dog !

Your ANT—.

154

Dec. 16, 1901.   (*Yalta.*)

Darling, I am quite well. I am bored to death with visitors, they stay all the time and I have no time to write to you. I am as cross as a dog. Take care of yourself, my darling, my joy. God help you.

I really am better, don't be anxious.

I kiss you warmly. Sasha Sredin, who has been sitting with me and now is going, will drop this letter in the post.

Your ANT—.

155

Dec. 17 (1901. *Yalta*).

My sweet popsey, I have no letter from you to-day, but may Heaven forgive you as I forgive you. I am getting better and better ; I am wearing a compress on my right side, I am taking creosote, but my temperature is normal and everything is going well. I shall be a man again.

I had visitors yesterday, they stayed a long time. I was raging. I have just heard over the telephone that a tourist— a Hungarian who visits all the authors—is on his way in a cab to see me. He does not know that I am not an author now but a gardener, a married gardener, with no encumbrances as yet but hoping for them.

Mother is well, but I can see that my illness has tired her out. Masha is coming to-morrow and everything will be set right.

I have had a letter from Kuprin from Petersburg; he is warm in his praise of you, but not enthusiastic about the Art Theatre. The Hungarian is coming. He 's coming ! No, I was wrong. Kuprin writes that one is conscious of the manager in Stanislavsky's acting, just as in the acting of Solovtsov, who is a manager too.

Why, surely you are not staying in the old theatre ? Oh, the barbarous wretches ! Well, my popsey, I kiss and embrace you. You, too, kiss your old man. The hair has been cut off the back of my head. My coat has not been brushed. I am not drinking Ems.

My love to your mother and to your Uncles Karl and Sasha and to your aunt. Keep well. I expect a description of the Saturday evening party.[1]

Your ANT—.

I believe the Hungarian is coming.

[1] O. L. wrote, Dec. 10 and 11 : ' I am thinking of having a party on Saturday and inviting all the company. I must do it, they insist upon it. If it 's lively and not stiff I shall be delighted. . . .' ' I am cancelling the

156

Dec. 18 (1901. *Yalta*).

My sweet actress, I am alive and well and hoping this finds you the same. There is no blood-spitting, more strength, almost no cough, the only trouble is an enormous great compress on my right side, and if only you knew how I think of you, how I regret you are not with me when I have to put on that huge compress, and when I seem to myself so helpless and lonely. Of course, that's not for long; as soon as the compress is on, then I'm all right again.

I am writing nothing, nothing. I am doing nothing. I have put off everything till next year. You see what a man you've married, what a sluggard!

What sort of a reception had Nemirovitch's play? It must have been a noisy one. The Moscow public loves him. I keep dreaming of writing an amusing play, full of rollicking fun. I don't know whether anything will come of it. Here in Yalta I am so sickened, so dummified by the view from my big window that I believe nothing will come of my writing. Well, we shall see.

How is Vishnevsky getting on? Does he officiate in Nemirovitch's play? I will write to him soon.

I love you, my puppy, I love you very much, I miss you terribly. In fact, it seems to me incredible that we shall ever see each other again. Without you, I am good for nothing. My darling, I kiss you warmly and embrace you a hundred times. I am sleeping splendidly, but I don't count it sleep since my sweet missis is not by me. Life is passing so stupidly.

Don't be bored, work hard, be a good girl, don't be depressed —it doesn't suit you. When you are merry, you look ten years younger.

Well, I kiss you once more. Write, my joy.

Your ANT—.

party for Saturday the 15th as the next days will be very hard; there is a dress rehearsal of " In Dreams " and " Three Sisters " in the evening. . . .' ' It seems I must give the supper party. I did try to get out of it, but Moskvin and Luzhsky were so downcast and said that they were already beginning to prepare their turns and were longing for a spree.'

157

Dec. 19 (1901. *Yalta*).

Greetings, dog! Masha came yesterday evening, to-day she keeps running up to the windows and going into raptures. 'Oh! how splendid to live here!' I am quite well, though I still wear the compress, which I shall leave off on Friday, the day after to-morrow. I am still doing nothing.

Thanks for the sweets, only I am sorry they are from Fley's and not from Abrikosov's; it's not that Abrikosov's are any better, but I'm used to them.

This is badly written because I can't see.

Darling, my good wife, it will soon be Christmas and we are not together. It is really incredible. Be in good spirits, don't be depressed, be merry and joyful, think about your husband who loves you more than ever. My nice little goose, my granny, I love you. . . . Masha brought a ham but it is not particularly nice, though I am eating a lot of it. I finished the line on the second sheet because it just happened so.

Write me a description of the first performance of ' In Dreams,' it must have been a great success. You are a good girl to feast your comrades and get up a party like that; I approve, my darling, my angel, my wonderful wife. I love such parties.

Well, I embrace you, I press you to my heart and kiss you. God be with you. Sleep well.

Your ANT—.

158

Dec. 20 (1901. *Yalta*).

My kind dog, this is what Nemirovitch writes to me : ' It seems that the theatre question is on the way to be settled. We shall most likely take Omon's theatre for twelve years and re-build to suit our needs. I am opening negotiations, I am inspecting the place and spend all my free hours with the architect, and so on.'

So there you are ! He writes, too, that Gorky's play will be produced.

To-day I am taking off the compress, which has bothered me like a corset.

Orlenev, who has come here on tour, came to see me to-day. My rooms were swept and dusted to-day.

My darling, my golden one, write, don't abandon me. I kiss you many times, I hug you and shut my eyes to see you.

Be well and happy.

Your husband ANTON.

159

Dec. 22 (1901. *Yalta*).

My sweet darling, all day long I have been expecting a telegram about Nemirovitch's play, and none ! Apparently it must have been so successful that you have all forgotten me.

I keep forgetting to write to you : if you need money take from Nemirovitch as much as you want. Make your own arrangements, darling, do what you think best. Oh, how I need you, if only you knew ! How I need you ! It's bad, it's bad without one's wife.

It's hot to-day in Yalta. Masha is delighted, she is walking about the garden without coat or hat ; one can hardly believe that there is snow and frost in Moscow now.

I love you. Do you know that ? My health is perfectly restored. I gave up the compress yesterday. To-morrow Altschuller will put on two plasters and that is the end of the treatment. I am eating a great deal now and can boast of an appetite.

Well, my darling, be merry and well. Spend the holidays in good health and spirits, think of your husband sometimes and write to him every day if possible.

I kiss and embrace you since there is no chance of doing anything more. Will you come the first week of Lent ?

Your ANT—.

You promised to send your photograph ; don't forget.

160

Dec. 23 (1901. *Yalta*).

My sweet dog, why, I haven't yet wished you a Merry Christmas! Don't think I am impolite; on the contrary, I have a great respect for my spouse.

I wish you all that is best and most remarkable, my darling.

The weather goes on being lovely. Bright and warm like summer.

I have received your telegram. I had one from Nemirovitch too.

How did you act? Well? Was it a dazzling success? You see the play was dazzling, sensational. When do you begin to rehearse ' The Petty-Bourgeois ' ? I don't like the fourth act [1] either. He ought to make it the first, and the third the fourth, then it would have balance.

My darling, I am quite well now, or almost quite. I eat a great deal, I sleep very well. I am in good spirits; there is only one thing I lack—my wife! The day after Christmas, I shall sit down and write. I went out yesterday and again to-day.

Well, be happy, be well! I love you very much. Good-bye till to-morrow. I write to you every day and so your phrase that ' at last ' you have received a letter from me means nothing. I write to you every day and rarely miss a day.

Your husband ANT—.

161

Dec. 24 (1901. *Yalta*).

You see, actress, I write every day. To-day is a fête for us, Mother's name-day, to-morrow is Christmas, and the sun is as hot as summer and the air is still. I can't go out to-day as I have two plasters on. I shall take them off in the evening and to-morrow I shall go out, perhaps I shall go to see Tolstoy and Gorky.

I have received your holiday programme. Samarova is not

[1] O. L. wrote, Dec. 18 : ' I haven't yet read Gorky's fourth act, Stanislavsky doesn't like it.'

once acting in my plays, Stanislavsky not once in 'Three
Sisters,' nor Marya Petrovna either. In fact, the plays seem
neglected. I can't digest M., but she appears every time in
'Three Sisters.'

It would be interesting to know when we shall see each
other. In Lent ? At Easter ?

I got your telegram, but still I don't know how Nemirovitch's
play went off. Do describe it more in detail, darling. Write
about K. too.

This summer we will go abroad, but in 1903, if we are alive,
we will spend the summer near Moscow. Is that right ? Yes ?

Naidyonov's play ' Vanyushin's Children ' was very much
praised. Is it really something out of the common ? If so,
why has the Art Theatre missed it ? I fancy that Nemirovitch
lets a great deal slip. Now, if I read the plays, your list would
be a great deal richer. What do you think ?

It 's rather hard living without you, particularly for a man
like your husband. I am very fond of you, darling, very.

Keep well. Don't overtire yourself.

Your ANT—.

162
Dec. 26 (1901. Yalta).

To-day no letter from my sweet love. I expect it is delayed
in the post. You need only scratch out the Moscow address
and then put Yalta on the letters that come for me and drop
them in the post, there is no need to put stamps on them. This
is apropos of a letter from the bank you sent me on yesterday.
Will they produce Gorky's play this season ? Nemirovitch
has had a great success ; I am very glad, that will attach him
still more to the theatre. The failure of this play would, I
believe, have meant the failure of the theatre.

You had a talk with Syeverov [1] from the 'Novoye Vremya'?
Wasn't it Snyessarev ? If it was, it 's not a very valuable
acquaintance, my darling.

I have had a letter from Tchaleyeva from Deutschland

[1] Syevertsov-Polilov.

(Hohenhonnef am Rhein), she has gained a great deal in weight and is recovering; she is much pleased with the sanatorium.

I have had a telegram from Samara : ' A happy Christmas to Olga Eleonardovna and Anton Pavlovitch. Kaboeva.' That was the sister of mercy, wasn't it ? I have had one from Nice, from Vassilyeva. What I can't endure are these congratulatory telegrams. Why, sending these telegrams must delay important ones. Your telegram came in the nick of time, though; I was very depressed yesterday. It rained, time dragged on very slowly, I was a little unwell and pining for my wife . . . you know I am married, darling ?

When, when shall we see each other ?

Be well, happy, merry, don't be faithless to your husband, if you can help it. I am not faithless to you, and indeed I couldn't be, my joy. God be with you. Keep well, I kiss you and embrace you.

Your ANT—.

163

Dec. 27 (1901. Yalta).

And so you acted well, Knipperusha.[1] I am glad, my clever girl. If the husband does nothing, let the wife keep it up for two.

I send you a cutting from a newspaper, what rot it is ![2] I haven't been on the sea-front for six weeks and no one has seen me.

[1] O. L. wrote, Dec. 22 : ' Katchalov was much liked and I was praised. To-day Samarova reported that the whole Little Theatre is resounding with my name and Katchalov's. In the notice in one newspaper they mention that they specially distinguish Knipper and Lilina. Rokshanin in his notice picked out no one else, but merely said : " I cannot pass over the brilliant acting of Knipper; this remarkable actress, who has hitherto played parts with a mood, now takes rank with the best modern actresses. She shows a mastery of dramatic art. . . ." I send the cutting.'

[2] The cutting referred to was called ' The Worship of Authors.' ' In Yalta, where A. P. Tchehov is living now, there exists, in the words of the " Saratov News," a complete army of senseless but insufferably ardent adorers of his genius, known locally as Antonovkas. The saintly creatures run along the sea-front of Yalta after the author, study his dress and his walk, try in every way they can to attract his attention and so on. In fact, perform no end of antics. The ideal of these harmless creatures is very modest : " To see Tchehov, to look at Tchehov." '

You stayed at the restaurant till 8 o'clock in the morning.[1]
Mind, it doesn't take long to ruin one's health. Nadyezhda
Ivanovna [2] was here yesterday. She told me a great deal about
you and about Moscow in general. Then I went to bed and
dreamed of you.

Mirolyubov [3] (who was the singer Mirov) has arrived in
Yalta. He came to see me to-day.

Our servants, Masha and Arseny, are going to the theatre
and will take this letter. They are giving ' The Forest ' [4] at
the theatre, Madame Tatarinov is acting. I read in the ' News
of the Day' a parody of Nemirovitch's play. Rather crude.
Now Luzhsky will most likely take to calling Nemirovitch
Anikoy-Voin.

Well, I kiss you, dog, kiss you and hug you again. Don't
forget me.

Your husband ANTON.

164

Dec. 29 (1901. Yalta).

You are silly, darling. Never once all the time that I 've
been married have I reproached you about the theatre ; on the
contrary, I have been delighted that you have work, that you
have an object in life, that you are not aimlessly hanging about
like your husband. I don't write to you about my illness
because I 'm quite well.[5] My temperature is normal. I am

---

[1] O. L. wrote, Dec. 22 : ' Afterwards we went, rather a big party, to
the Hermitage without the Stanislavskys. There we had supper, reeled
off speeches as though we were at home, did not want to separate and
decided to stay till the newspapers came. We sang and Alexandrov
danced. At 7 o'clock in the morning the newspapers were brought, we
read them aloud and were almost satisfied with them, and at 8 o'clock
began to disperse.'

[2] N. I. Sredin.

[3] V. S. Mirolyubov, the editor of the ' Journal for All,' was at one time
a singer.

[4] A play of Ostrovsky's.

[5] O. L. wrote, Dec. 23 : ' Antontchik, my darling, are you well again ?
Why don't you write me more about your illness, what your temperature
is and whether you have been long in bed ? I expect you have grown fearfully thin. You are eating nothing. How can we make you eat a great
deal ? It is such anguish to me to think that I can't be beside you, to

eating five eggs a day, I am drinking milk, not to speak of
dinner, which since Masha came has been very nice. Work,
darling, and don't worry, and above all don't be depressed.

Don't order the ' World of Art,' I shall have that magazine.
It is warm here in Yalta, everything is coming out and if this
weather goes on for another week everything will be in flower.

Masha is angry that you write nothing to her.

I am sending a photograph, a portrait of two Boers.[1]

Altschuller, the doctor, will soon be in Moscow and I am
advising him to dine with you. He will come to the Congress
in Moscow on Wednesday. Tell Masha, your cook, that if you
are out she must tell him when you will be at home.

Are they going to produce ' The Petty-Bourgeois ' ? When ?
This season or next ?

Well, my little dowdy, good-bye, take care of yourself !
Don't dare to be depressed and doleful. Laugh ! I embrace
you and am sorry that 's all.

There was no letter from you yesterday. What a lazy
wretch you 've grown ! Ah, you dog, you dog !

Well, my darling, my good splendid wife, I kiss you warmly
and warmly embrace you once more. I think of you very,
very often, you too must think of me.

Your ANT—.

165

Dec. 30 (1901. Yalta).

My little darling, give the enclosed letter to Rayevskaya.[2]
If you see Altschuller, buy a pound of sweets at Abrikosov's
and send them by him. Buy some *marmelad* too.

nurse you, change your compresses, feed you and comfort you. I can
fancy how you have been suffering. I give you my word that this is the
last year of this, my precious. I will do everything to make your life
pleasant, warm, not lonely, and you 'll see, you 'll be happy with me and
you 'll write and work. I expect in your heart you are reproaching me
for not loving you enough. It 's true, isn't it ? You are blaming me for
not giving up the theatre, for not being a wife to you ? I can fancy what
your mother thinks of me, and she is right.'

[1] Tchehov and a friend of his who have come out in the portrait with
very dark faces.

[2] An actress at the Art Theatre.

I am dull without you. To-morrow I shall go to bed at 9 o'clock in the evening on purpose not to see the New Year in. I haven't you, so I have nothing and I want nothing.

The weather has changed for the worse. Windy, cold and a smell of snow. Evidently winter is beginning. I am going to write to Nemirovitch.

My darling, write to me, I beseech you. Did I wish you a happy New Year? No? Then I kiss you warmly and whisper all sorts of silly things in your ear.

Don't forget your husband. You know what a temper he has, he soon comes to blows! Well, I embrace my spouse.

Your husband ANT—.

166

Dec. 31 (1901. *Yalta*).

My dear wife, I am perfectly well, perfectly! I am eating enough for ten, I have already begun to grow fat and my stomach is working superbly—which has not been the case for a long time past. Don't worry yourself, my own; on my word of honour, I am not lying, I am speaking the truth.

The pianist, Samuelson, was here to-day. He is getting up a concert in Yalta; his brother, who keeps a chemist's shop in Autka, is doing very badly, taking about six roubles a day. Complaints.

Altschuller is not going to Moscow.

I have had a letter from Meierhold. He writes well, even with some talent, and better than he used to. He ought to write for the newspapers.

A new actor, a certain Dr. Balaban, has appeared in Yalta. Did I write to you about him? He recites magnificently, reels my stories straight off by heart, and he is an actor apparently, a good real actor. I am advising him to go to Moscow and show himself to Nemirovitch.

No letter from you to-day! You have no conscience!!

It 's lovely weather in Yalta again; to-day I sat on the seat in the garden and enjoyed the air.

Well, my joy, I kiss you warmly. Don't forget me, think of

me, my little crocodile, and I 'll reward you for it.   I embrace you, darling.

Your ANT—.

I have ordered ' Art and Drama.'

I have sent a letter to Nemirovitch. I did not write much about his play, but in a friendly way, to the effect that it, the play, has had a great success and that all is right with the world.

167

Jan. 2 (1902. *Yalta*).

My sweet, delightful, incomparable wife, yesterday I had a dejected letter from you and to-day nothing ! You have begun to miss writing, evidently you have been going the pace in the holidays. Oh, how flat it is without your letters ! The day before yesterday I sent a telegram to the Art Theatre with wishes for the New Year, a long one, but addressed to Nemirovitch, and as Nemirovitch, according to the reports in the papers, has gone abroad I 'm afraid my telegram has not been received. Do find out, darling.[1]

Will the knaves let you off at the end of January ? Oy, look out, they 'll cheat you ! Give Roxanova your part in ' Lonely Lives,' then they will have more plays that they can do in your absence. Indeed, you act too often without a rest and that 's not good. It 's bad both for soul and for body. You ought not to play oftener than two or three times a week.

Darling, lovely woman, my treasure, write and describe the performance you will give for the doctors. I have read that the doctors want to give you a dinner to show their gratitude. Is it true ? Try your utmost, play your best, and let Samarova play the nurse.[2]

I meant to go into the town to-day to have my hair cut and

[1] O. L. wrote, Jan. 1 : ' At 1 o'clock I went to the Theatre, where we all met together for the New Year messages. We had champagne, tea and bread and butter. They read your telegram and liked it. Sanin proposed your health with a speech and they all clinked glasses with me.'
[2] M. A. Samarov, at that time an actress in the Art Theatre (she died in 1919), played the old nurse in ' Uncle Vanya ' in the original cast.

washed my head yesterday with that intent, but it 's cold, only three degrees above freezing. I must put it off.

I wake up and go to bed every day thinking of my wife. I think and think. . . . I kiss and hug you, caress and kiss your hands and stroke you all over. Keep well, my darling, and write to me.

Your husband ANT—.

168

Jan. 3, 1902. (*Yalta.*)

Two letters came at once to-day, my darling. Thanks! And Mother has had a letter from you too, only you have no need to be so doleful, you know that you are living in Moscow not by your own will but because we both wish it. And Mother is not in the least vexed or cross with you.

To-day I have had my hair cut! I have been in the town for the first time since my illness. I went in spite of the frost (—2 degrees) and I 've had my hair cut and my beard, that 's in case of your arrival. You are so severe, you see, I must have a decorous, well-bred appearance.

Masha has found a cook. I, I may say, am writing nothing, absolutely nothing! Don't be distressed, all in good time. You know I have written eleven volumes already, awful as it sounds. When I am forty-five I 'll write another twenty. Don't be cross, darling wife! I am not writing, but, on the other hand, I am reading so much that I shall soon be as clever as the cleverest Jew.

Now it 's January and loathsome weather is beginning here, with winds, with mud, with cold, and then February with fogs. The position of a married man who has no wife during these months is particularly deserving of compassion. If only you would come as you promised at the end of January!

Gorky is in a gloomy state of mind, apparently unwell. He is coming to-day to stay the night.

Do you feel, dog, that I love you? Or don't you care? I love you cruelly, so understand that!

Well, my splendid wife, my little German, my actress, take care of yourself. God keep you. Be serene, energetic, merry. I kiss you and embrace you.

Your husband ANTON.

169

Jan. 5 (1902.　Yalta).

Olya darling, no letter from you to-day.

I fancy that you actors haven't understood ' The Petty-Bourgeois.' Luzhsky can't play Nil; it 's the leading part, the hero. It is exactly right for Stanislavsky.[1] Tyeterev, now, is a part of which it is difficult to make anything through four acts. In every act he is exactly the same and says exactly the same thing, and, moreover, it 's not a living character, but a made-up one.

Congratulate Ella and Volodya.[2] I sincerely wish them health and happiness, and hope that when he becomes a singer he may not be unfaithful to Ella, or, if he is, that it may not be noticeable, and that Ella may not grow fat. Above all, that they may live together.

Yalta is covered with snow, it 's beyond everything; even Masha is down in the mouth and she no longer praises Yalta, but holds her tongue.

To what parts has Nemirovitch gone ? To Nice ? What 's his address ?

They have engaged a cook. She seems to cook well. Granny gets on with her, that 's the chief thing.

I dreamed of you last night, but when I shall see you in reality is quite uncertain, and it seems to me remote. You know they won't let you off at the end of January ! There will be Gorky's play and one thing and another. Such it seems is my destiny.

Well, I 'm not going to grieve you, my good marvellous wife. I love you, and shall love you even if you beat me with a stick.

---

[1] Apparently Tchehov had misunderstood. O. L. wrote, Jan. 1, about the cast, saying that Sudbinin was playing Nil.

[2] O. L.'s brother Vladimir and Ella Bartels (afterwards Rabenek) were at that time betrothed. Vladimir Knipper had given up the bar to become a singer.

There is nothing new except the snow and the frost, everything is as of old.

I embrace, I kiss, I caress my dear one, my wife ; don't forget me, don't forget me, don't drift away from me !

The roof is dripping with a sound like spring, but look out of window and it 's like winter.

Come to me in my dreams, darling !

Your husband ANT—.

Did you get the photograph of two Boers ?

170

Jan. 7 (1902. *Yalta*).

My prodigal wife, do sit at home for one short week at least and go to bed in good time ! Staying up every night till three or six o'clock in the morning—if you go on like that you 'll soon grow old and get scraggy and ill-tempered.

Tell Masha, your cook, that I congratulate her on her approaching marriage and that Masha, the mistress, will soon be in Moscow and give her the help she asks for. As for Alexandr's [1] having been a private detective, that 's the cook's utterly absurd gossip, and you shouldn't believe it. But if he is for ever hanging about the kitchen, that 's bad.

The holidays are over. I am very glad. Perhaps I shall begin to do some work. My health is grand, I couldn't wish for better. I eat enough for ten. My only trouble is I have no wife and live like an archimandrite. I get very few letters, even Dr. Tchlenov (your friend) writes me nothing.

However, in spite of your behaviour, I love you, I love and embrace my darling, and I always shall love you in spite of everything.

Only fancy, there are five and a half degrees of frost in Yalta ; yesterday there was high wind, uproar, a snowstorm. Masha is evidently disillusioned and no longer sings the praises of Yalta. In my rooms it 's cool, downstairs warm. I don't go out of the house.

How you are messing about with ' The Petty-Bourgeois ' !

[1] The future husband.

You 'll have to make haste for the season will soon be over. Luzhsky won't make much of the father. It 's not his part. And Subdinin will quite spoil Nil, the leading part. I expect the men's parts will fall flat, but the play will pick up on the women's.

My sweet darling, if any one else, not Samarova, plays the nurse in ' Uncle Vanya ' on the 11th of January I 'll break with the theatre for ever.[1] They 'll be making N. N. play in it next, that awful actress. It is dreary without you. But at the same time I am not miserable as you write, but full of hope. I have been in good spirits all this time, and the nearer the spring and the longer the days, the livelier I am.

My good, good wife, keep well and merry, don't be agitated, don't be depressed, take care of yourself. Christ be with you ! I stroke your shoulder, take you by the chin, kiss you on both cheeks. Don't forget me.

Your ANT—.

Vishnevsky has sent me a letter praising ' In Dreams,' praising himself in that play.

171

Jan. 9 (1902. *Yalta*).

My sweet pet, to-day it is raining, cold and horrid, and the day before yesterday there was a frost of eight degrees, so they say in the paper. I don't go out, I sit in my study and fancy that I have been in Kamtchatka for the last twenty-four years. I write nothing. I spend my time over trifles. Yesterday we had visitors the whole day, and I had a headache ; it 's still morning, there 's no knowing whether there will be visitors, but my head doesn't ache to-day.

It has begun snowing. The day after to-morrow you 'll be doing ' Uncle Vanya ' for the doctors. You must write and tell me how the play goes, how the doctors behave and so on and so on. Elpatyevsky is a good fellow, but he knows very little about medicine ; besides he left Yalta when I was still all

---

[1] The performance for the doctors at the Pirogov Congress.

right.[1] I wrote to you about Altschuller ; he hasn't gone to Moscow.

I have had nothing from Samarova.[2]

Our new cook, apparently a very nice woman, was taken ill yesterday ; they thought it was typhoid, but it turned out only a feverish attack. To-day she is on her legs, but taking quinine.

We will spend May and June in Yalta, July abroad, August (the second half) in Yalta, September and October in Moscow. I might spend May in Moscow, but you must come to Yalta and fetch me. Spending the summer in a sanatorium is not good enough. One sees nothing. How I should enjoy going with you to somewhere very far away, to Baikal, for instance ! It 's a marvellous lake ; if you saw it you 'd remember it all your life.

Christ be with you, my treasure. Only imagine, the sun has come out ! Be merry and well, don't forget me. Good-bye, my sweet goose, my marvellous dog. I love you very much.

Your ANT—.

172

Jan. 11, 1902. (Yalta.)

My sweet actress, be nice to Kurkin,[3] that 's right. I 'm not jealous. He is a very good man and an old friend of mine, and he is ever so much bigger than he seems.

---

[1] O. L. wrote, Jan. 4 : ' Elpatyevsky came to see me to-day, he stayed a good time and talked, of course, a great deal about you. He too says that you could quite well spend the three winter months in the neighbourhood of Moscow, that what matters is not the climate but régime, which, I repeat, I shall undertake, and I shall be a despot about it, but you will be all right.'

[2] From the same letter : ' Samarova calls you " my gentleman "; will you send her a note ? You say she sent you something. Thank her for the dish with the verses she presented to us—I wrote to you about it.'

[3] O. L. wrote, Jan. 6 : ' To-day I had a letter from Kurkin (the doctor), in which he informs me that the Congress of Doctors sent a telegram of greeting to you—our pride and glory—is that so ? He is nice, that Pyotr Ivanovitch. I was touched by the letter. And at the opening of the Congress Kurkin was so amiable to me, took me in, put on my wrap.'

I didn't write to you about seeing in the New Year, because I didn't see it in, though I wasn't asleep at midnight.

To-morrow Masha is going and I shall be left alone again. She has fed me up so that I have grown much fatter. And there is more order in the house when she is here.

To-day I am a little unwell. But that is by the way in passing ; I shall be all right again to-morrow.

How has the performance for the doctors gone ? Did they make some presentation ? I read in the newspapers they were going to present the company with my portrait. Why on earth my portrait ? Where will you put it ? Ah, my dear actress, when, oh when, shall we see each other ? I am so wretched without you that I shall soon begin screaming. Nothing interests me in Yalta, I might be an exile in the town of Beryozov. I want to live in Moscow, near you, I want to see life and watch it, I want to live in Moscow and there dream of going to the Crimea or abroad.

Elpatyevsky, do you say, liked ' Three Sisters ' ? Oh, no, my dear, excuse me.

I am drinking milk, two glasses a day. But Masha can tell you how I am living, if she wants to.

Well, my pet, my popinjay, my dog, my actress. Take care of yourself and God keep you. I love you, remember that ! Mind you remember it, dog ! How are the rehearsals of ' The Petty-Bourgeois ' going ? Will the play come off ?

I bow down to your little feet.

Your ANT—.

173

Jan. 13, 1902. (Yalta.)

My sweet darling, as far as I can make out from your last letters you are not coming to Yalta now. There 's the performance of ' In Dreams ' and the rehearsals of ' The Petty-Bourgeois.' I understand, darling, and I 'm not complaining. If you can't, well, you can't.

Masha went off yesterday ; to-day it 's cool and cloudy. I am quite well, and I eat a great deal, though I see no use in that. Elpatyevsky rang me up to-day ; when I told him that you were worried and troubled about the dinner, he was surprised and said he hadn't promised to dine with you at all. . . . [1] He has been very busy in Petersburg over his son [2] and has been successful, of which I am very glad, as apart from everything else his son is a capital fellow.

You are never tired of pressing me to come to Moscow. My dear, I should have come long ago, but they won't let me. Altschuller even forbids my going out in bad weather, though I did go out to-day as I was sick to death of being indoors.

To-day I have had two letters at once, and yesterday not one.

Well, God be with you, keep well and merry. My love to your people. Don't forget

Your ANT—.

174

Jan. 15, 1902. (*Yalta.*)

My sweet Olyusha, my popsey, I received one letter of yours through Dolgopolov,[3] and to-day I have had another in which you write about the same doctor.[4] Thanks, my own. God give you health and great success.

I had a telegram from the doctors, you know about that. Very pleasant, of course. But what is very unpleasant is that they, I mean the doctors, presented the company with a portrait of Braz's manufacture, a most hideous portrait. Why could they not buy one at Opitz's ? However, all that is not of consequence.

[1] O. L. wrote, Jan. 7 : ' There has been a silly misunderstanding with Elpatyevsky to-day. He promised to come to dinner and I told him that I would wait till five o'clock ; I did wait till half-past five and at last made up my mind to have dinner without him as I had to go to the theatre at six. . . . I was just ready to go when all at once a ring at the bell and he appears ! Oh horror ! I couldn't stay. . . .'

[2] Elpatyevsky's son was forbidden to visit Petersburg or Moscow.

[3] N. Dolgopolov was a doctor from Nizhni-Novgorod.

[4] O. L. wrote, Jan. 10 : ' Dolgopolov was here to-day ; he chattered endlessly and I thought with horror how he would wear you out with his babble. He abused me roundly for not giving up the stage. I was nervy, I spoke candidly to him, almost shed tears and afterwards was sorry for it.'

Solovtsov [1] is dead. I cannot believe it. I have had tremendous telegrams from him. Sometimes congratulatory, sometimes on business. I used, through him, to earn at least two hundred roubles a year—and all at once !

To-day I heard the spring notes of the birds for the first time. It is warm, sunny, still, and there is the timid, uncertain twittering of the bird which at the end of March flies away to Russia. There was a fire last night. The white house which stands just facing the windows of my study, on the further side of the river, built by Shapovalov,[2] was burnt. It is smoking still. They say that the alarm bell was rung in the night, but I didn't hear it.

You shouldn't have sent the foreign letter in yours. All you have to do is simply to scratch out the address, write Yalta and drop it in the post-box. Do you understand ?

Dolgopolov has not been to see me yet, he will come and he will talk a great deal and for hours—save us, oh heavenly cherubim ! In all probability he will come to-day. And, by the way, his wife is ugly, ill-tempered and elderly, but every nine or ten months she presents the world with a new baby. He advised you to leave the stage—it was just his silly babble ; he said that because he can't keep his tongue from wagging.

Yesterday I had no letter from you, and to-day I 've had a short one in which you write of not being well. Don't be ill, God forbid, or you 'll be beaten by your stern husband.

Well, my child, God keep you. I kiss you and embrace you, be well and merry, keep up your spirits.

Your ANT—.

I was limp and seedy yesterday, but to-day I feel splendid.

175

Jan. 16 (1902. Yalta).

Sweet pet, greetings, it 's my name-day to-morrow. I have the honour to congratulate you on it. Dolgopolov has been here to-day, he held his tongue but he stayed for hours.

---

[1] The well-known producer, who had his own theatre at Kiev.
[2] The architect who built Tchehov's house at Autka.

To-day, just as yesterday, the weather is most exquisite, like spring. Keep well, my angel, be merry. Don't have gloomy thoughts about me—I am quite well, you know. I love you desperately, my pet, my popinjay. I kiss you warmly.

Your ANT—.

Write me more fully about Gorky's play. He was here to-day and I had nothing I could read him.

176

Jan. 19 (1902. *Yalta).*

My darling, if I write often to you about the weather, it is because I imagined that it would interest you. Forgive me, I won't do it again. Then you are angry, too, that I don't share anything with you.[1] But what have I to share ? What ? I have absolutely nothing, or at any rate it seems as though I have nothing. There is no news whatever, my health is magnificent, I am not writing. The day before yesterday I went to see Tolstoy.

Tell Masha to buy five pounds of clover-seed and send it when she can to Yalta. Arseny needs it.

Be well and happy. Thanks for your letters. I forgot to say that Dr. Zevakin has been to see me. He is living, and is going to live, in Yalta. Many kisses.

Your ANT—.

177

Jan. 20 (1902. *Yalta).*

How foolish you are, my darling, what a silly ! Why are you whining ? What 's it about ? You write that it 's all immensely exaggerated and that you are utterly worthless, that I 'm tired of your letters, that you feel with horror that your life is growing narrower and so on and so on. You silly ! I didn't write to you about my future play, not because I 've

[1] O. L. wrote, Jan. 14 : ' Write me more about yourself. I don't know what is in your head, what occupies your thoughts, it is all far away from me, it is all apart from me. You write to me about the weather, about which I can read in the paper. . . .'

no faith in you, as you say, but because I 've no faith yet in
the play. It 's only faintly dawning in my brain like the very
first streak of sunrise, and I don't know myself yet what it 's
like, what will come of it, and it changes every day. If we were
together I should talk to you about it, but I can't write of it
because one would write nothing, merely talk all sorts of
nonsense, and then grow cold to the subject. In your letter
you threaten that you will never ask me again about anything,
that you 'll never meddle in anything.[1] But what is that for,
my darling ? No, you are my kind girl, your wrath will give
way to mercy when you see again how I love you, how close
you are to me, how I cannot live without you, my little silly.
Give over moping ! Laugh ! I may be permitted to mope,
since I live in the wilderness, since I have nothing to do, see
no one and am ill almost every week ; but you ? Your life is
full, anyway.

I have had a letter from Stanislavsky. He writes a great
deal and very nicely, he hints that Gorky's play may, perhaps,
not be produced this season. He writes about Omon, about
' Mesdames, ne vous décolletez pas trop.'

By the way, Gorky is just setting to work upon a new play
dealing with the life of a common lodging-house,[2] though I
advise him to wait a year or two, not to be in a hurry. A
writer ought to write a great deal, but he ought not to be in
a hurry, isn't that so, my spouse ?

On the seventeenth, my name-day, I was in a vile humour
because I was unwell and because the telephone kept ringing,
bringing me telegrams of congratulation. Even you and Masha
did not spare me, you sent me a telegram.

---

[1] O. L. wrote, Jan. 15 : ' How angry I am with myself, how miserable
when I act badly; I feel that I 'm not an actress at all, that it is all immensely
exaggerated and I 'm utterly worthless. It is very bitter. Why have I
no belief in anything ? I somehow think that you are tired of my letters.
. . . I feel with horror how my life is growing narrower ; wherever one
thrusts oneself, everywhere there are barriers. . . . From Masha's hints
I understand you have been telling her about the play you are thinking
of. You have never even dropped a hint of it to me, though you ought
to know how much it is to me. Well, God be with you, you have no faith
in me. I will never ask you another question. I will never meddle again.'

[2] ' The Lower Depths.' Also known as ' The Doss-house.'

By the way, when is your Geburtstag ?

You write : Don't be sad, we shall soon see each other ! What does that mean ?   Shall we see each other in Holy Week ? Or sooner ?   Don't upset me, my joy.   You wrote in December that you were coming in January, upset me, threw me into a turmoil, then you wrote that you would come in Holy Week— and I bade my soul be still, be calm, I suppressed myself, and now you are raising a storm in the Black Sea again.   What for ?

The death of Solovtsov, to whom I dedicated my ' Bear,' was a very unpleasant event in my provincial life.   I knew him well.   I read in the papers that he made corrections in ' Ivanov,' that I, as a dramatist, was guided by him, but that 's not true. And so, my wife, my nice, good golden girl, be in God's keeping, well and merry, think of your husband at least in the evenings when you are going to bed.   Above all, don't be depressed. Why, your husband is not a drunkard, nor a spendthrift, nor a rowdy.   I am quite a German husband in my behaviour.   I even wear all-wool pants.   I embrace my wife a hundred and one times and send her endless kisses.

Your ANT—.

You write : ' Wherever one thrusts oneself, everywhere there are barriers.'   But where did you thrust yourself ?

178

TELEGRAM [1]

Jan. 21 (1902.   *Yalta*).

Well greetings to cross dog ANTONY.

179

Jan. 21 (1902.   *Yalta*).

My sweet Olyuha, no letter from you to-day.   Are you cross with me ?   Or out of humour altogether ?   Yesterday I sud-denly had a telegram from you.   My darling, if I am taken ill, I will be sure to telegraph.   Don't be anxious.   If you hear

[1] An answer to O. L.'s telegram of Jan. 20 : ' No letters uneasy telegraph OLYA.'

nothing from me about my health, it means I am quite well, strong as an ox.

How disgusting our second-rate papers are ! Every day they write about me and about Gorky and not a word of truth. It 's sickening.

It is a pity that you have forbidden me to write about the weather when there is so much that is interesting in that department. There is no help for it. I must hold my tongue.

You are only rehearsing the second act of ' The Petty-Bourgeois ' and now it is near the end of January. Evidently the play will not come on this season. Or will you have time ? Gorky is setting to work on a new play as I have already reported to you, but Tchehov has not yet done so.

Sredin has arrived. . . .

My good nice, clever darling, be sweet, don't be bored, don't be miserable, and excuse me if at times my letters give you nothing. It 's not my fault, or only partly my fault, but you be merciful, don't punish me if sometimes I don't please you with a letter. If only you knew how I love you, how I dream of you, you would never write me anything sour.

I embrace and kiss my wife, which I have a perfect right to do as I am legally married. I even stroke you down your broad back. Keep well and merry.

Your husband in all-wool pants,

the German ANT—.

180

Jan. 23, 1902. (*Yalta.*)

Why is it, my good dog, you have grown so sparing of your endearments, why do your letters strike me as rather dry ? Are you angry with me ? What for ? Don't hide anything, my joy, and if you really have anything amiss in your heart, write and tell me.

I am taking ' Russia ' [1] this year.

Well, Sulerzhitsky came yesterday and brought the sweets and *marmelad* from you and told me a great deal about you.

---

[1] The paper edited by A. V. Amfiteatrov.

He told me that you have grown thin and are worn out. He stayed the night and went off this morning to Oleiz to see Gorky. To-day I had the letter from you in which you write that you will come the first week of Lent.[1] Is that so that you may go on the Wednesday of the same week to Petersburg ? Oh, don't torture me, my sweet, my dear one, don't frighten me !

Nemirovitch won't let you off, or if he does he will certainly contrive somehow, in some way, that your leaving Moscow will be impossible without the theatre having to be closed. But perhaps I 'm mistaken, I don't know.

To-day Sulerzhitsky, Balaban, A. Sredin and Tolstoy's son Andrey have been here. Balaban is the plague doctor, he is a capital reader and actor. He reads my stories superbly, acts on the stage, and has lately played in ' The Storm ' and ' The Forest.' [2] He came to say good-bye as he is going off to Petersburg. He will be in Moscow ; I gave him your address. Masha knows him.

. . . as though I were travelling and asleep in the train. However, you won't understand that !

Do me a favour, darling. The doctors presented you with that damnable portrait of me. It 's not like me and besides I hate it from associations ; ask them to take it out of the frame and put in Opitz's photograph instead. Speak about it to Tchlenov, who took the leading part in arranging it. I loathe that Braz portrait. My greetings to the mouse who is living in my study so-called.[3]

Where did you get the idea that I 'm miserable ? [4] I am bored, that 's true, but a good way still from misery. When

[1] O. L. wrote, Jan. 17 : ' Perhaps they will arrange a holiday for me at the end of January, perhaps a bit of Carnival week, the first week of Lent.'

[2] Plays of Ostrovsky's.

[3] O. L. wrote, Jan. 18 : ' In the corner of the big room which is called your study, there is a little mouse living, I have seen it and like its being there. At night when I sit quite alone writing to you, it rustles in the corner and at first it frightened me, but now I find it pleasant. I am fond of mice.'

[4] In the same letter : ' Forgive me, Anton, for your being alone and your being miserable.'

you are with me of course I am infinitely happier, and you understand that very well, though you are a dog.

Do let me write to you about the weather!

I kiss my little German and embrace her. Keep well, enjoy yourself, dine at Morozov's, or where you like, I give you full permission. When is Nemirovitch coming back? Write.

Your ANT—.

I know Dr. Frantsen, I know I. I. Shtchukin, too. I think the first is a silly fellow, the second is interesting. I dine with the second every time I am in Paris.

181

Jan. 25, 1902. (Yalta.)

And so I shall now write to you very rarely, as you are coming soon. You are a practical, strong-minded German and will come on Monday in the first week and leave on Wednesday or even Tuesday in the same week. . . . What a life you lead me!

Yesterday Shtchurovsky, the Moscow doctor who has come to see Tolstoy, was here. He came to see me not as a doctor but as a visitor. Tolstoy was very bad yesterday, his temperature went up to 39 and the pulse was up to 140 with palpitations. His chief complaint is old age, but there is also an intermittent fever which he caught many years ago.

There were visitors here the whole day yesterday. The whole day! And when you come, the place will be crowded and there's no doing anything.

Sulerzhitsky is living at Oleiz. He is somehow spiritually run to seed and has lost his freshness, but physically he is all right. He will live another fifty years.

I'm not going to tell you that I love you, dog! I have spoilt you enough! I must keep a stern hand over you. I must be severe with you, or you won't come at all, or will only come for half-an-hour.

Keep well, my dog. Well, there it is, I embrace you and kiss you. Madame Tatarinov has just rung me up.

Write!!

Your ANT—.

182

Jan. 27 (1902. *Yalta*).

My sweet popsey, I didn't telegraph to you ' cross ' dog but ' sweet ' dog, they must have got it wrong in the telegraph office.

Tolstoy is in a very bad way ; he had angina pectoris, then pleurisy and pneumonia. I expect you will hear of his death before you get this letter. I feel sad and heavy at heart.

Tell me on which day, which day of the month, you will set off. If you can't come, then you needn't ; stay at home and do your work. We will see each other in Holy Week. I am quite well.

I kiss you, my darling, tenderly and many times. Do write ; there is no letter from you to-day.

Your ANT—.

183

Jan. 28 (1902. *Yalta*).

Bring ' Vanyushin's Children ' [1] with you. Masha has the play. Do you hear ?

Tolstoy is bad, very bad. Pneumonia. Keep well, my joy. Behave yourself.

You have had no letter from me for three days ? That 's not true. I sometimes miss two days (and that 's only happened once), I sometimes miss one day, but I have never rested from letter writing for three days. I believe that you won't come. That can be seen from Nemirovitch's letter, not from anything in the letter, but just from his writing it.

If you don't come, send ' Vanyushin's Children ' registered. I kiss and embrace you.

Your ANT—.

184

Jan. 29 (1902. *Yalta*).

On the spree again, prodigal ! Well, that 's right, that 's capital ! I love you for it, only don't tire yourself too much.

[1] S. A. Naidyonov's play, which had been performed with great success at Korsh's Theatre.

How inappropriate to have given me the Griboyedov Prize !
It brings me nothing but Burenin's [1] abuse; besides I am too
old for these marks of approbation.

You are coming for two days ? Is that all ? It's like
giving only a teaspoonful of milk to Tanner after his forty
days' fast. It will only upset us, give us another separation
to endure—and my darling, think, isn't it better for you to
put off coming till the end of Lent ; think. To come for two
days is cruel, do understand ! Two days—that is Nemirovitch's
favour. Thanks very much ! Since I have endured till February I 'll endure till the end of Lent, two days are just enough
to exhaust you with the journey and put me in a turmoil with
expectation, and then at once parting ; no, no, no !

Your last letters were very nice, darling. I read them more
than once. I love you, dog. I can't help it.

Write to me. I 'll write regularly.

Your ANT—.

I embrace my prodigal. If you don't give up your plan of
coming at the end of Carnival week, understand that I consent
if you come for five days, not less ! Five days and six nights.

185

Jan. 31, 1902. (Yalta.)

Greetings, my sweet Olya, how are you ? I am getting on
pretty well since it 's impossible to live differently. You are
enthusiastic over Lunatcharsky's [2] play, but you know it is a
dilettante play written in a solemn classical style, because the
author can't write simply and from Russian life.

I believe that Lunatcharsky has been writing for some time,
and if I rummaged I believe I could find letters from him.

Bunin's [3] ' In Autumn ' is the work of a stiff, constrained

---

[1] The critic of the ' Novoye Vremya,' who wrote severe criticisms on
Tchehov's works.

[2] Now Minister of Education under the Soviet Government.

[3] O. L. wrote, Jan. 26 : ' Masha is already asleep. Before they went
to bed, I read them aloud Bunin's sketch " In Autumn." I liked it, the
mood is well sustained. We began reading Kuprin's " In the Circus,"
but were bored. I went off to write to you.'

hand; in any case Kuprin's ' In the Circus ' is far superior.
' In the Circus ' is a free, naïve, talented thing, written too by
a man who unmistakably knows what he is talking about.
Well, never mind them. Why are we discussing literature ?

Give Vishnevsky the receipt. Tell him that the money
was given long ago to the treasurer, but I only sent for the
acknowledgment yesterday. Who was it presented him with
my books ?

Tolstoy was better yesterday, there is some hope now. I
received your description of the party and the *affiche*; thanks,
my darling. I laughed so much. I was particularly amused
by the wrestlers, Katchalov's gaiters, and the orchestra con-
ducted by Moskvin. How gay you are and how drab it is
here ! Well, take care of yourself, my joy, God keep you.
Don't forget me. I embrace and kiss you.

Your German ANT—.

Tell Masha that Mother has recovered and is up and about
again. I write this on the 30th of January after tea, I wrote
mine to her in the morning.

186

Feb. 2 (1902. *Yalta*).

Dear shareholder, my business-like, practical wife, I had a
letter to-day from Morozov ; I will write to him that I agree
and that I will give ten thousand only, to be paid in two instal-
ments on the 1st of January and the 1st of July 1903.[1] You see
how I 've plunged.

---

[1] O. L. wrote, Jan. 28 : ' The future fate of our theatre is being decided,
Anton. During the third act Nemirovitch told me about it all. Our
meeting is on Sunday. Stanislavsky, Morozov, Nemirovitch, Luzhsky,
Vishnevsky, Simov, Artyom, Moskvin, Katchalov, Alexandrov, Samarova,
Lilina, Andreyeva, Knipper-Tchehova and, I believe, Stanovitch are all
shareholders. We are subscribing three thousand roubles, that is, we
are giving I.O.U.'s for that amount. Morozov will do up Lianozov's
theatre in Kamerhersky Place, let us have it for 10,000 roubles, and is
giving us a subsidy of 30,000 roubles. We make up the board of management. I write to you what I can make out of it as nearly as possible.
They count on you among the shareholders and are very anxious to have
you. Nemirovitch will write to you. You can imagine how excited we
all are ? How will it all be settled ? how will it all be arranged ? '

I send you a photograph : in it is Tolstoy, the old man and his wife, in the background his daughter and Boulanger (I believe), and in the foreground your spouse.

Boborykin, who was at your theatre, has gone and abused me in the ' Vyestnik Yevropý.' Over ' Three Sisters.' In his novel my play is abused by Gryazev, the professor, that is, Timiryazev, a man whom, by the way, I greatly respect and like.

I have had a very long letter from your friend Dr. Tchlyenov, he said he had been to see you and had heard Lunatcharsky and was reduced to despair.

You want me to write to you about the weather ? Oh, I daresay ! I 'll only tell you that to-day there is no wind, the sun is shining brightly, the quince is in flower and so are the almond-trees, but I say nothing more.

Good-bye for now, Olya, and God keep you from evil. Write to me every day, but as for your coming, I don't believe in it.[1] I kiss you, embrace you and so on and so on.

Your ANT—.

187

(Feb. 4, 1902. Yalta.)

My darling, mein lieber Hund, when you see Sytin tell him to buy me twenty mats and send me by *petite vitesse*, and you pay him for them. I have no matting and there is nowhere you can buy it here.

I have visitors, Sredin, Sulerzhitsky and others. I love you, my good spouse. I kiss your hand, your brow, your cheeks and so on, I embrace you. Write ! !

All are well.

Your German, A. TCHEHOV.

188

Feb. 6 (1902. Yalta).

My darling, my dog, my Olyusha, greetings ! I have written to you about Tolstoy's health already and more than once.

---

[1] O. L. wrote: ' I am coming for certain at the end of Carnival, and shall go straight on to Petersburg the week after.'

It was very serious, but now one may say with certainty that
the end has retreated into the distance, the patient is better
and no one can say what will be.   If he died I would telegraph
to you like this :—The old man is gone.

And so you have decided to come.[1]   You have been gracious
and merciful.   Nemirovitch telegraphs that you will set off on
the 22nd, but must be in Petersburg on the 2nd.   Obviously
I must not lose an instant, if I 'm to be in time to see you ; I
shan't even have time to kiss you, and don't dare think of anything more.

I wrote to you yesterday about mats.   Tell Masha not to
bother about them, I shall buy them myself in May when I
shall be in Moscow.

It 's very warm in Yalta, everything is coming out, the
quince is in flower, the almond 's in flower and every one is
afraid that more frosts will come and be sure to ruin it all.
To-day and yesterday I was pruning the rose-trees and, alas !
after every bush I had to rest ; evidently my health has greatly
changed for the worse this winter.

I received an azalea on my name-day, it 's flowering now.

I am reading the proofs of ' Sahalin.'

Well, woman, take care of your health.   I embrace you.   All
day yesterday I had visitors.   All day I had a violent headache.   To-day I am all right.

All the same I can't believe you are coming.   Ah, why
didn't I beat you when I was in Moscow !   I have to pay for
it now !

The Lord preserve you, my wife, I kiss you.

Your ANT—.

189

Feb. 7 (1902.   *Yalta*).

Greetings, popsey !   It 's nasty weather to-day.   Snow almost
knee-deep, but you are soon coming, so everything is all right,
everything is glorious.   In Sevastopol drive straight from the

[1] O. L. wrote, Feb. 1 : ' They are letting me off on the Thursday in
Carnival week.   Are you grateful ?   It was said before witnesses.'

station to the posting-yard, get straight into a carriage, wrap
yourself up and off. Or, perhaps, you 'll come by Simferopol ?
That will be newer for you and I believe it 's nearer and you 'll
get home sooner. Masha will explain to you.

Tolstoy will probably not live through it. Altschuller told
me to-day over the telephone that the old man's heart is
working badly.

How depressing it is to look out of window ! It 's not
weather, but beastliness.

No letter from you to-day. But I am writing, you see. So
I am a good, attentive husband.

Don't bring *marmelad*. If you want to bring sweets from
Abrikozov's, let me tell you that I don't want pine-apples or
fruits. I never eat them. Bring some cooked sausage from
Byelov's. I don't want caviare. Well, good-bye for now,
popsey. I kiss you on the shoulders, on the forehead, on the
cheek.

Did you read or hear that I telegraphed to Morozov ? Even
if you have ceased to love me, you might write all the same.
It doesn't matter.

Olyusha is coming to me soon !

Your ANTON AKTRISSIN.

190

Feb. 9 (1902. *Yalta*).

Dear Olya, dog, did I write to you to bring me ' Vanyushin's
Children ' ? Get it from Masha. You can read it on the
journey, by the way. Drive from Simferopol, hire posting
horses, go halves with some one or come by yourself, only
make haste to come ; it will be cold, remember that, wrap
yourself up well or you will be beaten.

Snow, cold—hateful !

Yesterday I was told over the telephone that Tolstoy is quite
well again, there has been a crisis, now the temperature is
normal again.

My good darling, I embrace you and kiss you. Why are
you acting Gorky's play with a peasant accent ? What are

you about ? ! ! It's as vulgar as Dosky's [1] speaking with a Jewish accent in Shylock. In 'The Petty-Bourgeois' every one speaks as you and I do.

Are you really coming soon ? I'm hoping, hoping, hoping ! And the weather is horrid, horrid !

Once more I kiss my wife, my little German, my shareholder.

Your husband A. AKTRISSIN.

191

Feb. 10 (1902. *Yalta*).

Popsey, dog, if you set off on the 20th, as you promise, you may catch the steamer from Sevastopol (it goes on Friday). It's awful driving now, while on the steamer you will have dinner and get a little nap ; it probably won't be rough, or, if it is, only a little. So do, darling, I entreat you, manage to get off on the 20th ! I entreat you !

I wrote to Nemirovitch that for the theatre to be a joint-stock company is a good thing, but the constitution of the company is devilish bad. Why should Stahovitch and I be shareholders and not Meierhold, Sanin, Rayevskaya ? Names are not what matter, but principles ; it ought to be laid down that every one who has served not less than three or five years, every one who receives a salary not below a certain figure, should become a shareholder. I repeat : what you want is not names, but rules, or everything will come to grief.

To-day they caught a Greek near our post-office pulling out a letter. I must own I was delighted. When you begin scolding me for not writing to you often, I shall fall back on that Greek now.

My darling, my own, my precious, my beauty, I entreat you, I bow down to your feet, do set off from Moscow on the 20th and be here by Friday, do what I ask you ! Show that you are a kind wife. Beg your master, Nemirovitch, he'll let you off. We've a good cook now, a God-fearing one ; she has brought peace and quiet into the kitchen. She is very religious.

[1] A former actor at the Art Theatre who in their first season played Shylock.

It 's revolting weather here. Snow.

I read in the newspapers that your company is not going to Petersburg, is it true ?

Well, I kiss and embrace you. Keep well.

Your ANT—.

I am sending off this letter on the 11th of February. There are all sorts of rumours here about Petersburg and Moscow. Mind and write to me if anything happens.[1]

192

February 13 (1902. *Yalta*).

Darling, dog, I am not coming to the harbour to meet you, as probably it will be cold. Don't be anxious, I will meet you in my study,[2] then we will have supper together, then we will have a long talk.

Yesterday I unexpectedly received a letter from Suvorin.[3] This after three years' silence. In his letter he abuses the theatre, but praises you, since it would have been awkward to abuse you too.

I believe Ekaterina Pavlovna [4] has already gone to Moscow. If there is no performance she will at least see the rehearsal and will have an idea of it.

Tell Tchlenov that I will be sure, absolutely sure, to write to him in a day or two.[5] I have nothing to write or I should have written long ago. Letters take five not three days to reach Yalta. This letter which I am sending on the 13th of

---

[1] Referring to the students' demonstrations.

[2] O. L. wrote, Feb. 8 : ' Write that you will not meet me at the harbour, but will wait for me in your study.'

[3] O. L. wrote, Feb. 6 : ' We are playing " Three Sisters." I expect Suvorin will see it. He came to see us to-day, stayed a very long time and apparently was very well pleased. He chattered a great deal . . . talked of the present disturbances, of the students. To-day he was told on the telephone from Petersburg that the University is closed.'

[4] Gorky's wife. O. L. writes in same letter : ' To-day I had a letter from E. P., she wants to know when " The Petty-Bourgeois " is coming on, she wants to come to it. Nemirovitch will write all details to Gorky. I will write to her too.'

[5] O. L. wrote, Feb. 8 : ' Tchlenov turned up after dinner and was troubled at your not writing to him.'

Feb. you 'll get on the 17th or 18th. You 'll see ! So I shall write you one little letter more to-morrow, and after that— Stop ! And a little later I shall enter upon my matrimonial duties. When you come, please don't say anything to me about diet. It 's boring, especially in Yalta. Since Masha went away, everything is topsy-turvy and going on as of old, just as before Masha came, and it is impossible it should be otherwise.

I am reading Turgenev. One eighth or one tenth of what that writer wrote will survive, all the rest will only be of historical interest in twenty-five or thirty years. Can you possibly have once liked the ' Budilnik ' artist Tchitchagov ? [1] Fie ! Fie !

Why, oh why, does S. Morozov admit aristocrats to see him ? Why, they just stuff themselves at his expense and then laugh at him behind his back, as they would at a Yakout. I 'd drive the beasts out with a stick.

I have some scent, but not much, and very little eau-de-Cologne. I kiss my darling, my precious wife, and am expecting her with impatience. To-day it 's overcast, dull and not warm, and, if it were not for the thought of you and of your coming, I think I should take to drink.

Well, I embrace my little German.

Your ANT—.

193

Feb. 14, 1902. (*Yalta.*)

Olya, my sweet, are you still in Moscow ? This is what I want to put to you, my popsey : if when you get to Sevastopol, you find there is a high wind or you are told at the station of its being stormy at sea, drive straight from the station to the posting-inn and there hire a trap, a covered one of course, or, better still, a carriage. But that only in case of extreme necessity ; remember that coming by sea is far more com-

[1] O. L. wrote, Feb. 3 : ' I met there (at the ball at S. T. Morozov's) the lame man Tchitchagov, who used to visit at our house as a high-school boy, and I used to be enchanted with his caricatures ; he knows you too. . . .'

fortable now than driving, even if it's not particularly good
weather.

Dr. Shtchurovsky has been with me to-day. Gorky has been
here.   He told me that ' The Petty-Bourgeois ' will not be given
in Moscow this season but will be given in Petersburg.
Nadyeshna Ivanovna Sredin has been.   She was laughing at
her daughter-in-law. Elpatyevsky and Dr. Sredin have been,
too. You see how many visitors I have. As soon as you come
they will be flocking to us from morning till night. Well, my
granny, I expect you on Friday.   Mind now and don't deceive
me. If you're late, even by one day, I'll divorce you.

Keep well.   Think of me.

Your ANT—.

194

TELEGRAM

Feb. 18 (1902.   *Yalta*).

Take as much as you like [1] expecting ANTOINE.

195

TELEGRAM

Feb. 19 (1902.   *Yalta*).

Bring my coat.

O. L. arrived in Yalta on February 22, *and spent five days
there, returning on February* 28.

196

Feb. 29, 1902.   (*Yalta.*)

My wife, my sweet Olyusha, what sort of a journey have you
had ?   I am uneasy, my heart's in my mouth . . . and then
this fiendish weather has poisoned the whole day for me and
I shall not be at rest till I get a letter from you.   How are you
faring ? For God's sake, write fully, darling.   Write, my
sweet. The weather still goes on being cold and nasty and I

---

[1] In reply to a letter of O. L., to take from the theatre funds to pay a debt.

picture you at this moment driving up to Baidaray, shrivelled up with cold and very cross.

Do come, darling, as soon as possible, I can't get on without my wife.

Write as fully as you can what happens in Petersburg and how everything goes, whether you are successful, what news there is, what rumours there are and so on and so on. If you see Mirolyubov give him my greetings, tell him that I got his telegram to-day.

I heard to-day that the son of Hirschman, the Harkov professor I knew at Nice, is dead.

It is snowing. As soon as it's warmer I will go and obey your orders, have my hair cut. But what I am to do about baths I really don't know. I shall have to go to Moscow to wash myself. Write to me, by the way: how were the baths burnt and how much was burnt?

Lavrov [1] arrived after you had gone away.

I keep fancying that you will lose your money on the way and be left without a farthing. I tell you once for all, take from Nemirovitch as much as you want without asking me.

Don't get into debt and don't be miserly. When you are sad, remember that you have a docile husband who loves his smart little wife. If—which God forbid—you are ever ill, come straight away to me, I 'll nurse you.

Well, I kiss and embrace my dog; remember me.

Your holy man ANTONY.

197

March 2 (1902. *Yalta*).

My sweet dog, it 's loathsome out of doors to-day : frost, high wind, snow, in one word—Tfoo !! I am busy correcting proofs, but all the same I am bored and raging. It 's intensely cold indoors.

I am impatiently expecting your letter from Petersburg. Do write everything fully, don't be lazy : don't make me beat you every day for laziness and negligence. I implore you, write!

[1] The publisher and editor of the magazine ' Russkaya Mysl.'

My room and my bed are like a holiday cottage forsaken by
its inmates.   I kiss my inimitable wife and embrace her.

Your German AN—.

198

Tuesday (March 5, 1902.   Yalta).

My marvellous darling, you telegraph Kirpitchny Street 8,
while to the best of my knowledge there is no Kirpitchny
Street in Petersburg, there is only Kirpitchny Place.   Hasn't
the telegraph office got it wrong ?   Perhaps it should be
Kirotchny not Kirpitchny.   I am anxious, my angel, very.

The weather has been most vile, now it 's sunny again, but
still it 's not warm.   I am quite well, very cross.

How has your first performance gone off ?   I know nothing.

I await a letter with your address ; as it is, I 'm not inclined
to write, I keep feeling that my letter won't reach you.   I
would eat a lot, but I have no appetite to-day at any rate.
Let us wait till the summer.   Don't wear yourself out, rest as
much as you can.

Suppose I should want to get my fee for the Moscow performances the second week in Lent, to whom and where should
I apply ?   Find out for me, precious.

I kiss and embrace you 1600 times.

Your old German A—.

Write ! ! ! !   I implore you !

199

March 8 (1902.   Yalta).

My cruel wife, here it is Friday already and I know nothing
about your company and what you are doing in Petersburg ! [1]

Evidently either the company has come to grief or my wife
is faithless.   Nemirovitch grudges money and time, I understand that, but I am bored, and I am as interested in the
fortunes of your company as all of you are.

---

[1] O. L. had written on the journey, also letters from Petersburg on
March 4, 5 and 6.

The weather is better, but it's cold. I don't care to look at anything. I am eating a great deal; Altschuller was here yesterday, he sounded me. He told me to put on a plaster, which I did. I am coughing less. I have received the proofs of my story[1] from Mirolyubov, and now I am taking steps to prevent the story from being published as the censorship has spoiled it frightfully. I shall begin to take steps and get a divorce if I find my wife is not behaving herself and not resting enough.

Ah, you dog, you dog! Write to me every day, write fully, circumstantially; why, anyway I am all you have and except me you've not a soul in this world, remember that.

I stopped writing this letter, I've begun again after reading the newspapers. In the Moscow papers I have read a telegram that the Art Theatre has had a ' colossal ' success.

I congratulate you, darling! All the same it would be desirable to know details.

I embrace you, poppet, and kiss you. God keep you.

Your AN—.

I have had my hair cut, did I tell you that?

200

March 9 (1902. Yalta).

My darling insect, I read to-day in the papers of your triumphs, of the performance of ' In Dreams,' and I read a telegram about ' Three Sisters.' Finally I read your letter, which grieved me. It seems from all you say that I shall have a lame wife coming to me at the end of Lent.[2] I received a parcel of newspapers from Petersburg, the address not written by you, one two-kopeck stamp on them. They write that the influence of Tchehov was apparent in the play ' In Dreams.' What rot!

It's sunny and not raining. I haven't yet decided where we should go for the summer. I don't want to go for a koumiss cure. By the way, my cough is less now and my health is mending. I would with pleasure move now to the Arctic Circle

---

[1] ' The Bishop.'
[2] O. L. had complained in her letter, March 5, of a pain in her legs.

somewhere in Nova Zembla or Spitzbergen. As soon as you
had gone, on the very same day, there was an influx of females,
the Girls' High School and Bonnier and Nadyezhda Ivanovna.
And they all had the same little smile, ' they hadn't liked to
intrude.'

Darling, give my greetings to our koumiss acquaintance
A. Give my love to Misha [1] and his family too. And ask
Vishnevsky to write to me at least one line.

There 's a God-fearing atmosphere in our kitchen, peace and
order, but yet I should be glad to dine away from home. They
won't make me rice soup, do what you will ! And other soups
don't suit me.

How piggish ! how base it is ! Not to send me one telegram !
Can Nemirovitch be so busy as all that ? You know, I am
interested, keenly interested, and after all I am a shareholder,
hang it all !

You thought that Gorky would refuse to be made an honorary
Academician ; [2] where did you get that idea ? On the contrary,
he was apparently pleased. If I don't get a letter to-morrow
I 'll smash you.

Well, my spoilt spouse, take care of yourself. I kiss and
embrace you a million times.

Your German husband An—.

201

March 10 (1902. *Yalta*).

My Olya, my wife, greetings. I write to you from having
nothing to do and from boredom, and I don't know what to
write about. My health to-day is superb, as it has not been
for ages. I cough hardly at all and feel perfectly well in myself ;
and this I put down to the weather, which is sunny and almost
warm. If only I could get quite well so that I could live in
Moscow ! They are already trying to find a house for us on
the Volga for the summer ; my requirements are : A house
and garden furnished, no wind, and to be near a harbour ;

---

[1] Tchehov's youngest brother, Mihail.

[2] O. L. wrote, March 4 : ' Many people thought Gorky would refuse
to be made an Academician. I had the same idea.'

best of all would be a lodge on some one's estate, so that I
could flirt with the young ladies. It would be nice to have
a little lodge where you could do the housekeeping and I could
give you orders and be very exacting.

To write reviews, and in 'Novoye Vremya' too—that is not
the job for Misha.

I have just been brought an enormous play in five acts for
me to read !! It's an outrage.

Well, I kiss you, pet you and embrace you. My greetings
to Tihomirov and tell him to send the papers, even the
notices which seem to him worthless. I am so bored I read
anything.

Your German husband whose trousers are threadbare in
the seat,

An—.

202

March 11 (1902. *Yalta*).

Wife, greetings; be so good as to thank Tihomirov for the
newspapers and tell him not to send 'Novoye Vremya,'
because I get that paper. Also give him some two-
kopeck stamps, because he only sticks on one and I have
to pay excess.

How sorry I am Marya Petrovna is not playing, but instead
of her there is my favourite Mundt !

No letter from you to-day. That's not generous. Write
and tell me whether Marya Petrovna is going to play, how she
is and what's the matter with her. My love to everybody,
Nemirovitch among them ; tell him that I've received his
photograph—Merci.

There is a curious telegram about Gorky in the papers
to-day.

So, my darling, be well and happy. I love you and shall
love you even though you turn from a dog into a crocodile.
I kiss my pigeon a thousand times.

Your An—.

203

March 12 (1902. *Yalta*).

My sweet, good darling, why such a depressed, gloomy letter ? [1]
And I am not up to much myself to-day either, far worse
than yesterday ; probably the weather is changing. My good
darling, don't be despondent, don't be dreary, you know we
shall soon be together again and I will try to make you
happy.

Why don't you get my letters ? I send to the address, Kirpitchny Street ; there is no such street and I'm afraid my
letters don't get to you. You might telegraph or something.

I have known Lika [2] for years. She is a good girl anyway,
clever and a thoroughly good sort . . . but there, it's all a
question of fate.

Write to me more fully. I am dreary without you. You
write that you are sick of the stage, that you are playing
without excitement, feeling bored. It's because you are
exhausted.

The weather is not so good to-day, but yet I have been
sitting all day long in the garden.

You write I have not written to you for two whole days, and
write in a tone as though I had already abandoned you.

My darling, if I didn't write to you for two hundred days let
me tell you I cannot abandon you and shall not abandon you
whatever happens. I embrace you, child, and kiss you.

Your German A—.

204

March 13 (1902. *Yalta*).

So at last, my crocodile, my sweet rogue, you have received
my letter. I write to you every day, you can take that for

---

[1] O. L. wrote, March 7 : '. . . This is the second day without a letter
from you, that is two days, and to-day makes the third—to-day I ought
to get a letter. . . . I woke up with a heavy head, I must have caught
cold, I will take some quinine. It's a grey disgusting day, everything
is dismal and I'm depressed.'

[2] L. S. Mizinov. See ' Tchehov's Letters to his Family and Friends.'

granted. Though I don't write much, I write. To-day I am
better than I was yesterday but not so well as the day before.
The barometer is falling, it looks like rain. It is spring or
something like spring.

I'm not going to write to Misha.[1] He likes Suvorin, and if
Suvorin has praised him that means more to him than anything. And he has a high opinion of Burenin too, and I
believe he is a little afraid of him. Let him write what he
likes about the company, don't worry yourself about it, my
darling. Marya Petrovna's absence is far worse than any
notices, it's a blow for the theatre, or anyway for the
season.

Leonid Sredin has been taken ill and his temperature is over
39. Alexin rang me up and told me this. Grandfather [2] is
recovering and is sitting up and in good spirits. Did you read
' The Peasant ' with his preface ? [3] There is nothing special
about it, but it's good, except the preface, which seemed to me
rather crude and inappropriately captious. I'll give it you to
read in the summer.

I should have liked to see Meierhold and to have had a little
talk with him and to cheer him up ; why, it won't be easy for
him in the Herson Theatre ! There is no audience for plays
there, all they want is a pantomime.

I am looking for a cottage on the Volga ; did I write to you
about it ? I am looking for a little lodge on a farm. It would
be nice not to have to eat a dinner ready cooked by our land-
lady, but to cook for ourselves. I want you to be well fed and
contented.

Well, I kiss my darling. God be with you, sleep well, think
of me and of the summer. I hug you tight, tight, I long for
letters. Be kind and good. Don't be depressed. Will you
be producing ' Uncle Vanya ' ? No ?

Your German, your stern husband A—.

---

[1] O. L. wrote, March 7 : ' Darling, you should write to Misha not to
put in notices of our company and particularly of me ; it's not nice, you
know, really.'

[2] Tolstoy.

[3] Von Polenz's novel with Tolstoy's preface.

205

March 14 (1902. *Yalta*).

Darling, you write that all the while you have been in Petersburg you have only had two letters from me. I write to you
every day to Kirpitchny Street 8, N. 30. Now I don't know
how to write to you, or whether to write at all. My letters
have evidently been lost. Can't you make inquiries at the post
one day ? Though they, I mean my letters, are already out of
date and of little interest.

I have had letters from you every day (except one day).
To-day there is a fog. I am better to-day than yesterday, I
feel all right.

Keep well, my darling. The Lord guard you. I kiss and
hug you.

Your holy man A—.

Send your address ; evidently Kirpitchny 8 is not correct.

206

March 16 (1902. *Yalta*).

My sweet, silly little puppet, my unkind, horrid wife, yesterday
I had no letter from you. Except yesterday I have written to
you every day ; evidently my letters don't reach you and I
congratulate you on it.

Well, darling, to-day there is a lovely spring rain. It is the
first this season. My mother went to communion to-day.
Arseny has an edifying expression. I am well, I am coughing
less and am in fairly good spirits. I am not writing my play,
and I don't because there are such a lot of dramatic writers
nowadays and it is becoming a boring, commonplace pursuit.
You ought first of all to produce ' The Inspector-General,' with
Stanislavsky as the mayor and Katchalov as Hlestakov ; that
would be for Sundays. And you would make a splendid
mayoress. Then ' The Fruits of Enlightenment '—also for
Sundays and to fall back upon in case of need. Only you ought
to engage two or three more decent actresses and as many
actors, who must be decent ones too. If the leading parts are

even occasionally taken by people like N., or even N. N., your theatre will come to grief in two or three seasons.

No one comes to see me, though indeed Marya Ivanovna Vodovozov came yesterday. Apparently she has made it up with me, for which I am very sorry.

How is the fourth act of ' The Petty-Bourgeois ' going ? Are you satisfied with it ? Write to me, darling.

Why haven't I had a single telegram ? I am expecting one every evening. Evidently Nemirovitch has lost heart, he is fretting over his notices.[1] But you, little silly, don't you put faith in those vulgar, stupid, crass reviews written by absurd people. They write not what they feel or what their conscience dictates, but just what fits in with their own inclinations. All the reviewing in Petersburg is in the hands of overfed, neur-asthenic Jews, there is not one real, true man among them.

Now it is the fourth week of Lent ! Soon you will be coming. I am going to give you the room where the piano is as well as the one downstairs where you were last year. So you will have two rooms. I will even give you three rooms, only don't go to Suvorin for 1000 roubles a month ![2]

Write, darling, don't be lazy, be a good wife. I hug and kiss you warmly. Write, my own ! Write longer letters, you are clever in your letters.

Your hen-pecked husband A—.

My greetings to Madame Andreyevsky, the one we met at the koumiss cure.

The day before yesterday, after reading your letter telling me you have not received my letters, I wrote to you at the Panaev Theatre.

207

March 17 (1902. *Yalta*).

My sweet crocodile, to-day I received two letters from you. One of them was written on March 11 and the postmark is

[1] In connection with his play ' In Dreams.'

[2] O. L. wrote, March 10 : ' . . . you know, Nemirovitch tells me that he had heard Suvorin was ready to give me 1000 roubles a month if I would go into his service.—Take that in ! '

March 13, evidently somebody has been carrying it about in his pocket.

My cough goes on getting better. You see, darling, how good I am. To-day there is a wind and a feeling of spring, everything is coming out and bursting into flower after the rain.

If you see A. A. Potyehin again, give him my greetings and tell him that I have a great respect for him.[1] Let my fee be paid to Masha; write to Zotkin [2] or to her, as you think best, oh dog !

So you will soon become a famous actress ? A Sarah Bernhardt ? So you will dismiss me ? Or will you take me about with you to keep your accounts ? Darling, there is nothing in the world better than to sit on a green bank and catch fish or to stroll about the fields.

I am eating well. You need not worry. You have had only three letters from me, so you say, while I have certainly sent you at least twelve !

Mother was for some reason highly delighted when she heard that you had been to see Misha and that he and his wife had been to see you.

And so ' Uncle Vanya ' will not come on ? Oh, how bad that is !

Good-bye for now, my poppet, I kiss you most warmly. Keep well and merry.

Your stern husband A—.

I have nothing against your being famous and earning 25 or 40 thousand a year, only first do your best for little Pamfil.[3]

208

March 19 (1902. Yalta).

My sweet, wonderful darling, yesterday I missed writing to you and only yesterday, while you continually leave me without

---

[1] A playwright. O. L. wrote, March 13 : ' Old Potyehin kept kissing my hand and thanking me.'

[2] The cashier of the Art Theatre.

[3] Tchehov and his wife were hoping for a son, and invented all sorts of names for him.

a letter. To-day, for instance. Can you expect me not to beat you after that ?

I am as strong as a bull. The weather is very decent. I spend almost all the time out of doors. Last night Leonid Andreyev and his wife came to see me, and she, I mean his wife, struck me as very uninteresting ; I should certainly run away from a woman like that.

Yesterday Madame Korsh came. What more am I to write to you ? What about ? Well, that I have observed that 'Novoye Vremya' has begun to take a different attitude to your theatre, evidently wrath has been turned to loving-kindness. What beasts they are !

I shall soon begin looking forward to your coming, my precious little German. I am deeply grateful to Tihomirov.

And Vishnevsky writes nothing to me, though I should very much like to hear what his Petersburg impressions are like.

I kiss my dog and hug her a million times.

Your despot A—.

L. Sredin is better ; he had pneumonia. Tolstoy is very much better.

209

March 20 (1902. *Yalta*).

My sweet darling, you ask why I don't take money for the translation of my works. Why, because it is not given me. Your friend Tchumikov wrote to me six months ago that somebody would send me 100 marks for his translation, but that somebody is in no hurry. You would do very well not to be at home to that Tchumikov. As for Marks and his 300,000, he talks nonsense. Countess Tolstoy never thought of bargaining with Marks, that 's all a lie.

I go about in threadbare breeches on purpose to show people how you are ruining me. You wait a little, I shall soon be going about without any breeches at all !

One word more about Tchumikov. You know I gave him an authorisation ; he has been translating me for years and he now dares to say that I refuse a fee ! What a brute !

Everything is out in flower here. Your room, with the piano, is waiting for you. You will soon be coming now. We will spend a little time in Yalta, then go to Moscow, then to the Volga. I want to have a look at your flat in Moscow, I am told it is very nice.

Old Madame Sredin and her younger son send you their greetings.* Do you know them? It would be nice for me to go on my travels next winter, up the Nile, for instance. What do you think? I would write you long letters from Africa, my darling!!

Well, be happy. God give you health and everything of the best. I hug you.

Your ferocious husband A—.

* She has only just been, and her son too; he talked in a quiet, gentle voice.

210

March 22 (1902. *Yalta*).

My dear wife, what they are trying to find for us is a completely furnished house, with everything provided, so that you won't have to bring pots and pans. It won't do to bring Anna Yegorovna,[1] God forbid—that would be losing our freedom, tying ourselves down. Steamers leave Sevastopol on Tuesdays, Wednesdays, Fridays and Sundays.

We might go to Finland, but not for more than a week and to as remote and wild a place as possible, so that nobody may be able to come and see us, not a single soul.

To-day Kupernik was here, Tatyana's[2] father; yesterday Kashkin,[3] Zevakin and Mme. Korsh.

Sredin is better. Dasha Ozarovsky — formerly Mussin-Pushkin and also Glebov—cannot be seriously considered as an actress.

It is spring-like weather, but no rain, dry.

To avoid all bother with the luggage, tell some one to meet you at the Nikolaevsky station and take your luggage home for

[1] The old cook in the Knippers' family.
[2] The authoress Shtchepkin-Kupernik.
[3] A musical critic.

you and you go on straight to the Kursk station and then to the south.

I am going to the dentist ! Keep well, darling, and Christ be with you. I embrace you.

Your A—.

211

March 23 (1902. *Yalta*).

My sweet dog, I have no time for letters, every day I go to the dentist and have my teeth stopped and all the rest of it. Muratova's drawing is splendid.[1] I will send Rayevskaya a book when she returns to Moscow and when I know her address.

Darling, I am ready to go to Switzerland even, only one can't fish there ! And I want to fish awfully. We ought to buy a cheap little estate near Moscow so that we may stay there in the summer and go fishing. Only near Moscow visitors would come.

Well, child, the Lord bless you. Don't be depressed, write to me. I kiss you with abounding love, my splendid one.

Your stern husband A—.

212

March 25 (1902. *Yalta*).

To-day, my darling, I went again to the dentist, and would you believe it ! I did not find him at home. To-morrow I shall go again and the day after to-morrow again—and go on like that for a whole week.

My dog, there is no rain ! I am splendidly well, could not be better. I know N. Kotlyarevsky very well, I have seen him several times. I have corresponded with F. Batyushkov ; those two—Kotlyarevsky and Batyushkov [2]—are very good and useful men, only they are rather arid and both have something about them that reminds one of I. I. Ivanov.[3]

What news is there ? Do write, darling. Or, better still,

---

[1] An actress of the Art Theatre, who died in 1921.
[2] University professors.　　　　　　　　　[3] A literary man.

make haste and finish your season and come to your husband's embraces.

Well, God bless you.   I kiss my darling.

Your spouse A—.

213

March 27 (1902.   Yalta).

Greetings, wife !   My health is completely restored and all that is wrong now are my teeth and I am going to the dentist every day.   In your last letter you ask me whether I think you clever in other things as well as your letters.   My darling, my treasure, my dog, I think you are a little silly, but I keep it a secret from every one.   You have been going it, though, in Petersburg, you have a lot of friends—I envy you !   You meet Madame Tchumin every day. . . . Is it true that she has an affair on with Vishnevsky ?   If it is true I wish them both all happiness.

I have had a telegram about ' The Petty-Bourgeois.'   Now I shall expect to hear a full account of it from you.

To-day, would you believe it ! it is raining.   I have nothing more to write about, give me my wife !   I am sick of writing.

It is real spring now.   I go about in my summer overcoat and no goloshes.

Well, make haste and come !   Here is the list of the steamers for you :

Monday .	.	. Batum.
Tuesday .	.	. Pushkin.
Wednesday	.	. Yalta.
Friday .	.	. Grand Duchess Xenia.
Sunday .	.	. Grand Duke Alexey.
Monday .	.	. Sevastopol.

These are the days on which steamers leave Sevastopol for Yalta.

Good-bye, actress, the Lord keep you !

I hug and kiss you.

Your A—.

214

March 28 (1902. *Yalta*).

Greetings, you rake ! To-day is cloudy, it looks like rain, it is coldish. I haven't yet finished with my teeth, but I soon shall. Bunin is coming in a day or two with Nilus, who is going to paint my portrait.

Grisha Glinka is the son of Baroness Ikskul. I sailed with him from Vladivostock; I think of him with pleasure, a nice boy. If the Ostrogorsky who proposed my health at the supper is the editor of ' Culture,' it is the bad Ostrogorsky, he has not a very good reputation. He published a story by Kostomarov in his magazine and gave it out as Tolstoy's.

I want you, my little German, make haste and come. I want to be off on my travels as soon as I can, and I want to consult you about it.

You say that you have upset your digestion. You shouldn't drink champagne.

God bless you, my pet, holy angels keep you. Don't forget your husband, think of him at least once in the twenty-four hours.

I hug you, my tippler.

Your husband, who wears ragged trousers but does not drink,

A—.

215

March 31 (1902. *Yalta*).

My sweet darling, I am just going to Tolstoy's. It is glorious weather. Are you sick of Petersburg ? Dull ? Cold ?

About the honorary Academicians nothing is settled yet, nothing is known [1] ; nobody writes to me and I don't know how I ought to act. I shall talk to Tolstoy about it to-day.

Gorky's play was a success, wasn't it ? Bravo, all of you !!

And so good-bye for now, darling. If necessary I will telegraph ; this is my last letter unless I write again to-morrow.

[1] Referring to the cancelling of Gorky's election as an honorary Academician, in consequence of which Tchehov and Korolenko resigned their membership of the Academy.

I am perfectly well, I shall finish with the dentist to-morrow. On Wednesday Nilus, the artist, Bunin's friend, will begin painting me.

And so, good-bye, wife ! We will meet and then no brute shall tear us apart till September or October.

I hug and kiss you a million times.

And so ' The Wild Duck ' was a disgrace ?

Your faithful husband A—.

No letter from you to-day.

216

TELEGRAM

5/IV. (1902.   *Yalta*).

Telegraph details of health.

217

TELEGRAM

6/IV. 1902.   *Yalta*.

.   .   .   .

218

TELEGRAM

9/IV. 1902.   *Yalta*.

.   .   .   .

219

TELEGRAM

10/IV. (1902.   *Yalta*).

Nemirovitch arrived keep the midwife as far as Sevastopol come alone telegraph impatiently expecting you.

O. L., exhausted by her work and her social engagements, was suddenly taken ill in Petersburg, was laid up for a fortnight and had a miscarriage, after which she travelled to the Crimea accompanied by a nurse.   As soon as she had made a partial recovery, Tchehov went with her to Moscow, but there she collapsed again and he was nursing her until June 17, when he went with S. T. Morozov for a fortnight's trip on the Volga and the Kama.

220

June 18, 1902.

My good, dear wife Olya, I slept splendidly all night in the train, now (at 12 o'clock in the day) I am sailing down the Volga. It is cool and windy, but very, very nice. I sit all the time on deck looking at the banks. It is sunny. Morozov has brought with him two good-natured Germans, one old and one young. Neither of them knows a word of Russian and I am forced to speak German. If you change your place on the deck at the right moment you can escape the wind. And so I am in good spirits, German spirits; the journey is comfortable and pleasant, I am coughing much less. I am not uneasy about you because I know, I am certain that my dog is well, it must be so

Give my love and thanks to Vishnevsky [1]; he has rather a high temperature and is frightened and depressed—that is because he is not used to it.

Respectful greetings to your mother and I hope she will be comfortable with us and that bugs won't bite her. My greetings to Zina. [2]

I will write every day, my darling. Sleep well, and think of your husband. The steamer is rolling and it is hard to write. I kiss and embrace my inimitable wife. Telegraph what Dr. Strauch says,

Your A—.

221

(*June* 19, 1902.   *Perm.*)

My sweet darling, I got the telegram at Kazan; many thanks, a thousand kisses. Now I am going up the Kama. The weather is exquisite, serene and warm. Morozov is in very good spirits. They say we shan't see Pyany Bor as we shall be there at five o'clock in the morning. That's a disappointment. There is a lot of water in the Kama. I am writing this and looking out of window ; we are approaching Lapshevo.

[1] Vishnevsky had been devotedly helpful during O. L.'s illness.
[2] An old servant of the Knippers.

Take care of yourself, my little stick.[1] Don't move into the country without me, I shall soon be back, before July 5. I am well, have plenty to eat and am warm. Don't be cross or depressed but keep up your spirits. My love to your mother, Volodya and Ella, and if you see Uncle Karl and Uncle Sasha give my love to them too.

I kiss you and embrace you. God keep you.

Your A—.

June 19, *near Lapshevo.*

We have passed Lapshevo, there was no post-box at the landing-stage.

222

June 21, 1902. *Sarapul.*

My sweet darling, I am writing this at Sarapul. It is hot to-day. Here I received your telegram sent to Tchistopol and I paid a rouble and ten kopecks excess on it. Take care of your health at least until July, don't eat rye-bread and so on.

To-morrow I shall be in Perm. I kiss and embrace my little stick. I am very well.

Your A—.

My warm greetings to Vishnevsky.

223

June 21-22, 1902.

Darling, I have not posted my letters but given them to people to post. Do you receive them ?

I did not take the sweets, I forgot them at home. Keep well ! Greetings to your family, child.

Your A—.

To-day is Friday and still I have not sent off the letter. Forgive me, darling, it has not been my fault. To-day is hot and lovely. At 4 or 5 o'clock we shall reach Perm. I have met on the steamer that same priest, the fair-haired man, who travelled with us as far as Pyany Bor last year.

[1] O. L. had become extremely thin during her illness.

224

June 22 (1902. *Perm*).

My sweet darling, my little stick, I am now at Perm. I reached here yesterday, spent the night at the Club Hotel ; at twelve o'clock to-day I am going by the steamer up the Kama to Usolye, from there to Morozov's estate, then back to Perm and at last to Moscow. I don't know on what day you will get this letter, probably not soon, but let me tell you on July 2nd I shall be back in Moscow. I am horribly tormented by jealousy, I don't trust my wife and so I am in haste, great haste. I 'll give you a drubbing.

Kama is a wonderful river. Some day we must hire a steamer for the whole family and travel in a leisurely way to Perm and back again, and that would be the best possible holiday, such as we never dreamed of. Let us think of it.

Do take care of yourself, my little stick, be a good girl. If Stanislavsky's lodge is ready, let us move there on July 3rd or 4th. We won't waste any time. Thanks for your kind telegrams.

Well, I am just going to the steamer, it is time to be off. I shall be sailing to-day and to-night, then by twelve o'clock we shall get into the train : I kiss you and if you behave yourself I embrace you as well. My greetings to Vishnevsky and Zina. Give your mother my love if she is still with you.

I have sterlet soup every day. By the time I arrive you must be fatter and as plump and crummy as the proprietress of a theatre.

I kiss you once more.

Your A—.

225

(*June* 23, 1902. *Usolye*.)

My dear, I write to you from Usolye. I have been a long time getting here in a stuffy, uncomfortable cabin, and now I am sitting and waiting for the train which will come in four or five hours. It is very hot now. By three o'clock to-day I shall be in Vilva, Morozov's estate, and there I shall sleep to my heart's content.

By July 2 I shall be in Moscow. That 's according to our reckoning.

Take care of yourself, darling, don't catch cold and don't upset your equilibrium. I greatly regret that I am not with you but alone. I am spoiled.

Well, my little stick, live and keep well, don't be depressed. We shall soon move into the country. Christ be with you.

Your AN—.

226

TELEGRAM

28/VI. (1902. *Perm*).

Telegraph to Kazan Kamenskys' landing-stage arriving July 2.

Soon after his return to Moscow, Tchehov moved with his wife to Lyubimovka, about 18 *miles from Moscow, where they stayed in a little lodge on Stanislavsky's estate. Owing to the state of his health Tchehov returned to Yalta on August* 15, *leaving O. L. at Lyubimovka.*

227

(*Aug.* 15, 1902.)

Dear Olya, I am writing to you in the train, forgive the scrawl. I have just passed the station Byelgorod. I am having a good journey. It is hot. At Kursk I saw M. V. Krestovsky,[1] she told me to remember her to you, she is in raptures over you. Shehtel's [2] wife and children are travelling in the same carriage with me. Don't be dull, darling, be cheerful, play patience and think of me. Forgive me, when I was in Moscow, not having a key, I broke open your table drawer with a knife and a chisel to get my papers. The lock is unhurt. I cleaned my boots. There turned out to be no vest in the wardrobe.

[1] The well-known authoress.
[2] The architect who had been commissioned to build the Art Theatre in Kamerhersky Place.

I bought a lot of provisions, a whole boxful, I am taking them now to Yalta. I had not time to buy cucumbers.

It's dusty in the train. Though you told me not to write about coming, still I shall soon be coming, very soon. Don't be angry with your fisherman. I kiss you warmly, be well and merry. Give my love to Elisaveta Vassilyevna,[1] Marya Petrovna,[2] Dunyasha,[2] Yegor [2] and the Smirnovs.[3] I shall write again at Lozovaya.

Your A—.

228

(*Aug.* 16, 1902. *Lozovaya.*)

I am at Lozovaya. Greetings, my sweet. It's already evening, it has got dark and is hot and stuffy. I drank a glass of milk at the station. Take care of yourself and God keep you. I shall expect to find letters from you at home. I kiss and embrace you.

Your A—.

229

Aug. 17 (1902. *Yalta*).

At last I am at home, my darling. I had a good journey. It was comfortable, though it was very dusty. I found a great many acquaintances on the steamer, the sea was calm. At home they were very much delighted to see me, kept asking about you and scolding me for your not having come ; but when I gave Masha your letter and when she had read it, there followed a silence, Mother was grieved. To-day they let me read your letter, I read it and felt no little embarrassment. Why did you scold Masha ? I swear on my word of honour that when Mother and Masha urged me to come home to Yalta, they did not ask me to come alone, but with you. Your letter is very, very unjust, but what has been written with the pen can never be effaced, there's no help for it. I tell you again :

---

[1] Stanislavsky's mother.
[2] Stanislavsky's servants.   [3] Relatives of Stanislavsky.

I swear on my word of honour that Mother and Masha invited you and me and never once me alone, that they have always felt warmly and cordially towards you.

I shall soon return to Moscow, I am not going to live here, though it is very nice here. I am not going to write the play.

Yesterday evening I arrived covered with dust, I spent a long time washing just as you told me. Washed the back of my head, my ears and my chest. I put on an open-work vest and a white waistcoat, now I am sitting reading the papers, of which there are very many, enough for three days.

Mother is entreating me to buy a bit of land near Moscow, but I say nothing, I am in a very bad humour to-day, I shall put it off till to-morrow.

I kiss and embrace you, keep well, take care of yourself. My greetings to Elisaveta Vassilyevna, write as often as you can.

Your A—.

230

Aug. 18 (1902. Yalta).

My sweet darling, it is awfully hot in Yalta, so hot that I can do nothing, and I have already begun thinking whether I had not better get away from here. And people have begun coming already, visitors stay for hours—and I rage in dumb desperation. To-day they gave us a very sweet cold soft melon at dinner, I ate it with great relish, after dinner I drank cream.

Forgive me, darling, yesterday I sent you a horribly dreary letter; don't be angry with your husband.

Altschuller has come, he insists on my being obedient, absolutely insists on it, and is coming to-morrow to sound me. I am sick of it all.

Our garden in Yalta has not dried up, only the grass is dry. I have not yet had any letters from you and I don't know how you are getting on. Be as gay as you can.

I embrace you a thousand times if you permit it and kiss you. I kiss every finger on your hand.

Your A—.

My special love to Kubyshka and Tsygan.[1]   Write every day.

S. P. Sredin was seen the other day in Moscow, her husband is still staying at the Sokolovs'.[2]   Yartsev,[3] so I am told, is being sent out of Yalta by administrative order, but what for no one knows ; he is the most harmless and indolent of men. Nadyezhda Ivanovna, looking annoyed, with tear-stained eyes, is going in a day or two to Moscow to her artist.   Manefa is not in Yalta, the head-mistress is alone now.

My darling, write ! !

231

Aug. 20, 1902.   (*Yalta.*)

Greetings, my darling, my wife !   Yesterday I received from you two greasy, crumpled letters ; evidently both had been posted at the same time by one and the same person.   How are you getting on ?   What is the weather ?   To-day it is a little cooler in Yalta, one can breathe.   Last night it was stifling and altogether horrid.   A Tatar woman died in the neighbourhood and all night long and all to-day her relations have been keening for her.

I have not received the debt.

Mirolyubov and I agreed to go together to Nervi at the end of November or beginning of December.   Till I go to Nervi I shall stay all the time in Moscow.

Ah, if you only knew how my hair is coming out !   I shall be bald directly, then you will cease to love me.   Yesterday I washed my head, but to-day the hair is coming out more than ever.   I suspect that it is all due to the soap prescribed me by your dear friend Tchlenov.

There is no news, everything is all right.   If you really will not be taking part in rehearsals in September, ask Taube [4] to let you come to Yalta.   There is no rain here at all, everything is dried up, but by September we may expect that the

---

[1] The house dogs at Stanislavsky's lodge, of whom Tchehov was very fond.

[2] The sister and brother-in-law of Stanislavsky.

[3] An artist and physician who had a house in Yalta.

[4] The doctor who had attended O. L. in her serious illness in the spring and part of the summer in 1902.

heavens will be merciful and give us a sprinkle. And I shall be very happy with you.

What is happening about Naidyonov's play ? Has Nemiro-vitch read it ? Do write more fully, my darling.

Tell Elisaveta Vassilyevna that I think of her every day and thank her for the peppermint lozenges. Has Marya Petrovna arrived ?

Write about everything, dog.

I left my penholder at home in Moscow, I left my spectacles, which are in your cupboard—in fact, do what I will, I shall have to come to Moscow.

I kiss and hug you and remain

Your bald-headed husband A—.

Write, darling. Why no letter to-day ? What is this fast for ? Don't be lazy, my child.

232

Aug. 22 (1902. *Yalta*).

My dear, good darling, I have had no letters from you for a long time, three days, but one has come to-day. As before, the heat has been insupportable, enough to make one scream. Yesterday evening for the first time there was a little rain, just a drop for three minutes.

I send you an advertisement which Masha has given me. Read it. Perhaps if there is a big pond there we might buy two or three dessyatines.

I have a cold in my head. My hair is coming out as it never has before, and the skin on my head smarts. I shall wait a little and if it doesn't stop I shall shave it off, that is, shave my head.

M. S. Smirnov asked me to buy some Tatar slippers, but she did not give me her size.

When I arrived here I paid all my small debts, but I haven't received the debts owing to me, so I am not paying S. T. Morozov the five thousand. I will write to him.

I know nothing about Naidyonov's play. What is it like ? Nemirovitch is very cold to him for some reason, and as I have thought, and still think, does not do him justice. Naidyonov, by the way, is far superior to Gorky as a playwright.

There is a regular drought here, a complete failure of the crops. Marya Fyodorovna, the schoolmistress from Melihovo, is going away to-morrow. Now she is with us. She has become a caution.

Don't be angry with me, my wife, don't be angry, dear. Really everything is not so horrid as you think. I am coming. We shall be together till December, then I shall go away and come back not later than March, and after March I am entirely yours if only you want me.

God bless you, I kiss you warmly and embrace you.

I miss you dreadfully. I have not had one attack of blood-spitting here in Yalta, while in Lyubimovka I had them almost every day the latter part of the time, though my weight increased.

Are you coming to Yalta ? Speak to Taube.

I kiss you once more. Be well and calm, my ginger dog.

Your A—.

233

(Aug. 23, 1902. Yalta.)

Copied : ' Adelaida Yulyevna Reed Konstantin Ludwigovitch Andreoletti betrothed. Tiflis. August 1902.'

This was sent to Yalta, addressed to you. No letters from you.

I am quite well. It is windy to-day. To-morrow I will write.

Nadyezhda Ivanovna has gone to Moscow.

Your A.

234

Aug. 24 (1902. Yalta).

My darling, it is now three or four days since I had a letter from you. If you don't want to write, that is your affair, but do get some one to send news of your health, I entreat you.[1]

---

[1] O. L. wrote on Aug. 14, 15, 18 and 20.

This is the fourth day that a dry, hateful wind has been blowing. At last I am beginning to get used to it and am sitting down to my table and writing a little. There has been no blood-spitting. But on the other hand I have a desperate cold in the head. Every day I drink cream, rather good cream too. I don't go to the town.

Masha returns to Moscow on the 4th of September. We are eating melons, there are no grapes yet; or rather there are, but they are poor.

Karabtchevsky [1] is here.

My joy, don't torture me, don't worry me needlessly, let me hear how you are a little oftener. You are angry with me, but what for I can't make out. Is it because I went away from you? But you know I had been with you ever since Easter without a break, never moving a step away from you, and I should not have left you, if it had not been for business and the blood-spitting. I have not received the money owing to me, by the way, but I am not spitting blood now. Don't be angry with me, my own.

It was cool last night, but this morning it is hot again.

When are you moving to Moscow? Write. Have you been to the doctors? What did they say?

I kiss you warmly, I embrace my joy, be calm and serene, and I implore you, don't be cross with your husband.

Your A—.

235

Aug. 27 (1902. *Yalta*).

My darling, my perch, after long suspense, at last I have received a letter from you. I am leading a quiet life. I don't go into the town, I talk to visitors and from time to time write a little. I am not going to write a play this year. I have no heart for it. And if I do write anything of the sort, it will be a farce in one act.

Masha didn't give me your letter, I found it in Mother's room on the table, picked it up mechanically and read it—and

---

[1] The well-known Petersburg barrister.

saw then why Masha was in such low spirits. The letter was awfully rude and, worst of all, unjust ; of course, I saw your state of mind when you wrote it and I understand. But your last letter is somehow strange, and I don't know what is the matter with you and what you have got in your head, my darling. You write : ' It was strange to expect you in the south when once they knew that I was laid up. It showed clearly the desire that you should not be near me when I was ill.' Who showed that desire ? When did they expect me in the south ? In my letter I have sworn to you on my word of honour that they never once urged me to come south without you. This won't do, this won't do, darling. One must be afraid of injustice. You must be blameless on the score of justice, absolutely blameless, the more so as you are kind, very kind and understanding. Forgive me, darling, for these scoldings, I won't do it again. I am afraid of it.

When Yegor sends in his bill, will you pay it for me ? I will pay it back in September. My plans are : I shall be in Moscow until the beginning of December, then I shall go away to Nervi and I shall stay there and at Pisa till Lent, then I shall come back. I have a cough in Yalta such as I had not in dear Lyubimovka. Not a bad cough, it is true, but there it is. I am drinking nothing. Orlenev was here to-day, also Nazimova. Doroshevitch has arrived in Yalta. I saw Karabtchevsky the other day.

Did I write to you about ' The Sea-Gull ' ? I wrote a tearful letter to Gnyeditch,[1] begging him not to produce ' The Sea-Gull.' I have received his answer to-day : he can't avoid producing it, because new scenery has been painted for it and so on and so on, so there will be a storm of abuse again.

Don't tell Masha that I read your letter to her. However, do as you think best.

There is a chilly feeling about your letters, and yet I go on pestering you with endearments, and think of you endlessly. I kiss you a billion times and hug you. Write to me, darling, oftener than once in five days. You know I am your husband

[1] A playwright and one of the managers of the Alexandrinsky Theatre in Petersburg.

anyway. Don't part from me so soon without having lived with me properly, without having borne me a little boy or girl, and when once you have a baby, then you can behave exactly as you like. I kiss you again.

Your A—.

236

Aug. 28 (1902. *Yalta*).

My dear dog, Madame Adel asked me when she was going to give her some commission to you, so I am sending part of what I should have had to bring myself. I am afraid she may crush the things or be angry with me for giving her so many.

It 's already cold in the evenings in Yalta. One resents the summer being already over. You enjoy fishing, you sit for hours together without moving ? So you are growing like me. I kiss you, my precious darling, and hug you.

Your A—.

Write and tell me if you get the things and whether they are all right.

237

Aug. 29 (1902. *Yalta*).

My dear wife, my actress, my dog, greetings ! You ask for answers to questions you put in your last letter.[1] Very well ! Yes, visitors are already boring me. Yesterday, for instance, they were coming from morning till night—some on business, some just to call. You write that I like having these visitors, that I am coquetting when I say that it enrages me. I don't know whether I am coquetting or not, only I can't work and I

---

[1] O. L. wrote, Aug. 23 : ' So visitors are boring you already. But I have come to the conclusion that you like it and that it is just coquetting when you say it enrages you. Am I right ? I am very glad that you are so pleased with Yalta and that you are so happy there. Stay there and don't hurry back here. You had better remain in Yalta altogether for the whole autumn, that will be very nice for you. Altschuller will be very much pleased ; write to me what he has said to you, do you hear ? Write me all about it, make yourself. What is your state of mind, how do you feel in yourself ? Write more about yourself, I entreat you. How did you stand the journey ? '

am sometimes greatly exhausted by conversation, particularly
with people I don't know. You write : ' I am glad that you
are so pleased with Yalta and that you are so happy there.'
Who told you that I am so happy here ? Why do you ask
what Altschuller said to me ? That doctor often comes to see
me. He wanted to sound me, tried to insist on it, but I refused.
My state of mind ? Excellent. How do I feel in myself ?
Yesterday I felt horrid and took Hunyadi, but to-day pretty
middling. As usual, I cough more than in the North. I stood
the journey very well, only it was very hot. Your hair is
turning grey and you are growing old ? [1] That is owing to your
bad temper, because you don't appreciate your husband and
love him enough. I sleep as I always do, that is, very well. I
couldn't wish to sleep better. Yartsev was here yesterday, he
chattered away gaily, telling us how nice the land is that he
has bought in the Crimea near Kokkoz ; apparently everything
is all right about the Benevolent Society too, as the whole
business has been cleared up and the Board of Management saw
that it (that is, the Board of Management) had been deceived
by false witnesses.

It is hot, there is a wind. I am drinking Narzan furiously.
To-day I had a letter from Nemirovitch and received a play
from Naidyonov. I haven't yet read it. Nemirovitch asks for
a play, but I am not going to write it this year, though the
subject is splendid, by the way.

Masha has had a letter to-day from Alupka from Tchaleyeva. She writes that she feels dreary, that she is ill and has
nothing to read. Not a cheerful letter.

Masha will arrive in Moscow on the 16th of September and
will bring wine. My good darling, find out whether Colonel
Stahovitch [2] could not give me a letter (from himself or some
one else) to Zenger, the Minister of Popular Education, asking
for the admittance of a Jew to the Yalta High School. This
Jew has passed the entrance examination for the last four years

[1] From the same letter : ' My hair is turning grey and I believe I am
growing old.'
[2] A. A. Stahovitch, afterwards director and actor in the Moscow
Art Theatre.

and always gets full marks, and yet they don't admit him though he is the son of a Yalta house-owner. They accept Jews from other towns. Do find out, darling, and write me as soon as possible. Write me a couple of words about your health, dear old woman. Are you fishing? That's a good girl.

I don't know whether you have enough money to pay Yegor for the dinners. Hadn't I better send you some? What do you think? Write to me more fully, dog, be a wife to me. Our dinners are worse than they were in Lyubimovka, the sturgeon is the only thing that's good. I eat much less, but I am drinking milk. I drink cream too, fairly decent.

There's no rain, everything is so dry in the Crimea that it drives one to despair. Doroshevitch came to see me yesterday. We talked for hours of all manner of things. He is very enthusiastic over the Art Theatre and over you. He has seen you only in ' In Dreams.'

I take my dog by the tail, swing her to and fro a few times and then stroke her and pet her. Keep well, child, and may the Lord keep you. If you see Gorky at the rehearsals congratulate him and tell him—but only him—that I am not an Academician now, that I have sent in my resignation to the Academy. But only tell him, no one else. I hug my darling.

> Your husband and protector.

238

Aug. 31 (1902. Yalta).

Why don't you get my letters, darling? I don't know. I write to you almost every day, I rarely miss a day. At first I wrote to Tarasovka,[1] but now, at your bidding, to Alexeyev's house. Well, these last three or four days I have been unwell and coughing and aching all over, but now it seems all right, only the cough remains. In fact, I cough more here than in the North. You write : ' How can you ask me to come to Yalta when you say yourself that I mustn't travel? I don't

---

[1] A station half a mile from Stanislavsky's country house.

understand, in fact I don't understand anything.' I did ask
you to come to Yalta and, at the same time, wrote that you
were to consult Taube and Strauch.[1] It wasn't I that told you
you mustn't travel, but the doctors. You write that, in fact,
you don't understand anything. What is it exactly you don't
understand ? Do I express myself metaphorically ? Am I
deceiving you ?

No, no, no, darling, that 's all wrong.

I have had a letter from M. S. Smirnov with photographs
and also one from Lily.[2] I doubt whether I am ever going to
answer them ; tell them that I don't write because I shall
soon be coming and shall see them. Tell them that Marie and
Natalie had better send the sizes of their feet, I can't buy them
slippers without the size.

It is hot in Yalta, there is no rain at all and it looks as
though there would not be. At night I am bathed in per-
spiration. The ink is drying up. And you know to-morrow
is September ! The trees in the garden have not perished, but
they have not grown one inch.

If the police-officer would let us have his bit of land,[3] still we
shouldn't have the river bank. And we can't do without our
own bank. Then it would be better to take something near
the Stanislavskys, from the Crown property. Best of all would
be to wait for an opportunity.

I haven't read Naidyonov's play yet. Somehow I am not
drawn to it. I read the ' theological magazines ' and magazines
in general.

Well, take care of yourself, my darling. Now I have begun
getting letters more often from you, thank you for it. Do
write, don't be lazy, my good dog, my splendid little girl. I
kiss you and hug you many times.

Your A—.

---

[1] The celebrated gynaecologists, who were attending O. L.
[2] An Englishwoman living in the Smirnovs' household.
[3] O. L. wrote, Aug. 26 : ' I went over to the factory to ask the director
about land, he promised to do his best. He says that the place we looked
at near Tcherkizovo is very fine, dry and beautiful. If we could get an
acre or two from the police-officer, would you like it there or not ? '

239

Sept. 1 (1902. *Yalta*).

My dear, my own, again I have had a strange letter from you.
Again you hurl all sorts of things at my head. Who has told
you that I don't want to go back to Moscow, that I have gone
away for good and am not coming back this autumn ? Why,
I wrote to you, wrote clearly in plain Russian, that I was certainly coming back in September and should be staying with
you till December. Didn't I write it ? You charge me with
not being open and meanwhile you forget everything I tell you
or write you. And I simply can't imagine what I am to do
with my wife, how to write to her. You write that you shudder
when you read my letters, that it is time for us to part, that
there is something you don't understand in it all. It strikes
me, my darling, that neither I nor you are to blame for all this
muddle, but some one else with whom you have been talking.
Distrust of my words and my actions has been put into your
mind and everything seems to you suspicious—and against
this I can do nothing, nothing, nothing ! And I am not going
to try to persuade you and convince you, for it is useless.
You write that I am capable of living beside you and always
being silent, that I only want you as an agreeable woman and
that you yourself as a human being are living lonely and a
stranger to me. My sweet, good darling, but you are my wife,
you know, do understand that at last. You are the person
nearest and dearest to me. I have loved you infinitely and I
love you still, and you go writing about being an agreeable
woman, lonely and a stranger to me.[1] . . . Well, there it is, have
it your own way !

[1] O. L. wrote, Aug. 28 : ' So you don't want to come back here ?
While I, like a fool, have been dreaming of it. Why didn't you tell me
straight out that you were going away for good ? I was right in my
presentiment. Why didn't you tell me openly that you were going away
on account of blood-spitting ? that is so simple and easy to understand.
So you concealed it from me. How it hurts me that you behave to me
as to a stranger, or a doll that mustn't be upset ! I should have been calmer
and more self-controlled if you had been open with me. So you feel that
we have lived together long enough. Is it time to part ? Good. I don't

I am better, but I cough desperately. There's no rain, it is hot. Masha is going on the 4th, she will be in Moscow on the 6th. You write that I shall show Masha your letter, thank you for your confidence. By the way, Masha is absolutely not to blame in any respect, you will be convinced of that, sooner or later.

I have begun reading Naidyonov's play. I don't like it. I don't feel inclined to finish it. Telegraph when you move to Moscow. I am tired of writing other people's addresses. Don't forget my fishing-tackle, wrap the rod in paper. Be cheerful, don't be depressed, or, at any rate, pretend to be cheerful. Sofya Petrovna Sredin has been to see me, she told me a great deal that wasn't interesting ; she knew already that you had been ill, who was with you and who was not. Old Madame Sredin is already in Moscow.

If you are going to drink wine, write to me and I will bring some. Write whether you have enough money or whether you can get on till I come. Tchaleyeva is living in Alupka ; things are in a very bad way with her.

We are catching mice.

Write what you are doing, what parts you are learning, what good things you are studying. You are not lazy like your husband, are you ? My darling, be a wife, be a friend, write me good letters, don't give way to the dismal dumps, don't torture me. Be a kind, splendid wife, as indeed you are in reality. I love you more than ever and as a husband have not been to blame towards you in any way, do understand that at last, my joy, my scribble-scrabble.

Good-bye for the present, be well and merry. Write to me every day without fail. I kiss you and hug you, my puppet.

Your A—.

understand something in all this. I simply don't understand—something must have happened ; though your letters are affectionate, why is it that a shudder runs through me when I read them several times ? . . . But you know that you are capable of living beside me and always being silent, and I sometimes feel myself superfluous ; I have felt that you want me only as an agreeable woman, and I myself as a human being live lonely and a stranger to you.'

240

Sept. 3 (1902. *Yalta*).

Olya, my sweet, my precious, my darling, yesterday I received your glorious letter, read it and was comforted. Thank you, my own. I am getting on pretty middling. I shall probably arrive on the 20th of September if nothing happens ; if anything does, then I shall come a little later.

Masha goes to-morrow. Now I shall feel dreary. I have no appetite at all, I eat little compared with before (at Lyubimovka), very little, but the letters I get are even less. I kiss my glorious wife and embrace her. Write at least every four days. When am I to leave off addressing my letters to the Red Gate ?

Your A—.

241

Sept. 5 (1902. *Yalta*).

My good darling, I write to you and keep fancying for some reason that my letters don't reach you—and so I have no inclination to write. When am I to begin writing to Neglinny ? [1] That address to Alexeyev's house seems to me extremely misty, though, of course, that is my mistake.

Suvorin, who is now in Yalta, has been coming to see me. He is going to-day. Mirolyubov and Doroshevitch come sometimes.

Write to me a little more. I gave Madame Adel your things because she asked to take them herself.[2]

Well, darling, do change your address. The heat here is impossible, there is no rain and it looks as though there won't be any. I am worn out, I may say.

God keep you ; I kiss you and embrace you.

Your A—.

People keep coming in incessantly, it 's impossible to write.

[1] Tchehov and O. L. had a flat in Neglinny Place.

[2] O. L. wrote, Aug. 31 : ' Tamara Adel was waiting for me, she brought a parcel and a basket of grapes, which her mother sent me and which are very good. I felt a little awkward at your having given them such a big parcel to bring. Masha might have brought it. I felt ashamed, to tell the truth '

242

Sept. 6 (1902.   *Yalta*).

My little crocodile, my marvellous wife, the reason why I
have not come to Moscow as I promised is this.   As soon as I
arrived in Yalta my physical barometer began to fall, I took
to coughing fiendishly and completely lost my appetite.   I was
not equal to writing or travelling, and then, as ill-luck would
have it, there was no rain, not a drop ; whatever happens, one's
soul is parched with the heat.   I wanted to take Hunyadi Janos
as usual, but in Yalta it seemed not to be the real thing and
gave me palpitations for two days afterwards.

You see what a tiresome person your husband is !   To-day
I feel much better, but there is no rain and it does not seem
as though there ever will be.   I would come to Moscow, but I
am afraid of the journey.   I am afraid of Sevastopol, where
I shall have to sit half the day.   And don't you come here, I
shouldn't like to bring you here into this baking, dusty desert.
And indeed there is no particular necessity, as I am already
better and as I shall be soon coming to Moscow.

A hundred roubles a dessyatin is an insane price, absurd.
Give up looking at houses, darling, nothing will come of it.   Let
us wait for something to turn up, that is the best plan, or we
will take a cottage every summer.

What letter of Nemirovitch's are you writing about ?   A
letter to Strauch ?   What 's it about ?

In case you want to come to Yalta, bring the spittoon, the
dark blue one.   I forgot it, and my pince-nez ; don't bring any
shirts, but bring my woolly things, the Jaeger ones.

Suvorin was here two days running ; he told me all sorts of
things, a great deal that was new and interesting, and left
yesterday.   I had a visit from Nemirovitch's admirer—Fomin,
who delivers public lectures on the subject ' " Three Sisters "
and " Three of Us," Tchehov and Gorky,' an honest and candid
but apparently not very intelligent little gentleman.   I talked
a lot of lumbering nonsense, told him I did not consider myself
a playwright, that there is now in Russia only one playwright,
that is Naidyonov, and that the play ' In Dreams ' which he

likes so much is a bourgeois production and so on and so on, and he went away.

I write to your own Moscow address, as, if I may believe your last letter, you have already moved to Moscow. And a very good thing too.

I kiss the mother of my future family and hug her. Tell Vishnevsky to write me a couple of lines of one thing and another. . . .

Your A—.

243

Sept. 8 (1902. Yalta).

To-day, darling, it has turned cool, one can breathe freely, and my health might be called magnificent. I am even hungry to-day.

I have had a letter from Valeriya Alexeyev asking me to give her permission to translate my stories for America. You, I remember, have written to me already about this absurd nonsense. I can't give her permission, as I believe I have given permission to others already ; besides she can translate them without permission.

Are you looking for a flat ? Write me all about it.

It looks like rain, but I believe it won't rain, it's simply enough to make one scream.

Keep well, my sweet little sparrow.

I kiss you, my precious darling.

Your A—.

244

Sept. 10 (1902. Yalta).

My dear little chubby, don't worry about the young Jew, he is already a pupil at the High School. We have no rain, no rain, and it doesn't look as though it ever would rain. There is no water. An invisible dust hovers in the air and of course that does its work. But all the same I have recovered, I am much better ; I am coughing less and beginning to be hungry.

I refused to take shares from Morozov, because I hadn't

received the money owing to me, and apparently I shan't get it soon or shan't get it at all. I don't care to be only nominally a shareholder as a distinction. You are an actress and earn less than you deserve, and so you can be a shareholder on credit, but I cannot.

Are you walking now or able to go in a cab ? Do you sometimes go to the theatres ? In fact, what are you doing ? What are you reading ? If any one is coming to Yalta, let him bring the spittoon and my spectacles.

This year I shall certainly go abroad. I can't spend the winter here, for many reasons.

Has Strauch given you leave to have children ? Now or later ? Ah, darling, my darling, time is passing ! By the time our child is a year and a half old, I shall most likely be bald and grey and toothless, and you will be like your Aunt Charlotte.

Oh, if only it would rain ! It is nasty without rain.

I kiss and embrace my old woman ; write to me, don't be lazy, be kind.

When will the rebuilding of the theatre be finished ? Write, darling.   Your husband A—.

245
Sept. 12 (1902. *Yalta*).

My sweet, darling, you write that the 9th of September was your birthday. Why didn't I know it ? I congratulate my newborn wife, and, of course, apologise, because there is nothing left for me to do but apologise. In your last letter among other things you reproach me for deceiving you and staying in Yalta.[1] But could I have come ? Why, I have been coughing furiously, brutally, I have been aching all over, I have been cross and creaking, like an old waggon with ungreased wheels. With you there's snow, while here the weather is vile, not a drop of rain, a dry, dusty wind blowing and very cold in the evenings. And so now it's a question hard to settle whether I am to stay here or come to Moscow.

[1] O. L. wrote, Sept. 8 : ' Who was it assured me that he was going to Yalta only for a few days, and who did not believe it ? And who has turned out to be right ? '

L. Sredin has arrived and been to see me.   Mirolyubov will
soon be in Moscow and will come to see you.   Probably I shall
come soon too. since staying here is not lively, and in any case
I must go away, there's nothing for it.   There has been no
blood-spitting.

You write that, according to Strauch, you are quite well
again, but yet you don't go in a cab, but are still walking
everywhere.   Why is that ?   Or are you better but not quite
well ?

Write more fully about your health—I have asked you, and
I ask you emphatically about it on the strength of the law by
which a wife is bound to be in subjection to her husband.

My darling, I kiss you on the forehead and the nape of your
neck and I miss you desperately.   Behave yourself, don't catch
cold, don't be depressed.   God bless you.

Your A—.

246

Sept. 14 (1902.   Yalta).

Greetings, dog !   My general health is not so bad now, I am
coughing much less.   I didn't catch cold in the bathing-shed,
please don't imagine things.[1]   It was simply the accentuation
of the process in the lungs in consequence of the heat and
inconceivable dust in Yalta.   Now it has turned cold and
I have revived.

Again I repeat I did not take you with me because Strauch
forbade it.[2]   And I fancy, in any case, you would not have
come with me.   You were already absorbed in your own
interests, the theatre, the Actors' Congress, lively conversation,
and by then you were in no mood for Yalta.   Oh well, it
doesn't matter, my wonderful darling.   We shall soon see each
other, most likely.   I shall go from here to Nervi by way of
Moscow and shall stay in Moscow by my spouse for as long a
time as possible.

[1] O. L. wrote, Sept. 10 : ' I imagine that your being ill is connected
with the storm during which you sat in the bathing-shed.'

[2] From same letter : ' I cannot tell you how it wounds me that you
were so harsh and would not take me with you.'

I congratulate you on the grand piano.[1] Play on it a bit, and if it turns out to be really good, shouldn't we buy it for our own ? Think about it, dog. I 'll come and then we will decide. Nikolasha wouldn't choose a poor instrument, of course.

I didn't send you any wine because I will bring it myself. I cannot write a play, I am drawn just now to the most common-place prose.

It 's cold, the barometer keeps going higher and higher, it doesn't rain and it doesn't look as though it ever would. I have taken to eating a great deal. There are a devilish lot of flies now indoors (it is cold for them outside), they drop even into the coffee and the soup. The sea is rough ; it is dusty.

Mirolyubov is gone, he will bring 200 roubles from me— that 's for your board and Masha's. He will either give you the money now or send it from Petersburg, that is, according to circumstances.

Every day I eat water-melon.

Good-bye for now, my child. I kiss you and embrace you and kiss my actress again.

Aren't there any new plays ? Are there none in view ?

Your A—.

247

Sept. 16 (1902. *Yalta*).

My darling, my bird, greetings ! How are you getting on ? What news ? We have none unless it is the weather, which has turned warm and grown decent. But still there is no rain and it doesn't look as though there ever would be.

Why should I write to Valeriya Alexeyev ? What am I to say to her ? since, in the first place, I don't know whether she can translate, and, in the second, I don't even know how to address her as I don't know her father's name. What makes you want me to be published in America ? And in a lady's transla-

[1] From same letter (Sept. 10) : ' Nikolasha (N. T. Sokolovsky) has got me a wonderful little instrument from the factory for 12 roubles a month ; it is a pity that I can't buy it. I should have to pay 200 roubles down and 20 roubles a month ; it 's not an upright piano but a little grand.'

tion too, which means a very bad one ?   Give her some sort of
answer yourself.

Tell M. S. Smirnov that I won't answer her letter till she
sends me her Moscow address and the size of her sister Natalie's
foot.

Have you been in the new theatre ?   Well, what did you
think ?

To-day I had a very happy letter from Vishnevsky, who,
evidently, has revived at once, as soon as he plunged into
theatrical work again.   I very much want to see you and to
touch your cheek and your shoulder.   You know I am your
husband and have a right to do anything I like to you.   Keep
that in mind.

Are you going to rehearsals ?   Are you working ?

Are ' The Pillars of Society ' going well ?   Write me everything, everything in the fullest detail.

I kiss my little chubby and embrace her.   God bless you,
darling.   I love you.

Your A—.

248

Sept. 18 (1902.   *Yalta*).

My splendid spouse, there has been a real event—in the night
it rained.   When I walked about the garden this morning, it
was already dry and dusty again, but still it has rained and
in the night I heard the sound of it.   The cold is over, it has
turned hot again.   My health is completely restored, at any
rate I am eating a great deal and coughing less ; I am not
drinking cream because the cream here upsets me and is very
cloying.   In short, you need not be anxious, everything is
going, if not very well, at any rate no worse than usual.

To-day I feel sad, Zola is dead ; it 's so unexpected and, as
it were, so inappropriate.   As a writer, I did not care much
for him, but as a man, I thought very highly of him in the
last few years, when the Dreyfus case was at its height.

And so we shall soon see each other, my little beetle.   I will
come and stay with you till you turn me out.   I shall have

time to bore you, you may be sure of that.   Tell Naidyonov,
if the subject of his play comes up, that he has great talent—
in any case.   I am not writing to him, because I shall soon
talk to him—tell him so.

I wrote to Morozov the same thing as I wrote to you ; *i.e.*
that I retire from being a shareholder through lack of money,
because I have not been paid the debt I had reckoned on
receiving.

Don't be depressed, it does not suit you.   Be merry, my
darling.   I kiss both your hands, your forehead, cheeks and
shoulders, I stroke you all over, I embrace you and kiss you
again.

Your A—.

Mother sends her love and keeps complaining that you don't
write to her.

249

Sept. 20 (1902.   *Yalta*).

Olya, my sweet, greetings !   In your last letters you were
plunged in melancholy and perhaps you have already turned
into a nun, while I am so longing to see you !   I am coming
soon, very soon, and I repeat I will stay until you turn me out,
even until January.   Mother is leaving Yalta on the 3rd of
October—so at least she was saying yesterday.   First she will
go to Petersburg and then, on her way back, will stay in Moscow
with Ivan.   That is what I advise her to do.

Why are you so worried about my taking shares from Morozov ?   As though it mattered ?   When I come to Moscow, I will
have a talk with him ; and meanwhile leave it alone, darling.

And so I shall travel to Moscow without a spittoon, and that
is so inconvenient in the train.   Don't send it or perhaps it
will come too late.   Tell Masha on the day of my arrival to
fry a veal cutlet, the sort that costs 30 kopecks.   And let there
be some of Stritsky's ' Export ' beer.

By the way, I am eating a great deal now, yet I have very
little strength and energy, and have been coughing again, have
begun drinking Ems again.   But my spirits are pretty middling,
I don't notice how the day passes.   Oh well, that 's all nonsense.

You write that ' if we lived together without parting you would bore me, as I should grow used to you as to a table or a chair.' ' And you and I are both somehow incomplete people.' I don't know, darling, whether I am incomplete or not, only I am certain that the longer I lived with you the deeper and broader my love would become. So just know that, my actress. And if it were not for my illness, a more settled man than I it would be difficult to find.

There were a few drops of rain the night before last, a very few in the day-time yesterday and not a drop more. The sun is as scorching as ever, everything is dry. About your intestinal trouble you should speak to Taube. Has he come back from abroad ? Have you consulted him ? You know anything wrong with the intestines induces melancholy, keep that in mind. When you are old, thanks to that affliction, you will beat your husband and children—beat them and sob as you do it.

Altschuller is coming to-morrow and will sound me—it is the first time this autumn. I have kept refusing to let him, but now it is somehow awkward. He keeps trying to scare me and threatening to write to you. Here in Yalta for some reason every one imagines that you are very severe and keep me in subordination.

What next ? Well, next I kiss my little beetle. Write more fully about your health. I tell you again : see Taube and then write. And so I kiss you and stroke your back and then embrace you. Till we meet ! !

Your A—.

Stritsky's beer is called ' Export.' If you will be ordering twenty bottles, order ten of Martovsky and ten of ' Export.' I will telegraph before I come.

250

Sept. 22 (1902. *Yalta*).

My dear philosopher, my little German, greetings ! I have had a magnificent letter from you to-day—the description of your expedition to Lyubimovka, and I rejoiced that

I had such a good, nice wife. Altschuller came to see me yesterday and examined me for the first time this autumn. He
tapped and listened. He thinks that my health has consider-
ably improved, that if one may judge from the change that has
taken place since the spring, the disease is being cured ; he even
sanctioned my going to Moscow—it was so splendid ! He says
that I must not go now, I must wait for the first frosts. So
you see ! He says that creosote did me good, and the fact that
I spent the winter in Yalta, but I say that it was the holiday
in Lyubimovka that did it. I don't know which of us is right.
Altschuller insists that I must leave Moscow as soon as I get
there. I said : ' I will leave in December when my wife will let
me.' Now the question arises where to go ? The point is that
there is the plague in Odessa and it is very possible that when
I am coming back from abroad in February or March I may be
detained for some days, and afterwards in Sevastopol and Yalta
I shall be looked upon as a leper. I can't return in the winter
except by way of Odessa. What am I to do now ? Think it
over !

We have no rain. It is windy.

I have read August Scholz's article on the Art Theatre.
What rubbish ! A typically German, eulogistic rigmarole in
which more than half the information the author doles out to
the public is pure falsehood ; for instance, the failure of my
plays at the Moscow Imperial Theatre. Only one thing is
good : you are called the most talented Russian actress.

My jackets and trousers are very shabby. I have begun to
look like a poor relation. You will be ashamed to go about
with me in Moscow, and there, to please you, I had better
pretend in the street I don't know you—until we buy some new
trousers.

Well, my joy, take care of yourself. Don't be depressed and
don't give way to your nerves. I embrace you and slap you
with all my might, let me tell you. We shall soon see each
other, darling.

Your A—.

And so then, I am all right. Take that in.

251

Sept. 24, 1902.   (*Yalta.*)

My wonderful darling, we have had rain, a rather good rain, it is muddy.   So I shan't write to you again about the rain.

I saw Adel on the steamer when I gave his wife the parcel. I liked him, though we had not long to talk.   I teased Madame Adel about Bartels' pies, saying he ought to be put in prison, but he, *i.e.* her husband, took it seriously and began defending Bartels and your brother.[1]

Don't forget, dog : when I come to Moscow we 'll buy some ' Houbigant ' scent, a very big bottle or two or three small ones, and send them to Altschuller.   Don't forget, please : remind me.

Mother is going to Moscow on the 1st of October, or, at very latest, the 3rd.   She is taking the cook, Polya, with her and the housemaid is leaving ; I shall be left with Granny and Arseny. It is assumed that I am going to dine in the town.   On the 15th of October, *himself* comes to Moscow.   Tremble.   I shall bring my autumn coat, my cap and my hat.   If it should be cold you will bring my fur-coat to the station.   But I expect the overcoat will be enough.   I shall bring my rug too.

I shall stay in Moscow till December or even longer according to circumstances.   If there is still the plague in Odessa in the winter I shan't go abroad—owing to causes of which I have written to you already.

In Moscow I shall do nothing but eat, drink, be nice to my wife and go to the theatre, and in my free time sleep.   I want to be an Epicurean.

Don't mope, my treasure, that 's not good.

Vishnevsky is boarding with you and paying 20 roubles a month.   Upon my word !

If you come to the station to meet me, do come alone, I en-treat you.   If it is still not good for you to go in cabs, don't

---

[1] Bartels kept the best baker's shop in Moscow, and the reference is to some alleged poisoning through his pies.   O. L.'s brother was at that time engaged to Bartels' daughter.

dare to come, stay at home and I will come by myself. Again I entreat you.

I have had a letter from Suvorin. He is producing one of his plays in Moscow, another in his own theatre in Petersburg.

So he will be in Moscow, will come to see us and talk about the theatre.

Well, God keep you, my dear wife. I bless you, kiss you, turn you upside down, throw you up by one leg and then by your shoulder and embrace you a thousand times.

Your A—.

Don't forget me. Write. Your last letters were very good. Thank you.

252

Sept. 26 (1902. Yalta).

Greetings, dog! In your last letter you complain of palpitations of the heart, say that you feel as it were over-excited, and that you are giving up coffee. Coffee won't hurt you, my darling. The whole trouble is in the bowels, which are sluggish and stiff. You ought to try taking milk, that is, drinking five or six glasses of milk a day in addition to all the rest of your food. But there, we will soon talk of that.

Tell Gorky that I am soon coming to Moscow so that he may be at the first performances. I have not yet seen ' The Petty-Bourgeois,' you know, I have not seen ' In Dreams.' Now I shall see everything, my little beetle, and praise my wonderful wife.

Mother is going by a mail train because the mail train stops more frequently : she can neither stand nor move about in the carriage when the train is in motion.

Yesterday Kuprin, who is married to the daughter of Madame Dayvdov (who edits ' Mir Bozhy '), was here and he told me that his wife is in tears several times every day because she is with child. And the owls scream at night and she fancies that she will die when the baby is born. And I listened to him and made a note of it. I thought : when my wife is with child, I will whack her every day so that she may not be capricious.

I go on coughing, but nôt very much. Everything is going well. One of these days I shall go and have my hair cut

because Olga Leonardovna does not like her husband to have
long hair.

And so keep well and merry.   Don't drive yourself over your
work, you have plenty of time.   Take example from me.

Your A—.

253

Sept. 28 (1902.   *Yalta*).

Actress, every day, literally every day, you go and buy
furniture for your dressing-room (it is evident from your
letters), but you never think of buying a big wicker armchair
to rest in, an armchair with a sloping back, in which you could
sit in the intervals when you are not playing.   Then you need
a good sprayer, and a rug which could easily be lifted from the
floor when the room is swept every day.

I am perfectly well; so there is no reason for me to stay
in Yalta, and I shall come on the 15th or 16th of October, or if
the theatre opens later, then on the 20th.   In fact I shall come
not later than the 20th and most likely before the 20th, even
perhaps before the 15th.   Living without one's wife and at the
same time being a married man is extraordinarily dreary.

Mother will be in Moscow on the 4th of October.   It is persistently asserted that a railway will soon be constructed
between Yalta and Sevastopol, and that even now tickets from
Sevastopol to Moscow will be sold not at Sevastopol, but at
Yalta.

I love you, my little duffer, my peasant-wench, my actress.
God be with you!   Keep well and serene.   Be merry.   I kiss
and embrace you.

Your A—.

I sent a letter to Meierhold to-day.

254

(*Sept.* 30, 1902.   *Yalta.*)

Actress, guess who has been to see me to-day!   You won't
guess right for any cakes.   At four o'clock yesterday afternoon

your doctor, Strauch, suddenly turned up, dressed like a swell, with a striped tie ; it appears he was performing an operation at Gurzuf. He told me that you were completely recovered and can act as much as you like.

Yesterday I remodelled an old farce of mine.[1] To-day I shall copy it out and send it to Marks.

Mother is going to-morrow. I shall be left solo.

My health seems to be getting better and better. I eat enough for ten. Only I don't drink, for there is no decent beer and the wine here is heavy and unattractive.

Mother will bring half a bottle of red wine for you to try. Masha and you try it, and if you like it I will bring some. I fancy it 's not bad. Only make haste and write, for it is very possible I may start soon.

So I shall be at the first performance.[2] And what if there is no seat for me and I have to sit in a box together with N. !

Well, my little duffer, I embrace you warmly. Don't forget that you have a husband. Think of it at least once in two days. If you think of changing your flat, try and get one higher up in the same block. If it 's a hundred or two hundred roubles dearer that doesn't matter. What do you think ?

Your A—.

255

Oct. 2 (1902. Yalta).

Actress, what do you want a fly for ?[3] There are no decent flys in Moscow, you know. One is always sick in a fly. Let us simply take an open cab. I shall be in my autumn overcoat and perhaps there will be no need of a fur-coat. I shall have my rug and goloshes.

Mother went off yesterday meaning to travel to Moscow by the mail train. I didn't telegraph to you because I don't know for certain whether she will get a ticket at Sevastopol or

[1] ' The Injurious Effects of Tobacco.'   [2] ' The Lower Depths.'
[3] O. L. wrote, Sept. 28 : ' I absolutely must come to the station, I will bring your fur-coat ; and, if it 's a bad day, let me meet you in a little closed fly. Do let me, darling, I will get a clean one.'

not. They say the trains are full and all the tickets sold for the next fortnight.

It really is bad that Nemirovitch was sick. Anyway, it was a bad sign. When you see him, tell him that I am very anxious and hope for his speedy recovery.[1]

They say in the newspapers that all the tickets for the express train and the extra one have been sold up to the 15th of October. What a state of things if that is true ! I have written to Sevastopol, perhaps a little place will be found. I am living all alone in the house. I don't mind it. I did think of setting up a mistress, but thought better of it. After all, I am going away so soon !

Keep well, my good dog, my mongrel. If you come to meet me at the station, take a cab there and back.

Well, I bow down to your feet and embrace you. Think of me or you will be beaten. You know how stern I am.

Your A—.

My love to Mother and Masha.

256

Oct. 5 (1902. Yalta).

Greetings, my actress ! Mother set off on the 1st of October, then I had a letter from her by which I learnt that she missed the train, and stayed the night at Sevastopol, and probably she spent the night in some cheap scoundrelly inn. Where she is now, I don't know. Perhaps she is still staying in Sevastopol. So you went on the 4th to meet her at the station ! There, you see what comes of not listening to me ! Why, I wrote to you not to go to meet her because she may not reach Moscow before the 27th of November, and then will probably arrive in the fourth class of a goods train. Darling, for God's sake, see that she goes to Petersburg first class in the mail train or else in the train which leaves and arrives half an hour after the mail train.

As soon as you learn from my letter or telegram that I am

[1] Nemirovitch-Dantchenko had been suffering from inflammation of the ear and was taken with vomiting after an operation on it.

coming, send at once to the chemist and get for me half a pound of pure refined cod-liver oil and ten grammes of *creosoti-fagi.*

Do you understand ? I shall come either the 14th or the 17th. I am told *all* the tickets are sold up to the 15th and, if so, I cannot come till the 17th. Anyway, I have written to Sevastopol and am now waiting for an answer.

I am dining well. Granny prepares soup and meat. I eat water-melons. Tell Mother, if she has arrived, that Nastya has not gone yet, for which I am glad, as there is some one to set the table and show in visitors. The cranes are well-fed and contented. All day long they rest, but from what work I don't know. The dogs eat and sleep all day. It is sunny, warm—even hot.

Well, Christ be with you, my joy. Be serene and merry and I 'll love you more than ever for it.

Your A—.

257

Oct. 8, 1902. (*Yalta.*)

My actress, if you don't get a telegram from me, know that I am leaving Yalta on the 12th and arriving in Moscow on the 14th of October. You can reckon on it. The ticket has already been bespoken and my departure definitely settled. So then I shall be in Moscow on the 14th.

Why, you have gone crazy ! ! ! Give a farce to the Art Theatre ! A farce with only one actor in it who does not act at all but only speaks ! ! [1] I will write a play for your theatre, that will be better.

The luckless Smirnovs told me to buy some Crimean slippers for them and I can't get them ; Sinani bought some to-day and sent them by Arseny, but they are ordinary peasant-shoes. I don't understand why he bought them, it is simply waste of money.

So expect me. I am coming. I shall be badly dressed, so don't come near me in Moscow, don't recognise me ; instead of saying ' how do you do ' at the station, I shall just give you a wink.

[1] ' The Injurious Effects of Tobacco.'

It 's warm weather in Yalta.

To-day they gave me coffee with a fly in it—a cooked fly—so disgusting !

Well, doggie, keep well and merry.   I embrace and kiss you one million three hundred thousand times.

Your A—.

Tchehov apparently left Yalta two or three days after this letter, and remained in Moscow almost to the end of November.

258

(*Nov.* 27, 1902.   *Tula.*)

My darling, it was hard to part with you.   Soon after Moscow Shubinsky,[1] the husband of Yermolova,[2] came and sat by me : we chatted, talked of the theatre, of his wife, and of the artists, that is, all of you.

I have already had lunch, thanks to you, my darling.   God bless you.   Live quietly, don't fret, don't get angry.   I kiss you.   I believe I have forgotten nothing, I have taken everything.   I will post this letter at Tula.

I kiss and embrace you.

Your A—.

259

(*Nov.* 28, 1902.   *Lozovaya.*)

I am writing this at Lozovaya.   It 's cold, 10 degrees of frost and sunny.   I am well, eating cucumber soup.   I pine for my missis.   My sweet darling, write to me about everything, don't be lazy.   Shubinsky only left me this morning.   The train is almost empty.

The Lord bless you.   I kiss and embrace you.   My love to Masha.

Your A—.

---

[1] A Moscow barrister.
[2] The famous actress at the Moscow Imperial Little Theatre.

260

Nov. 80 (1902. Yalta).

My joy, my darling, yesterday evening I arrived in Yalta. I have had a good journey, not many people in the carriage, only four ; I drank tea, had some soup and eat what you gave me for the journey. The further I got south, the colder it became ; in Sevastopol I found frost and snow. I came on to Yalta by the steamer ; the sea was calm, I had dinner and talked to a general about Sahalin. In Yalta I found cold and snow. Now I am sitting at my table writing to you, my inimitable wife, and am conscious of not being warm, of its being colder in Yalta than in Moscow. From to-morrow I shall begin expecting a letter from you. Write, darling, I implore you, or I shall soon perish of ennui in the cold and silence here.

Mother got home comfortably, though she did drive. I found everything at home in good order, everything safe ; though some precious apples which I left at home till December (they only ripen in December) had been put by Arseny and Granny in the sour cabbage. When they heard that you were bringing a terrier, they were very much delighted. A dog is greatly needed. Would not the terrier like to come with Masha at Christmas ? Think it over.

Don't be bored, my treasure. Work ; go everywhere ; sleep as much as you can. How I long for you to be well and in good spirits ! During this last visit you have grown even more precious to me. I love you even more dearly than before.

Without you, going to bed and getting up is very dreary, somehow absurd. You have spoilt me dreadfully.

Altschuller is coming to-day and I will give him your pocket-book. Doggie, my poppet, I kiss you an endless number of times and embrace you warmly. George [1] has come. Keep well and write to me.

Your A—.

You put a very great many shirts in my trunk. Why so many ? There is a perfect mountain of them in my cupboard.

[1] A cousin of Tchehov's.

My love to your mother.   Thank her for the sweets and give
her all good wishes.   My humble greetings to Uncle Karl,
Uncle Sasha, Volodya and Ella too.

261

Dec. 1 (1902.   *Yalta*).

My joy, my darling, my sweet, my wife, how are you getting
on without me ?   What are you feeling, what are you thinking
about ?   Everything is all right with me, I am well, I am not
coughing, I sleep well and I eat well.   I pine for you cruelly,
my granny, and it makes me cross and ill-humoured.   Altschuller was here yesterday.   He was very much delighted
with your present, about which he will no doubt write to you.
The head-mistress of the High School has called.   There is no
snow to-day, there is a thaw.   It is sunny.   The cranes are
calling.   Soon, in a month or six weeks, it will be spring here.

As soon as you get the dog write and tell me what it is like.

A devilish heap of newspapers have accumulated.   I shall
never fold them all up ; what a lot of lies of all sorts in them !
Yesterday I ate sturgeon with the horse-radish I brought with
me.   Tell Masha to be sure to buy horse-radish at Byelov's and
bring it with her, also a smoked ham and anything else of the
same sort.   To-morrow I shall sit down to write.   I shall write
from morning till dinner-time and then from after dinner till
evening.   I shall send a play in February.   I shall embrace my
wife in March.

Don't be lazy, darling.   Write to your spiteful, jealous husband, make yourself do it.

There is a new church here in Yalta.   They are chiming the
big bells, it is pleasant to hear because it is like Russia.   In a
day or two the question of the railway will be settled, they will
begin constructing it in the winter.   Tell Masha that we have
plenty of water, we can drink as much as we like.   They are
laying the Autka water-pipes only in one direction now—in ours.

My good granny, the Lord bless you !   I hug you many times.
Don't forget your husband.

A—.

262

Dec. 2 (1902.   Yalta).

Greetings, my good wife! Your first letter came to-day,
thank you for it. Without your letters I am utterly frozen
here, indoors just as in Yalta it is cold. Only, darling, you
must stick up your letters better, in different envelopes.

Sredin was here yesterday and Sofya Petrovna, who has
grown much thinner and looks older. And Madame Bonnier
has been. There is a great deal of scandal talked here, goodness only knows what they say about Moscow people. They
keep asking how Leonid Andreyev is, for some one has spread
a rumour that he has gone out of his mind. Though to the
best of my belief he is quite well.

I send you cuttings from the newspapers. Give them to
Vishnevsky or Tihomirov after you have read them. They
are from the Odessa papers.

You write that your heart aches for every unpleasant
moment you have given me. My dear girl, we have not had
unpleasant moments. We have behaved ourselves very well,
no married people could wish to do better. . . .

I congratulate you on Snap. Send him to Yalta. We have
no one to bark here.

The Archbishop here, Nikolay, visiting the High School
praised Gorky to the skies, saying that he was a great writer,
but disapproved of me—and the teachers for some reason are
keeping that a secret from me.

And so, behave yourself well as befits my wife. The Lord
bless you. I hug you, pat your head and kiss you.

Your ANT—.

263

Dec. 4 (1902.   Yalta).

Greetings, my cross dog, my furious pup! I kiss you in my
very first line and stroke your back. There is no news, everything goes on as before, everything goes well. It is as cold
as ever. To-day the dedication of the new church took place.

Mother was there and came back cheerful, joyous, very much pleased at having seen the Tsar and the whole ceremony; she was admitted by ticket. The bells in the new church chime a *basso profondo* pleasant to hear.

The new towels are soon wet through, it is uncomfortable to dry oneself with them. I have only two towels, though I thought I took three with me. I am eating very well, I am writing something or other, and sleeping eleven hours out of the twenty-four. The copy of the agreement signed by me with Marks is probably in the keeping of the head-mistress of the High School, I have not found it at home. When I went away, I gave all my important papers to the head-mistress to take care of. And indeed I don't care for bothering over that agreement. Nothing will come of it. Once you have signed an agreement, you must stick to it honestly, whatever it may be.

My good creature, think of me, write. And remind Nemirovitch that he promised to write to me every Wednesday. All my visitors are in raptures over the sow with the little pigs that you gave me.

Write what news there is at the theatre, how Marya Petrovna is, whether they are proposing to produce any play. If they are, let Vishnevsky write me full details.

I am ordering the ' World of Art '—tell Masha about that. My darling, my missis, I left behind in Moscow the black soap with which I wash my head (the soap for scurf and scalp irritation), give it to Masha to bring. Don't forget, my own.

When you begin thinking about me, remember that I am thinking of you, too, and that I kiss you and hug you.

God be with you. Be merry and joyous. Don't forget your husband.

A—.

264

Dec. 5, 1902. (*Yalta.*)

My sweet darling, dog, I am very dreary without you. It snowed all last night, now it is pouring with rain, pattering on the roof. The time passes with wearisome slowness. I sit and think that next year I will spend the whole winter in Moscow. My health does not make itself felt, *i.e.* it is not bad. It is cold in my rooms.

I have had a telegram from Shalyapin's admirers, supping after the benefit. I have had a long letter from Smolensk from a priest, or priest's son, written by a man who has evidently suffered a great deal, thought a great deal and read a great deal ; the letter is one unbroken hymn of praise in my honour. I have received an honorary ticket from the students of the Technical Institute. In short, my life has gone back into its usual rut.

To-day I have had no letter from you, but I dreamed of you. Every night I dream of you.

The weather in Yalta is most horrible ; the invalids feel bad, so the doctors say.

I kiss my superb wife. I hug her, I pet her. Don't be unfaithful to me, dog. Don't be carried away. And then I won't beat you, I 'll be kind to you. Write to me about everything, don't conceal anything, you know I am the person nearest to you in the world, though I do live far away.

I have some scent, three-quarters of a bottle, but still I shall say thank you, if you send me another little bottle by Masha. I have eau-de-Cologne and I have soap too. The hair-brush is used daily.

I have brought the clock quite successfully. Now it is in its place and going well.

Well, my poppet, I kiss you once more. I bless you. Do write, don't be lazy.

Your A—.

I have not once yet been to the town. It is cold, there is a furious wind blowing.

265

Dec. 6 (1902. Yalta).

My darling, your telegram has come. I have no one to send with an answer, they have all gone to church, and, indeed, an answer is hardly necessary since by now you will have received my letter.

I have no document dealing with the conditions of breaking my contract, and I never have had, and I remember when the agreement with Marks was drawn up we made no such conditions at all. I cannot send a copy with the authorisation given to Sergeyenko either, as I have not got it and have never had it. I have only a copy of the agreement, of the same deed which Pyatnitsky has already, as you write. On my honour, darling, I have no such documents, don't imagine I am deceiving you and hiding them.

Madame Solovyov was here yesterday ; she invited me to come and see her.

I have already settled to work. I am writing a story.[1] It is cold in my room, no wife here, no one brushes my coat, some one has taken away all the magazines that came in my absence. . . . I am not losing heart, though, but looking forward with hope to the future when we shall meet again and be living together.

Your envelopes are good for nothing, your letters arrive almost open. Do spend 5 kopecks on plain envelopes and throw away those aristocratic things. Or buy thin English paper and envelopes to match—at Muir and Merrilees. To-morrow I will send you a letter on English paper.

How is Suvorin's ' Question ' going ?[2] And is Tchirikov writing a third play already ? What a wealth of plays ! The theatre will grow fat if it goes on like this.

The weather is very horrid.

See, my heron, how devoted your husband is, he writes every day ! Two letters came from you to-day ; the one in which you write about Poltava was probably detained.[3] Mother

---

[1] ' Betrothed.'

[2] The play ' The Question,' which was being performed at the Little Theatre.

[3] O. L. wrote, Nov. 30 : ' This morning a pretty young woman, a native of Poltava, came to ask you and me to help by getting up a concert or something ; seven persons are being exiled to the Far East for the disturbances of last March in Poltava. Among the seven is her husband, and she was forbidden to visit the capital. I am sorry for her. She told me a great many things. It is awful. They are sending them out in December and twelve peasants too. I have promised to speak to Gorky Korolenko has done a great deal for them already.'

kisses you and thanks you for the hat. She asks whether you won't send the hat by Masha. Cannot Masha bring it ?

Well, God be with you. I embrace you. Don't be depressed, write more fully, don't be stingy.

Your A—.

266

TELEGRAM

Dec. 7 (1902. *Yalta*).

Well everything satisfactory ANTONIO.

267

Dec. 7 (1902. *Yalta*).

Greetings, dog ! This is the English paper about which I wrote to you yesterday. They have it also unruled, that perhaps is better.

I had heard about Madame Mayer,[1] but I have not seen her account and I have not had it. If it is good, the very best thing would be to give it to Goltsev, that there may be a review of it in ' Russkaya Mysl.' To send it to the ' News of the Day ' would be no use.

There has been no sun ever since I came back here, so I have not yet had a chance of basking in the sun. The weather is nasty altogether, not kindly, one has no inclination to work. I feel well.

Tell Masha to put down in her list 5 roubles 10 kopecks from O. M. Gribkova. Let her take it from my money, or I will repay her when we meet in Yalta.

I have not once been into the town yet. I take my cod-liver oil regularly.

[1] O. L. wrote, Dec. 3 : ' A young lady has come from Petersburg and wanted to see you. She brought the account written by Sister Mayer, who is working in Sahalin, where she went through the impression made upon her by Tchehov's book on Sahalin . . . please read it. This Mayer is certainly a wonderful person. Only, she has absolutely no helpers and she would like to make this account known to the public. I am thinking of sending it to Efros, in the hope he might at least put in extracts from it, especially as he has already written enthusiastically about this Mayer.'

I am continually thinking about you, dog. It seems to me
that I am going to grow more and more attached to you. I
embrace my little dove, my heron.

Your A——.

Will ' The Sea-Gull ' be produced this year ?

268

Dec. 9 (1902.   Yalta).

My treasure, you are angry with me, but speaking quite
sincerely I am not in the least to blame. I know that Gorky
had a box at Shalyapin's benefit night, I heard nothing of a
box for literary men, and in any case I should not have gone
to the benefit night.[1] As for letters, I write them and send
them to you every day (I have missed only two days), and why
they don't reach you at the proper time I don't know and can't
understand ; probably they are detained for a day or two by
the spies, whose name is legion. Don't be angry, darling, don't
be offended, everything will come right, the winter will pass
and the present discomforts and misunderstandings will be
forgotten.

To-day at last the sun has come out. My health is good,
but it was better in Moscow. I have had no spitting of blood,
I sleep well, I eat splendidly, I play patience in the evening
and think of my wife.

Your letters are short, cruelly short. You know your life
is rich and varied, you have something to write about, and at
least once a week you might rejoice my heart with a long letter.
You know every letter you send I read two or three times over !
Understand that, my darling.

I have written to you already that I have not those papers
that Pyatnitsky wants. I have only a copy of the agreement
and nothing else. And Pyatnitsky, as you write, already has
that copy.

To-day I changed my linen. In fact, I carry out your

---

[1] O. L., Dec. 4, spoke of having missed Shalyapin's benefit performance because she did not know there was a special box for literary people,
as she was not told of it.

orders precisely. There are a very great many shirts, day and night, heaped up in my cupboard—disgracefully many—so that I have sorted out half a dozen and given them to Mother to make away with.

Tell Masha to bring some white tape for the windows. It is ordinary tape, let her bring several bundles. One has to heat beef dripping, dip the tape in the dripping and then stick up the windows; it turns out very well, you do not need paste.

And fate has glued me to you not with dripping or paste, but with a cement that grows stronger every day. I embrace my darling. God be with you. Write about everything.

Your A—.

269

Dec. 10, 1902. (*Yalta.*)

My sweet little crinoline, greetings! Your kind, good-humoured letter with the news that you have received my letters has come, and thank you for it.

Mother asks Masha to bring some arrowroot biscuits, the same that we had last time.

If Masha sees Sytin, let her remind him about the calendars for Mother. I will write to Masha separately to-morrow.

It is a good thing that you go sometimes to see Taube. He is a very conscientious and exact man, mind you don't fall in love with him.

Keep well, my little duffer. Congratulate Volodya on his 200.[1] So then, he is a regular barrister by now. Write and tell me when his wedding is to be, and how and at what time I am to send the telegram.

I press Fomka's paw.[2] I am afraid he may devour our cranes.

I embrace my lawful wife and kiss her a thousand times.

Your A—.

---

[1] O. L.'s brother had won his first case in the law-courts and had been paid 200 roubles.

[2] The terrier, also called Snap.

270

Dec. 12 (1902. *Yalta*).

Greetings, my actress. Madame Schwabe [1] has come ; I have received the soap, thank you for it. I spoke to Altschuller over the telephone and from what he says she is consumptive and seriously ill. To-day I am sending you Mayer's manuscript. Of course, she is a very good woman and her work is a holy work ; if possible, it would be a good thing to talk of her account both in ' Russkaya Mysl ' and in the daily papers and in the ' News of the Day ' if you like, but better still, in the ' Russian News.' By the way, tell Efros to send me the ' News of the Day ' for the coming year, 1903, and also tell the ' Courier.' Leonid Andreyev has influence on the ' Courier.'

They are shooting in Yalta. The cold has driven the thrushes here, and now they are shooting them. They don't think of the duties of hospitality.

I am writing a story, but it is turning out so terrible that I am even outstripping Leonid Andreyev. I should like to write a farce, but can't set about it, besides it is cold for writing ; it is so cold in my rooms that I have to keep walking about to warm myself. It was ever so much warmer in Moscow. It is disgustingly cold here indoors, and when one looks out of window there is snow, frozen heaps, a leaden sky. There is no sun and still no sun. The only comfort is that from to-day the days begin to grow longer, so we are moving towards spring.

My nails are long and there is no one to cut them. A tooth has broken in my mouth. A button has dropped off my waistcoat.

In the holidays I will be sure to write to you every day— even twice a day ; that is so that you may be less bored.

Matvey Strauch has received an order of merit.

They came to-day about the purchase of Kutchukoy. I said that it was not my business, that Masha will soon be here and that they may apply to her.

---

[1] A teacher from Moscow, and a friend of Masha Tchehov's and O. L.'s.

I have not once yet been into the town !! I embrace my superb, well-behaved, clever, wonderful wife—embrace her and kiss her warmly.

Your A—.

Mother keeps coming and thanking you for the hat. She likes the hat very much.

271

Dec. 14 (1902. *Yalta*).

My darling, dowdy, dog, you certainly will have children, so the doctors say. All you need is to recover your strength completely. Everything is all right and correct in you, set your mind at rest, all you lack is a husband who could live with you all the year round. But, there, I am going to arrange somehow to live with you for a year without parting or going away, and you will have a little son who will break the crockery and pull your terrier by the tail, and you will watch him and be comforted.

Yesterday I washed my head and most likely I caught cold a little, for to-day I can't work, my head aches. Yesterday I went for the first time into the town ; the dulness there is awful, none but ugly faces in the streets, not one pretty woman, nor one interestingly dressed.

When I set to work on ' The Cherry Orchard ' I will write to you, dog. Meanwhile I am working at a story, rather uninteresting—for me at any rate ; I am sick of it.

In Yalta the earth is covered with green grass. When there is no snow, it is pleasant to see.

I have had a letter from Efros. He asked me to write what opinion I have of Nekrassov. He wants it for his paper. It 's revolting, but I shall have to write it. By the way, I am very fond of Nekrassov, and for some reason there is no other poet whose defects I forgive as readily as his. So that is what I shall write to Efros.

A cruel wind is blowing.

It will be cold now for Fomka to travel to Yalta, but perhaps he might be brought in the railway carriage, or perhaps the dogs' compartment is heated. If Masha does not bring him with her, perhaps Vinokurov-Tchigorin, the Gurzuf school-master, who has gone to Moscow to-day, might bring him.

One ear has peeled off the sow you gave me.

Well, my treasure, God be with you. Be a good girl, don't be depressed, don't mope, and think a little oftener of your lawful husband. In reality, you know there is no one in this world loves you as I do, and you have no one but me. You should think of that and make a note of it.

I embrace you and kiss you a thousand times.

Your A—.

Write a little more fully.

272

Dec. 15 (1902. Yalta).

My beloved woman, to-day I received your letter on two little sheets. Here are the answers to your questions. I take cod-liver oil and creosote regularly, since it is almost my only occupation. I have no dressing-gown ; I made a present of my old one to somebody, but to whom I do not remember ; but I do not need it, since I don't wake up at night. My jacket has only been brushed once all this time. Now, that you mayn't be angry, I will take steps. I washed my head lately. I changed my shirt this morning. My socks I'll change immediately, this very minute. But none of the towels seem much use to me. They are wet through as soon as you take hold of them ; probably they were cheap. I want shorter, rougher towels, thicker and more shaggy.

There was a fall of snow last night. It is rather scurvy out of doors.

Darling, if you are a wife to me, do have a fur-coat made for me when I come to Moscow, of some warm but light and handsome fur, for instance of fox. You know my Moscow fur-coat almost kills me. It is quite a hundredweight. Without a light fur-coat I feel like a beggar. Do your best for me, wife ! Why I did not get myself a fur-coat that last visit, I can't understand.

In the holidays I shall write to you every day. Set your

mind at rest. I am happy myself when I am writing to you.
You know you are my wonderful, delightful, well-behaved,
clever, rare wife, you have not a single defect—from my point
of view, anyway.

You have, though, you are hasty, and when you are in a bad
temper it is dangerous to come near you. But that is of no
consequence, it will pass with time. We have one common
defect—that is, that we have married late.

Last year and before that when I woke up in the morning I
usually felt in a bad humour, my arms and legs ached, but this
year there is nothing like that, it is as though I had grown
younger.

I have had a letter from Vishnevsky ; tell him that I will
answer him in the holidays.

I embrace my darling, I kiss her and bless her.

Write to me more fully, don't be lazy. Now the days are
already growing longer, spring is coming, so we shall soon see
each other. Well, God be with you.

Your A—.

273

Dec. 17 (1902. *Yalta*).

My actress, greetings ! Your last two letters were not cheerful : in one you are in the dumps, in the other your head aches.
You ought not to go to N.'s lecture. You know N. is a dull-
witted, conservative person, though he does consider himself a
critic and a liberal. So the theatre develops passivity, does
it ? Well, what about painting ? and poetry ? Why, the
spectator who looks at the picture or the man who reads the
novel cannot express his sympathy or lack of sympathy with
what there is in the picture or in the book. ' Hail to the light
and perish darkness ! ' That is the canting hypocrisy of all these
out-of-date deaf impudent fellows. Bazhenov [1] is a charlatan,
I 've known him for years ; Boborykin is old and embittered.

If you don't want to go to the club and the Teleshovs', don't
go, darling. Teleshov is a nice man. . . . But, as a rule, it is

---

[1] A Moscow alienist.

tedious with all these fellows who have anything to do with literature, with very few exceptions. How behind the times and stale all our Moscow literary world is, old and young alike, you will see later on in another two or three years when the attitude of all these gentry to the heresies of the Art Theatre becomes clear to you.

There is a furious wind blowing. I cannot work. The weather has worn me out, I am ready to lie and bite my pillow.

The water-pipes have burst, there is no water. They are mending them. It is raining. It is cold. And it is not warm in my rooms. I pine for you desperately. I have grown old, I can't sleep alone, I often wake up. I read a notice of ' Uncle Vanya ' in the ' Perm Gazette ' ; it said that Astrov was very drunk ; probably he was staggering about through all the four acts. Tell Nemirovitch that I haven't answered his telegram hitherto, since I have not thought yet what plays to produce next year. I think there will be plays. It would not be amiss, as I said, to stage Maeterlinck's three plays with music. Nemirovitch promised to write to me every Wednesday, and even put his promise into writing, but so far not a single letter, not a sign.

If you see Leonid Andreyev, tell him to send me the ' Courier ' in 1903. Please do ! And tell Efros about the ' News of the Day.'

My clever girl, my dove, my joy, my dog. Keep well and merry. God be with you. Don't worry about me, I am in good health and well-fed. I embrace you and kiss you.

Your A—.

I am going to take the ' Citizen.' I have received a volume of poems from A. M. Fyodorov. The poems are all poor (or so it seemed to me) and trivial, but there is one I liked very much.

Below in the street the hurdy-gurdy is droning,
My window is open. The twilight is falling,
The mist from the fields floats in at my window
And like a caress brings the soft breath of spring.
I cannot tell why I feel my hand trembling,
I cannot tell why there are tears on my cheek.
My head sinks on my arms. With deep sadness and longing
My heart yearns for thee . . . thee, so far, far away !

274

Dec. 19 (1902. *Yalta*).

Dear actress, I can't write a long letter; I have been at the dentist's, I feel very much exhausted, I feel as though I had been pulled to pieces. Forgive me, darling. To-morrow I will sit down and reel off a long letter to you.

Madame Bonnier is here. Yesterday we had Madame Solovyov, whose acknowledged adorer I am becoming. You have nothing against it, have you ?

I was working and getting on well, but for the last four or five days I have been doing nothing, as my teeth would not let me forget them, and a break in the story followed.

I embrace and kiss you. You seem as it were surprised that our letters are tender; how could they not be, heron ? Why, don't you love me ?

Well, God be with you.

Your A—.

275

Dec. 20 (1902. *Yalta*).

My dear little friend, to-day I had a telegram from Stanislavsky as follows : ' Gorky's play and the theatre had a great triumph. Olga Leonardovna topped the list with a critical audience.' Rejoice, darling. Your husband is very much pleased and will drink to your health to-day, if only Masha brings some porter with her.

I am having a bother now with my teeth. I do not know when all the stupid business will be over. Yesterday I had a letter from you almost unstuck (again !), and to-day is a sad day for me, as Arseny has brought no letter from you by the post. And the weather is sad to-day : warm, still, but no breath of spring. I have been sitting on the balcony in the sun thinking of you, of Fomka, of crocodiles, of the lining of my coat, which is torn. I have thought you need a little son who would occupy you and fill up your life. You will have a little son or daughter, my own, believe me, you need only wait a little to be quite normal again after your illness. I am not telling you lies, I am not concealing a scrap of what the doctors say, on my word of honour.

Misha sent some herrings. What else is there to tell you ? We have a great many mice again. Every day I catch them in the trap. And the mice are probably accustomed to it now, as they behave placidly and are no longer afraid.[1] There is nothing more to write about, there is nothing, or at any rate it is not apparent, life is passing dingily and rather emptily. I am coughing. I sleep well, but all the night long I dream as befits a sluggard.

Write me all sorts of little details, child, that I may feel that I don't belong to Yalta but to the North, that this dreary and empty life has not yet swallowed me up. I dream of coming to Moscow not later than the 1st of March, that is in two months, but whether it will be so I don't know. God keep you, my good wife, my ginger-haired dog. Imagine that I pick you up in my arms, and carry you about the room for two hours, and kiss and embrace you. My love to your mother, to Uncle Karl, to Uncle Sasha, to Volodya, to Ella, to Zina. Thank Stanislavsky for his telegram.

I will write to-morrow. Sleep well, my joy, eat as you should, and think of your husband.

Your A—.

276

Dec. 21 (1902. *Yalta*).

My actress, again to-day I have had no letter. Well, there 's nothing for it. I will sit without a letter, as smokers sometimes sit without tobacco. I have received from Gnyeditch the information that I am to have not 8 but 10 per cent. on ' The Sea-Gull,' that ' The Sea-Gull ' is drawing good houses and so on and so on. I have had a letter from Suvorin, two full sheets. By the way, 'Old Theatregoer,' writing in the 'Novoye Vremya,' is himself, Suvorin. In every article he abuses

[1] Tchehov used to catch the mice and then let them out again over his garden fence.

Stanislavsky, who obviously worries him and haunts him every night in his dreams.

I have had no information yet about ' The Lower Depths,' but I know that the play is going splendidly. That means that the season is saved, you will have no losses, though, indeed, losses would have been no great harm to my thinking, for your theatre is in a very secure position. It could go on very well for a long time.

I bow down to your little feet for the scent. I kiss my darling for the sweets, which had melted. In the cup there turned out to be a surprise of a very trivial kind—an Eiffel Tower, worth a farthing. I have not seen the towels, Masha sent them to the wash. The scent is very good.

By now holidays have begun ; I congratulate you, my darling. Are you dull ? You are all alone now in the flat, and that worries me a little. When you go out, from six o'clock in the evening Xenia[1] plays the concertina—and that every evening ; I used to be worn out. One might have been in a tavern. That goes on probably now, and now every evening our flat is full of noise. You might take Zina to stay with you for the holidays. I am very uneasy. Forgive me that I am not living with you ; next year everything shall be properly arranged, I will be with you, that is certain.

But my lines and my letters are all crooked, I must light a candle. I have lighted it.

Write to me, write every day, at any rate during these days. I kiss you, my own, and embrace you. God be with you. I am sending the fur-coat abroad,[2] Arseny is going to the harbour with it. Do write.

Your A—.

277

Dec. 22 (1902. *Yalta*).

My dear little fatty, the newspapers have come to-day with ' The Lower Depths.' I see now what an immense success you

---

[1] A maidservant in the Tchehovs' flat.

[2] On his way back from Nice, Tchehov had been obliged to borrow a fur-coat from friends, and it was a long time before he could send it back.

have all had. It means that one can say for certain that you will go on for the rest of the season with a full house and in excellent spirits. If only you all keep well. Here I am seedy to-day, I shall probably have to take my inexpensive remedy —castor oil. It is raining, you are far away, I am a little sad, but still I feel better than I did last year.

' The Pillars ' are hardly likely to be a remarkable success, but now you don't care, now you feel the sea is only knee-deep. Now whatever you produce this season, everything will be good and interesting.

Well, how are you spending the holiday, my child ? I am glad your brother has come, now I am not anxious about you ; only don't let him go away, let him stay with you.

I awfully want to write a farce, but never seem to get time, I can't settle down to it. I have a kind of presentiment that the farce will soon come into fashion again.

To-morrow I am going to the dentist, the pain will probably be frantic. And the man's hands are unwashed, his instruments are unclean, though he is a real doctor, not a mere dentist. Tell me about the supper after ' The Lower Depths,' what you all eat and drank there for your 800 roubles, describe it all as fully as possible. What sort of humour is Bunin in ? Is he thinner ? Is he pining away ? Is the Wanderer [1] still hanging about without work ?

Yesterday they rang me up to say that L. Sredin has a temperature of 39. The invalids are mostly feeling pretty bad, the weather is so nasty. Is Balmont in Moscow ? Have you seen him ? . . . In fact, he is a passionate person.

I kiss you and caress you, and taking your head in my arm, bent in a loop, listen to what you are telling me.

Have I wished you a Happy Christmas ? Yes ?

Your A—.

Mother is very much pleased with the hat and is still thanking you for it.

[1] Petrov (*nom de plume* ' The Wanderer '), a writer.

278
Dec. 24 (1902. *Yalta*).

My dear old woman, your old man is a bit unwell. I slept last night very badly, uneasily ; aching all over my body and feverish. I am not hungry and to-day there 's the pie. Oh well, it does not matter.

I have had a very nice letter from Kurkin about Gorky's play, so nice that I am thinking of sending a copy of it to Gorky. Of all I have read about the play, it is the best criticism. Unreserved enthusiasm, of course, and many interesting remarks. You were praised in the newspapers, which means that you did not overdo it but acted well.

If I had been in Moscow, I should certainly, at all costs, have gone to the Hermitage after the play and have stayed there till morning and have fought with Baranov.[1]

Yesterday I wrote to Nemirovitch. My ' Cherry Orchard ' will be in three acts. So I think ; however, I have decided nothing finally yet. I shall soon get well and begin considering it again, now I have cast everything aside. The weather is most vile. Yesterday the rain was lashing all day, and to-day it is overcast and muddy. I live like an exile.

You say that my last two letters were good and that you like them very much, while I am always afraid as I write that I am writing uninterestingly, tediously, as though it were a duty. My dear old woman, my dog, my pup, I kiss you, I bless you, I embrace you. I shall send your company a telegram for the New Year. I will try and write a little more at length and more lightly. Mother has received your note and is very much pleased.

Keep well. Act as much as you like, but do rest, don't overtire yourself. I embrace my darling.

Your A—.

---

[1] An actor at the Art Theatre, formerly a singer. In her letter O. L. described the supper, which ended in rude behaviour on the part of Baranov, who was a little elevated.

279

Dec. 25 (1902. *Yalta*).

Your letter to Mother came just in time, that is, yesterday, her name-day. My health is not up to much, but better than yesterday, so I am on the way to recovery.

If only you knew, darling, what a clever creature you are! That's clear from your letter among other things. It seems to me that if I could lie only half a night with my nose tucked into your shoulder it would do me good and I should leave off moping. I can't live without you, say what you like.

I saw all your portraits this morning in the ' News of the Day ' in Gorky's play, and was delighted. Moskvin, Stanislavsky and you are wonderful, Vishnevsky very bad, stupidly bad. I was quite moved—it is so good. You are a fine set.

At last I have sent that fur-coat back to Nice and I no longer feel like a scoundrel.

Dear dog, why am I not with you ? Why haven't you a flat in Moscow where I could have a room, in which I could work hidden away from friends ? Take a house for the summer in which I can write ; then I would get up early. And let us be alone in the house, if not every day, at least three times a week.

Little German, you must describe what the wedding [1] is like. It will, no doubt, be very proper and solemn.

What did Baranov do at the Hermitage ? What was it all about ? What was the scandal ? Do describe it all, darling.

I embrace my heron and kiss her.

Your A—.

280

(Dec. 27, 1902. *Yalta.)*

I cut this little mug out of ' Drama and Art ' [2]—which by the way is a vulgar, paltry little magazine, probably published for the sake of profit. How are you getting on, little beetle ? How

---

[1] The wedding of O. L.'s brother, Vladimir, with Ella Bartels.
[2] A reproduction of a photograph of O. L. is enclosed.

did you enjoy yourself at the wedding ? To-day I had a telegram of congratulation from Stanislavsky's mother. I will send her one in reply for the New Year.

I am better but still not quite right. Altschuller says that I have had influenza. Yesterday evening, apropos of nothing, I began to have a dizziness before my eyes and a headache which still persists. We spent the first day of the holiday as usual, there was nothing out of the way, spiritless and uninteresting on the whole. We are expecting Bunin and Naidyonov, who according to the newspapers have gone to Constantinople. Madame Bonnier ordered some geese and ducks for us from Kursk, but these birds were stranded at Sevastopol. Altschuller told me yesterday that he had received the scent from Muir's and, moreover, 60 kopecks change.

So half the season is over ; soon the other half will pass ; so again we shall be living together and feeling as if we had only been married yesterday.

Did I tell you that I had a first-rate criticism of ' The Lower Depths ' from Kurkin ? I have taken a copy of it and sent it to Gorky. I have had a letter from Stanislavsky, I am going to write to him. Apparently he is in no great spirits. And my spouse, too, judging from her last letter, is not ecstatic. You silly little thing, you are working, toiling, and that 's the chief thing. If I worked all day I should be both satisfied and happy.

I have had a mass of letters to-day, with drawings, effusive congratulations—from all the Smirnov young ladies. The most naïve and talented of all was written by Natasha, the artist. But what a lot there are of them ! What if you have so many daughters !

Hullo ! Madame Bonnier has arrived, so I cannot write any more, basta ! Embrace me, darling, come close to me and I will whisper something silly in your ear.

Write, my actress.

Your A—.

You have good houses, is Vishnevsky triumphant ?
Forgive me these horrid smudges.

281

Dec. 28 (1902.   *Yalta*).

Greetings, dear actress, God be with you ! The wedding is over by now. I congratulate both you and the young people. You write that Volodya feels queer with the properties, *i.e.* with the dowry. I could well believe it ! Five rooms in *style moderne*, a grand piano of his own, a bath, an inkstand costing 80 roubles—all this bourgeois wealth must really seem queer for a young man beginning life. Now he needs as much work and anxiety as possible, or he will begin to grow fat and at forty will be expressing a genuine dissatisfaction with life.

My teeth are aching and crumbling, I have not yet finished bothering over them and most likely I shan't have done with it soon. I am coughing a little, but on the whole I am well.

Dyagilev [1] has sent me a letter, and No. 11 of the ' World of Art,' in which there is a long criticism of ' The Sea-Gull ' and of myself in general. Read it if you come across it.

You write with disgusting ink which sticks your letter together ; I have to tear it apart. And you don't seal up your letters.

My darling, when I begin the play I will write to you. The long-legged crane (as you call your husband in your letter) will provide a play, but who is going to act the old lady I don't know. I have read that Azagarova [2] has been asked to act at some provincial theatre, though, indeed, she would scarcely be suitable for the part.

Bend down and I will kiss you on the back of your neck and your head. I embrace you. I won't allow you to have a ' Spaniard ' and I won't allow you to become a ' Spaniard ' either. You have a Moor whom you ought to love, and that Moor kisses his darling.

Your A—.

How is Fomka ? Masha likes him, but she says he is not a real terrier but a mongrel.

[1] Editor of the magazine ' The World of Art,' in later years director of the Russian Ballet.

[2] An actress at that time playing at Korsh's Theatre.

282

Dec. 30 (1902. *Yalta*).

My dear actress, I went to-day to Ostrovsky, the dentist, to finish the business ; he examined the tooth he stopped a week ago and said he ought to change the stopping and do it better. He took out the stopping, and at that moment people came to him about business connected with the Jewish cemetery (he is a Jewish elder) and took him off to the dead, while I went home without a stopping in my tooth, furious and half-ill. How do you like that ?

I have had a charming letter from Batyushkov. In fact, I have had a great many letters during these last days. Masha has a bad headache to-day. The turkeys and ducks ordered by Madame Bonnier from Kursk have arrived, but they cannot be eaten because they stink.

Yes, darling, the new towels are good, thank you, my little housewife. The tenderness which you say resides somewhere in my depths I pour out all at once in love and caresses for those towels, for your letter and altogether for your being my wife. If you and I were not married now, but were simply author and actress, it would be incredibly stupid.

Varavka [1] has sent me two cards, one evidently for you. Again I am a bit unwell to-day. Well, never mind, it is nothing much. I bless you, my darling, and embrace you.

Your A—.

283

Jan. 1, 1903. (*Yalta.*)

A happy new year to you, my sweet actress, my wife ! I wish you everything you want and deserve, and above all I wish you a little half-German who would rummage in your cupboards and smudge my table with ink while you would look on delighted.

I am pleased with you for enjoying yourself so much at the wedding. Of course, it is a pity I wasn't there ; I would have

[1] The doctor at the sanatorium in which Tchehov and O. L. spent the summer of 1901.

watched you and indeed have whirled round myself. To-day
I have had a good many letters, among them one from Suvorin
and one from Nemirovitch. The latter sent me a list of the
plays which your company is intending to produce. Not one
that stands out conspicuously, though they are all good.
' The Fruits of Enlightenment ' and ' A Month in the Country '
must be produced that you may have them in your repertory.
You know they are good literary plays.

Masha saw the New Year in at Madame Tatarinov's, I stayed
at home. Madame Tatarinov has sent me a wonderful flower
of the cactus species—*Epiphyllum truncatum*. It has been
raining all day.

Write to me, my own, comfort me with your letters. My
health is splendid. The tooth is stopped, there is one left to
do. In short, everything is more or less all right.

I am unhappy without my wife ; one sleeps as it were on a
cold stove, that has not been heated for ages. Bunin and
Naidyonov are heroes now in Odessa. People can't make
enough of them.

They are calling me to tea. Keep well and merry, actress.
God be with you.

Your A—.

284

Jan. 3 (1903. *Yalta*).

Greetings, sweet actress ! Don't be uneasy, I have sent a
telegram to Stanislavsky's mother for the New Year. I sent to
all of them, even to Meierhold in Herson. I don't know Dr.
Mahotin or don't remember him. We will spend the holidays
of course without N., or I shall decamp. My health is pretty
middling, I have had my teeth stopped, now I can eat anything
and everything. You write that I am not so nice with you in
Yalta—aie, aie, darling, that is only your fancy ; most likely
you think so because you were ill in Yalta. I love you equally
everywhere, and I am everywhere equally yours.

Well, all this has been in answer to your thoughts in your
letter ; now I will write my own.

I have had a telegram from the young people; early in March I shall go and see them and congratulate them. They are both very nice, only I am somehow sorry that Volodya is married. He ought first to have been toughened, to have stood on his own feet; as it is now, I shouldn't wonder if he begins to grow fat. I did mean to make ' The Cherry Orchard ' into three long acts, but I may turn it into four; I do not care whether it 's in three or four acts—any way, the play will be monotonous.

Dr. Alexin is going to Moscow, he will come and see you. He took part lately in a concert for a charity and the piano would not play, the black keys refused to work, and he, Alexin, suspected Madame Tatarinov of having put something into the piano out of revenge; an altercation took place behind the scenes, Madame Tatarinov was taken ill and is still in bed with a high temperature. What t-r-r-agedies we go through!

So do your best to take a cottage for the holidays, my old woman, so that by the 10th of March I could stay there. I will stay alone in the cottage and write and my actress will come out and stay the night with me. That 's it, isn't it ? I will write and in the evening consult with my actress. In the summer we will go off somewhere together, we will travel for a fortnight and then go back to our cottage.

I have received an honorary ticket for the Exhibition. It is cold to-day, the sea is rough and it is not warm in my room. When you see Sasha Sredin, thank him for the telegram he sent me and tell him that I did not send an answer because I had not his address.

I kiss you, I embrace you and dream of you. Do write, darling, don't be lazy.

Your husband A—.

285

Jan. 5 (1903. Yalta).

My actress, I am quite well, no need to be better. Only I am dull, very dull, for two reasons, the weather is very bad and my wife is not here. And I have nothing to write about in my letters, life is grown so meagre, there is nothing interesting in this Yalta.

To-day Madame Bonnier arrived, she described how she had a quarrel with Madame Solovyov. Shapovalov (the architect) has been and Lazarevsky has been—in fact, my society is most lively.

We are now drinking white wine from Theodosia. I will bring some of it so that we may have something to drink in our cottage. I will bring 20 bottles. You are good in Lona,[1] I feel that, only don't change your voice. That you should have your hair short and walk with a stick, that is very good.

God keep you, my own. I kiss and embrace you. I can't do without you, keep that in mind.

Your A—.

286

Jan. 7, 1903. (*Yalta.*)

Actress, my sweet dog, puppy, greetings ! Things are going well with me, I am pretty middling, but just fancy, there is a plaster on my right side and the doctor has ordered me to put on a compress for two days. It is a slight attack of pleurisy. I am sleeping splendidly, eating magnificently and in good spirits, and the illness I am telling you about is of no consequence. Don't be uneasy, puppy.

You keep going to tea-shops and sugar factories, while I have been nowhere all the holidays. I stay at home and eat horse-radish. How I saw the New Year in has been written to you already. I did not see it in at all. In the cake I found good luck for you and me.

To-day I have received from your theatre a list of the plays they propose to stage. Among them is Ostrovsky's ' Every Wise Man is a Bit of a Simpleton.' That play seems to me quite unsuitable for you. It is the Russified Tartuffe you know ; it is the Crimean ' Bordeaux.' If you produce anything, let it be Tartuffe itself, or don't produce either. You should rummage about, dear ; couldn't something be found in

[1] O. L.'s part in Ibsen's ' The Pillars of Society.'

Victor Hugo ? For the holiday performances ? It would be a good thing, too, to produce Gogol's ' Marriage,' it might be an enchanting production.

If Halyutina [1] marries Andreyev [2] I congratulate her. . . . Ever since I became a German, *i.e.* your husband, marriages have become the regular thing at the Art Theatre; we led the way.

My own darling, I am not getting the ' News of the Day.' Do get it from Efros. It is piggish, every January I have to remind him. Don't forget, my own, remind him, make Efros feel that it is not nice of him.

Ah, dog, dog, if only you knew ! If only you knew how I pine for you, how I miss you ! If only you knew !

Your German A—.

287

Jan. 8 (1903. *Yalta*).

Dear puppy, to-day the ' News of the Day ' has come. Don't trouble, don't say anything to Efros. My health is excellent ; I have got the compress on, but I don't hear the rattle in my right side. Don't be uneasy, my darling, everything is all right. I have finished with the dentist, as I wrote to you. About the weather I wrote too, it is bad.

Masha is setting off on the 11th of January, so she will be in Moscow on the 13th. Yesterday Madame Tatarinov sent me an amaryllis in flower. Madame Bonnier has had a quarrel with Madame Solovyov, a bitter quarrel. And there is no other news at all.

When you see Gorky, thank him from me for giving you nothing to do in the second act of his play, so that you have time to write to me. Odd as it will seem to you, I do not read your letters, but devour them. I feel my actress in every line in every letter.

The last few days I have been clearing up and putting away last year's letters.

---

[1] An actress at the Art Theatre.
[2] An actor at the Art Theatre at that time.

Well, my pretty, I embrace you and kiss you on the forehead and the neck. Be careful of your health. Don't gad about too much. Lie down whenever you can. Don't eat anything hard. Don't eat any sort of rubbish such as nuts. Christ be with you.

Your A—.

288

Jan. 9 (1903. Yalta).

Dear dog, this evening, with the doctor's permission, I shall take off the compress. So I am well again and shall not write to you any more about my health. The creature that screams so horribly about whom you inquire in your letter is a bird; the bird is alive, but, for some reason, it is screaming much less this winter.

I have no document relating to breach of our contract, but it does not follow that Marks has not. To the best of my recollection I did not sign it, but perhaps my memory is deceiving me. Sergeyenko had the authorisation. Then Gruzenberg [1] asks me to send him a copy of my letter. What letter is meant?

I believe that if I were to write now to Marks he would agree to give me back my works from the 1st of January 1904 for 75,000 roubles. But you know my works are already cheapened by the ' Niva,' and not worth that sum, at any rate they won't be worth it for another ten years, until the ' Niva's ' supplements for 1903 rot. If you see Gorky talk to him about it, he will agree. I don't trust Gruzenberg, and it does not seem quite a literary thing to do to catch at a mistake or an oversight of Marks's and to take advantage of it ' legally.'

And, indeed, one must not, in any case, forget that when the question of the sale of my works to Marks was raised I had not a farthing, I was in debt to Suvorin and, with all that, being published abominably, and above all was preparing to die and wanting to put my affairs in some sort of order. However, it is not too late and it will not be directly; we must think

---

[1] A Petersburg lawyer.

it all over properly, and for that it would not be amiss for me to see Pyatnitsky in March or April (when I shall be in Moscow). You might write to him about that.

Masha is going the day after to-morrow, I shall be utterly dull when she has gone.

I kiss my dowdy and embrace her. It is a long time since I have written anything, I have been continually ailing, to-morrow I shall set to work again. I have had a letter from Nemirovitch.

Your A—.

Do I love you ? What do you think ?

289

Jan. 11 (1903. *Yalta*).

Actress, darling, I have written to-day to Batyushkov to send you, to Moscow, ' Mir Bozhy.' I have written to him that I do not need it in Yalta. The High School gets it and lets me have it. Masha went off to-day, and a high wind blew up before dinner. Tell her to write to me whether she had a rough crossing. Let her write, in fact, what sort of a journey she had to Moscow.

When I come to Moscow I must go and see Marya Fyodor-ovna Yakuntchikov. I like her, though I have seen very little of her. Darling, everything has got muddled up in my head during the holidays, as I have been unwell and done nothing. Now I shall have to begin all over again from the beginning. Mine is a hard lot. But there, it does not matter. Let your husband prattle away for another two years and then he will set to work again and write another fifteen volumes, to the horror of Marks.

I am ordering from Sinope a lot of flowers to plant them in the garden. That is because I have nothing to do and am bored. I have not my dog, so I must have flowers at least to amuse me.

To-day I have at last read ' Wanderer's ' poem, the one on account of which the 'Courier' was suspended. There is only one thing one can say about the poem, and that is that it is a very poor one, and why it scared them so I can't imagine. I am told that the Censor has been put under arrest ? What for ? I don't understand it. One must suppose that they are all in a funk.

Let Masha describe the visit of a certain Tarnani to us. I believe this is the second letter I have sent you covered with smudges. Forgive your untidy husband.

When is Consul Bernik [1] coming on ? Is Stanislavsky good in Bernik ? That my wife is good, magnificent, I have no doubt. In another two or three years, granny, you will be a thoroughly good actress, already I 'm proud of you and rejoice in you. I bless you, granny, and kiss you. Think of your husband.

Your A—.

290

TELEGRAM

Jan. 13 (1903. Yalta).

All is well ANTONIO.

291

Jan. 13 (1903. Yalta).

My dear Olya, at 11 o'clock in the morning, when Masha had gone, I felt not quite the thing ; I had a pain in my chest, sickness, 38 degrees, and yesterday it was the same thing. I slept well, though I was disturbed by pains. Altschuller has been. I had to be swathed in a compress again (it is an immense one). This morning the temperature was only 37, I feel weak and shall put on a plaster directly, but still I had a right to telegraph to you to-day that all is well. Now it is all right, I am getting better, to-morrow I shall be quite well again. I conceal nothing from you, do understand that and don't worry yourself with telegrams. If anything—not merely serious, but even approaching seriousness—happened, you would be the first person I should tell.

You are depressed ? Chuck it, darling. It will all come right in time.

[1] Ibsen's ' The Pillars of Society.'

To-day the earth is covered with snow. It is foggy, cheerless. I am sad that so much of my time has passed without work and that apparently I am no longer a worker. To sit in an armchair with a compress on and mope is not very cheerful. Will you get tired of me, darling ? In your yesterday's letter you wrote that you were losing your looks. As though it mattered ! If you were to grow a nose like a crane's, even then I should love you.

I embrace my own, my good dog. I embrace and kiss you again. Write.

Your A—.

292

Jan. 14 (1903. *Yalta*).

Actress, Pushkareva is not normal, keep that in mind. She came to me with her play twenty years ago or even earlier. She is the sister of the poet Pushkarev—a poet and playwright ; she used to be called ' Vanda ' in derision. Don't read the play, but tell Xenia or the cook, Masha, to give it back to the authoress when she comes, or you will suffer for it from her. I have had a letter from her, by the way.

There is snow here. You write that I am the only person who abuses the weather here. Why, does anybody praise it ? Who is the man ? I have had a letter from Kuprin, he has a daughter. Make a note of it. I have had a letter from Suvorin, an answer to the lecture I wrote him. He writes that he is worried to death by his son. I get the paper ' The Citizen ' ; in the last number Gorky is called a neurasthenic, and the success of his play is put down to neurasthenia. Well, he is a man who hasn't the faintest whiff of neurasthenia about him. After his success Gorky will have to endure an onslaught of envy and hatred for a long time to come. He has begun with success—and that is not forgiven in this world.

Madame Tatarinov has pneumonia.

Well, God be with you. Keep well, my splendid wife. Don't get excited. Don't be depressed, don't quarrel with any one, think sometimes of your husband. I kiss you on the shoulder.

Your A—.

293

Jan. 16 (1903.   *Yalta*).

Granny, you are slandering me ; I have never told you a lie about my health, I have never concealed anything and, indeed, I am afraid I have sometimes exaggerated things.   Here I write you a report again.   Before Masha went away I had a pain in my side, it was a slight pleurisy and apparently dry ; compress, plaster and so on, it got better.   But on the 11th of January, the day that Masha set off, I felt poorly : a pain in my right side, sickness, temperature 38.   It appeared that it was pleurisy, a slight effusion on the right side, again a plaster, powders and so on.   To-day my temperature is normal, but there is a little pain in the side ; there is still exudation, but, according to Altschuller, it is already being absorbed, what's left is nothing to matter.   I feel much more cheerful and am glad to sit up to the table, and I have a good appetite.   Again I repeat that I have never concealed anything from you and don't intend to.

Here is a cutting from the ' Citizen ' for you.[1]   Tell T. A. Tihomirov that in No. 4 of the ' Citizen ' there is a long article on Gorky's ' The Lower Depths.'   Let him cut it out and paste it up.

It has rained in the night, all the snow has melted.   To judge from what I see from my window and hear in the stoves the weather is not up to much.   There is no news ; the dogs and the cranes are growing fat, Arseny has become quite saintly, he will soon be beginning to go about in a cassock.   The study smells of your scent.

---

[1] The following cutting was attached to the letter : ' In Moscow they are called Maximists.   Among them is an individual who, in imitation of Gorky, calls himself " Wanderer."   Like Gorky he wears a Russian shirt and top boots.   He also sports a decadent belt and a golden pince-nez.   Recently at some philanthropic entertainment he read a poem invoking his audience to knock persons of property on the head.   Apparently this invitation has had no practical result.   But the author has won the heart of a lady who hails from the farther side of the river and who has offered him herself and her millions made in trade.   I am told that the Maximists are very popular with the merchant gentry of Moscow, and particularly so with their ladies.'

Well, I embrace my granny and kiss her 1001 times. Write
to me every day, be sure to. Our cottage for the summer must
have two essentials : the proximity of water for angling in
and the absence or remoteness of other habitations. It would
be desirable to have only two or three rooms so that nobody
could stay the night in the summer, and so on and so on.

Well, take care of yourself, Christ be with you.

Your A—.

294

Jan. 18 (1903. *Yalta*).

Greetings, my darling ! Do you know what I have been
thinking ? Do you know what I want to suggest to you ?
You won't be angry ? You won't be surprised ? Instead of
a cottage in the country, let us go this year to Switzerland.
There we would settle down and spend two months happily,
and come back to Russia. How does it strike you ? What do
you say ?

The schoolmaster arrived to-day and brought your presents.
First of all, a million kisses for your photograph, I bow down
to your little feet. You have pleased me, my darling, thank
you. The pocket-book is very nice, but I think I shall have
to put it away, as the pocket-book I have already is a souvenir
and very precious ; it was once given me by my dog. Besides
I fancy the new one is not so convenient, it would be easy to
lose money and papers out of it. I bow to you for the sweets,
too, though I fancy it 's the sort I do not eat ; Mother is very
fond of them, so I shall give them to her.

But poor Vishnevsky ! The judicious schoolmaster put
the beer he sent me in the luggage-van ; it froze and the
bottles burst. The schoolmaster ought to have been warned.
Altogether I have no luck with beer ! And who sent me the
fowl in a hat ? You or Vishnevsky ? An amazingly tasteless
Viennese product. It was evidently bought in a Vienna shop
—not Klein's, but is made by the Jews who are ruining Vienna
bronze ; they have nothing but these Jewish bronzes for sale
in Moscow now. Brrr ! I have thrown it in the stove, it makes

me sick to look at it. However, that 's a trifle, but I am sorry about the beer—I could scream, in fact.

Will you go to Switzerland ? Write to me, my own, thinking it over, and weighing everything, and if you decide that we can go, and perhaps shall go, begin to get ready, little by little, so that we get off by the end of May with our route planned out beforehand. Last night I read an article of Yevgeny Markov's about Venice, in the ' Vyestnik Yevropý.' Markov is an old-fashioned writer, sincere and full of understanding, and under his influence I suddenly felt such a yearning ! I longed to go to Venice, where we will go one day. I longed to go to Switzerland, where I have never been yet.

Now if only the schoolmaster had brought *marmelad* or peppermints from Tramblay's ; but there, never mind. Let us go, my own ! Think of it ! If for some reason you can't, let us put it off till next year.

There is a cruel wind blowing to-day.

Well, I embrace you and bless my joy. Make haste and answer about Switzerland.

Your A—.

295

Jan. 20 (1903. *Yalta*).

Madame Tatarinov has pneumonia, my darling, and I 'll get the photograph of the house when she is better, not before. I have made the pocket-book you sent me into a little case for manuscripts and notes ; each story has its own division. It 's very convenient.

Well, have you thought what you are going to say to me about Switzerland ? I think we might plan out a very nice tour. We might stay on the way at Vienna, Berlin, and go to the theatres. What do you think about it ?

Savina is producing my old farce ' The Anniversary ' for her benefit night. Again they will be saying that it is a new play and spitefully rejoicing.

It is a bright, sunny day, but I am sitting indoors as Alt-schuller has forbidden me to go out. My temperature, by the way, is completely normal. You keep writing, my own, that your conscience pricks you that you are not living with me in Yalta, but in Moscow. But what 's to be done, darling ? Think of it sensibly : if you were living with me in Yalta the whole winter, your life would be spoilt, and I should feel stings of conscience, which would hardly be better. You see, I knew that I was marrying an actress ; that is, when I married you I was fully aware that you would spend the winters in Moscow. I don't feel myself in one millionth fraction of a bit injured or cheated ; on the contrary, it seems to me that all is going well, or is as it must be, and so, darling, don't worry me with your conscience-pricks. In March we shall begin living again, and again we shall not feel our present loneliness. Set your mind at rest, my own, don't be agitated, but wait and hope. You must hope and nothing more.

Four boys have been suffocated by charcoal fumes in the bazaar in Yalta. The supplement to the ' Niva ' has arrived, my stories with a portrait, and under the portrait my signature, wonderfully nastily done.

Now that I am working, most likely I shall not write to you every day, you must forgive me.

Let us go abroad, do let us go !

Your spouse A—.

296

Jan. 23 (1903. *Yalta*).

My actress, greetings ! I have had a letter to-day from Nemirovitch, he writes about the plays which are to be produced, and asks about my play. That I am going to write my play is as certain as twice two makes four. If only I am well, of course ; but whether it will succeed, whether anything will come of it—I don't know.

You want Polya[1] to put on my compress ? Polya ? ! ! ! However, I am not putting on compresses now, I get off with nothing but plasters. My temperature was normal yesterday, and to-day I have not taken it. Now I am sitting down and

_____
[1] The Tchehovs' servant.

writing. Don't cast an evil eye. I am in the humour for it, I should like to skip off to a restaurant and have a spree there, and then sit down and write.

Why is ' Wanderer ' getting married ? What does he want to do that for ?

I keep waiting to hear what you will say about Switzerland. We might have a very good time there. Incidentally I might drink beer there. Think it over, my priceless darling, and don't protest too much, if you don't want to go.

The Gurzuf schoolmaster told me nothing about Moscow, but only sat and gnawed his beard. Perhaps he was grieved at the beer-bottles having burst with the frost. And, indeed, I wasn't well ; I sat waiting in silence for him to go.

Your sow with the little pigs on her back is standing on my table, she sends you her love. She is a jolly sow.

Oh ! what a mass of subjects there are in my head ! How I long to write ! but I feel that something 's lacking—either in my surroundings or my health. The ' Niva ' Supplement has come out—my stories with my portrait, and I feel as though they were not my stories. I ought not to live in Yalta, that 's the fact ! I might be in Asia Minor. What is the saintly Sasha Sredin doing in Moscow ? How is he and how is his wife ? Have you seen Balmont in Moscow ?

Well, doggy, take care of yourself, keep up your spirits, write a little oftener to your husband. I bless you, embrace you, kiss you. Shall I soon see you at last ?

Your A—.

297

Jan. 24 (1903. *Yalta*).

Yes, darling, I am better now, and to-day I am quite well, so well that I have even been out in the garden. It 's lovely warm weather.

I have had a letter from Alexandr Borissovitch, that student, the earnest Jew who was something like a vice-director in the Andreyevsky Sanatorium. He asks after my health, and informs me, by the way, that he is now a doctor. He asks to be remembered to you.

Two strange puppies have turned up in our yard, they bark all night and are already quite at home. How are we to get rid of them ? They are both mongrels.

Darling, forgive me for the advice : don't leave money at home, or lock it up safely. Or else you won't get off without some shocks. I won't write any more to you about this subject, forgive me.

Old Prince Liven spent yesterday evening with me. I embrace my dog and am eager to hear what you will say about Switzerland and Italy, about our summer altogether. We have not much life before us together, our youth will be gone in two or three years (if we can still call it youth, indeed), we must make haste, we must do our utmost to get something out of it.

Well, God be with you, don't be depressed.

Your A—.

298

Jan. 26 (1903. *Yalta*).

My wonderful darling, my sweet dog, so you agree about Switzerland and our going a tour together, in fact ? Glorious ! We will spend five days in Vienna, then stay a little in Berlin and Dresden, and then go on to Switzerland. In Venice it will most likely be very hot by then.

I liked your pocket-book very much and I do like it very much, I swear, but I didn't want to part with the old one which was yours. Now your pocket-book (the new one) is lying on my table and I have all sorts of little notes for stories in it. I write and keep going to the pocket-book to look things up.

Your Company has ceased sending me their repertoire.— Note that, madam.

I didn't like the cock in the hat because it is a sham product. One can't keep things like that in one's room. But there, the devil take it !—the cock, I mean.

The weather here is divine, to-morrow I shall drive into the town. There's only the faintest trace left of the pleurisy, it is almost all absorbed.

I have met Yevlaliya, I know her.[1] I sometimes read her husband's articles in ' Russkoye-Slovo,' but so far they are not very interesting.

I am writing a story [2] for the ' Journal for All ' in the old-fashioned style, the style of the 'seventies. I don't know how it will turn out. Then I have to write one for ' Russkaya Mysl ' and one for the ' Mir Bozhy.' Save us, O heavenly Cherubim !

What a glorious, perfect time we 'll have travelling together ! Oh, if only nothing prevents it !

I had a letter from Kommissarzhevskaya,[3] she asks for a new play for her private theatre in Petersburg. She is going to be the manager of a theatre, queer creature : why, she will only get on for one month, within a month all interest in her theatre will be over ; but it is awkward to write to her of that, and, indeed, I can't ; by now she is hopelessly involved in her enterprise. And what am I to write to her about the play ? Refuse it ? Speak to Nemirovitch *as soon as possible* and write me whether I may promise her ' The Cherry Orchard,' that is, whether you are going to act that play in Petersburg. If not, then I will promise it to her.

So then we are going off on our travels together ? My clever girl, now I will never cast you off. I embrace you so that all your little ribs crack. I kiss both your cheeks, your neck, and your little back and beg you to write to your husband.

Your A—.

Madame Tatarinov's daughter has gone to see you all. You won't come for Carnival, don't be a humbug. And indeed you had better not, my joy, you will only exhaust yourself and then get ill. Come for the whole of Lent, then I agree.

I have made a discovery in the new pocket-book, a very deep pocket, half-a-yard deep, evidently to put money in.

---

[1] Obviously a mistake. The lady referred to was called Illariya, the wife of A. V. Amfiteatrov, the writer mentioned by O. L. in her letter.

[2] ' Betrothed.'

[3] Vera Kommissarzhevsky, the famous actress, the sister of the well-known producer.

299

Jan. 28 (1903. *Yalta*).

Dear doggy, if I don't write to you every day it is not because I am angry [1] (God preserve me), but simply because I am sick of writing, I want to see you, see you, see you, and because I am settling down to write a story. So if you don't have a letter from me for two days you mustn't be anxious.

What idiotic ink all your letters are written with ! It 's as though you wrote with glue instead of ink. I have to unstick them.

Tell Pyatnitsky that, as far as I remember, I did not sign any note about breach of contract, and I don't understand what is meant by such a note ; Sergeyenko had an authorisation from me, but there was no sort of ' Agreement regarding Sergeyenko.' Tell Pyatnitsky that I shall see him in March or April and talk to him.

I am quite well now, I feel better, indeed, than I did in the summer. I am eating a great deal and pleased to talk to people. (When I am unwell, I don't want to eat, and talking to people is, at times, insufferable, but I control myself.) I write and read all day and with envy read over the letter in which you describe the sturgeon pasty and the sterlet soup, you dog. This winter I may say that I have had almost no blood-spitting and not a single haemorrhoidal catastrophe.

If you see Balmont again, tell him to send me his address. Why, I daresay there is no one so well disposed to that rascal as I ; I like his talent.

Aren't you getting the ' Mir Bozhy ' yet ? Why ? Tell Pyatnitsky to send me his new publications, among others Gorky's ' The Lower Depths.'

There was a storm yesterday, and to-day the steamer came late ; and it is rather rough to-day.

They are giving an anniversary dinner to Goltsev. It would please me if Masha or you were present at that dinner

---

[1] O. L. wrote, Jan. 23 : ' No letter for two days, and the last was so nervous, not nice ; what has happened ? are you displeased with me, are you angry with me ? '

or supper. If you are at the anniversary write to me all about it. You know I am Goltsev's senior, for I have been writing for more than twenty years (Goltsev is celebrating not his twenty-fifth, but his twentieth anniversary).

Well, my granny, I bless you with both hands and kiss you a hundred times. In the spring we will go to the Geltsers, we will go anywhere you like, to Madame Yakuntchikov's and Marya Petrovna's. If I am well, as I am now, I will be on the go the whole time. Ah, my fat little granny!

Your husband (retired from service) A—.

Tell Masha that the seeds have arrived, 7 pounds of grass seed.

300

Jan. 30 (1903. Yalta).

Well, my actress, yesterday I was in town for the first time after my long imprisonment; I had my hair cut and look eight years younger, but, I suppose because I have got out of the way of it, I was awfully tired. Every year now I grow more and more easily tired. I am writing a story,[1] but slowly, a tablespoonful every hour—perhaps because there are many characters in it, and perhaps because I got out of it and must get into it again.

Yesterday the actress who has been the object of your benevolence turned up and asked for Masha; when she was told that Masha was not here she remained in the kitchen waiting to see me. I sent her out a rouble; Arseny and Granny hid themselves, Polya was the only one who spoke to her. She stayed an hour or two and went away, promising to come again. She is either mad, or simply a fraud, but I expect we shall have a lot of trouble with her yet.

I am very well. Don't send beer, I will drink it abroad, but now I don't feel inclined for it; besides I can only drink when I am in company. I will write the play. I have had a letter from Geneva from Vassilyeva.

I have ordered all sorts of bulbs and perennials from Suhum. There is plenty of water now. Perhaps I shall make another

[1] ' Betrothed.'

tank to hold ten thousand gallons if it does not turn out to be too dear.

Don't worry about the above-mentioned actress, she has apparently settled in Yalta and she is hardly likely to get at me. I enclose her letter.

Are you making out the plan of our Swiss tour ? Climate and beautiful scenery are what matter most, keep that in mind ; excursions, walking exercise, combining pleasure with profit ! I am going to dance attendance upon you, too ; only, darling, give me your word not to be ill again. You must promise. Be a good girl as you were in Axyonovo.

To-day there is no letter from you.

Give my greetings to every one in the theatre, give my love to Masha and Vishnevsky. How is Nadyezhda Ivanovna ?

Well, doggy, I stroke you and pull you by the ears and the tail. I am not up to much without you, rather wretched in fact, I may say, but still it is nice to think that I have got you. Without you I should have grown old and gone to seed like a burdock under a fence.

I embrace my treasure and kiss her, kiss her a thousand times.

Your A—.

301

Feb. 1, 1903. *Yalta.*

My granny, if you want to send sweets, send not from Abrikosov's but from Fley or Tramblay—and only chocolates. Send also ten or, if they will take them, twenty herrings, and get them from Byelov's. You see, darling, what a lot of commissions I pile on you ! My poor, dear wife, don't be weary of such a husband, be patient, in the summer you shall be rewarded for everything.

Yes, darling, ' In the Mist ' is a very fine thing, the author has made an immense stride ; only the end, when the woman's stomach is ripped open, is done coldly, without sincerity. Zvantsova [1] shall be received, don't be anxious, I 'll even ask her to dinner.

[1] A painter, whom O. L. asks him to receive graciously.

The weather is most horrible, a high wind howling, a blizzard, the trees bending double. I am all right, quite well. I am writing, though slowly, still I write.

Darling, go to Hetling's, the chemist's, and buy there an ounce of *bismuth subnitici* and send it to me with the other goods if an opportunity arises. Get at Hetling's, also, a little five-kopeck box of the tiniest wooden toothpicks, a basket-work box. Do you understand ? Eau-de-Cologne I have, scent I have, soap I have also. If there really is an opportunity, get also (I have just thought of it) from Hetling *capsulæ operculatæ*; these capsules are for swallowing creosote—No. 2, English, one box.

I go on with this letter next day. Snow has fallen in masses, as in Moscow.

I have no letter from you. A mouse has been caught. I am just going to settle to work, I am going on with my story, but most likely what I write will be poor and spiritless as the wind is still blowing and it is insufferably dreary in the house.

When we go to Switzerland, I shall not take anything with me, not a single coat, I shall buy everything abroad. I shall take nothing with me but a wife and an empty box. I have read Batyushkov's article on me in the ' Petersburg News ' ; it is pretty bad. It might have been written by a promising boy in the Sixth form. The ' World of Art ' in which the new men are writing produces quite a naïve impression, too, as though angry schoolboys were writing it.

Well, dog, don't forget yourself. Remember that you are my wife and that I may any day demand you through the police. I have even the right to inflict corporal punishment on you.

I hug you so hard that you positively squeak, I kiss my darling, I implore her to write to me. Did Xenia [1] and Masha [1] like ' The Petty-Bourgeois ' ? What do they say about it ? I have had my hair cut and it feels strange.

Well, actress, the Lord be with you.

Your A—.

[1] The Tchehovs' servants in Moscow.

302

Feb. 3 (1903. *Yalta*).

Granny, sweet actress, I am alive and well and my face is not gloomy, as you write, but cheerful, for so far everything is going well. You say that we shall not be in debt to Morozov, as the shares will be covered ; but I don't owe Morozov anything as it is, as I have done what I said I would, *i.e.* when I received the money owing me I sent him three thousand roubles. You might, by the way, on occasion inquire whether he ever received that sum, he did not acknowledge it.

We shall go first to Vienna, stay there a day or two, then go to Switzerland, then to Venice (if it is not very hot), then to Lake Como, where we shall settle down properly. Do you understand, granny ?

Then, if there is time after all that, that is, if you are permitted to be with me till August 15th or 20th, we will go for two or three days to Paris and then by the quickest train to Moscow. Do you understand ? Yesterday Zvantsova came ; she said she was expecting me to go and see her, *i.e.* that I ought to return her call ; that means she won't come and see us again. Yesterday Prince Liven came, he stayed a long time and talked a long while of the past, how he was governor of Moscow, how he was a minister, etc. Altschuller, too, came yesterday, but he did not sound me this time, but only stayed a little as a visitor. Among other things I gave him a lecture for upsetting you with his letter.[1] In the first place, I fell ill not in Moscow but in Yalta, I know best about that ; and in the second, I shall go to Moscow when I choose.

Yesterday I received a photograph in a frame from Zvantsova—the garden at Melihovo, with my father working in a flower-bed. Did Masha send it ? Please thank her. But I will write to her myself to-day.

[1] O. L. wrote, Jan. 28 : ' I have had a letter from Altschuller, too, saying that you are better. But what does it mean ? You kept writing to me that your health has been no worse since you left Moscow, and judging from your letters you have been in good spirits, but the doctor says you have been in the dumps all the time and that that is the result of your stay in Moscow.'

Scribble me some news. Yesterday I did not write because the temperature in my room was only 11 degrees. A regular winter wind was blowing, then there was rain with the wind, it rained all night and now the snow is gone ; but the accursed wind is still blowing furiously.

Well, my darling, anyhow it is getting on for spring, soon we shall see each other, soon we shall go abroad. I embrace you, my joy, God be with you.

Your A—.

303

Feb. 5 (1903. *Yalta*).

My actress, it is two days and two nights since I had a letter from you. So then you have given me up ? You don't love me any more ? If that is so, write and tell me and I will send you your chemises that are lying in my cupboard, and you send me my winter goloshes. But if you still love me, let everything stay as it is.

Yesterday Shapovalov arrived, he brought the peppermints and the order of the Sea-gull from Stanislavsky.[1] I am eating the peppermints and I have hung the Sea-gull on my watch-chain. I bow down to your little feet for your kindness.

For the last few days the temperature in my study has been 11° or 12°, never higher. Arseny does not understand heating a stove and it is cold weather—first rain, then snow, and the wind has not dropped yet. I write six or seven lines a day, I can't do more, not if my life depended on it ! I have diarrhoea every day, but still I feel well, I don't cough much, my temperature is normal, not a trace left of the pleurisy.

In two or three months' time you will be used to me, and then we will escape abroad, like Giron and Louise, and go everywhere.

Why has ' The Lower Depths ' been forbidden in Petersburg ? Do you know ? And will your company be allowed to perform it if you go ? There is nothing to object to in the

---

[1] A golden sea-gull, a badge inscribed ' To A. P. Tchehov from K. S. Stanislavsky.'

play, in any sense whatever. It has even been praised by the
'Citizen.' And here Suvorin's 'Question' is being done in
Petersburg with Savina in it, and great success. It 's a pleasant
town, I must say!

My darling, why don't you write to me? Why? Are you
angry? But what for? I am uneasy and dull without your
letters. Write even if you are angry.

If you can't write an ordinary letter, write an abusive one.

I have received a medallion, too, with a glass and a frame
for a portrait. From whom is that? From Vishnevsky?
Thank him, darling, I am very much pleased with it.

Is Marya Petrovna playing? Bravo!

Well, I kiss you on the neck and both hands and I embrace
my joy tenderly. Keep well, laugh, hope.

Your passionate husband A—.

304

Feb. 7 (1903. Yalta).

My pup, I have received everything but the cup that you
write about. I haven't yet received Madame Tchumin's poems.
Vladimir Vladimirovitch Tchehov is the son of my father's first
cousin, the well-known alienist; he is an alienist too. I don't
like Goltsev's anniversary either; to begin with, they have not
elected him an honorary member of the Society of Lovers of
Russian Literature, and they haven't collected enough money
for a scholarship in his honour. A reading-room near Ruza is
nonsense! There is nobody to read there and nothing to read—
everything is prohibited.

Olga Mihailovna Solovyov brought me nineteen herrings and
a pot of jam. When you see her, thank her, tell her that you
are touched. The herrings are good. Tell Masha that there
were six degrees of frost yesterday in Yalta, this morning the
same; it is an idiotic state of things when one has to huddle up
to the stove and do nothing. There is no letter from you to-day,
the sky is grey and cold. My health is pretty middling, I don't
complain of it.

Suvorin's 'Question' has had an immense success in Petersburg, his witticisms are thought very amusing. So the old man has made a hit. I have read that an envoy has been sent by your company to Petersburg to negotiate for a theatre for the week after Easter. Is that true ? And will they allow you to play ' The Lower Depths ' ? I fancy the censor is making a dead set against Gorky, and not through fear of him but through hatred. You see, Zverev, the head censor, was reckoning on the play being a failure, and told Nemirovitch so, and here it has made a sensation, and such a sensation !

Time is passing quickly, very quickly ! My beard is turning quite grey and there is nothing I wish for, I feel that life is pleasant and at times unpleasant—and there I stop and don't go beyond it. Your sow, with three little pigs upon its back, stands before my eyes, the elephants, white and black, are standing there too—and so it is every day. Anyway, darling, write to me whether the Art Theatre is going to Petersburg and for how long. Then, I did not write to you that I want to let Kommissarzhevskaya have my play before the Art Theatre has it. She wants the play in the autumn or the winter, and I want to know whether I may promise it to her for any time next season if only after Christmas.

But I am boring you, my pup. Forgive me, my pet, I am just finishing. Only let me kiss your hand and embrace you. It 's cold !

Your A—.

Speak to Nemirovitch again about Kommissarzhevskaya, I must give her an answer.

305

Feb. 9 (1903.   *Yalta*).

Dear actress, Madame Tchumin's poem may be good,[1] but— ' one concordant impulse ' ! Can one use such scurvy words as ' concordant ' in poetry ? One must have taste, you know. I am not going to Sweden, for I want to spend two months at least with you alone.[2] If you like, we 'll go there, but only by

[1] The poem was dedicated to Tchehov.

[2] O. L. wrote, Feb. 3 : ' To-day Stanislavsky has suggested that we should join them in a trip to Norway. He wants to write to you about it himself.'

ourselves. I know Arbenin ; he is that tall, lanky, unsuccessful actor who turns novels and articles into plays ; his wife, a brunette with a little forehead, made my acquaintance twenty years ago in Odessa, where I hung round the company of the Little Theatre when it was acting there and took out the poorest actresses, who got very little salary, to dinner and for walks—but did not seduce a single soul and did not try to. What next ? You say that you will send me peppermints by Kossovitch. But I have had the peppermints already.

There is no frost, but the weather is still nasty. I cannot get warm any way. I tried writing in my bedroom, but it was no use ; my back was hot from the stove while my chest and hands were cold. I feel that my temper is ruined and I am ruined altogether in this exile.

I like Balmont, but I can't understand what Masha is so enthusiastic over. His lectures ? But you know his delivery is very absurd and affected, and, the worst of it is, that it is hard to understand him. He can only be understood and appreciated by Madame Sredin, perhaps, too, by Madame Balmont. He only speaks well and expressively when he is drunk. His elocution is original, that 's true.

I have Batyushkov's lecture,[1] I believe I have written to you about that already—I wrote that I didn't much care about it. There is almost nothing in it. Forgive me, my own, I am frozen and I expect that 's what makes me so severe. But when I am warm I shall be more gracious.

I have had a nice letter from Marya Petrovna. I will write to her to-morrow. I keep forgetting to tell you, two puppies, mongrels, took to living in our courtyard ; all night long there was an incessant joyful barking. After I had begged and insisted for many days, Arseny put them in a sack and carried them off to somebody else's yard ; they haven't come back.

What more is there to tell you ? To-morrow the Yartsevs [2] are going to Moscow, they will tell you about life here and beg you to get them seats at the theatre. Well, take care of

[1] On Tchehov's work.
[2] The family of the artist and doctor, G. F. Yartsev.

yourself, my own. Make haste and carry me off. I kiss and embrace you, my sweet.

Your A—.

306

Feb. 11 (1903. *Yalta*).

My incomparable wife, I agree! If the doctors allow it we will take a house near Moscow, but it must be furnished and heated.

In any case, here, in Yalta, I am hardly ever in the open air. But there, we will soon talk it over thoroughly, my darling.

You wrote that you had sent me Batyushkov's article, I haven't received it. Have you read S. A. Tolstoy's [1] article on Andreyev? I have seen it and it threw me into a fever, the absurdity of that article was so glaring. It 's positively incredible. If you had written anything like that I would have kept you on bread and water and beaten you every day for a week. There is one person who will be crowing now and grow more impudent than ever—that 's Mr. Burenin, to whom she gives a testimonial.

No letter from you to-day. You 've grown lazy and have begun to forget your husband. My darling, I wouldn't worry myself about M. and N. She is not a lady of culture, and he is an alien, it 's excusable in them.

If only there is a play and if only there are full houses, all the rest is really of no consequence. And Marya Petrovna should not harp on it and tune her spouse to a minor key.

My body is beginning to ache a little, I suppose the time has come to take castor oil. You write that you envy my temper. I must tell you that I am naturally hot-tempered, I am hasty and so on and so on, but I am accustomed to control myself, for a decent man ought not to let himself go. In old days I used to carry on like anything. And my grandfather, you know, was a bitter partisan of serfdom in his convictions.[2]

The buds have already turned white on the almond, soon the

---

[1] Sofya Andreyevna, Tolstoy's wife.

[2] This, of course, is by way of a joke; in reality, his grandfather was himself a serf.

garden will be in blossom. To-day it is warm and I have been out for a walk in the garden.

I am dreary without you, my own. I feel that I am a lonely sluggard, I sit for ages without moving, and all I need is a long pipe to complete the picture. I shall begin to write my play on the 21st of February, you will have the part of a foolish girl. And who is going to play the old mother, who? We shall have to ask Marya Fyodorovna.

Anatoly Sredin has just been; he brought the cup, chocolate, anchovies and a necktie. Thanks, my own, thanks. I kiss you a thousand times, I embrace you a million times.

Do you know, I fancy that S. A. Tolstoy's letter was not the genuine thing, but a fake, some one has imitated her style for a joke. Well, my joy, keep calm and well.

Your A—.

307

(Feb. 12, 1903. Yalta.)

This letter was written in Yalta, but posted in Moscow by Grigory Fyodorovitch Yartsev, who wants to see you. I have told him that he may find you at eleven o'clock in the morning. If he does not find you at that time let Xenia or Masha tell him when you will be in.

L. V. Stredin has been ill. Grigory Fyodorovitch will tell you the details. Keep well, best wishes for Carnival.

Your A—.

308

Feb. 14 (1903. Yalta).

My dear poppet, my wonderful wife, a happy Lent and happy holiday. I have got out of working order and I have not written to you for a long time, forgive me. There's not something to write about every day; besides I haven't time, I am writing a story which I shall finish in two days. So you are going to Petersburg with the company for Easter? And you will be there till Whitsuntide? And after that the rehearsals?

There was very little peppermint in the lozenges from

Tramblay, they don't even smell of it, but the chocolate was very good.

We have had warm weather now for two days, so the trees will soon be out. I have had from A . . . a very boring letter, like herself; she asks for a story for a public recitation. The lady aforesaid is publishing some book about the late A. I. Urussov and asks me for his letters.

I have had diarrhoea all this time. I have been low-spirited and felt like being cross and crying, but now I am all right, I am better and feel well. Write and tell me when, that is, what day and what month, you will be completely free, so that we can go away. We will take a single passport (that is so that you won't run away from me abroad) and we will get a sleeping carriage to the frontier or Vienna.

Is ' Wanderer ' married ? Who 's his bride ? Is it true that she is a rich tradesman's daughter ? Is it true that Gorky's wife is coming to Yalta ? I was told so by Stanislavsky's niece (the daughter of Zinaida Sergeyevna Sokolov), who came to see me the other day with Anatoly Sredin.

Next winter if I can't live at Moscow or near Moscow I shall go abroad for the whole winter, at anyrate till the middle of February. It 's tedious living here.

When I come to Moscow don't forget that we must order a fur-coat, a very warm and especially light one. I have never yet, in my life, had a tolerable, in the least presentable, fur-coat costing more than fifty roubles.

Our beauty, Olga Mihailovna, will be with you in Lent, upon which I have the honour to congratulate you. And now what is very possible, and what I expect, indeed, the poet Balmont will take to coming to see you, then he will begin swearing that he loves you madly ; a curious fellow, that Balmont.

Without you it 's not well with me in any way, take that in. My own, do write to me every day. I know that you have a new important part that you love, I know and appreciate that, indeed I love Lona myself, just because you are playing her ; but all the same, actress, write to me every day, I entreat you ! I embrace you and kiss you.

Your A—.

309

Feb. 16 (1903. *Yalta*).

Dear actress, I am sitting all day long in the garden in the open air and so I don't write to you. Forgive me, my own, don't think that I have been faithless. And so you are going for Easter to Petersburg and will be playing there. And what plays ? If you only take one of my plays, take ' Uncle Vanya.' And next year ' The Sea-Gull.'

It has turned warm, soon the quince will be in flower. I am reading the ' Missionary Review,' a journal published by a General of the Order of the Russian Jesuits, and a very interesting journal. Ah, my darling, I say it sincerely, with what pleasure I would give up being a writer now ! But there, that has nothing to do with the question.

I am told that ' The Lower Depths ' is already out. I shall have to go to Sinani's to buy it. Plays never satisfy me when I read them, though ; I have no understanding of the stage and I don't know how to read them. But still it would be interesting to read ' The Lower Depths.'

People tell me that there have been disturbances in the Moscow University. I say that it is not true or my wife would have written to me about it. Write and tell me how Leonid Andreyev has taken S. A. Tolstoy's letter. Write and tell what ' Wanderer ' is doing and how he is. Bunin has, for some reason, gone to Novo-Tcherkassk. I am well, everything is all right ; it is true that my bowels are in a bad way, but still that doesn't matter. I take nothing but soup and roast meat. I have eaten nothing else for the last two months. I eat nothing that could possibly upset my stomach, and if there is continual diarrhoea, I can't tell why it is myself.

Do I sicken you ? Forgive me these medical details, my darling.

The head-mistress came yesterday, the teacher from Gurzuf came too ; that gentleman always stays a very long time and pinches his little beard, and I wait in agony for him to go. Soon, in the second week of Lent most likely, our cousin Lyolya, George's sister, a girl between twenty-three and thirty,

is coming and will stay with us probably till the autumn.   Give
Masha the joyous news.

Well, I embrace my sweet actress, God keep you.   Be well
and merry.   Wait for your husband who has been starving so
long and is therefore fierce and passionate.

Your A—.

310

Feb. 17 (1903.   Yalta).

Darling, why did you send me the post-office notification ?
You need only have written or told the postman my address,
that 's all.   Herewith find the same notification and at once
have it dropped into a post-box without sticking on any stamps
or putting it in an envelope.   Do you understand ?

Why are you so pleased at succeeding in the part of the
virtuous woman ?   It is only cross and incompetent actresses
who play the virtuous characters, you know.   That 's one for
you, make the most of the compliment.   Anything better than
the parts I have written for you (' The Sea-Gull,' for instance)
you are hardly likely to find.   I don't say the part is well
written, but you play it magnificently.   To invite Kommissarzhevskaya [1] for ' The Sea-Gull ' would be not at all amiss.

I am quite well, I have nothing more to tell you about
myself.

Well, I kiss my granny.   Keep well, think sometimes of your
husband.

Your A.

311

Feb. 19 (1903.   Yalta).

Oh my darling, greetings !   It 's glorious weather, I sit out
of doors almost the whole day and I feel very well.   There is
no news.   Arseny says that two ladies or girls came to call on
me, but were not admitted, of which you, as a strict spouse,

[1] O. L. wrote, Feb. 12 : ' Every one is asking for " The Sea-Gull " there
(in Petersburg).   Nemirovitch suggests inviting Kommissarzhevskaya to
four performances of " The Sea-Gull." '

ought to approve. I have received the plants from Suhum, to-morrow I shall plant them. If only the weather were always like this in Yalta ! Then life would be possible.

So your company is going to Petersburg ? It is definitely settled ? Well, a good journey to you !

I am writing a little, I am reading a little. For about six hours out of the twenty-four I am always in very low spirits for reasons of which I will not speak, for they are very trivial. Now that it is Lent, Granny cooks for us ; Polya is going to church. Well and so on and so on.

Mirolyubov is coming to Yalta. In fact, people are ' begin-ning to arrive,' as they say. You will write me fully and minutely how ' The Pillars of Society ' go.

I can't see to write, it is getting dark. God bless you, my priceless wife.

Yours A—.

312

Feb. 20 (1903. *Yalta*).

Dear puppy, I would not let Suvorin [1] have one of my plays for his theatre even if he offered me a hundred thousand roubles. I despise his theatre, I regard it as rather noxious.

The almond is already in flower, the quince is in flower. To-day I am not very well. You want to bring me to Moscow to see Dr. Strauch ? Well, I am ready. Let him examine me, but I do not imagine myself that my health will be the better for it. Altschuller is not treating me, he is only carrying out what Dr. Shtchurovsky prescribed for me, my darling. Per-haps you are mistaken about Varnek.[2] I have received the cup and am already drinking out of it. I put the necktie on every day ; it will have to be shortened, it is long enough for a fat man. Thanks for not allowing me to mope any more ;

---

[1] O. L. wrote, Feb. 14 : ' Nemirovitch has just told us at the theatre that nothing will induce Gorky to give Suvorin his play, and Suvorin will only let us have his theatre on condition of his having the play. So we shall not be at Suvorin's, and the Panaev theatre, they say, is taken. I don't know how it will end.'

[2] O. L. had written about an unsuccessful operation performed by Varnek, the gynaecologist.

when I am with you I never do mope, except when I am unwell, as I am to-day. I spent the whole day downstairs in the garden, they were planting the Japanese and the German irises.

Well, my precious, I kiss you on the nape of your neck, and on your little back, and bless you.

Your A—.

313

Feb. 22 (1903. *Yalta*).

Greetings, my little grey pup ! Yes, you are receiving bouquets there from Yermolova while I sit unwashed like a Samoyed, I am even beginning to growl like one. You ask, do I at least wash my neck ? My neck I do wash, but all the rest is as grubby as a golosh. I want to go to the baths and Altschuller won't allow me.

I have had a very nice letter from Nemirovitch ; he writes about my illness and about my play. My illness is well known, and I know everything I ought to do and ought not to do, but about the play I can say nothing. I soon will say something. Your part is a perfect fool. Do you want to play the part of a fool ? a good-natured fool.[1]

I am not likely to miss taking castor oil, my darling, I believe it is more than a week since I have had any appetite. I ought to be a fasting monk, it is very easy for me not to eat.

I have had a volume of plays from Fyodorov. Among others ' A Force of Nature.' I like that play, there is a million times more talent in it than in the whole of Timkovsky.[2] Now I 'll tell you what I think : he has architectural abilities enough and to spare, but very little material to build with.

Now there is a plague of Egypt beginning for me : that is getting my fees for ' The Sea-Gull ' from the Government Bank. There is no possibility of getting the money. Apparently I ought to stick a stamp for sixty or eighty kopecks somewhere, but where I don't know.

---

[1] Tchehov supposed that O. L. would play the part of Varya in ' The Cherry Orchard.'

[2] A playwright, whose plays had a great run,

I have received two packets of postcards, snapshots from ' The Petty - Bourgeois ' and ' The Lower Depths.' Thank Stanislavsky, darling. Write and tell me, is Vishnevsky getting married or not ?

It is beginning to be cold, there is a little wind sprung up. It was quite nice before dinner.

Well, my wonderful duffer, my incomparable spouse, my marvellous actress, I embrace you an infinite number of times and kiss you as many. Don't forget me, you know we have only a little life left, we shall soon be old ; keep that in mind ; write, my good child.

Your A—.

314

Feb. 23 (1903. *Yalta*).

Dear dog, if there will be a room for me, that is a room in which I could keep out of sight and be in nobody's way, and in which I could work, in Korovin's Building, take the flat.[1] If it is a little high up that is no drawback, or not a great drawback ; I will go up gently without hurrying.

I tell you nothing about the stories I am writing, because there is nothing new nor interesting in them. One writes, reads it through and sees that one had done that already, that it is all stale, stale . . . one wants something new, something a little acid !

I want a little room, but it must be warm and, above all, one in which I shall not hear N. and M. when I don't want to hear them, and I shall not hear how X. eats soup.

It has turned cool. I am a little unwell. I was coughing all night. I keep avoiding castor oil, putting it off, but I expect I shall come to it. How is Misha's little girl ? [2] Well, granny, I bless you. You will take steps about passports. I can never arrive at anything but unpleasantness. You must tell the young ladies who are going abroad to study : (1) To finish their studies in Russia first, and then go abroad if they

---

[1] Tchehov's wife and sister were looking for a flat with more sun and air for Tchehov.

[2] His brother Mihael's child had scarlet fever.

want to devote themselves to a learned career ; our educational institutions for women, for instance the medical courses, are excellent. (2) Do they know foreign languages ? (3) Jews go abroad to study of necessity, because they are restricted here ; but why are they going ? [1] You must discourage those young ladies, in fact. Very many of them go abroad because they do not know how to study.

Write to me, granny, don't stand on ceremony, you can write me anything you like, you know, because you are my wife.

I scratch your spine.

Your A—.

I envy you, you wretch : you have been at the baths ! !

315

Feb. 25 (1903. Yalta).

Dear actress, I have just received your telegram. So ' The Pillars ' had a middling success ? So you stayed on at the Hermitage until the morning, so now you are all in middling, that is not very high, spirits.

Yesterday at last I did take castor oil and to-day I am beginning to creep out of my seediness. I write to my wife about nothing but castor oil, she must forgive her aged husband. There is nothing new here, everything goes on as before. Shwabe didn't simply leave Yalta, she fled. She fled from the boredom of Yalta, from the attractions of the place. To-day I have had no letter from you, I have only had a telegram— whether from you or from Nemirovitch I could not quite make out, as there was no signature.

Have you read Burenin's article on ' The Lower Depths ' ? I thought he would begin picking holes in your company, but God was merciful ; evidently he looks forward (it is quite possible !) to producing a play with you, for instance ' Poor Heinrich,' in his translation.

You have been at the mushroom market, I do envy you, dog ; if only I could stroll about !

[1] O. L. wrote, Feb. 18 : ' A girl comes to beg for help for her friend who has to be sent abroad ; she asked me to ask Morozov.'

Tell Masha that the stove downstairs, the iron one, smokes every morning. Did she buy a new one such as she wanted ? There is no living with ours ; it uses a lot of coal.

How is Misha's little girl ? Mother and I are very uneasy ; scarlet fever, and in Petersburg too, is no joke.

Well, hold out your little hand to me, and I 'll kiss it tenderly. I keep dreaming of the time when you will meet me at the station. I shall go straight to the baths from the station. Only I am so dirty that I daresay they will charge me quite eighty roubles. Well, never mind, you will pay for it for me and then I 'll try and be a good deserving husband.

I kiss and pat my dog and pull her tail and ears.

Your A—.

316

Feb. 27 (1903. Yalta).

Greetings, actress. It is dark, cloudy weather, but still I wander about the garden and prune the roses ; I am just sitting down, a little tired. It is warm and nice. About the play, I will write you definitely about the 10th of March, that is, whether it will be written by the end of March or not. I have not forgotten about Switzerland, I remember it, for I am eager to be alone with you as soon as possible. My health is pretty fair.

About ' The Pillars ' I have read nothing yet in the papers, I know nothing, and judging from your telegram you are not quite satisfied. If that is so, I can only give you one piece of advice : Don't mind it, darling. Why, it is Lent now, time to rest and live, and you go on ruining your nerves and straining yourself, there is no saying what for. And your only satisfaction is that Vishnevsky is putting an extra thousand in the theatre's banking account, and what the devil is that thousand to all of you ?

I remember that when the Art Theatre was beginning the idea was not to pay attention to the monetary success ; Nemirovitch used to say that if the company liked the play (not the audience but the company itself) they would produce it thirty or forty times, even if they only sold twenty roubles' worth of tickets. . . . Just fancy now writing a play and thinking all the time, and fretting oneself with the thought, that if the takings are fifteen hundred and eighty and not sixteen hundred roubles the play won't run, or, if it does, it will be a disappointment.

I have scent, I have eau-de-Cologne. I have soap for washing my head.

Did I write that I had received the postcards of ' The Petty-Bourgeois ' and ' The Lower Depths ' from Stanislavsky ? If I didn't, keep it in mind, and thank Stanislavsky when you see him. Do you understand ?

I have nothing more to write about, little duffer. There is only one thing I want, to take you by the ear, pull you to me and kiss you twenty times on your forehead and your little chin. Write me longer letters, yours are shorter than a bug's step. My greetings to your brother and nephew if they have not gone away yet. I embrace my own good darling.

Your A—.

317

March 1 (1903. *Yalta*).

Dear actress, the Yartsevs have arrived; they tell me that they did not like ' The Pillars,' but that you were very good in it. I read praise of it in the ' Russian News ' to-day. As a rule I put no faith in the newspaper men and I don't advise you to. Efros is a good fellow, but he is married to Selivanova,[1] hates Stanislavsky, hates the whole Art Theatre—which he does not conceal from me ; Kugel, who does the dramatic criticism in a dozen papers, hates the Art Theatre because he is living with Holmskaya, whom he regards as a very great actress.

Our camellia is in flower, tell Masha about that.

Well, how are you getting on, darling ? how are you feeling ? Yartsev says that you have grown thin, and I don't like that at all. It is the theatre exhausts you. I have had a letter from Nemirovitch ; he writes that it is a long time since he had

---

[1] At that time an actress in the Petersburg Alexandrinsky Theatre.

any letters from me, though as a fact I wrote to him a very little while ago. His address is Nyemtchinov's Building, Great Nikitsky Street, that's right, isn't it ? It is cool here, but I sit in the open air all the same. Sofya Petrovna Sredin is much thinner and looks much older. Leonid Sredin no longer gets up, he keeps his bed, and that has been so for a long time now. I received the herrings, thank you. Here Olga Mihailovna has brought me two dozen herrings, too, and I am eating them all the time.

They say that Gorky is coming soon to Yalta, that they are getting rooms ready for him at Alexin's. Tchirikov is, according to rumour, coming also. So I expect I shall have no time to write the play. And your favourite, Suvorin, is coming ; as soon as he comes, he will be here from morning to night, day after day.

When are you going to take me away to Switzerland and Italy ? My darling, won't it really be before the first of June ? You know it is wearing, it is fiendishly dreary ! I want to live !

You are angry that I tell you nothing about my stories, about my writings in general. But, my darling, I am so sick of it all, that it seems to me as though you and every one else are sick of it, too, and that you only speak of it out of consideration for my feelings. It seems so—but what am I to do if it seems so ? One story, ' Betrothed,' was sent to the ' Journal for All ' long ago and will most likely appear in the April number ; another story is begun, and a third is also begun, but the play —well, I have laid out the paper for the play on the table and written the title.

Well, God be with you ! I bless you affectionately, kiss you and embrace my darling.

Your A—.

318

March 3, 1903.   Yalta.

My pet, I was only just going to write to you, when the head-mistress came, and not alone, she brought a teacher with her. Now they are downstairs having tea, while I hurriedly write you these lines. I am quite well, no aches, I am coughing less. It is dull. The weather is worse. Yalta is in a flutter, every one is expecting Gorky, and it makes me feel not exactly bored, but dispirited, to think that I shall have to talk to his wife, to see the governess, to hear Maxim yelling. I have grown old ! They are coming ! ! Keep well !

Your A—.

319

March 4 (1903. *Yalta*).

My sweet darling, we are having grand doings here in Yalta ; a branch of Cuba's, the real Petersburg Cuba, has been opened. I am going to-morrow to see what there is in it and I will write and tell you ; perhaps, now we may not need to bring all sorts of provisions from Moscow.

You give me a scolding for my play not yet being ready and threaten to take me in hand. Do take me in hand, that is a nice threat, it attracts me, there is only one thing I desire—to get into your hands ; but as for the play, you have most likely forgotten that from the days of Noah I have told each and all that I would set to work on the play at the end of February or the beginning of March. My laziness does not come into it. Why, I am not my own enemy and if I had the strength I would write twenty-five plays. And I am very glad that the play is not ready, as now you will not have to rehearse it, but will have to rest. To work so immoderately, it is piggish, to say the least of it.

It is cool, but still not bad. About next winter I have decided nothing so far, but I am not building particularly roseate hopes upon it. The only thing I can say so far is that I shall stay in Moscow until December (especially if you get me a fur-coat), and then, most likely, I shall have to dash off abroad to the Riviera, or to Nervi, or something, till the 15th of February, then back to Yalta. We shall remain separated, but there is no help for it ! There is no finding any way out, however one racks one's brains. If you should be with child, then I would take you with me to Yalta in February. Would you like that, darling ? What do you think about it ? I would consent to winter even in Archangel, I shouldn't care about anything then, if only you were a mother.

Will you be going to Petersburg ? Yes or no ?

And so to-morrow I shall go to Cuba's to have a little sniff at European civilisation. Are you moving into your new flat ? On which storey ? If it is very high then I shall be half an hour getting up ; that does not matter, I have nothing to do in Moscow anyway.

A bathroom is all very well, but all the same I shall go first of all to the baths. I shall miss your Gonetsky flat, it was so near the baths.

Well, my granny, I embrace you and with you in my arms begin dancing about the room, then I kiss you on your neck and on your back and flip you on the nose, my darling.

Your A—.

320

March 5 (1903. *Yalta*).

My darling, actress, as I am no longer a literary man, but a gourmand, I set off to-day to Cuba's shop, which is now open. There I found marvellous caviare, immense olives, sausage of their own make, which has to be fried at home (very delicious !), dried sturgeon, ham, biscuits, and mushrooms. In fact, there will be no need now to bring anything from Moscow except cereals and millet. I think we ought to buy even the smoked ham for the holiday at Cuba's. I write you about all this because Altschuller was here to-day and he assured me that I must not go to Moscow under any circumstances whatever until the middle of April. My sweet, my wife, actress, own darling, won't you find it possible to come to Yalta for Easter, or if you go to Petersburg, for the week after Easter ? We could have a glorious time together, I would give you splendid things to eat and drink and ' The Cherry Orchard ' to read, and then we would set off together for Moscow.

Altschuller says that my pleurisy is not yet absorbed and that I must not go on any account. Do come, my own ! The company will give you a holiday, I 'll get it out of them, if your entreaties are not enough. Write that you are coming ; above all, think it over. Think what is best and most convenient for you. But I am so dreary, I so yearn to see you, I so long to devour you alive that I have no patience left, I beg and beg you to come. Don't be angry, darling, but first think it over, consider it. And if you decide to come, then go at once and bespeak a ticket (at Neglinny) or you won't get one for the holiday. And write to me what you decide.

In ' The Cherry Orchard ' you will be Varvara Yegorovna, or Varya, the adopted daughter, aged twenty-two. Only please don't be angry. Don't write, telegraph one word : ' Coming ' or ' Impossible.'

You write that you don't know how we shall meet, while I feel exactly as though we had parted yesterday and I shall meet you exactly as though you had never ceased to be mine for one day.

There is no letter from you to-day.

March 6. I am writing next day. From your letter received to-day, it seems that the Petersburg question is not yet finally settled, that you may still go. If so, come to Yalta after Petersburg ; consider everything thoroughly, and if you don't think it necessary or possible to come, then so be it, I submit, and will come myself without any more talk. You must decide, for you are a busy, hard-working person, while I loaf about the world like a fribble.

There is a high wind to-day, it is disagreeable. If my play does not turn out as I have conceived it, you may hit me on the head with your fist. Stanislavsky has a comic part and so have you.[1]

Well, poppet, take care of yourself. I love you, you may feel as you like. Your photograph is in the window of Volkov's shop.

I embrace and kiss you.

> Your retired husband A—.

Don't buy any more peppermints, there is *marmelad* at Cuba's.

[1] Tchehov assumed that Stanislavsky would play Lopahin and O. L. Varya.

321
March 10 (1903.   *Yalta*).

I am both sad and a little annoyed, my darling, that Masha and you keep me in uncertainty ; have you moved into your new flat or not yet ?   And where is this Korovin's Building of which you write ?   Is it in Pimenovsky Place, or somewhere else ?   I am sending this letter to the theatre, and I shall give up writing to you until I receive the new address, or the news that you have not yet moved.

I have received the photographs to-day, the snapshots of the *foyer* and others, many thanks !   Tell Tihomirova,[1] who sits in the office, that the book (Gorky's ' The Lower Depths ') is to be sent registered and not simply parcel post, and that she must not put letters in parcels.   In every one of the three parcels I have received there was a letter.

You say that by now I have forgotten what you are like. Yes, darling, I don't remember whether you are fair or dark, I only remember that at one time I used to have a wife.   Either Marya Petrovna will fall ill or Stanislavsky will break down in Petersburg, and so I am not building hopes on the three thousand of which you write.[2]

One letter I sent to Pimenovsky Place, and now I am afraid that it has not reached you.

I don't know Krasov, I have never seen him.

Well, God be with you, keep well and merry.   I kiss you and embrace you.

Your A—.

322
March 14 (1903.   *Yalta*).

My own darling, you cannot go on like this !   I have sent one letter to Korovin's Building, Pimenovsky Place, and yesterday

---

[1] Sister of one of the actors and an assistant in the office of the Art Theatre.

[2] O. L. wrote, March 5 : ' So they are going to Petersburg. I expect you will get over three thousand roubles, the takings there will be four thousand six hundred.'

Korsh the student told me that Korovin's Building was in Petrovka.   To-day I get a letter from you, a delightful description of your new flat and my room with a bookshelf, but no address.   Well, what would you have me do ?

We are having magnificent spring weather in Yalta, everything is in blossom, I go almost every day into the town.   And it seems I must have changed a good deal during the winter, for every one I meet looks at me sympathetically and says all sorts of kind things.   And I have asthma.   And I have a bad wife who conceals her address.   Yesterday Altschuller was here and he kept teasing me, and I began to suspect that you had bribed him to keep me in Yalta as long as possible.

I entreat you, darling, do send your address !   I cannot endure sending letters to the theatre.

And what Turgenev play are you producing ?   You ought also to do ' The Inspector-General ' and ' Marriage,' and you might look through Pisemsky, I daresay something in the style of ' Bitter Destiny ' might be found in him.

Mother is going to church, to-morrow she takes the sacrament.

Madame Goloushev has just arrived bringing a letter from Masha.   And no address again ! !

Well, my darling, God keep you, I kiss and embrace you a thousand times.

Your A—.

323

March 17 (1903.   *Yalta*).

My joy, I have not had your address and by now I despair of ever having it, and so I am writing to you again to the theatre. Many thanks to Uncle Karl for the table and the sofa, but as we are going away in the summer, and shall be making new plans for the autumn, we shall scarcely need now either the table or the sofa.   And to drag that furniture which is very cumbersome from place to place would be very uninteresting.

Now, my joy, my good dog, I have a favour to ask for which you will not thank me.   The point is that the head-mistress is going to Petersburg and will, of course, attend the performances of the Art Theatre. She begs me to ask you to book a box in the first row for ' The Lower Depths ' and also one for ' Uncle Vanya,' two in all. My darling, do take them if it is not too late. Please do.

For some reason I don't feel sure that this letter will reach you. And altogether I am sad that my correspondence with you is so stupidly upset, and for what the devil only knows, on account of an address, the name of a street, since you have written already that it is Korovin's Building. But what street is the damned house in ? Is it in Petrovka ?

You are very busy, of course, but it would not be much trouble to Masha to send the address. Oh well, never mind.

It is warm here, there are mists, I sit in the garden sometimes thinking, sometimes fuming. I have had a letter from Teleshov, too, about Scholz.

I bless you and kiss you.

Your A—.

324

March 18 (1903. *Yalta*).

My wonderful darling, at last you have sent your address, and everything is straight again. Thanks, darling. The tearful letter in which you abuse yourself before setting off to Tchernigovsky,[1] I received this morning. I looked through it, no address. I was on the point of applying for a divorce when at midday I had your telegram. So I shall come to Moscow the week after Easter, I shall come before your return from Petersburg, I shall meet you, I shall meet you not at the station but at home after I have been to the baths and have finished writing my play, and by the way, I am not getting on with it quite well. One of the leading characters is not sufficiently thought out and hinders it ; but by Easter I expect the character will be quite clear and I shall be rid of my difficulties.

If Masha has not yet gone, tell her to bring a little ready-cooked sausage. Do you hear ? all the rest we will get at

---

[1] About three miles from the Troitse-Sergiyevsky Convent, where the Stanislavskys usually went for the Lent holiday and where O. L. went that year.

Cuba's. The photograph [1] you write about I shall most likely
send you to Petersburg by the head-mistress. If the boxes don't
cost more than thirty or, say, forty roubles, then book them for
her for ' The Lower Depths ' and ' Uncle Vanya,' but if there
are none as cheap or no boxes at all, then, my darling, don't be
cross with your stupid husband, but take two stalls at three
roubles each for her for each of the plays. I adore you, my
own, I love you.

To-morrow I will write again. Don't talk nonsense, you are
not in the least to blame for not living with me in the winter.
On the contrary, we are a model couple if we don't interfere
with each other's working. You do love the stage, don't you ?
If you did not love it, then it would be a different matter. Well,
Christ be with you ! Soon, very soon, we shall see each other,
and I shall hug and kiss you forty-five times. Keep well, child.

Your A—.

325

March 19 (1903. Yalta).

Greetings, my actress, you must excuse me, but our prolonged
separation is having its results. I am in correspondence with
Mlle. Pushkarov. How it will end, what this correspondence
will lead to, I don't know, but meanwhile congratulate me : she
has promised to send me her play. I remember that I have read
that play already in the eighties. Anyway I have written to
her not to send me her play, as I understand nothing about
plays, but to send it to Nemirovitch. Warn him, tell him about
the play, let him tell her authoritatively that she, Pushkarova,
must write no more, or that she must produce her plays somewhere in the provinces, if it really isn't utterly hopeless.

I am well, the last few days I have begun coughing a little,
but I expect it is of no consequence. I feel cheerful, I sit in
the garden or work a little in my study, I think of you, of our
tour in Switzerland and Italy. When we are abroad, we will
eat a great deal and drink a great deal of beer. You know I
have drunk nothing all the winter.

---

[1] The portrait of O. L.'s mother which she left behind.

The 17th of March was Gorky's name-day. His wife arrived for it. She and he talk of you with enthusiasm ; they say that you have made immense strides during the last few years and are acting magnificently. As I listened I rejoiced that I had such a wife and made a note of it.

I sent one letter to Pimenovsky Place, did you get it ? Ah, darling, how distressed I was over the address !

So don't forget to tell Nemirovitch about Pushkarova. In my letter to her I praised him to the skies, so that, if he read it, he would be highly delighted.

Send me your Petersburg address in good time. From Petersburg you will send me long telegrams at my expense, for which I am setting aside twenty-five roubles.

Do you know, darling, I don't care at all for ' A Month in the Country,' [1] the play is out of date, and if it is not liked people will say that it is your fault and not the play's.

I have got out of touch with people and with life in the winter. I have nothing to offer now, absolutely nothing, so you had better take on somebody else. . . . Darling, you agree, don't you ? No ?

I embrace you and kiss you, write to me every day. Don't torture me.

Your A—.

326

March 21 (1903. *Yalta*).

My darling, your last letter is simply revolting. You say ' in how many letters I wrote that we were moving to Petrovka Korovin's Building.' While I have *all* your letters intact and only in one you casually mention that you are moving into Korovin's Building—and I was left to suppose that you had moved to Pimenovsky Place. I knew that you would blame me for it in the end. And I have kept all your letters, I will show them to you. Oh well, God be with you. I have had so much distress over that address for the last fortnight that I can't get over it even now.

---

[1] A play of Turgenev's.

We have no rain. ' The Cherry Orchard ' will come off ; I
am trying to make as few characters as possible ; it will be
more intimate so.

Well, I can't write more, forgive me.

Your A—.

You write that I read your letters inattentively. What
makes you think that ? I 'll bring all your letters and you 'll
see for yourself that not one letter has been lost, and that there
is no address in any one of them.

327

March 22 (1903. *Yalta*).

My good darling, I tell you what you must do for me before
you go to Petersburg : see what underclothes I have got in
Moscow and let me know exactly. How many shirts, how
many pants and so on. You will telegraph from Petersburg.
Among other things you must telegraph on what day you will
be back in Moscow ; if you will be back, let us say, on Tuesday,
I will be in Moscow by the Monday. I shall not come and
meet you at the station, but shall wait for you at home with
open arms.

My sweet darling, how could I need Shahovskoy's [1] table
until the autumn ? Why, we shall be travelling until the
autumn, and have you no fear of other people's furniture,
with the locked drawers, and the talk afterwards of the furniture having been ruined at the Tchehovs' ? We must not have
it, we mustn't ! We will buy a writing-table and a sofa, we
will have everything of our own. If we want a cow or a horse,
we will buy them too.

You write that a great many people are coming to Yalta, so
that I shall not be dull. I want my wife and not visitors, my
darling, and I don't care to see anybody.

I have given the head-mistress the photograph of your
mother, my mother-in-law. My own, do write to me a little
more ! I entreat you on my knees ! I ask you in earnest !

[1] S. Shahovskoy had offered to lend them his writing-table for the
summer.

Don't be lazy, don't pay attention to a headache, but sit down and write, write about what you like, every line is precious to me.

Well, I kiss you, my little German Knipsha, I embrace you and kiss you once more.

Your A——.

328

March 23 (1903. *Yalta*).

My dear granny, you are cross with me about the address, you keep declaring that you did send it and even several times. Wait a little, I'll bring you your letters, you shall see for yourself, and meanwhile we will drop it, we won't say anything more about the address, I have got over it. Then you write that I ask you again about Turgenev's plays and that you have already written to me about them, but that I forget what you say in your letters. I don't forget the least thing, darling, I read them over several times, but the trouble is that there is never less than ten days between my letter and your answer. I have read over almost all Turgenev's plays. ' A Month in the Country ' I have told you already I don't like, but ' The Bread of Others,' which you are producing, is all right, it is not badly done, and if Artyom does not drag it out and does not make it monotonous, the play should go fairly well. You will have to shorten ' The Provincial Lady ' a little, won't you ? There are good parts in it.

I have had no piles the whole winter, but to-day I am a regular titular councillor. The weather is divine. Everything is in flower, it is warm and still, but there is no rain, I am afraid for the plants. You write that you will hold me in your arms for three days and three nights, but how about dinner and tea ?

I have had a letter from Nemirovitch ; thank him very much. I am not writing to him because I sent him a letter lately.

Keep well, mongrel. I have already written to you about Gorky ; he has been to see me and I have been to see him. He is pretty well. I cannot send you my story, ' Betrothed,' because I haven't it ; you will soon read it in the ' Journal for All.' I have written stories like it already, written them many times, so that you will gain nothing by reading it. . . . Write or I will call you a wretch.

Your A—.

329

March 24 (1903. Yalta).

My own, don't forget to see Modest Tchaikovsky [1] in Petersburg and to ask him from me to return me his brother Pyotr's letters which he had from me for his book. If Modest Tchaikovsky is not in Petersburg, then find out from Karabtchevsky, or some one of the literary people, where he is, and whether you can get his address if he is abroad. Do you understand ? If you do, you are my clever girl. ' It 's the Weakest Link that Snaps ' was written at the period when the best writers still showed the influence of Byron and Lermontov, with his Petchorin ; why, Gorsky is just the same Petchorin ! A rather thin and vulgar version, but still Petchorin. And the play may seem uninteresting ; it is rather long and only of interest as a record of old days. Though I may be mistaken, which is very possible. You know how pessimistic I was in the summer about ' The Lower Depths ' and what a success it has been ! I am no judge.

Soon, soon we shall see each other, my dear priceless old woman; I shall embrace and pet you, I shall walk up and down Petrovka with you.

I shout ' Hurrah ! ' to you and remain for ever your neglected, faded and dingy husband.

A—.

You are praised in the ' World of Art,' Knippusha. I have sent you to-day the copy in which you are praised. I am proud, my darling, I am proud !

[1] A literary brother of the composer Tchaikovsky.

330

March 26 (1903. *Yalta*).

Greetings, my darling ! the Gorkys have been here to-day.
A. Sredin has been and Zvantsova ; I don't know whether I
shall have time to write this letter for it to go to-day. I am
alive and well, there is no news and nothing particular has
happened or is going to happen. I have had no letter from
you for three days, but I am not huffy about it, only grieved.
It is windy to-day and most likely that is why I have been
coughing all day.

You must (1) write to me exactly which day you are leaving
Moscow, (2) to what address I must write to you in Petersburg,
(3) on what date you will return to Moscow. This last you
should telegraph to me a good while beforehand, so that I may
book a ticket for the journey in time.

I kiss and embrace my darling. Write to me if you have
not yet forgotten me. Well, God be with you.

Your A—.

Telegraph when you leave Moscow ; in fact, don't grudge
money for telegrams all this time.

331

March 28 (1903. *Yalta*).

My amazing actress, I am desperately sunburnt and now I am
afraid that when you see me you will fling up your hands and
ask for a divorce. While I so long to live with you. Just for a
little bit. I have received the chicken and have put it in a
conspicuous place like the sow (with the little pigs on her back).
Thanks, darling ! The Easter cake did not make a great impression upon me, I gave it to Mother. You write that you
will make me wash my neck. My own darling, I do wash my
neck even in Yalta, but how about the rest of me ?

The head-mistress came to-day to say good-bye, she is going
to Petersburg. I gave her the address of Batyushkov, 15
Liteyny St., from whom she will learn your address.

Before going away to Petersburg, take the bulbs off the

electric light, and put them away, so Masha says. This must be done or they will play pranks when you are away and use the electric light. And Masha tells me that you are playing ' Uncle Vanya ' with wretched scenery, and a lady to-day abused Petrova and Savitskaya very severely ; the first she abused in general and the second for her acting in ' The Pillars.' Leave Snap at your flat ; if I had known he was such a nice dog, I should not have insisted. Let him stay in Moscow, I shall see him there. To-day there is a little rain. I am rather unwell.

I am drinking kefeer every day.

Before this year had properly begun I was already making plans how we, that is you and I, would spend the next. You have already forgotten what I am like, but I remember you and think of you continually, as though we had only parted yesterday. While Sasha Sredin is delighted that he is parted from his wife. And Madame Goloushev is glad that she is parted from her husband. So there you are !

Well, my little Zulu, I am expecting a telegram to tell me when you will be leaving for Petersburg and another telegram with your Petersburg address. Good-bye for the present, my spouse, I kiss you on the back.

Your A—.

Try and get hold of the letter I sent to Pimenovsky Place.

332

TELEGRAM

April 8 (1903. *Yalta*).

To-day at last telegram received all well sending letter write fully when we shall meet telegraph Black Phiz.

333

April 8 (1903. *Yalta*).

My incomparable darling, my own, Christ is risen ! to-day I got your telegram with the address and have been meaning to write to you all day, but visitors have not let me have one free minute and won't let me, though it is evening now. . . .

I kiss you, my joy. Mirolyubov will drop this letter in the post-box at once.

Do write to me a little oftener and a little more fully ; write when you will be in Moscow that I may have time to book a seat in the train and arrive in time.

I embrace and kiss you a thousand times.

Your Black Phiz.

334

April 9 (1903. *Yalta*).

My superb darling, I cannot manage anyhow to write you a long letter. There are visitors without end, and when there are no visitors one runs out into the garden to sit still a little and rest. I am looking forward with longing and impatience to the moment when I shall at last see my actress. When will you be in Moscow, what day ? Write or telegraph exactly.

I will write the play in Moscow, it is impossible to write here. They won't even let me read my proofs.

It is real spring ; everything is out in flower now. Bunin has gone to Odessa, Fyodorov too. Gorky is here. Kuprin has gone away, he was pining for his wife. And why will people get married ! !

There has not been one letter from you yet from Petersburg. Yesterday I sent you a telegram. I am expecting an answer, though there is nothing to answer in it.

I 'll bring your sheets, darling, set your mind at rest.

I embrace you, my own, hug you, lift you in the air and kiss you. Keep well, don't exhaust yourself.

Your A—.

Tell Stanislavsky and Rayevskaya that I have not answered their telegram of congratulation because I don't know their addresses.

335

April 11 (1903. *Yalta*).

Greeting, my wonderful dog, and many thanks to you, I have just received two letters from you. And yesterday I had a telegram about ' Uncle Vanya ' from Nemirovitch and Stanis-lavsky. My head aches, I am coughing, visitors sit on for ages, yesterday one bearded individual stayed on for four and a half hours beside my table, but still I feel tolerably and am think-ing of our meeting. So I shall be in Moscow on the 24th to meet you on the 25th. As soon as I arrive I shall go to the baths. I think that I shall be comfortable now in Moscow. I have my own room—that is, a great thing, there is no Xenia, who used to oppress me in the evenings playing the concertina as though we were in a pot-house. The only trouble is getting up the stairs! And this year I am so troubled with breathlessness. Well, never mind, I shall clamber up somehow.

I read to-day in 'Russkoye-Slovo' about the first performance of ' The Lower Depths,' about the crowded audience, the hysterics and so on. The notice struck me as uneasy.

I have had a long letter from Masha Smirnov, she asks me to write her something. The author Kozhevnikov is coming to see us to-day. I have received a manuscript to read—in fact, I might as well shoot myself.

Will you have an actress for the part of an elderly lady in ' The Cherry Orchard ' ? If not, then there will be no play, I am not going to write it. It is cool and windy in Yalta, there is no rain, growth has stopped in the garden. After the cold and the wind a sultry heat will begin.

Maklakov and Shehtel are here. L. Andreyev has been here a long time, but he has not been to see me. And Pyatnitsky is here.

Well, my own darling, it is time we were off to Switzerland ; get ready ! I kiss you, God be with you.

Your A—.

336

TELEGRAM

April 12 (1903. *Yalta*).

Black Phiz well eating much leaving twenty-second.

337

April 15 (1903. *Yalta*).

My inimitable darling, my little duffer, you have no need to be cross with me for my silence ; in the first place, you wrote yourself that you were leaving Moscow in the beginning of Holy Week; and in the second, I do write pretty often. Besides, what is the use of writing since we shall see each other soon, so soon, since I shall soon be pinching your back and so on ? The ticket is already bespoken, I shall leave on the 22nd and be in Moscow on the 24th.

I shall go straight to the baths as soon as I arrive. I will bring you the sheets. Why are you all singing the same tune as the ' Novoye Vremya,' why are you ruining ' The Lower Depths ' ? Oy, all that is not right. I don't like your tour in Petersburg at all. I have no great desire to write for your theatre, chiefly because you have not an old lady. They will be foisting the old lady's part on you, though there is another part for you, and besides, you have already acted an elderly lady in ' The Sea-Gull.'

Well, there was a little rain yesterday, we are having a fine spring, only cool and boring.

Dr. Bogdanovitch has died in Yalta. Did you know him ?

To go to Odessa and Kiev is a good idea.[1] And I will go with you on tour. You will have crowded houses in Odessa, and it will be nice to stay in Kiev and meet the spring there.

Why don't you perform ' The Petty-Bourgeois ' ? That is liked, you know, in Petersburg.

I shall write you one more letter and send you one more telegram, and then good-bye until we meet soon afterwards. I am as dark as an Arab. It is nice in our garden. I sit there all day long and am fiendishly sunburnt. Have you seen Modest Tchaikovsky ? Have you seen Suvorin ? Does Misha come to the theatre ? But you will answer these questions in Moscow, my faithful spouse.

I kiss you on the muzzle and pat you on the back.

Your Black Phiz.

[1] O. L. wrote, April 10 : ' We are all dreaming of going together with you next spring to play in Kiev and Odessa.'

338

April 17, 1903. (*Yalta*.)

And so, my incomparable wife, my ginger dog, I send you my last letter for this season. On the 22nd of April I shall leave Yalta, on the 24th I shall be in Moscow. That's settled, the ticket is already bespoken. It is no good your pressing me to come to Petersburg, since it will not be quite easy for me even to get to Moscow, and I should have to be travelling quite twenty-four hours longer to get to Petersburg. And, indeed, what is there to do there ? I have received P. Weinberg's review ; he wrote just the same thing about ' The Sea-Gull,' and yèt ' The Sea-Gull ' is still hobbling along. Our old men are full of spite, that 's bad. And Minsky [1] is false and affected.

Keep well, my darling; I shall meet you looking quite clean as I shall go to the baths. Ilyinskaya was here to-day, she made me a present of a little cash-box.

Well, take care of yourself and be happy, my own. The play is taking shape little by little, only I am afraid my tone on the whole is out of date. I fancy so. I kiss my bird, I tweak her by the beak and the claws.

Your A—.

339

TELEGRAM

April 18 (1903. *Yalta*).

Arriving Moscow twenty-fourth ticket taken don't want to go Petersburg well.

340

TELEGRAM

April 20 (1903. *Yalta*).

Received lovely present thanks my own.

As arranged, Tchehov went to Moscow and O. L. returned there from Petersburg. They were kept in town by rehearsals at the

[1] A well-known Russian poet.

Art Theatre until June.   Tchehov went for two days to Petersburg
on business during this period, and sent his wife the following
letter and telegram during the journey.

341

May 13 (1903.   *Spirivo*).

Greeting, darling, you see I write to you.   Now the train is at
Tver, I shall post this letter at Bologoye.   I was very sad to
part from you.   At Bologoye I shall dine to your health.   It
is hot.   I am sleepy.   From Petersburg I will write or telegraph
to-morrow, not later, if I don't leave to-morrow.   I don't
expect anything good from the German.   Well, darling, Christ
be with you.   I kiss and embrace you.   Keep well and merry.
Your A—.

342

TELEGRAM

May 15, 1903.

To-day by the Sevastopolsky.

The Tchehovs abandoned their plan of going abroad owing to
the great heat.   Instead they spent June and half of July on the
Yakuntchikovs' estate.   They were anxious to find a small country
house in the neighbourhood of Moscow where Tchehov could spend
the winter, as the Moscow professor, Ostroumov, had sanctioned
his doing so.   The latter part of the summer was spent in the
Crimea, where O. L. remained until September 18.

343

Friday, the day of your departure.

My sweet darling, my horsey dog, what sort of a journey have
you had ?   How did you spend the time at Sevastopol with him
of the ginger moustaches ?   Has everything gone well ?

I came back from the steamer not well ; I have no appetite,
there is a tedious stupid feeling in my stomach, and it is not

particularly pleasant to walk about, my head aches like anything. I don't know why it is. But the worst of it all, of
course, is your going ; I shall not soon get used to your absence.

If you have not yet managed to send off the parcel to Yalta
you might add gaiters—they will soon be wanted.

I read to-day in the papers that ' The Cherry Orchard ' will
appear in December. If that is correct, very good, I agree,
only let the play appear at the beginning of December, not the
end. I shall work at it to-morrow.

Nina Korsh and her little girl dined with us to-day. I am
a little worried at your having taken only seventy-five instead
of a hundred roubles from me. So I owe you twenty-five
roubles, darling.

' Novoye Vremya ' still goes on picking Gorky to pieces, I am
afraid it may lead to a scandal.

Write to me, my own, my precious, you are convinced now,
you know how I love you.

To-morrow I shall write to you again, but now you must
rest, you must talk, you must unpack your boxes. Give my
greetings to every one I know, don't leave any one out. Write
and tell me how ' Julius Caesar ' is going, whether anything
has been heard concerning it, and so on and so on. How
is Vishnevsky ?

I embrace you, I kiss your little paws, God be with you.

Your A—.

I fancy my handwriting is smaller than ever, isn't it ? To-
day I shall play patience solo.

344

(Sept. 19, 1903. *Yalta.)*

My dear pony, dear little dog, dear wife, greetings, darling !
I kiss and embrace you a million times ; write and tell me with-
out delay how and what, and whether everything is all right in
Moscow.

Once more I embrace you, pony. God be with you.

Your A. T—.

I shall soon be coming.

345

(Sept. 20, 1903. *Yalta.)*

How cruel this is, my darling ! All yesterday evening, then in the night, then all to-day I have been expecting your telegram from Sevastopol, and only this evening (Saturday) I get from Shaposhnikov [1] : ' Your wife set off safely ' and so on ; and I have been imagining that the steamer had gone down, that you could not get a ticket and so on and so on. It is wrong of you, dear spouse ; another time, don't promise.

I am better to-day, but yet I am not quite well. Weakness, a nasty taste in my mouth, no appetite. To-day I managed my washing by myself. The water was not cold. Your absence is very, very noticeable. If I were not cross with you about the telegram I could say a great many nice things to you and I would tell you how I love my pony. Write to me every detail relating to the theatre ; I am so far from everything that I am beginning to lose courage. It seems to me that I have already outlived my day as a writer, and every sentence I write strikes me as good for nothing and of no use at all ; this by the way.

I have not yet seen Mihailovsky, I have not seen Panov [2] either. If I see them, of course, I will tell you. I forget to take the pills, though I put them under my very nose ; but still I remember them in time and correct my error.

I kiss you, my little wife, darling. If my letters are horrid and pessimistic, don't be distressed, my own, it is all of no consequence.

Your A—.

346

Sept. 21 (1903. *Yalta).*

My splendid wife, to-day I feel a little better, evidently I am coming back to the normal ; I no longer look wrathfully at my manuscript, I am already writing, and as soon as I finish

[1] Director of the Government Bank in Sevastopol and a friend of Tchehov's, who saw O. L. off at the station.
[2] An artist and friend of Mihailovsky's.

I will telegraph to you at once. The last act will be merry,
and indeed the whole play will be merry and frivolous ; Sanin
won't like it, he will say I have grown shallow.

I get up at eight o'clock in the morning. I wash. To-day
there was cold water and I had a good tub. It is warm out of
doors, almost hot. Everything goes well in the house, Sharik
has not yet learnt to bark, while Tuzik has forgotten how to. I
feel almost frightened sleeping without you.

Kostya [1] has not come once since you went away.

Your letter written in pencil came to-day. I read it and
sympathised with you, my joy. Drinking champagne ! driving to the Bratsky Cemetery ! Oh, darling, it is those long red
moustaches have fascinated you so or you would not have gone.

I shall send the play addressed to you and you must hand it
on to the authorities. Only don't be too downhearted when
you read it and think it bad.

I kiss you, my pony, I pat you and stroke your nose. Be
merry, don't be depressed, don't be too clever, and try to waste
rather less money. God be with you, be merry, I repeat.

Your A—.

347

Sept. 23 (1903. *Yalta*).

Greetings, darling, my better half ! To-day two postcards
came from you, I am very glad and pleased to have them. I
had reckoned on getting a telegram from Moscow, but there,
bless you, I put myself in your place and understand. What
new ideas have they at the theatre ? They are not tired out,
are they ? They are not disappointed ?

The fourth act in my play will, compared with the other
acts, be rather meagre but effective. I think the end of your
part isn't bad. In fact, you must not lose heart, it will all be
all right.

Your brother has not been to see me once since you went
away. I am not in the least offended, I only tell you of it
just so that you should know ; your parcel is lying here await-

[1] Her brother Konstantin, who was in the autumn of 1903 working
with Mihailovsky-Garin in the south of the Crimea.

ing his arrival; his address is Yalta, Derekoy, at Mustafa-Bey's. Panov was here yesterday, smartly dressed, pleased with life and happy; he stayed a long time. He told me that Mihailovsky has in all probability gone with Kostya to Syuren. Mihailovsky will be here on Thursday.

Madame Tatarinov's son died as they were bringing him home from abroad. The funeral is to-day, Masha has gone to the church.

I am managing my tub quite well. I get them to give me a can of ordinary water from the tap and a small jug of ice. Then I mix them and get just what I want. I am slow over my dressing, either because I have got out of the habit of dressing myself, or because I am hindered by breathlessness. Nastya puts out a fresh suit for me every day. I clean my teeth. I use the sprayer. What else? I write to my wife almost every day.

P. I. Kurkin will come and see you in a day or two. He will tell you what he wants and you must think a little and give him advice. It is a very important matter.

Sharik is growing, but he does not bark yet. You forgot your cat when you were going away; do you want me to send it?

My greetings to Vishnevsky, and tell him to acquire all the softness and elegance he can for his part in my play.[1]

Well, poppet, I bless you, don't be cross, don't frown, don't scold your husband. We shall soon see each other. I shall come as soon as ever the frosts begin in Moscow.

Your A—.

348

Sept. 25 (1903. *Yalta*).

My dog without a tail, this letter will probably reach you after you have received a telegram to tell you that the play is finished. The fourth act is getting itself written easily, it seems to hang together quite well, and that I have not finished it quickly is because I keep on being rather ill. To-day, it is

---

[1] He assumed that Vishnevsky would play the part of Gaev.

true, I am better than yesterday, but at eleven o'clock my legs
and back began aching and I began coughing. All the same
I fancy that now things are going to get better and better.
The day before yesterday 'your enemy,' as you call him,
Altschuller, turned up ; I did not let him sound me, but I told
him about my morning tub. He threw up his hands in horror
and forbade my having a sponge bath. And now I have to
wash myself in the old way, so that in three or four days my
neck will be grey again. For the last two mornings I have
not had the tub, but the state of my health is the same as
before, though I fancy I do feel stronger.

Yesterday at last Kostya was here. He turned up good-
humoured, excited, grey and lean, in dark muslin trousers.
We gave him some dinner. He went away, but came back in
the evening with some dirt in his eye. I proceeded to perform
an operation on it. The operation was, I believe, unsuccessful,
but the eye got better. Early this morning he came to fetch his
linen. To-morrow the most difficult part of his work is over.
He gets on with Mihailovsky.

Nastya changes my suits regularly. Indeed, it is a very
nice, orderly plan. Altogether it is to be regretted that I
married you so late in life. When I send you the play, try to
manage that Stahovitch should not be present when it is being
read (at the *foyer*).

I fancy that there is something new in my play, however
dull it may be. There is not a single pistol shot in the whole
play, by the way. Katchalov's part is a good one ; find out
who is to play the girl of seventeen and write and tell me.

Yesterday I did not write to you and wrote very little altogether because I was not well.

I kiss you, my joy, and embrace you warmly. I send greetings to Vishnevsky, Nemirovitch, Stanislavsky and all the
good orthodox Christians. I am behindhand with the play,
tell them that I am very, very apologetic.

To-morrow there will be a letter from you—the first from
Moscow. I am expecting it with impatience. Well, poppet,
don't forget me, think of me sometimes.

Your A—.

349

TELEGRAM

Sept. 26, 1903. *Yalta.*

Four acts completely ready copying will send you health mending warm kiss you ANTOINE.

350

Sept. 27 (1903. *Yalta*).

My darling pony, I have already telegraphed to you that the play is finished, that all the four acts are written. I am now copying it out. My people have come out living, that's true, but what the play amounts to I don't know. Well, I'll send it you. You will read it and find out.

Mihailovsky and Panov were here yesterday. The first talked a great deal. I listened with pleasure. The second held his tongue. Then Kostya turned up. Though he does not agree with something or other, he is apparently well pleased. Mihailovsky was warm in his praise of him.

The day before yesterday your extraordinary friend with the red moustaches, Shaposhnikov, turned up. He was here again to-day. He dined with us and after dinner he went off with Masha to Suuk-Su, to see Madame Solovyov. He is incredibly boring, so boring that one wants to put out one's tongue as one listens.

If only you were to think, pony, of sending me a telegram after the first performance of ' Julius Caesar ' ! I am writing ' The Cherry Orchard ' on the paper Nemirovitch gave me and with the gold nibs I had from him too. I don't know whether there will be any improvement owing to that.

Ah, poor Volodya,[1] why does he listen to his relations ? He will never make a singer, while he had already made a good and zealous lawyer. And why is it that you are all so scared of the career of lawyer ? Isn't it as good to be a decent lawyer as to sing tenor at the theatre for ten years at 4500 roubles a year

---

[1] O. L.'s brother Vladimir.

and then to be on the shelf ?　Evidently none of you have any notion what is meant by a solicitor, a lawyer.

The sea is rough, though the weather is fine.　Panov has already left.　Mihailovsky and he will be at the first performance of ' The Cherry Orchard '—so they said.　Give my love to Snap and thank him from me for not giving you a fright by having his neck broken.[1]　Sharik is pleased with life.　Tuzik sinks at times into pessimism.

Sredin is painting you ?　But that is a pleasure . . . why, you have been painted by him—by Sredin—already !

Well, pony, I stroke you, I brush you, I feed you on the very best oats and I kiss you on the forehead and the neck.　God be with you, write to me, and don't be very cross if I don't write to you every day.　Now I am copying the play, so I deserve indulgence.

Greetings to all.

Your A—.

351

Sept. 29 (1903,　*Yalta*).

My wonderful wife, pretty sleek little pony, greetings !　The play is finished, but I am copying it slowly, as I have to make changes and think points over ;　I shall send it off with two or three passages incomplete, I will put them off until later—you must excuse it.　In all probability Masha will bring the play.

Your brother has not appeared again.　I cough less, I feel well, only I am often in a rage (with myself) and I don't eat very much, I have no appetite.　I change my suit every day, I wash in the old way, I sleep very well, I clean my teeth, I eat *marmelad.*

Yesterday evening it rained, my darling, and turned nice and fresh and soft.　The roses are in flower.　E. P. Gorky [2] has not been to see us yet.　In fact, no one comes, though indeed your friend Madame Bonnier has been.　So you have taken to going to the theatres ?　and to Timkovsky's plays too ?　Why, Pashalova is an old actress, my age at least, she used to play

---

[1] The dog had been run over.　　　　　　[2] Gorky's wife.

in Korsh's theatre ; she is quite a provincial actress, uninteresting, and I don't know why so much has been said about her.
Perhaps it is this : she is a Princess Tchegodayev by birth, and
the wife of the gentleman who killed Roshtchin-Insarov.

I love you, darling.

If my health would improve I would go off somewhere for a
long voyage.   It is essential, for at home one mopes and turns
into a Timkovsky.

Tell Bunin to come to me for treatment if he is unwell, I 'll
cure him.

Well, pony, I kiss you on the neck and stroke you.   Ah, if
only you would act the governess in my play, it is the best part,
I don't care for the others.

Keep well and be merry, Christ be with you.

Your A—.

352

Sept. 30 (1903.   *Yalta*).

My joy, I have just received the parcel from you : thanks, a
thousand thanks !   I have already put on the gaiters and feel
an extraordinary warmth in my legs, and that is very welcome
as to-day I am not the thing, my writing goes on quite badly,
and I have even rung up Altschuller to come.   Cough, no
appetite.   Thank God, that at least I sleep well, I sleep like a
Little Russian.   Altschuller will probably clap on a plaster.

Yesterday I was tired and I did not work, and if my play is
four or five days late, for goodness' sake, do all of you forgive
me.   I shall hardly be in time to send it off with Masha.

Our Sharik is growing ; they tell me that he barks well, but
I have not heard him once.   It is a dull cool day ; the stone
wall round the yard is growing higher and higher, I think it
will make it more snug.   Since it is so cold outside there are
lots of flies inside, I am sick of them.

After the first performance of ' Julius Caesar ' do write me
a full account of it.   You know I am very, very much interested,
darling.

Our newspaper announces to-day, in big letters, that the fleet has gone to Korea with sealed orders. Oy, doesn't that mean war ?

Keep well, my pony, be merry and eat lots of oats. I am appallingly dull without you.

Temperature is 37·5.

It is drizzling. God keep you, I embrace you.

Your A—.

353

Oct. 2, 1903. (*Yalta.*)

Greetings, pony, thank you for your letter about ' Julius Caesar ' and the rehearsals, you have described it all so well, I am very much pleased. I keep expecting more and more letters, I am a discontented beast. Write, darling, write, my own.

To-day my temperature is normal. Altschuller has prescribed me pills which will save me for seven days from having to put on my dressing-gown and trot off. There is still weakness and cough. I write every day, though only a little, still I write. When I send the play you read it and see what might have been done with the subject under favourable circumstances, that is, with good health. As things are, it is just a disgrace, one writes a couple of lines a day, gets used to what is written and so on and so on.

We are having summer weather, the roses are in flower. Yesterday evening your brother dropped in.

They have taken to feeding me up ; they stuff me.

Yesterday Altschuller had a long talk with me about my illness and spoke with great disapproval of Ostroumov for sanctioning my spending the winter in Moscow ; he besought me not to go to Moscow, not to live in Moscow. He said that Ostroumov was probably drunk.

My clothes are brushed every day, the soap you sent me is superb ; to-morrow I shall wash my head with a shampoo powder. How glad I am I married you, my little pug-face ! Now I have everything, I feel you day and night.

I have cut off half the girdle from my dressing-gown, as there were unpleasant incidents. Did I tell you that Mother is

delighted with your presents ? I have taught her patience
' Thirteen ' in the form that we played it.

God be with you. I kiss and embrace you. Keep well, my
pony.

Your A—.

Describe the first performance as fully as possible.

The head-mistress has come and Masha and Mother are
obliged to go into the town on very important business, so
what is to be done now ?

354
Oct. 3, 1903. (*Yalta.*)

Why do you write in such an offended tone about the sponge
baths, pray ? Altschuller has prohibited them, it is true, but
I have not been any better for his prohibition, and I will certainly take to them again as soon as I come to Moscow. Now
I am better, though my cough does not let me forget it, especially in the mornings, and I am quickly tired. All the same I
repeat I am getting better and better every day. Masha will
tell you how I am eating now. I eat like a tiger.

If you want money get it from Vishnevsky in the office on
account of future benefits. I am expecting a telegram about
' Julius Caesar ' ; the sun is already setting, but still there is
no telegram.

Mihailovsky has just been here with the celebrated Teitel,
the examining magistrate from Samara, a Jew. Teitel will
come to see you in Moscow to arrange somehow about a theatre
ticket. Your brother has been too, tired but in good spirits ;
we fed him with supper.

Don't be cross about the play, my darling, I am copying it
slowly, because I cannot write faster. Some passages I don't
like at all, I am rewriting them and copying them out again.
But soon, pony, I shall finish it and send it off. I shall let you
know by telegram when I send it. You see I am not so stingy
as a rich actress like you ; I have been waiting all day in vain
for a telegram from you.

Darling, forgive me about the play ! forgive me ! On my
honour, I have finished it and am copying it.

Masha will tell you how much fatter I am. Your husband will arrive a fat little man, you 'll see. I am sleeping grandly, I dream of bats.

Well, pony, I kiss and embrace you. Keep well and strong. Don't forget your fat husband.

A—.

355

Oct. 4 (1903. *Yalta*).

My good darling, my better half, I am writing to you on red paper and I think the paper is a failure, it is hard to write on it, and not easy to read. I have sent Masha off to-day; this morning I received your telegram about ' Julius Caesar.' You can't imagine, pony, how you delighted me with that telegram. So it is a success ? and a great success ? Bravo ! And your letter to-day is so nice, so full of fragrance, one can read it a dozen times and it does not pall. Do write to me, my fat little wife, I appreciate it !

They are feeding me furiously. And nature responds to the same rather unceremoniously. To-day I have been twice whither even kings go on foot. My court doctor, Altschuller, will be here to-day. However that may be, my health has improved and is improving.

I love you, pony.

I kiss and embrace you. Christ be with you.

Your A—.

I shall come at the end of October. The German singer will tell Volodya [1] all sorts of yarns, you 'll see.

356

Oct. 5 (1903. *Yalta*).

My darling, pony, I ask you to do me a favour. If there is an opportunity send me some tooth-powder, get it from Hetling's, and send me at the same time my cap that I may have something to put on in the train ; if I have two caps at home, send me the warmest one. Do you understand ?

[1] Her brother Vladimir had gone to Dresden to study singing.

My health is improving. To-day I have a plaster on. For four days I shall have to fuss about with ointments. I am taking pills, powders and drops, I am eating like a boa-constrictor. I am afraid I may eat you up when I arrive. Pervuhin, a Yalta author, has been here to-day, he stayed a long time. At first I was cold with him, then I was kinder and began talking to him sincerely ; he became most effusive. His wife has inflammation of the kidneys ; they are going to Cairo.

October the Sixth. I am going on next day. Mother bids me tell you that she likes the comb very much, only it won't stay on her head, she must have something rather simpler.

It is glorious weather again to-day. I got up with a head-ache and spent a long time over the plaster, which had to be taken off. I am in a good mood and I am going to work to-day. It is morning, I am expecting the papers of October the 3rd and shall read about your company. My windows are open.

I will soon send the play. They wouldn't let me write at all yesterday. Your letter has come about ' Julius Caesar,' thank you, darling ! You write : ' I am terrified by my loneliness and by my existence being of no use to any one.' As for loneliness I understand that and admit it, but as for the uselessness of your existence—excuse me, you are not a pony, but a puppy, you have no more logic than one.

I love you. You know that, don't you ?

I have had a letter from Gorky.

Well, don't be depressed, don't mope, keep well. Greetings to all.

Your A—.

357

Oct. 7 (1903. *Yalta*).

My superb darling, my enchantment, greetings ! Yesterday N. N., a handsome lady, called upon me, she had to talk to me about business, about the Board of Management of the Gurzuf School ; we only talked of business for five minutes, but she stayed three hours literally. Literally, I am not exaggerating one minute, and I don't know how much longer she would have stayed, if Father Sergiy [1] had not come in. When she went away I could not work, my inside was all of a shake, and meanwhile my play is not yet copied, I have only just managed to drag on to the middle of Act III. It drags on and on and on, and because it drags on, it seems to me that my play is immensely long, colossal. I am horrified and have lost all relish for it. However, I am copying it to-day, don't be uneasy. I am better, though I am coughing as much as ever. I have had an affectionate, friendly letter from Tchirikov to-day. He is witty over two pages, but his witticisms are not amusing. He has sent me his photograph and that of his daughter, whom he calls 'Tchirikov's Novella'; that for some reason is not funny either, but he is a kind and warm-hearted fellow. He will send me his play,[2] which Gorky praises very highly.

When you happen to be at Muir's, buy an eighteen-kopeck packet of paper, not writing-paper, and send it to me at the next opportunity together with the cap. I am going to wash my head with your shampoo-powder to-day.

Why are you depressed? It is so unfair, you know! You are at home, you are at the work you love, you are strong and well, you have not your husband, but he is coming soon. You must be sensible!

I have not been to the town since you went away. I have not grown thinner since last year, and I believe I am fatter. The Jaeger vest with the buttons on the shoulder is tight for me, very tight. To-day I put on a clean shirt. My suit is brushed every day. It is drizzling with rain. It is warm. Well, pony, forgive me, I must write. I must end my letter. Keep well, my little dear, God be with you. I write to you often, almost every day, don't be lazy.

I kiss you on the nape of your little neck.

Your A—.

---

[1] The priest at the Autka Church. [2] 'The Chosen People.'

358

Oct. 8 (1903. *Yalta*).

My darling, I cannot write an appeal from the women students, since we have to do with the private petition of the one female student Shtchedrin and not with the petition of all the students. You consult Goltsev,[1] he 'll tell you what to do, or else wait until I come.[2]

You write that a friend who returned yesterday from Yalta told you that Kostya's son is very ill and that Kostya is very much upset. It is all nonsense. Kostya's son has been ill with a common childish ailment of no consequence, and Kostya had a letter a long time ago telling him that his son was well again. I repeat it is all nonsense. It is Kostya's way to tell alarming stories to every one.

There has already been an appeal to the papers asking for subscriptions to be sent to Stasov for the women students. We ought to make haste and produce my play and give a performance for their benefit. My play is making progress, to-day I finished copying the third act and began upon the fourth. The third act is the least dull, but the second is dull and monotonous as a spider's web.

Madame Smirnov sent me a letter but forgot to put on a stamp ; I had to pay the excess. She asks me to write to her. Tell her that I am forbidden to write letters because I am busy with my play.

I have had a letter from Nemirovitch.

I am better to-day, I am coughing less, but I have had to

[1] The editor of the magazine ' Russkaya Mysl.'

[2] O. L. wrote, Oct. 5 : ' Shtchedrin, the girl from the Women's Medical Institute of whom Kurkin spoke, has been to see me. I gave her a card to Morozov (Savva Timofeyetch, a director of the Art Theatre), and he promised to give three hundred roubles in the spring ; he says that everything has been apportioned for the season. Myeshkov is not in Moscow ; I promised her to arrange for an appeal in " Russkoye-Slovo " and in the " Courier," and will you be so good as to write to Sobolyevsky not to refuse to publish an appeal in the " Russian News," and to say that subscriptions should be sent either to the editor of the paper or to Dmitri Vassilyevitch Stasov, 20 Forshtadsky, St. Petersburg, for the needy students attending the Medical Institute ? Can you do this ? '

run out twice already.   It must be that the Yalta water con-
tains something which has a laxative effect on me.   I tell you
the holy truth, darling, if my play is not a success you can throw
the whole blame on my intestines.   It is so revoltingly nasty !
It is ages since I have had a normal motion, I don't remember
when I had, in fact.

Forgive me, my pony, for boring you with these nasty details.

Kostya was here yesterday, we spent a long time talking ;
he is a nice, good-natured fellow.

Who, who will play my governess ?

Gorky's theatre [1] in Nizhni will not come to anything, that 's
not a business for Gorky nor for Tihomirov, though Tihomirov
may well gad about the world a bit, that will do him no harm.

Shall I kiss you, my joy ?   Very well.   I kiss you on your
neck, on the back of your little head, on your forehead and on
your lips.   Don't scold your husband, he can still stand up for
himself.

Your A—.

359

Oct. 9 (1903.   Yalta).

My pony, don't write me angrily dismal letters, don't forbid
me to come to Moscow.[2]   In any case I shall come to Moscow,
and if you don't let me come to you I shall stay somewhere in
an hotel.   You see I want very little in Moscow—in the way
of conveniences—a seat at the theatre and a spacious *vater-
kloset*.   My darling, my health is much better, I have grown a

---

[1] O. L. wrote, Oct. 5 : ' Only fancy, Gorky is getting up a sort of
affiliated branch of the Art Theatre in Nizhni, he has got together a company, he is taking our Tihomirov as manager, he is inviting people to take
hundred-rouble shares, he has asked me, but you know I never have a
hundred roubles to spare ; Gorky with his hair cropped, wearing a jacket,
looks younger.'

[2] O. L. wrote, Oct. 6 : ' My dear, I simply don't know what to write
to you.   I know that you are ill, that I am for you simply a nonentity,
who comes, stays with you and goes away.   There is such a horrible
falsity in my life that I don't know how to live . . . and here I go about
desolate, I scourge myself, I blame myself on every side, I feel I am in
fault all round.   There is something I cannot cope with in life . . . of
course you must not come to Moscow at all.'

little fatter from the diet, I am coughing less and by the 1st of November I hope all will be quite well. I am in a very good mood. I am copying the play, I shall soon finish, darling, I swear I shall. I will telegraph as soon as I send it. I assure you every extra day is only to the good, for the play is growing better and better and the characters are clear now. Only what I am afraid is that there may be passages which will be struck out by the censorship; that will be awful.

My own, dove, darling, pony, don't be anxious, everything is not so bad as you think, everything is going quite well. I swear that the play is ready, I assure you a thousand times; that I have not sent it hitherto is simply because I am copying it very slowly, and making alterations as I always do when I am copying.

It is raining and cool to-day, two live quails have been brought us.

Darling, I shall *certainly* come to Moscow, whatever you do to me; and I should come even if I were not married; so if I am run over by a cab in Moscow it won't be your fault.

Act well, carefully, study, darling, be observant, you are still a young actress, don't gave way to depression, please. For God's sake!

I washed my head (did I tell you?), but the liquid didn't froth. I must have used too much water.

Madame Gorky and Madame Sredin were here yesterday. Dr. Sredin has nephritis, and he has begun to have dropsical swellings on his face. He is in great anxiety evidently, for he keeps looking how much albumen he passes.

I embrace my joy. God be with you, be calm and cheerful.

Your A—.

360

Oct. 10 (1903. *Yalta*).

Greetings, pony. To-day I have no letter from you. I am proud, it seems I am more exact than you; my health is not bad to-day, in fact it is extremely good, I am not coughing much and I have not run out at all. I am copying the play once more and will *without fail* send it within three days, whereof I will inform you by telegram.

Kostya was here to-day ; he spent a long time yesterday in a restaurant and noted down the phrases used at billiards for my play.

Set your mind at rest, all is well.

I kiss my darling. I have read that Luzhsky is to act Brutus instead of Stanislavsky. What is that for ? Do you want the receipts to go down to six hundred roubles ? I have written an appropriate part for Luzhsky, it is a short part but just the right thing for him.

My poppet, I embrace you.

Your A—.

361

Oct. 12 (1903. *Yalta*).

And so, pony, hurrah for my long-suffering and yours ! The play is finished, finally finished, and to-morrow evening, or at the latest on the morning of the 14th, it will be sent to Moscow. At the same time I shall send you some comments of a sort.

If alterations are needed they will, I fancy, be very slight. The worst thing in the play is that I wrote it not at one sitting, but over a long, a very long, period, so that it is bound to seem spun out in a way. Oh, well, we shall see ! My health is mending, I am no longer coughing much and no longer have to run out. Since Masha went away my dinners are, of course, not so good ; to-day, for instance, mutton, which I must not eat now, was served for dinner and so I had to do without meat. I eat a very nice sort of jelly. The ham is very salt, it is hard to eat. I eat eggs.

Darling, how hard it was for me to write the play !

Tell Vishnevsky to find me a job as an excise-officer. I have written a part for him, only I am afraid that after Antony the part created by Anton will strike him as inelegant and uncouth. However, he will play the aristocrat. Your part is only worked out in the third and the first acts, in the others it is only sketched in. But there again, it does not matter. I am not downhearted, and Stanislavsky ought to be ashamed to be in a panic ! Why, he began so valiantly, played Trigorin just as he pleased, and now he is crestfallen because Efros does not praise him. Well, my little growler, don't grumble at me, bless you. I love you and shall love you. I may beat you, too. I embrace you and kiss you.

Your A—.

362

TELEGRAM

Oct. 14, 1903. (*Yalta.*)

Play sent off well kiss greetings ANTONIO.

363

Oct. 14 (1903. *Yalta*).

Why do you keep grumbling so, granny ? [1] I sent for Altschuller myself as I did not feel quite the thing and was sick of trotting out. He ordered me to eat eight eggs and pounded ham. And Masha has absolutely nothing to do with it. Without you I am helpless as though I were on a desert island.

And so the play is sent off, you will probably get it at the same time as this letter. I enclose an envelope of notes which you must read when you have made acquaintance with the play. Telegraph at once after reading it ! You will give it to Nemirovitch and tell him that he, too, must send me a telegram that I may know all about it. Ask Nemirovitch to keep the play a secret so that it may not get to Efros and the others before its production. I don't like unnecessary talk.

Your letters are not cheerful, you are depressed. That is not good, my darling. And to-day there is no letter from you

[1] O. L. wrote, Oct. 10 : ' Have you at last taken your health in hand ? Why is it that when I am there it is always so difficult ? Why is it you torment me and never do anything ? . . . but as soon as I go away or as soon as you go away from me then remedies are taken and you begin feeding up and Masha can do anything for you.'

at all. If there is anything wrong in the theatre, why, you know, failures are so natural, and there will inevitably be a year or two when your company will have to put up with nothing but failures. You must stand firm. Stanislavsky was firm last year, but now he has been shaken and has begun to be despondent.

My health is all right. The day before yesterday my stomach began aching in the evening and ached all day yesterday. But to-day all is well again. To-day I have knocked off the eggs and am only going to eat half as much. Altschuller was here yesterday, he sounded me and sanctioned my going for a drive in the town. Don't I sicken you with my medical talk ? Don't I really ?

I have read that the telegraph wire is broken down between Moscow and Harkov, my telegram will be very late. To-morrow I shall sit down to write a story without haste. I can hardly believe that I am no longer writing my play. Would you believe it, I made a fair copy of it twice. Your husband has grown old, and if you take on an adorer I shall have no right to complain.

If it is proposed to produce anything new, do write and tell me, my own, write me everything.

Keep well, pony, read the play, read it attentively. There is a horse in my play, too. I bless you and embrace you many times, God be with you.

Your A—.

I. Lyubov Andreyevna will be played by you since there is no one else. She is dressed with great taste, but not gorgeously. Clever, very good-natured, absent-minded; friendly and gracious to every one, always a smile on her face.

II. Anya. Absolutely must be played by a young actress.

III. Varya. Perhaps Marya Petrovna will take this part.

IV. Gaev is for Vishnevsky. Ask Vishnevsky to listen to people playing billiards and to note down as many of the terms used as he can. I don't play billiards, or rather did play once but have forgotten it all now and it is all put down at random in my play. We 'll talk it over with Vishnevsky later, and I 'll put in all that is necessary.

V. Lopahin. Stanislavsky.

VI. Trofimov, the student. Katchalov.

VII. Simeonov—Pistchik. Gribunin.

VIII. Charlotta—is a question mark. I will put in some more of her sayings in the fourth act. Yesterday I had a bad stomach-ache while I was copying Act IV. and I could not put in anything fresh. Charlotta plays a conjuring trick with Trofimov's goloshes in the fourth act. Rayevskaya could not play it. It must be an actress with a sense of humour.

IX. Epihodov—perhaps Luzhsky.

X. Firs—Artyom.

XI. Yasha—Moskvin.

If the play will do, say that I will make any alterations required by stage conditions. I have the time, though I confess I am awfully sick of the play. If anything is not clear in it, write and tell me.

The house is an old mansion ; at one time people have lived in a very wealthy style in it, and this ought to be felt in the staging. Wealthy and comfortable.

Varya is rather crude and rather stupid, but very good-natured.

364

Oct. 15 (1903. *Yalta*).

Greetings, pony! Kostya has only just been to see me ; he rode over. Now he speaks well of Mihailovsky and praises him. By the way, Kostya moved to Madame Bonnier's the other day ; he is staying there, and I told him that I should write and tell you and that you would tease him. She has been here and was very warm in her praises of him.

I am uneasy, the telegraph wires have been broken by the storms and my telegram has probably not reached you yet. About my play I have no definite expectations. I am tired of it and so I don't like it. Now I am resting.

My health is better and better. Yesterday I ate little, I gave myself a rest, but to-day I am eating like a whale. Poor woman to have such a voracious husband !

Yesterday I demanded from the cook the list left by Masha (the programme of my dinners) and it appeared that she (the cook) had never once prepared them by the list. They have been continually giving me roast beef and mutton, salt sturgeon, soup with unmashed potato, and these were not in the list. I made a scene and asked them to cook me nothing, it ended in a reconciliation, and to-day, for the first time, I am eating a dinner according to prescription.

I ought to go and have my hair cut, darling, but it is nasty windy weather. I am told that the sea-front is flooded.

Well, write to me, my pony, scratch off a rather longer letter with your little hoof. I love you, my treasure, I embrace you.

Your A—.

Tell Masha Mother is quite well.

365

Oct. 17 (1903. *Yalta*).

Pony, I was in the town yesterday, I had my hair cut and look eight years younger. To-day I sat a long time in the garden till the sun was hidden in the mist.

I have had a telegram from Gorky, he asks for my play for his Annual and offers me fifteen hundred roubles a signature. And I don't know what to answer since, in the first place, I have had no answer yet from Moscow, and in the second, by the terms of my agreement with Marks I can only give my works to periodical publications (*i.e.* newspapers and magazines) or annuals published for a charitable object.

There are some alterations and finishing touches needed in my play, but I think they won't take more than fifteen minutes. Act IV. is not quite finished, and there ought to be a little more movement in Act II., and perhaps two or three words at the end of Act III. should be changed or it may be too much like the end of ' Uncle Vanya.'

If the play is no use now, don't be downhearted, pony, don't grieve, in a month I will so transform it that you will not know it. You see I was wearisomely long over it, writing it at long intervals with diarrhoea and a cough.

So far the cooking is all done according to the list. All quite correct.

Our Arseny sits beside Granny and is at peace with all the world, but does very little work. Write and tell me how the tickets are going for ' Julius Caesar.'

I have had a letter from Ivanenko.[1] I am expecting telegrams but don't get any. I embrace you, my own.

Your A—.

366

Oct. 19 (1903. *Yalta*).

My dear pony, darling, greetings ! I didn't write to you yesterday because all day long with a flutter at my heart I was expecting a telegram. Late last night your telegram arrived and this morning one from Nemirovitch of a hundred and eighty words. Many thanks. I was all the time in a funk, terrified. What I was most frightened about was the lack of movement in the second act and a certain incompleteness in the student Trofimov. You see Trofimov has been in exile over and over again, he is continually being sent down from the University, and how is one to express these facts ?

Darling, tell them to send me the repertoire, for I am not getting it. If there is an opportunity don't send me my cap, send me a packet of the precious paper, some tooth-powder, a packet of notepaper (the cheapest) and something interesting besides. I am living well, the cooking is scrupulously correct, though yesterday evening they did give me salt sturgeon and roast beef again, which are not on Masha's list. Tell Masha, by the way, that my digestion is getting better every day and Mother feels well. The weather is very fine, better indeed than it was.

Is my play going to be produced ? If it is, then when ?

[1] A young man who had stayed at Melihovo with the Tchehovs, to whom he was much devoted.

I have had a very nice letter from Stanislavsky, warm and sincere. Will ' The Pillars of Society ' come on this season ? You know I have not seen them yet.

I am coming early in November. I shall, in all probability, publish the play in the Gorky Annual, only I don't know how I am to get round that German, Marks.

The Odessa newspapers give a version of the contents of my play. Nothing like it.

My darling, pony, a thousand roubles for a bath ! I pine for a bath, already ferns and fungi are growing all over me.

Meanwhile do find a very good tailor who would undertake to make me a fur-coat, and do choose some soft fur. Write to me in detail on a separate sheet what things I must bring with me to Moscow. Write and tell me, too, who is to play Charlotta.

In ' Novoye Vremya ' (Wednesday) I have just read the actor Rossov's article on ' Julius Caesar.' He warmly praised Katchalov and Vishnevsky, and that 's strange as last year Rossov wrote of the Art Theatre with hatred and haughty aversion.

Mihailovsky and Kostya are here. They have just come.

Your A—.

367

Oct. 21 (1903. *Yalta*).

My dear pony, did I write to you about my failure ? The shampoo-powder won't make a lather, that is, it doesn't froth. We followed the directions on the wrapper ; the first time we thought we had used too much water, but the second time we did not know what to think. Tell us what to do.

Morozov is a good man, but he ought not to be allowed to touch matters of vital importance. Of acting, of plays, of actors, he can only judge as one of the audience and not as a manager or director.

To-day I had a telegram from Stanislavsky in which he calls my play a work of genius ; that means over-praising the play and robbing it of a good half of the success it might have under favourable circumstances. Nemirovitch has not yet sent me the list of the actors who are to take part in the play, but I am still uneasy. He has already telegraphed that Anya is like Irina, evidently he intends to give Anya to N. N.

And Anya is just as like Irina as I am like Burdzhalov.[1] Anya is first and foremost a child, light-hearted all through, knowing nothing of life, and not once crying except in Act ii., and then she only has tears in her eyes. And you know N. N. will whine through the whole part, besides she is too old. Who is playing Charlotta ?

I feel pretty middling, though my cough does not stop. I cough more than I did this time last year.

I am coming early in November ; Mother will come in the middle or at the end of the month ; she is very dull here.

Alexandr Pleshtcheyev [2] is going to publish a theatrical magazine in Petersburg after the style of ' Art and Drama.' He will smash Kugel. In January I shall send him a farce, and let him publish it. For a long while I have been wanting to write a rather silly farce.

When will the rehearsals of my play begin ? Do write and tell me, darling, don't tantalise me. Your telegram was very short ; you might, at least, try now to write a little more fully. You know I am like an exile here.

For some reason or other I keep thinking every day of our life at Madame Yakuntchikov's.[3] Such a hideously idle, absurd, tasteless way of living as in that white house, it would be hard to meet again. The people live exclusively for the pleasure of seeing General Gadon in their house or going out with Prince Obolensky, the deputy minister, and how can Vishnevsky, who looks up to these people as though they were gods, fail to understand it ? There are only two good people deserving respect in the place, Natalya Yakovlyevna [4] and Maxim.[5] The others are . . . But let us drop the subject.

[1] An actor at the Art Theatre.
[2] The son of the poet Pleshtcheyev.
[3] On whose estate Tchehov had spent part of the previous summer.
[4] N. Y. Davydov, an artist.
[5] The old footman at the Yakuntchikovs'.

And Natalya Yakovlyevna has forgotten her promise to make a little town for me.[1]

Madame Bonnier is preparing to go to Moscow, she has already ordered a white dress specially to wear at the Art Theatre.

When will your letter come at last ?   I long to read about my play, an impatience which you would understand if you lived like me in this Siberia.   However, I am beginning to get used to Yalta ;   may be, I shall train myself to work here.

Well, my pony, my good Hungarian, I embrace you and kiss you warmly ;   don't forget me, you know I am your husband and have the right to beat you, to whack you.

Your A—.

368

Oct. 23 (1903.   *Yalta*).

You write, pony, that Efros can do no harm by his lying ; however, all the newspapers, literally all the provincial ones, have republished what he says, and to-day I have seen it in the ' Moscow Courier.'   What a mischievous brute he is !

You write that Vishnevsky cannot play Gaev.   Who, then ? Stanislavsky ?   then who will do Lopahin ?   You can't give it to Luzhsky . . . he must play Epihodov.   No, you mustn't slight Vishnevsky.

It is growing colder, there is a scent of the winter.   Yesterday tall Olga Mihailovna was here, she talked about love and promised to send herrings.

There is absolutely no news.   I get up in the morning, I get through the day one way or another, and I go to bed in the evening and fall asleep quickly, and that is all.   Scarcely any one comes to see me.

Nemirovitch writes that I have a great deal of crying and some crudities in my play.   Do write and tell me, darling, what you think not right, and what they say, I 'll correct it ; it is not too late, you know, I could still remodel a whole act.

---

[1] This artist promised Tchehov a model of an old Russian town carved out of wood, and presented it to him on Jan. 17, 1904.

So the actors like Pistchik ? I am very glad. I think Gribunin will play him splendidly.

My darling, I make you a low bow, I kiss you and embrace you. Be merry and content. So far all goes well in the kitchen, that is, they cook me things from the list Masha left. I am all impatience to come to Moscow, I so long for salt meat and veal cutlets. Especially salt meat.

And I long to pet my pony, too.

Your A—.

369

Oct. 24 (1903. Yalta).

My darling, pony, what is the object of translating my play into French ? [1] Why, it is a wild idea ! the French will make nothing of Yermolay, or of the sale of the estate, and will only be bored. There is no need, darling, there is no point in it. The translator has the right to translate it without the author's permission, there is no copyright with Russia ; let Korsov [2] translate it, so long as I am not responsible for it.

No letter from Nemirovitch so far. I have diarrhoea again to-day. I ran out three times this morning ; however, I paid no attention to it, but drove out to the town, where I bought ham and so on.

The weather is cold and nasty.

If, as you write, Vishnevsky is not going to act Gaev, what part will he act in my play ?

Tchirikov's play ' The Chosen People' has been much praised, but it appears to be very mediocre and even poor. Gorky puffed it tremendously and has even arranged for its translation into foreign languages.

I read in the papers to-day that your mother, Anna Ivanovna,[3] has received a medal. I congratulate her; don't forget to tell her that if it depended upon me I should bestow a diamond medal on her. If my play comes on, I shall have the

[1] O. L. wrote, Oct. 20 : ' Korsov wishes to see me, he wants to translate " The Cherry Orchard " into French for the Parisian stage.'

[2] Korsov was a baritone in the Imperial Opera.

[3] O. L.'s mother was a professor at the Moscow Philharmonic.

right, so to speak, to order a nice fur-coat. Make a note of that. Look at furs and at tailors so that there may be no delay. What most matters is that the fur-coat should be warm and soft. I shall walk about Moscow arm in arm with my wife in a new fur-coat. If only I don't have diarrhoea. I love you, pony, and therefore I shall whack you.

My own darling, when will you listen to me ? I have asked you a thousand times to stick up your envelopes better, your letters come to me almost open.

Write to me every day as fully as possible, don't hide anything from me.

I embrace and stroke my dear wife. Don't be dull, keep well and merry.

Your A—.

370

Oct. 25 (1903. Yalta).

My dear pony, to-day the ' Crimean Courier ' and the ' Odessa News ' reprint the article in the ' News of the Day ' ; it will be reproduced in all the papers. And if I had known that Efros's performance would have such a bad effect upon me, nothing would have induced me to let the Art Theatre have my play. I feel as though I had been soused in slops and made to drink them.

I have not had the promised letter from Nemirovitch so far. And, indeed, I am not particularly looking forward to it ; Efros's sallies have spoiled my whole mood, I have grown cold and feel nothing but ill-humour.

Ekaterina Pavlovna [1] and Madame Sredin were here yesterday. Mihailovsky has been, too. I abused Tchirikov's play in a letter to you, and it turns out that I was in too great a hurry ; it was Alexin's fault, he abused the play over the telephone. Yesterday evening I read ' The Chosen People ' ; it is nothing very particular, but it is not so badly written, one might mark it three and a half.[2]

---

[1] Gorky's wife.　　　　[2] Out of a maximum of five is meant.

No, I had never meant to make Lyubov Andreyevna subdued [1] by suffering, nothing but death could subdue a woman like that. But perhaps I don't understand what you mean. It is not hard to act Lyubov, you have only to take the right tone from the very first; you will have to think of the smile and manner of laughing, you will have to know how to dress. But there, you can do it all, if only you want to, if only you are well.

I refuse to know Efros henceforward.

I am eating a great deal. Tell Masha that Arseny's brother (Pyetunka as they call him in the kitchen) has come back, he is living in our kitchen. He is a splendid gardener, would not one of our acquaintances like to have him? Tell Madame Morozov that this gardener has completed his studies in horticulture, is sober, young, well-behaved, and competent to plant a magnificent garden (not a flower-garden but an orchard). Now wouldn't she like to have a sumptuous orchard of her own of sixty to ninety acres? Seriously, do speak to her. I will answer for him, for I understand the subject very very thoroughly. They shouldn't lose the chance of him.

Marks has sent a telegram, he asks to publish ' The Cherry Orchard.'

It is cloudy. It is cool. Sredin is passing a lot of albumen. It is a bad look-out. They made an analysis for me lately but they found none. I look every year. On the other hand, I am coughing more and worse than in past years.

The leaves are still on the trees, they are not falling. I bought caviare, herrings and pilchards, but forgot to buy anchovies, so when Masha sends Granny the boots she might put in anchovies. No need, though; that was just a slip of the pen. There are anchovies at Cuba's.

Well, pony, I kiss you and embrace you; comfort me with your letters. I love you.

Your A—.

[1] O. L. wrote, Oct. 21 : ' You did mean at first, darling, to make Lyubov Andreyevna subdued by suffering; do you remember, you showed me her words in Act II., and how hard it is to play her.'

371

Oct. 27 (1903. Yalta).

Greetings, pony! You say that you write to me every day, but I didn't get a letter yesterday. The chrysanthemums are flowering furiously,[1] abundantly. The roses are in flower, too. The weather is remarkably mild and pleasant to-day.

It is now fifteen days since I sent off the play and I have not had a single letter yet, not counting yours. Altogether I have had no luck with that play. Even if it is not coming on this season they ought to have written to me all the same. Tihomirova might have written anyway. And I don't get the repertoire. Oh well, God be with you all.

I sit in the balcony every day for two or three hours. I don't go to your nook where the hammock is, it is autumn there already and desolate. The wall was finished long ago, before Masha left.

Kostya is a little unwell, he says it is fever, but he is in good spirits. You think he has a little affair on with Madame Bonnier? It may be so. She has become so light-hearted and happy. He has had your letter. But apparently writing is difficult to him, just as reading is, indeed. . . . Oh, dear Hungarian, how dreary I am! shall I go abroad or what? What do you think?

If you want your letters to arrive punctually, you should drop them yourself in the post-box. The letter which did not reach me yesterday is probably being carried about in somebody's pocket now.

I kiss you, my pony, I embrace my darling.

Your A—.

372

Oct. 28 (1903. Yalta).

My pony, I have written to you about the cap and the tooth-powder already, you have forgotten. I wrote that I don't

---

[1] O. L. wrote, Oct. 23: 'Are the chrysanthemums in flower? you don't tell me anything. What is happening in the garden? Is the wall finished? what is the weather like? is everything still green? Do you sit on the balcony, do you go into my nook where the hammock is? Answer about everything, I entreat you.'

want the cap and the tooth-powder, but that I want toilet-paper. Your photograph came to-day, and I paid twenty-eight kopecks excess on it as there were only two stamps on it instead of four. Photographs ought to be sent in a registered packet.

Pistchik must be played by Gribunin, God forbid that N. should be given that part. Firs will be done by Artyom, Yasha by Moskvin or by Gromov, who would make a very original Yasha. But Moskvin, of course, is better. And if only Marya Petrovna [1] would consent to play Charlotta, what could be better! I had thought of it, but did not dare to suggest it. That she is frail and short does not much matter. But the great thing is that N. should not play Pistchik, God forbid! Leonidov I don't know. No one but Stanislavsky ought to play the merchant. You see, it is not a merchant, in the vulgar sense of the word, that must be understood.

Still no letters from your company. I don't receive the repertoire and I have not received it. I am not likely to be lying about it.

So Naidyonov has come to grief with his 'No. 13'? Well, he ought to have listened to me and not have written a play oftener than once in five years. Why, 'Vanyushin's Children' will keep him going for a long time yet, so he need not have been in a hurry.

Efros persists in keeping himself before the public. Whatever provincial paper I open I see the hotel room, I see Tchaev.[2]

So you did go to T.'s, you did hear the recitation? Well, now blame me for not reciting my stories and plays! But if the supper was good, one can forgive anything. It is a long while since I had a good supper, by the way.

I have already written to Gorky, the play will be published in his Annual. He offers me fifteen hundred roubles a signature.

[1] Madame Stanislavsky.
[2] N. E. Efros had published a distorted version of 'The Cherry Orchard' in which Act III. was said to take place in a hotel instead of in the drawing-room, and Gaev was called Tchaev.

How does he make it out seven thousand roubles ?[1]   Why,
there are only two signatures in the whole play.

Give my greetings to Bunin and Baburin (*i.e.* Naidyonov).[2]
Remember me to Veressayev[3] if you see him ; tell him that I
like him very much.

If you order a fur-coat, please do it without the help of
Vishnevsky.   He behaves with such dignity in shops that they
always charge him three times the price. . . . And, by the
way, Vishnevsky has not sent me a single letter all this time ;
I shall drop his acquaintance.

Mother is greatly delighted with your card, only the word
' cross-eyed ' shocked her a little.

Windy.   Cool.   We have almost all the stoves in the house
going.

You see what long letters I write to you !   What do you say
to that ?   Ah, pony, pony, why, I have never once switched
you with a whip, all I can do is to pet you.   I embrace you, I
kiss you and embrace you once more.

Your A—.

Your letter with the photographs came three days late.
Evidently somebody had been carrying it about in his pocket.

373

Oct. 30 (1903.   *Yalta*).

You see what fine paper I write to you on, pony !   As to
my election to the Society of the Lovers of Literature, I can
make nothing of it.   If they have elected me a president, why
a temporary one ?   If temporary, for how long a time ?   Worst
of all, I don't know whom I ought to thank, to whom I ought
to write.   The other day I received an announcement, written
in a vile handwriting, and signed by somebody called Kallash,

---

[1] O. L. wrote, Oct. 22 : ' Gorky asks for the play for his Annual, says
that he will give it a philanthropic object so that you can give it to him
without breaking your agreement.   Why, Marks would not give you more
than a hundred and fifty roubles a signature, would he ?   And from
Gorky you would get over seven thousand, so he says.'

[2] A joke of Tchehov's referring to Turgenev's story ' Punin and Baburin.'

[3] A doctor and writer.

not written on a stamped form, so evidently not an official
notice; but how to address this Kallash and where he lives I
don't know, and so far I have not written to express my
gratitude for my election.

Stanislavsky will make a very good and original Gaev, but
then who will act Lopahin ? you see Lopahin, is the central
character.   If it is not successful the whole play is done for.
Lopahin must not be played as a loud, noisy man, there is no
need for him to be typically a merchant.   He is a soft man.
Gribunin won't do, he must play Pistchik ; the Lord preserve
you, don't give Pistchik to N., or perhaps he would like to try
his hand on Lopahin ?   I 'll write to Stanislavsky, I had a
letter from him yesterday.

To-day the Art Theatre is abused for ' Julius Caesar ' in the
' Citizen.'

Yesterday I had diarrhoea for no reason, to-day it is all
right.

If Moskvin wants to play Epihodov I shall be delighted, but
then what is there for Luzhsky ?

I 'll think a little and maybe I 'll come to Moscow, or I am
afraid Nemirovitch will distribute the parts on diplomatic
considerations.

I am dreary, I can't work, it is dull weather and cold and
one is conscious of the stoves indoors.

It appears that I need not have hurried with the play, I
might have spent another month on it.

What a misery it is cutting one's nails on one's right hand !
Without my wife I am in a bad way altogether.

I am getting used to the dressing-gown you sent me.   But
to Yalta now, I can never get used.   In fine weather it seemed
as though all was well, but now I see—it is not home ! it is just
as though I were living now at Birsk, the place we saw when we
sailed down the White River together.

Have you received the chrysanthemums ?   In what condition ?   If good I will send some more.

I kiss my little beetle.   Be a merry little thing.

Your A—.

374

Nov. 1 (1903. *Yalta*).

My darling, Hungarian, yesterday there was no letter from you and I was bored. Nothing new has happened except perhaps that I have ordered my dark-blue suit to be put away, and have changed it for something warmer.

I have had a letter from Nemirovitch. I had not received it, but I have received it at last. Vishnevsky absolutely can't play Pistchik, it is Gribunin's part. I don't know why Marya Petrovna so wants to play Anya; why, it is a meagre part, uninteresting. Varya, to my thinking, is much more suitable for her. Nemirovitch writes that she is afraid of Varya's being like Sonya in ' Uncle Vanya.' Whatever resemblance is there ? Varya is a nun, a foolish creature.

To-day it is windy and cold. They are celebrating my literary jubilee, they evidently want to do me honour, that is, to tell even more lies about me; and meanwhile my jubilee (twenty-five years) will be in another two or three years, not before.

Write me a list of what I must bring with me to Moscow, else I shall bring nothing.

Write to me, pony, every day, as on the days when there is no letter from you I am as glum and cross as a toothless old dog.

Your shampoo-powder was no use, it won't make a froth and doesn't lather the head.

Well, take care of yourself, and be merry, my wife. As soon as you write ' Come ! ' I 'll come at once ; I want to go to the baths ! to the baths !

Your A—.

You can send one packet of toilet paper in a registered parcel, only take off the string and make it into a roll.

375

Nov. 3 (1903. *Yalta*).

Greetings, my darling ; soon, very soon I shall come, though I don't believe that my play will come on in December; they will put it off until next season, that 's what I expect.

About Efros I hope that I shall write to you no more, forgive me, my own. I feel just as though I had brought up a little daughter and Efros had taken and outraged her. But it is ridiculous that to-day Nemirovitch in the ' News of the Day ' answers some provincial paper that Efros has given the contents of my play quite correctly. Either Nemirovitch has not read Efros' account or he is afraid of Efros, or he has some special view of his own. In any case, it is nasty.

To-day it is still and damp. The stoves are heated. My intestines are still in a bad way.

I have given Gorky the play for his Annual. That Tchirikov is going to publish or edit a magazine in Moscow I hear for the first time from you. What 's that for ? Who wants Tchirikov as an editor ? He should go on writing his stories. And Gorky is getting up a theatre.

The sun has peeped out.

I remember that when I was with Marks in the summer he offered me five thousand roubles ; I think of it and regret that I did not take it. Tell Masha that our neighbour, Mandrazhi, has sold his land for forty thousand to some Petersburg gentleman.

If you see Gorky tell him to get the play from Nemirovitch for printing. By the way, you write that you have got the play. You know that is the only copy, mind you don't lose it, or it would be very ridiculous. I have already burnt the rough copies.

Nemirovitch is evidently in a very nervous state, he ought to have a rest. Where is Sulerzhitsky now ? What is he doing ? What is he dreaming about ? Does he still want to buy land ?

The chrysanthemums are in flower, the trees are still green, but there is snow on the mountains. I long to walk up and down Kuznetsky and Petrovka in a new fur-coat.

Well, I embrace my pony warmly and kiss her. I can imagine how Muratova and you laughed [1] when you played in ' Julius Caesar.' God be with you.

Your A—.

---

[1] O. L. wrote, Oct. 29, describing how she and an actress, Muratova, had come on in the crowd of ' Julius Caesar ' and how funny every one had thought it.

376

Nov. 5 (1903. Yalta).

My darling, marmot, I had a letter from you yesterday about a rug, and to-day I went myself into the town. You write about ' a pale yellow quilt with a greenish shade in it, light coloured,' while I have rummaged among all the Bokhara rugs and I did not find a single light one, they are all more green with a yellowish tone. And the salesman told me that they never have pale yellow ones on sale. There was nothing for it, I took one. If it does not do, fly into a rage, and fling it away.

It is very nice out of doors to-day, soft and bright. Don't give my play to Tchlenov, don't give it to any one, don't read it aloud. To-day I have had a letter from Stanislavsky, with inquiries about the house, whether it is built of stone or wood and so on and so on ; I will answer him. . . .

The Moscow Repetilov [1]—the alienist Bazhenov—is here, and has already been to see me. He hates the Art Theatre, from partiality for the Little Theatre.

I have had a letter from Vishnevsky which is not quite pleasant. He complains that they are not giving him a part in ' The Cherry Orchard ' and so on and so on, and twice underlines some sentences. A queer letter.

You can see better what the Moscow weather is ; when you tell me, I shall come. Write to me how ' Lonely Lives ' has gone, whether there was a full house, whether Luzhsky was good. Your brother, Kostya, is still in Yalta, he is waiting for Mihailovsky, who has gone to Petersburg. I don't think he will get out of Yalta before the 15th of November.

I have read Nemirovitch's letter in the ' News of the Day,' and only now grasp how the misunderstanding has arisen. He writes that there are no errors in the review, apparently there are a great many slips of the pen in my play, and that the drawing-room is called an hotel room. If so, bid them correct it, darling. Because they play billiards it does not follow that it is in an hotel. But can it really not be clear from the context ?

---

[1] A character in Griboyedov's ' Woe from Wit.'

However, I can make nothing of it. I don't imagine that Nemirovitch would tell a lie simply to shield Efros. So do write to me what there is in my play, if it is an hotel or a drawing-room ; if it is an hotel, telegraph.

I shall come to Moscow, and at once to the baths, then supper, then sleep. Ah dog, dog !

God be with you. There is nothing new except the rug I bought for you. I embrace you, my precious pony.

Your A—.

377

Nov. 7 (1903. *Yalta*).

My darling, pony, greetings ! There is no news, everything is all right, absolutely everything. I don't want to write, I want to come to Moscow, but I am waiting for your permission.

Von Polenz, author of ' A Peasant,' a delightful writer, is dead. I have had letters both from Nemirovitch and from Stanislavsky, both of them are apparently in perplexity ; you told them that I did not like my play, that I was anxious about it. But do I really write so unintelligibly ? There is only one thing I am anxious about—that is that Simov should not paint an hotel room for Act III. They must correct that mistake. I have been writing about it for a month, and they only shrug their shoulders by way of answer ; evidently they like its being an hotel room.

Nemirovitch has sent an express telegram asking for an express reply, to say who is to play Charlotta, Anya and Varya. For Varya he offers a choice of three names—two unknown to me and the third, Andreyeva. There was nothing for it but to choose Andreyeva. That was cunningly contrived.

It is a long time since Kostya has been here. Very likely he will come to-day. Mihailovsky will be detained in Petersburg, apparently Kostya won't go home very soon.

Darling, do rescue me from here. I have sent the rug off by Bazhenov, who came yesterday to say good-bye. If you don't like it, send it back, I will change it.

' The Bankrupt ' [1] is a failure at the New Theatre. I saw that play splendidly acted, I thought it an excellent play, and indeed so it is. The men's parts are written in a masterly way.

To-day I overslept myself and did not wake till nine. I feel pretty well, I think. The only thing is diarrhoea. I must make a change and lead a more immoral life—I must eat all sorts of things, mushrooms and cabbage and everything, and drink wine. What do you think ?

Tell Vishnevsky to take more exercise and not to get excited.

Well, my poppet, I embrace you. Make haste and rescue me.

Won't it really be interesting to see your husband in a new fur-coat ?

A—.

Don't write to me about roast duck,[2] don't torture me. When I come I 'll eat a whole duck.

378

Nov. 8 (1903. Yalta).

My darling, my little beetle, I have just received the letter in which you glorify me as a superman and lament your own lack of talent. Many thanks.

Yesterday I had a letter from a certain Yanina Berson, who writes that the students in Geneva ' have nothing to fill their bellies with, no chance of work and, as they don't know the language, they are starving like rats.' She is a friend of Gorky's. She asks for a copy of ' The Cherry Orchard ' in order to give a performance for their benefit. The students will act it, she says. As she says that she meets you at the theatre, please tell her that I cannot give any one ' The Cherry Orchard ' until it has been produced by the Art Theatre, as the play is not yet ready and may want some alterations, that she shall have the play in December or January, and meanwhile the students of Geneva had better act something else, for

---

[1] Björnson's play.

[2] O. L. wrote, Nov. 2 : ' We had crayfish soup, roast duck and Guryev's pudding. Nice ? '

instance Tchirikov's ' The Chosen People,' a very suitable play and a very decent one in every respect. Do you hear ? Tell her that. I am not answering her, for I do not know by what name to address her. She appears to be atrociously coarse.

We are having rain, 10 degrees of heat. To-day I am going to wash my head. Half my kingdom for a bath ! Kostya is dining with us to-day and so we are having duck and cauliflower for the occasion. But the ducks here are hard and stringy as birds of prey.

In the newspapers to-day they say that the Crimean Railway is to be laid not by Mihailovsky, but by some other engineer. Apparently it is Madame Bonnier's gossip.

Olga Mihailovna brought me some oysters and some herrings. Every one in the house was so horrified at the oysters, looked at them with such terror and superstitious awe, that I had to abandon all idea of opening them. The herrings are very good. In fact, life would evidently be impossible for me without Olga Mihailovna. Madame Bonnier is soon coming to Moscow and has ordered in Odessa a fur-coat and several dresses for the occasion.

My jubilee is an invention. They have never yet written the truth about me in the papers. I don't think the year of my jubilee can be earlier than 1906. And all this talk and preparations for a jubilee simply irritate me.

As soon as you write to me that I may come, I will get a ticket. The sooner the better.

Don't study your part too much, you must first talk it over with me, and don't order your dresses until I come.

Muratova can be amusing in everyday life ; tell her that she must be funny in Charlotta, that 's the chief thing. But I doubt whether Marya Petrovna can do Anya ; . . .

When shall I see you at last ? When shall I be beating you ? I embrace you, pony.

Your superman who runs so often to a super-watercloset.

A—.

379

Nov. 10, 1903. *Yalta.*

Dear Knippusha, my dog, greetings. If you are asking about Balmont's book ' Let Us Be as the Sun,' I received the afore-said book long ago. There is only one thing I can say about it : it is a very fat book. I received from Stanislavsky a letter to-day telling me that the rehearsals of ' The Cherry Orchard ' are beginning to-day, November 10, and that Sergey Savvitch Mamontov is going to Japan as the correspondent of ' Russky Listok.'

In his letter Stanislavsky says that there will be the same scenery for the third and fourth acts. And I am glad, glad not because the scenery will be the same, but because the third act will evidently not be in an hotel as, for some reason, Nemirovitch and Efros were so anxious that it should.

Here it is rainy, damp. I don't go out of doors. But I am continually trotting off—anyway it 's exercise.

As for my tidiness, don't be uneasy, darling. I change my shirt often, I change my suit every day, I clean my teeth, if not every day, at least oftener than once every two days. The only thing is that I don't go to the baths, but that is not my fault, not a bit. Hot baths make me weak and give me cold.

Do describe the rehearsals in your letters. There is no news, everything is all right. It is too dark to write, though it is only 3 o'clock in the day. If you have not yet been false to me, I embrace you and kiss you a number of times.

Your A—.

380

Nov. 12 (1903. *Yalta*).

Poppet, I read to-day in the papers about ' Lonely Lives ' and was rejoiced. Do your best, pony, you will have your reward. And with what pleasure I shall see ' Lonely Lives ' ! I shall see it not once but five times.

Two or three days ago I heard from Masha that the felt

over-boots were bought. I expected them yesterday, I expected them to-day, and at last I gave it up. Granny has rheumatism, and I am in a horrid plight, without toilet paper. And I have been asking for it ever since the beginning of September. Perhaps I don't write clearly. Last year there was the bother over the address and this year over a beastly 'hotel' and the paper. I simply can't understand what's the matter.

Madame Bonnier will soon be coming to Moscow, she is taking Mother with her. They had meant to go at the beginning of next week, but now it is evident they won't be able to get off till November 20. I shall remain *solo*.

To-day the weather is simply exquisite. Still and bright. About translating my plays, tell everybody that you know nothing about it, that I do not answer your questions and so on and so on. You see, I can't forbid it, let any one translate them who wants to, no good will come of it anyhow.

Tell Sulerzhitsky not to go away without seeing me, I must talk to him about his agricultural plans. He must buy himself a plot of land in the Moscow province and not in Tchernigov. One can grow even pine-apples in the Tchernigov province, but there is no market, while in the Moscow province every cucumber, however yellow, can be disposed of.

There is no gaiety in my letters, I am conscious of it, darling. I am in the dumps, I am cross, I cough and I keep having to run out. There is no news. Your brother is still in Yalta. Yesterday I told Madame Bonnier as a secret that he had won twenty-five thousand in a lottery; so there will soon be a paragraph about it in the papers.

We have just had dinner. It has been settled at dinner that Mother should go to Moscow with Nastya, our maid; she is to go next week, on Tuesday, by the mail train. That is, she will leave on November the 18th or 19th. She is sick of Yalta. You must arrange that she should see 'Lonely Lives' and 'Julius Caesar.' She will stay at Vanya's, and then she says will find rooms for herself, so as to stay in Moscow till the spring.

It will be rather hard for me to get up to the 3rd or 4th floor, especially in a fur-coat. Why haven't you changed your quarters ? But never mind, I shall stay indoors in Moscow, I shall only go to the baths and to your theatre.

I embrace you, pony, I stroke your little hoofs, I stroke your tail. Be well and merry.

Your A—.

Nastya is triumphant.

I remember I had a letter from Madame Flachs [1] and I remember I gave an evasive answer, I refused. I believe it was about ' Uncle Vanya.'

When are you going to send for me ?

381

Nov. 16 (1903. *Yalta*).

My sweet darling, I have not written to you for so long because I have been frightfully out of spirits and was afraid of saying silly things in my letter. To-day is Sunday, the air is still and I am in a better mood, though in reality nothing has changed, everything is as it was.

Don't come and fetch me in a covered cab, I am always sick in a shut-up carriage. Much the best is an ordinary sledge. I received the repertoire from the theatre on Monday and from you on Saturday, when it was already out of date. If Tihomirova has taken to sending it again, don't you trouble.

Mother is setting off the day after to-morrow, Tuesday. She will go by the mail train, she does not like the express. She will stay at Vanya's in Moscow.

If you have not yet sent off the felt boots and the paper, don't send them. I ought to have telegraphed to Muir and Merrilees in September, but I did not think of it.

Tell Masha that Mother will bring the English magazine and the apples. Nastya is wild with joy at going to Moscow.

My neighbour, Mandrazhi, has sold his land, they say to a Petersburg man. Olga Mihailovna has eaten too many oysters

---

[1] O. L. wrote, Nov. 7 : ' Tchumina asks me to tell you that a German literary man, Flachs, who has translated and produced Gogol's plays, is asking through the Vengerovs permission to translate " The Cherry Orchard " in order to produce it in the best Berlin theatre. . . . Flachs's wife is a Russian.'

and is ill. Her telegram about the teacher or governess was not meant for you, but for you to hand on to Masha—so she says, at least.

I have an unbearable temper, forgive me, darling. I kiss and embrace you warmly.

Your A—.

382

(Nov. 17, 1903. Yalta.)

Can you imagine, pony, that in my old age I am going to wear a fur-coat or a collar of imitation sealskin ? I want a fur-coat which should be

(1) Very warm and very light.
(2) Fastened with buttons like a coat.
(3) Should have a collar not of imitation or dyed fur, but of real good fur.

And the cap should be of the same fur as the collar. You are a miser, while I have never had a fur-coat made for me, though I have spent a tremendous lot of money. Surely there is nothing wrong in my having a fur-coat that will cost 300 or even 400 roubles (including the cap) ? Think it over with Vishnevsky.

The sleeves ought to be rather long, or at any rate not short. So you are ordering the fur-coat now ? Or will you wait till I come ? Do as you think best.

Mother is going to-morrow. The weather is perfectly calm, yet she is going to drive though she is not afraid of sea-sickness.

My jubilee will not be just yet, not for some years. I should have to look through my old letters and papers to see when I received my first cheque.

There is no news, everything is as always. I will bring the linen and all the contents of my trunk as you have written. I will not depart one millimetre from the list.

I am without toilet paper. I have been feeling fearfully irritable for the last three weeks.

Well, take care of yourself, God be with you. I embrace my pony and kiss her.

Your A—.

383

TELEGRAM

17/XI. (1908.   *Yalta*).

All is well.

384

TELEGRAM

20/XI. (1903.   *Yalta*).

Defer ordering coat await letter Antonio.

385

Nov. 21 (1903.   *Yalta*).

My dear, long-suffering wife, my pony, to-day at last the parcel has arrived.   Granny is delighted with the felt boots and the slippers, she has just been in to thank me ; I have put the other slippers on Mother's table ; and the shelf is very pretty, or at least I thought so.

Thank you, my own !   And forgive me, forgive my grumbling ; but I could not help it, since I was wretched all the time.

I have received the plan of the first act.   It will be a two-storeyed house, with two wings, also of two storeys,

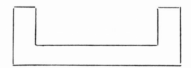

but you know in the yard formed by those wings there would be very little sun, cherries would not grow there.

I telegraphed to you to-day about the fur-coat.   I am so afraid you will order a coat the wrong shape, without buttons and with a dyed seal collar.   Wait a little, darling, I shall soon be coming.

N. was here to-day, she stayed an agonising time.

The shelf is just right to hang over the photographs.   You are mistaken in your supposition.   I have not quarrelled with

Mother. It pained me to see how miserable she was and I insisted on her going—that 's all. She is not fitted for life in the Crimea.

I embrace you, my kind, delightful, practical pony, I embrace you and kiss you. God be with you. Don't be cross if you think I don't write much to you.

I write little but I love much.

Your A—.

386

Nov. 21 (1903. *Yalta*).

My dear pony, all this time I have been displaying my nasty temper, forgive me. I am a husband and they say that husbands always have nasty tempers. I have just been rung up on the telephone, it was L. speaking from Sevastopol ; he told me he was coming to see me this evening and perhaps will stay the night, and again I shall be raging. Make haste, make haste and summon me to you in Moscow ; in this place it is bright and warm but I am already demoralised, I cannot appreciate its charms as I ought, I want the sleet and bad weather of Moscow ; I can't exist without the theatre and literature. And you must admit that I am married, I want to see my wife.

Kostya has gone at last. He is a splendid fellow, it is pleasant to be with him. Mihailovsky was here yesterday ; it was settled that Kostya will live in Yalta while the line is being constructed.

No letter from you to-day. Yesterday I telegraphed to you about the fur-coat. I asked you to wait for a letter. I am afraid you are cross. But never mind, we shall make it up. There is plenty of time before us.

The weather is quite like summer. There is no news. I am not writing anything, I keep waiting for you to allow me to pack and come to Moscow. To Moscow, to Moscow ! That is not said by ' Three Sisters ' but by ' One Husband.'

I embrace my little turkey.

Your A—.

387

Nov. 23 (1903. Yalta).

Greetings, Hungarian pony, how are you? How soon are you going to write for your husband? Yesterday the schoolmaster from Gurzuf, a very interesting young man who kept biting his beard and making efforts to talk about literature, was here from early morning till dinner time; after dinner, from 3 o'clock till evening, the very charming head-mistress was here, together with a *dame de classe* whom she brought to have a look at me; I have had L. too, who never for one instant ceased talking about literature. And how you caught it from me! I sat with my visitors, listened, fretted and was all the time swearing at you. Keeping me here in Yalta is simply pitiless.

When Mihailovsky was here last he told me that Kostya will be one of the principal people on the building of the railway, he will be living in Yalta. I tell you this in answer to your question about Kostya.

I have had a letter from Meierhold. He says he has been laid up for a week and has haemorrhage from the throat.

Stanislavsky wants to have a train pass in Act II., but I think he must be restrained from that. He wants frogs and corn-crakes.

Sharik is turning into a very good dog. He barks day and night. Only he has got sharp teeth, the rascal.

Mme. Sredin has arrived. Keep well, dear little soul. I was almost writing ' dear little fool.' It is getting dark. I embrace my ladybird.

Your A—.

388

(Nov. 25, 1903. Yalta.)

Darling, German pony, I sent you the testimonial you asked for. I believe I have written it all right. If it is not the right thing, Yegor must wait a little.[1] Tell him that I decided to wait a little longer, and if my wife does not send for me at last, I shall come to Moscow without any permission. Tell him that.

I have had a letter from Sulerzhitsky. He writes that things are not going quite well with your company, it seems there are some misunderstandings. If it is true it is a pity. But I imagine it is all nonsense, mere talk and rumour.

Olga Mihailovna has gone, by now she is in Moscow. Mother has arrived in Moscow, and you, *i.e.* Masha and you, are convinced by now that there have been no misunderstandings between us. She went away because she was very, very dull, I insisted upon it. I fancy that by December she will get tired of Moscow and then she can come back to Yalta with Masha.

The weather is amazing, like paradise, not one centipede, not one gnat, but I am afraid that as soon as I am on the steamer the wind will begin blowing. Arseny has grown fat and is enjoying life.

Sharik has grown big, he barks day and night. So Nemirovitch did not read my play to the Society of Lovers of Literature ? We began with misunderstandings and with misunderstandings we shall end—such, it seems, is the fate of my play.

If my fur-coat is heavy, don't ask for mercy, I shall beat you and smash you to smithereens. Tell them not to line it with wadding, wouldn't something like eider-down be better ? If you see Kostya before I do, tell him that Madame Bonnier has recovered.

Well, I embrace you—God be with you.

Your A—.

Nov. 25.

Don't be stingy, try to get the fur-coat as light as possible ; even my overcoat is too heavy for me now, you know.

389

Nov. 27 (1903. Yalta).

Darling, the dog in the first act must be long-haired, small, with no life in it, with sour eyes. Snap won't do. Apparently

---

[1] Yegor was a footman in Stanislavsky's service ; he wanted to get the job of a shopman in a wine-shop and through O. L. had asked Tchehov to give him a reference.

I sháll be permitted to go to Moscow next August, not before. My dear chief, my stern wife, I will live on nothing but lentils, I will get up respectfully when Nemirovitch or Vishnevsky comes in, only do allow me to come. You know it is revolting to live in Yalta and thanks to the Yalta water and excellent air have to be on the trot all day. It is time for you, cultured people, to understand that I always feel infinitely worse in Yalta than in Moscow. The sea has been still and calm but now it is raging, immense waves leap up almost to the sky, and you will keep me here till I shall not be able to leave here or to go anywhere.

I shall travel in a sleeping carriage; don't bring the fur-coat to the train, it will get cold, I shall put it on in the waiting-room.

How miserly you have grown! You will be sticking used stamps on to your envelopes next. Why don't you telegraph anything? I am afraid you will send my summons to Moscow by post and not by telegraph. I will give you ten roubles, only don't be stingy, telegraph, don't be a miser.

Tell Mother that the spectacle-glass was dropped by the head-mistress, who, by the way, has promised to come and see me again before I go away.

It has turned cold. I will wait a little longer and then if you don't write or telegraph I will go to Nice or somewhere a little more lively.

I embrace you, pony. God be with you, my joy. And so I am waiting and waiting.

Your A—.

390

Nov. 29 (1903. *Yalta*).

I really don't know what to do and what to think, pony. You persistently don't ask me to come to Moscow and apparently don't intend to ask me. You should write openly and tell me why it is, what is the reason, and I would not waste time, I would go abroad. If only you knew how depressingly the rain patters on the roof, how I long for a sight of my wife. But have I a wife? Where is she?

I am not going to write any more, say what you like. There is nothing to write about and nothing to write for.

If I get a telegram to-day I will bring you some sweet wine. If I don't you won't get a button.

Snap, I repeat, won't do; what is wanted is that mangy little dog you saw, or one of that sort. Or, there need be no dog at all.

Well, I embrace you.

Your A—.

391

TELEGRAM

30 XI. (1903. Yalta).

.　　.　　.　　.　　.　　.　　.　　.

Early in December Tchehov went to Moscow and remained there until February 15, 1904.

392

(Feb. 15, 1904. Near Oryol.)

My dear love, I am having a good journey, I had some very bad beetroot-soup, and I miss you. By now you know what is the matter with Lyova,[1] write to me exactly. Be well, serene and merry, my darling, don't think about your husband. I feel well, my health is magnificent, don't be uneasy, my dear. The line is clear, there are no delays, we are having a good journey. Do write to me, I beg you, write me long letters, I shall be dreary in Yalta, do understand that. Give my greeting to all 'The Cherry Orchard,' even Muratova.

Your A—.

393

(Feb. 16, 1904. Lozovaya.)

Greetings to you from Lozovaya, where I am sitting in the refreshment-room eating fish. So far all goes well, the weather

[1] O. L.'s nephew, who was seriously ill at the time.

is warm, there is not much snow.   To-morrow morning I will
write, and meanwhile I kiss you and embrace you.

Your A—.

394

(Feb. 17, 1904.   Sevastopol.)

Greetings, my incomparable pony ！   I write this on the
steamer, which is leaving in three hours' time.   I have had a
good journey, everything has gone well.   Nastya is on the
steamer with Snap.   Snap feels quite at home, he is very sweet.
In the train, too, he behaved exactly as though he were at home,
barked at the guards and amused everybody ;   he was highly
delighted at seeing me, now he is sitting on deck with his legs
stretched out behind him.   Apparently he has forgotten
Moscow already, mortifying as it is.   Well, pony darling, I
shall be expecting letters from you.   I can't exist without your
letters, let me tell you.   Either write every day or else divorce
me, there is no middle course.

I hear Snap overhead has begun barking at some one.   I
expect passengers are playing with him.   I will go and see.

And so all is well, thank God, couldn't be better.   I trust
the sea will not be rough.

I kiss my directress and embrace her a million times.   Write
fully, don't spare your ink ;   my dear, good, nice, talented
actress, God be with you.   I love you very much.

Your A—.

395

TELEGRAM

18/II. (1904.   *Yalta*).

Splendid journey.

396

(Feb. 18, 1904.   Yalta.)

My dear, nice, good darling, I love you very much.   How are
you getting on in Moscow ?   This is only my first day in Yalta,
yet I am already plunged into the *kur-ort* life here ;   the head-

mistress has been, my brother Alexandr and his family have arrived. The weather is pretty middling ; as for my mood, I can't tell you anything ; the new table has arrived ; I am busy now moving my things on to it.

To-morrow there will be a letter from you, I am looking forward to it and shall look forward to it with impatience. Visitors, visitors, visitors endlessly, they won't let me write, they spoil my mood, one man stays all day long in my study. I kiss you warmly, darling. Snap feels quite at home ; he does not fret, plays with the other dogs, altogether I fancy he is not particularly intelligent, or is even rather stupid.

My brother will stay over a month in Yalta. And his family too. The table has turned out all right, the same size as the old one.

My brother is staying not far away, at Horoshevitch's. My kind pony, I shall write again to-morrow.

Your A—.

397

Feb. 20 (1904.   *Yalta*).

My darling pony, it 's dreary, cold, uninteresting without you, and you have so spoiled me that I am afraid I shan't know how to dress and undress when getting up and going to bed. My bed is hard and cold, the rooms are cold, outside it is freezing, dreary, not a sniff of spring. All to-day I have been busy with last year's letters and old newspapers, I seem to have nothing else to do now. . . .

Snap is either deaf or stupid. He might never have been away from here, he jumps about with the other dogs and sleeps obediently in Mother's room. He is very good-humoured but does not understand much.

Nastya is doing the cooking, but not very well ; we ought to get a cook. To-day I had fried sturgeon, very rich and good, and soup that was like dish-water. And pancakes that were cold as ice.

I ate everything in the train (that is in answer to your question), all except a ham sandwich. I had a good journey.

The table is here, I am writing on it. The drawers are rather stiff to open. On the whole it is nice. But the other things have not come yet. 'Kashtanka' has arrived, an elegant edition, badly illustrated, one of Marks's.

I have not yet been into the town, I have not been out of doors. I have no wife, she is in Moscow, I live like a monk. I am sorry I did not bring the cup with me. The one I have here seems small; perhaps I am wrong about it. Arseny has grown lazy or forgetful, Nastya brushes my clothes; I keep my teeth clean. I shall go to the baths in May when I come to Moscow, till then I shall grow a crop of maize—anyway, I shall be making something.

To-day I had a letter from you—the first of the season. Thanks, my angel, I kiss you, I embrace you, I pat you.

I wish they would make haste and beat the Japanese, the papers seem so queer, and people too; there is a lot of lying, the exchange has fallen, interest in anything except the war has dried up in people.

What misunderstandings between us are you talking about,[1] darling? When did you irritate me? Bless you! We had an extraordinary, wonderful time together this winter, I feel as though I had come back from a campaign. I do thank you, my joy, for being so nice as you are.

Write to me, or I will beat you as my habit is. I kiss you and embrace you, my joy. Keep well and merry.

Your A—.

398

Feb. 22 (1904. *Yalta*).

Darling, German pony, how are you feeling? Here the cold is almost insufferable, it's windy, altogether it is a desperate climate. I think of Moscow as of the Riviera. Snap has completely settled down and turned into a yard-dog. He barks a great deal.

I have been in the town to-day. It is disgustingly cold.

---

[1] O. L. wrote on Feb. 15 asking whether she caused Tchehov many annoyances in Moscow.

How is Lyova ? What have they settled ? How awful it is,
you still keep buying him toys ! That's ruin for children.
But it is no good my writing that, you won't believe me.

You write that Lyova is running about and is all over the
place. How is that ? Why, Kostya said in one of his letters
to you, that he can't use his legs. . . . I am not having a very
good time. What do they say about Kommissarzhevskaya's
performances ? Have you been to them ? And what sort of
houses are you having, my darling ?

They talk all sorts of nonsense about the war here.

N. irritates you, but, my good darling, don't give way to
your irritation, don't forget that the woman is ill. My things
have not yet come. I am writing this letter at the new
table.

God be with you, don't forget your husband ; anyway, he
loves you probably more than all the rest put together.

Good-bye, my piccolo, I kiss you on the shoulder and embrace
you.

Your A—.

399

Monday (Feb. 23, 1904. Yalta).

My wonderful doggy from over the seas, I am alive and well
in spite of the disgusting weather. I am not coughing, I am
eating well and a great deal. To-day I had soup and sturgeon
for dinner, very nice. We have a new cook ; I have not yet
seen her, but so far I approve of her cooking.

Is Marya Fyodorovna leaving ? That's a pity, anyway.
It is true that she is not an exceptional actress, but you have
only to give her part to X to see the difference. I think she
will come back to the Art Theatre.[1] And I fancy that Gorky
has nothing to do with it.

Lyova won't be humpbacked.

So Kommissarzhevskaya is a success ? There you are !
The Efroses and Luboshitses are on her side, it seems.

[1] M. F. Andreyev had given notice of her intention to leave the
Art Theatre.

There is a mist over the mountains to-day, it is cloudy and cold.

If the Moscow flat were not so idiotically high up, I should be pining for Moscow now. My own darling, find out about Tsaritsyno.[1] And are there no other houses near the station ? I don't think we could think of anything better than Tsaritsyno. It is particularly nice there in the winter. Only it is not worth ten thousand ; taking into consideration the house itself, the lack of convenience (so necessary for a writer) and the fact that the lease only runs for another eleven or twelve years, and so on and so on, they ought to let us have it cheaper. We should have to lay out two or three thousand on repairs.

I embrace and kiss my darling. God be with you, don't worry. I have unpacked everything and put everything away, I have scarcely anything to do. I am sleeping well.

Your A—.

400

Feb. 24 (1904. *Yalta*).

My darling, my things have evidently been lost, there is no sight nor sound of them. So all these offerings have been for nothing, and for nothing I bought the mushrooms. I ought to have received them on the 16th or 17th (by passenger train) and now it is the 24th and none of the authorities have heard anything about the things. My trousers are lost, and the model town, and Stahovitch's inkstand.

Tell Vishnevsky that Ilnarskaya is going all over Russia with ' The Cherry Orchard ' and prints on her posters ' Performance is authorised by special permission of the author.' I have never given any sort of permission.

Why is Lyova going to Eupatoria instead of to Yalta ? The weather here is exceptionally bad, idiotic, and meanwhile the daisies are out and the almond-trees are just going to come out too. My darling, I like Tsaritsyno. Honour bright, I do !

I had a manuscript and a letter to-day from an author ; he begs me ' on his knees ' to read it, says that he is only twenty, that he is in despair.

---

[1] The Tchehovs had looked at a house in Tsaritsyno which they had some idea of buying.

There is no news, everything is as of old. The cook seems to cook pretty well. I am eating a great deal. Snap is in the yard all the time, he sleeps in Mother's room. He is thinner.

I sleep well.

I kiss my dog, I embrace her and give her a good stroking. Be well, merry, calm.

Your A—.

401

Feb. 25 (1904. Yalta).

My good, wonderful dog, thank you, I get letters every day. And to-day at last the things have come. I thought before that there would be a lot of them, and, after all, they do not amount to much; I 've hung them on the wall and arranged them on the table and one does not seem to notice them. But I am glad of the soap, to-day I will wash my head. The parcel has come and now I have nothing to look forward to.

Did I write to you? Marks sent me 1000 roubles instead of 250 for the story ' Betrothed.' You see what liberal gentlemen these Germans are.

With the things came the frog, which is standing on my table. The loathsome inkstand has come too.

And the weather is still awful. There are a few things in blossom in the garden, but I don't see them, I don't care to look at them. There is a mist over the mountains, it is cold, un-utterably damp. It is warm indoors. I am sleeping well though I fancy for some reason that my bed is hard. I am eating splendidly. I cough as much as I did in Moscow, that is, I scarcely cough at all. Altschuller has been to see me twice already; both times to call and chat. Dr. Dmitriyev, one of Yalta's oldest inhabitants, is dead.

Sofya Petrovna Sredin has come.

There is no other news, keep well and merry and the heavenly angels keep you. Remember that I love you, dog.

Your A—.

Snap is certainly not intelligent.

402

Feb. 27 (1904. *Yalta*).

My good spouse, you have no faith in me as a doctor, but still I will tell you that Korsakov [1] is inclined to be pessimistic, he always suspects the worst. I had a patient once, a little girl whom I attended for two or three months ; Korsakov was invited for a consultation, he declared she could not recover ; but she is alive to this day and has been married for years. If there is tuberculosis of a vertebra, that is still a long way from tuberculosis of the brain or of the spinal marrow. Only they ought not to take the boy about to see people or to allow him to hop about too much. And again, I ask, why did they pitch on Eupatoria ?

All the time I have been in Yalta, that is, since February 17th, there has not been one glimpse of sunshine. The damp is awful, the sky is grey, I sit indoors.

My things have come, but they have rather a dejected look. To begin with, there are fewer of them than I imagined ; and secondly, both the ancient boxes were cracked on the journey. Life is dull and uninteresting ; the people around are irritatingly uninteresting, they have no interests whatever, they don't care about anything. And ' The Cherry Orchard ' is being performed in all the towns three or four times ; it is a success, would you believe it ? I have just been reading about Rostov on the Don, where it is being given for the third time. Ah, if only you had not in Moscow M., nor L., nor A. ! A. acted fearfully badly, but I held my peace.

You write that you have not had letters from me, yet I write to you every day, only yesterday I did not write. I have nothing to write about, but still I write. Snap, the son of a bitch, is quite used to us ; he is lying in my study with his hind-legs stretched out ; he sleeps in Mother's room ; he plays with the other dogs in the yard and so is always muddy.

You have a lot of uncles, you do nothing but see them off ;

[1] A Moscow doctor for the diseases of children who was attending O. L.'s nephew.

mind you don't catch cold; do stay at home at least in the fourth week of Lent, when you are not acting.

Have you thought of anything for the summer ? Where are we going to live ? I should like to be not far from Moscow, not far from a station, so that we might do without a carriage, and without kind patrons and admirers. Do think about a house for the summer, darling, perhaps you will hit on some plan. You are my clever, sensible, practical girl—when you are not cross. I remember with such pleasure our journey to Tsaritsyno and back. Well, God be with you, my joy, my kind good dog. I miss you and I can't help missing you, for I have grown used to you. I kiss and embrace my wife.

Your A—.

403

Feb. 28 (1904. *Yalta*).

My darling, if you go to Tsaritsyno again, take Vanya and Masha with you, have a good look at the place all of you, consider it thoroughly and decide.

To-day for the first time the sun has come out. I have been to the town and bought provisions. I will send ' Kashtanka ' for you and Lyova, and also for Olga Mihailovna Andreyev's children ; I will send the copies by Yartsev, who is going to Moscow in a day or two.

Again it has clouded over, the sun has disappeared. I am sick of this nastiness.

I kiss you, my joy, and embrace you. I can't make the model town stand up anyhow, the wall will fall down. There is nothing new.

Your A—.

404

March 1 (1904. *Yalta*).

My dear little whale, I had several business letters yesterday, I was writing and writing till I got sick of it, so that I had not time to write to you. It is a fine, still day ; yesterday I cleaned my teeth, washed my hands before going to bed, had supper ;

to-day I had dinner. I am eating a great deal; I don't utter a single word at dinner as now it is Lent and I have dinner alone; I am satisfied with everything. My clothes are brushed every day; my boots have not been cleaned once yet. Why? I can't say.

I have new candlesticks in my bedroom : lions with the hind-quarters of dogs, a present from Stahovitch. Yesterday I went to Dr. Dmitriyev's funeral and to-day I have read of the death of Strauch. Can it be the same, our Strauch? Why did he die, and what of?

If only we could buy a house and move the superfluous furniture from your flat there, it would be just the thing. And Masha might move there, and the cook, Masha, too. It is spring now, a lovely time is coming; the rooks must have come back.

Tell Masha that Mother calls Snap Schwarz. And he, that is Schwarz, either walks about in the garden or sleeps by the hot stove downstairs and moans.

Tell Masha that Babakay, the contractor, came and took 300 roubles.

There is no news, darling. Yesterday, as it was Sunday, I put on my new suit; to-day, my old one. I am coughing very little, even less than in Moscow. I expect I shall grow stout and you will be ashamed of having such a fat husband. I am very sorry that I don't see Lyova ; though I am a poor doctor (in your opinion) yet I might have discovered something reassuring ; I expect they have frightened his mother.

I embrace my darling, God be with you. Remember me, think of me, I will reward you for it. Don't send the rug. Much better tell me, had I not better buy another one of the same sort for you?

Keep well, my dog.

Your A—.

405

March 3 (1904. *Yalta*).

My dear, wonderful better-half, I am alive, strong as a bull and in good humour, and there is only one thing I cannot get used to—that is my celibate state.

I have a favour to ask of you, darling. As I have said to you before, I am a doctor, I am a friend of the Women's Medical Institute. When ' The Cherry Orchard ' was announced, the women students appealed to me as a doctor to arrange a performance for their mutual benefit society ; their poverty is terrible, lots of them don't finish their course because they cannot pay their fees and so on and so on. I promised to talk to the directors, then I did speak to them and extracted a promise. . . . Before I left Moscow Nemirovitch told me that it would not be judicious to arrange for a performance in Petersburg at present, it is war-time now and the house might be empty ; he suggested that it might be better to get up for the students' benefit a literary matinée like the one that was got up for the Authors' Fund. I agreed with him and it ended in his promising to organise a literary matinée, only he asked to be reminded of this in Petersburg. So now, my own, do remind him in Petersburg, and insist that this matinée shall take place. Some of them will come from the Medical Institute to see you in Petersburg ; receive them, talk things over, be as gracious as you can and tell them how and where they can get hold of Nemirovitch.

I am getting a geographical atlas from Marks. I am expecting the boots of which you wrote me. I keep thinking about Strauch, why he should have died. The kingdom of heaven be his, he was a very nice man.

We shall beat the Japanese. Uncle Sasha will come back a Colonel and Uncle Karl with a new decoration.

If you decide to buy the house at Tsaritsyno, arrange to have proper sanitation put in at once. We must have the same sort of arrangement as in Yalta, drains laid down through the yard, then a fall into a cesspool which must be cemented, covered with sheets of metal with earth over them leaving an opening the size of a frying-pan, covered with a metal disc just like a frying-pan ; and we must buy a pump like the one in Yalta for irrigating the garden.

Do you understand ? Only that must be done at once. In the autumn I will begin building a bath-house. But that is all dreams, dreams !

What is Lyova's temperature ? Why don't you write and tell me ? Darling, my pony, keep well, merry and happy. I am afraid visitors may come. They are awfully boring, the people here who are not literary ; I have nothing to say to them and I can hardly see out of my eyes from listening to them.

Well, God be with you.

Your A—.

Forgive my references to drains. And by the way, you told me there were some workmen at the Art Theatre who understood drainage.

406

March 4 (1904. Yalta).

My very wise dog, write to Budkevitch [1] that ' The Sea-Gull ' and ' Three Sisters ' have been translated into German long ago, and ' The Cherry Orchard ' is being translated for Berlin and Vienna and will have no success there, as there they have no billiards, no Lopahins and no students *à la* Trofimov.

Thanks for your letter, my consolatory darling. I love you very much, you know it very well.

Has Uncle Karl reached the front ? Has he written anything ? From Uncle Sasha I had a letter signed by him and several officers at Krasnoyarsk. To-day, taking advantage of the fine weather, I have been to the town, there bought ham, caviare, cakes. Garin-Mihailovsky has arrived in Moscow, he will probably be coming to see me. He is going to the Far East to build a railway. Savina will be in Yalta.

Well, my little frog, I kiss and embrace you and pat you on the back. Keep well and merry, don't be depressed, think of your husband.

Your A—.

407

(March 6, 1904. Yalta.)

You ought to be ashamed to write with such awful ink, my little whale, my darling ! You wouldn't believe it, I had to

[1] A writer.

tear the letter from the envelope, it seemed as though it had been gummed together on purpose. And Masha sent me a letter gummed up in the same way. It's downright piggish. The letters are sticky, and in the letters you scare me with your presentiments—'something terrible is hanging over us' and so on. It is dreary enough here with the nasty cold weather. Snow on the mountains, snow on the roofs, the air colder than in Moscow.

Well, take the flat in Leontyevsky Place, it is nice there, near to everything. I will come two or three days before you are back from Petersburg. Do you understand? I have had a letter from Vishnevsky, he writes of the magnificent houses you are having in Petersburg, praises the flat in Leontyevsky Place and so on. Mihailovsky has been to see me, he is going to the Far East and says your brother Kostya is going there too, of course for an enormous salary.

Lyova will get well if, of course, there are no accidents.

I had such a disgusting dream! and it lasted more than an hour. There you are!

I long to see you, my darling, I want to talk with my wife, my only woman. There is nothing new, no one talks of anything but the Japanese.

Well, God be with you, don't be depressed, don't tire yourself, be merry. Where did you get the notion that I caught cold on the way to Moscow from Tsaritsyno? What tosh! excuse the expression! It is only in Yalta people catch cold. I have a desperate cold in my head. I embrace my little beetle and kiss her a million times.

A—.

408

March 8 (1904. *Yalta*).

Well, darling, I have had another letter stuck together from you to-day. I had to tear the plan of the flat from the letter. Where did you get hold of such noxious ink?

I congratulate you on your move, darling, I wish you in your new flat plenty of money and plenty of good moods. If there is a lift, that's very nice, but it's my luck that lifts are always out of order; whenever I have to go up, it is undergoing repairs.

How far the closet is from the kitchen on the plan!

So the cook has no concertina in the evenings now ? I am longing to be in Moscow, if only the summer holidays would come. Here the weather is disgusting, though the quinces and the almonds are in flower; I long for space and the air of the North. I shall come earlier than necessary, before you come back.

I have had a letter from Orlenev; he says that he is coming to Yalta, that he wants to repay me the hundred roubles he borrowed from me three years ago. We shall see. He is playing with Goreva in Ibsen's 'Ghosts'; they say, with success.

My brother Alexandr is sober, kind and interesting—altogether his conduct is a comfort to me. And there are hopes that he won't take to drink again, though of course one can't rely on that. He is a case like Uncle Sasha.

Darling, in the 'Russian News' there are excellent surveys of the war, especially of the naval operations, by a certain **V. M.** You train yourself to read it every day and you will soon develop a taste for it. V. M. it appears is not a sailor, an admiral, as I imagined, but a humble municipal statistician, who has had a craze for the navy from his childhood and who knows all the fleets in the world in the minutest detail. His conjectures turn out correct.

Well, my little whale, my grey dog, I stroke you, I embrace you, I kiss you.

Your A—.

409

TELEGRAM

9/III. (1904. *Yalta*).

Congratulations new flat rejoice it is so good greetings kiss ANTONY.

410

March 10 (1904. *Yalta*).

My dear pony, you don't telegraph anything about your health ; how dreadful it is and how stupid ! I was staggered at your postcard and now I am sitting and wondering and all sorts of ideas stray through my mind.

You let Loulou [1] go and did not tell her where, *i.e.* in what town, to stay. The day before yesterday I was rung up on the telephone. It was Loulou speaking from Sevastopol ; she asks where she had better stay, whether at Sevastopol or at Alupka. I could not make out why Sevastopol ? why Alupka ?

Why, whatever Yalta is, the climate is milder here than in other parts, there is drainage here, there are good doctors, and first-rate ones come sometimes, here it is comparatively cheap ; while at Alupka there is typhoid and at Sevastopol there is not a soul she knows and it is cold. I answered that she had better call on Shaposhnikov, address so and so, and if she can't settle in Sevastopol, she should come on to Yalta. No sight nor sound of her since, not a sign of life. By the way, tell me Loulou's Christian name and her father's name. And tell her that not to stay at Yalta is stupid, to say the least of it.

Is there really a gleam of hope at Tsaritsyno ? Darling, let Masha ask Vinogradov whether there are no houses to be sold with two or three acres of land. As a rule there is so little land. You, too, might look out for something and inquire. . . . But perhaps you are still in bed and are concealing the fact from me. Oh, how mean, how barbarous ! Why don't you telegraph ? You grudge the money ? Ah, my own, if only there were a house with land near a station !

It is cold and raining here. We are heating the stoves. My health is good, the climate of Moscow has evidently set me up.

I bless you, child ; don't be ill, take care of yourself, sleep as much as you can, and when you go to Petersburg wrap up

---

[1] The wife of O. L.'s brother Kostya. She had gone to the Crimea with her invalid child.

warmly. Do you hear ? You ought to have a husband who
would beat you every day ; you might as well divorce me, I
am no use.

I kiss you and embrace you twenty-six times.

Your A—.

411

March 12 (1904.   *Yalta*).

My darling, not a word from Loulou ; where she is, and
where are my new boots which you sent by her—I don't know.
Why she does not want to stay in Yalta, I don't know either,
though I should have thought Yalta was the only place that
doctors could have ordered.

You abuse Tsaritsyno, that is, write about fever there, but
I still stick up for Tsaritsyno. If the house-owner says that
there is no fever in her district, we must believe her rather
than G., who does not know one-tenth of what a doctor ought
to know. And if one did get fever at Tsaritsyno, it is only a
stone's-throw from Moscow, and there is no fever in the winter.
The great thing is that one can walk to the station and there
are many trains. Think it over, darling. Don't follow the
common herd. It is only their talk about fever, based on
vague rumours.

I write this not knowing where you are or how you are ;
what am I to think of your silence, to what address am I to
write—to Leontyevsky or to Petrovka ?—I am beginning to
wonder whether I hadn't better dash off to Moscow. Why,
oh why, haven't you sent me one telegram about your health ?
Why ? Evidently I count for nothing to you, I am simply
superfluous. In fact, it is beastly.

When are you going to Petersburg and where are you going
to stay there ? tell me.

I have had a letter from Sulerzhitsky, with an enclosure
from Ekaterina Pavlovna.[1]

It is cold and damp in Yalta, every morning I am woken
up by the sound of the rain, and that pleasant state of things

[1] Gorky's wife.

has been going on for ever so long. I don't go out. Snap lies all day by the stove.

Where is Uncle Sasha now ? Where am I to write to him ?

I still can't understand why you did not tell Loulou to come to Yalta. Why did you advise Sevastopol for her boy ? I don't understand it, I don't understand it. If it is such weather in Yalta I can imagine what it is in Sevastopol. And I can imagine what sort of lodgings Shaposhnikov will find for them ! In Yalta there are good doctors,—and anyway I am in Yalta—a relation, after all, and Masha will soon be coming. Oh, these prudent Germans !

Well, forgive me, darling, I won't say any more. I am upset, and that's intelligible or ought to be intelligible. I have been trying for a whole week to get rid of a corn, but I haven't yet been to the dentist though I ought to have gone long ago. If I am well at the end of June and in July, I shall go to the front, I shall ask you to let me go. I'll go as a doctor. Keep well, don't distress me by your silence, write, telegraph, let me hear from you a little oftener. God be with you, my joy, be a good wife, honour your husband

A—.

412

March 15 (1904. *Yalta*).

Dear doggy, to-day at last a letter has come from you, but in what a pitiful state ! It is written with such disgusting ink that it is all stuck together, and when I tried to pull the pages apart there was a rending sound, whole lines were stuck together and the letter was torn ; I don't know how to explain such nastiness.

Now you are in your new flat, I have congratulated you on it already ; now I congratulate you again, send you my love and thousands of greetings. I am wearing my new boots. Orlenev is going to play here to-morrow (in Ibsen's ' Ghosts '). I shall probably go if it is not raining. But it rains continually, it is cold and muddy, snow on the mountains. I bore you describing the weather, but what can I do, darling? I have no one but you to complain to.

You haven't yet told me what it is like in your new flat, whether it is nice and there is plenty of room.

Your sow with the little pigs on her back sends you her love. Snap is thriving, yesterday he ate too much raw meat (Granny fed him in the kitchen), he was taken ill, was sick and so on, now he is all right. We have no mice.

My own darling, my dog, be calm and well, don't be depressed, write to me oftener than once a week. Who knows, perhaps you have not ceased to love me yet. In any case, I kiss you a million times.

Your A—.

413

March 18, 1904. (*Yalta.*)

My sleek doggy, tell me at once when, *i.e.* on which day, you are going to Petersburg and also where I am to write to you there the first few days. You know you won't send me a telegram. You send telegrams to all your relations but you grudge spending sixpence on your lawful husband. Ah, I haven't beaten you enough.

Ostrovsky is no relation of mine, but is the son of the teacher of mathematics at my high school. He borrowed 15 roubles from me once and, of course, has never paid it back, and since then he has been to see me everywhere, he even turned up in Perm, but I was not at home; he pretends to be an actor.[1]

I saw Orlenev in Ibsen's ' Ghosts.' It is a rotten play and the acting was not up to much, you feel it is all a sham. I had a letter from Ivan to-day about Tsaritsyno, he likes it.

You have it warm, we have it cold, a cruel wind. Don't buy a bedstead, wait a little, we will buy it together when I come.

Not a sign of life from your Loulou. Tell Nemirovitch that the sounds in Acts II. and IV. should be briefer, much briefer, and should sound as though they come from very far away.

---

[1] Ostrovsky was an actor who called on O. L. pretending to be a relative of Tchehov's.

How mean it is they can't get such a trifle right, a sound, though it is put so clearly in the play !

And what news of Uncle Sasha ? His address is ' Manchurian Army,' then the name of his regiment and his rank. One can write without stamping the letter.

How is it you don't miss me, you dog ? That 's piggish of you. Well, I bless you, kiss you and embrace you. Christ be with you.

Your A—.

The boots are good, only for some reason the left one is a little tight, and they thump so when one walks that one doesn't feel like a civilised being. But they look handsome.

I went to the theatre in a frock-coat.

414

March 19 (1904. *Yalta*).

My dear wife, wretch, dog, why no letters ? You sent me a note in pencil and since then not one letter, and I don't know whether you are alive or dead or whether you have married somebody else. Good wives don't treat bad husbands like that, and you torture me with your silence, I don't know what to do, I am ready to rush off to Moscow.

This morning L. D. Sytin and the priest Petrov [1] turned up to see me. And the weather is bad, cold, grey ; they came south ' to have a breath of warm air,' to bask in the sun, and they have not taken off their fur-coats.

Madame N. came, sat here for two hours, goodness only knows what tosh she talked, she prevented my writing this letter. She has gone downstairs to have tea, I hear her sweet voice.

I have received the boots, Loulou sent them. Very nice, thank you, my joy. But the Jap [2] is vulgar, atrociously bad taste. Now I am a swell in my new boots, I rejoice that God has given me such a wife.

I embrace you, I kiss you, I bless you. I am afraid you

---

[1] A priest of liberal views who took to literature and was afterwards unfrocked.

[2] A toy.

won't tell me which day you are going to Petersburg. Let me
have the address, too, to which I can send my first letters (*i.e.*
those I shall write before I get your address).

No news from Loulou. Well, God be with you, my dear
better-half.

Your A—.

415

March 20 (1904. *Yalta*).

My sweet darling, dog, you have not yet gone away, so you
will get this letter. Tell Moskvin that he may put in the new
words and I will put them in myself when I read the new proof.
I give him *carte blanche*.[1]

Masha has arrived. She says they want eleven thousand for
the house at Tsaritsyno. Well, that's too much. What is
nice about Tsaritsyno is that it is only a walk from the station
—that's the chief thing. Are there no other houses there ?
Or near Butovo or Podolsk ? Only it must be near a station.
You have no time, darling, you are just going off, I ought to
see to the house question myself and help you ; things are too
stupid, I shan't be able to be in Moscow till May.

Snow is falling. It is cold.

Now I shall write to Moika 41. I shall address the letters
Tchehov-Knipper.

Greet Marya Petrovna, tell her I kiss her hand. I am glad
about Mundt.[2] . . . Of course, Meierhold has not got consumption, as I told you.

Well, my wife, allow me to kiss and embrace you. Tell
Moskvin I envy him [3] ; I would give ten thousand for a baby
now. I am very dreary without a living creature to comfort
me. But there, you will do your best, I rely upon you.

Your A—.

[1] O. L. wrote, March 16 : ' Moskvin implores permission to put in a
phrase in Act iv. when he squashes the hat-box. Yasha says, " Twenty-
two misfortunes," and Moskvin is very much tempted to say, " Well,
it 's a thing that might happen to any one." He said it once accidentally
and it went down with the audience. Will you allow it ? '

[2] She was engaged to be married.   [3] Moskvin had a son born.

416

March 24 (1904. *Yalta*).

My magnificent wife, Christ is risen !

I kiss you and embrace you, and desire, warmly, passionately desire, that my Olya may be happy, merry and rich. It is three days since I have written to you and I have missed writing very much.

To-day I had a letter from Lvov, he writes about the Tsaritsyno house ; he praises it very much and gives the same advice as you do, namely, to talk to his father-in-law, Martynov.[1] I certainly will see Martynov, and meanwhile you write to Madame Yezutchevsky ; write that the house is old, that it needs many repairs, that drains will have to be put in, that the lease has not many years to run and so on and so on, and that if she will let us have it for eight thousand it will be quite a fair price ; mention, by the way, that there are other houses for sale at Tsaritsyno, and in fact that there is a greater readiness to sell than to buy. If she agrees I 'll pay her part of the money at once, and Vishnevsky will pay the other part.[2]

I have not yet had the photographs you wrote of. Masha speaks well of them. Orlenev came to see me to-day and paid me back the hundred roubles. He is not drinking and is full of his plans for a theatre of his own in Petersburg. He is going on tour to Europe and America. Leonid Andreyev will be here this evening. See what lots of celebrities ! Orlenev carries a portrait of Stanislavsky in his pocket, and swears that he dreams of entering the Art Theatre company ; I advise him to join you, he would come in very appropriately and so would Kommissarzhevskaya.

It is rather cold. Snap has been unwell, but he is all right again now ; he is all day long in the yard, in the evening he sleeps in my easy-chair and at night in Mother's room. He goes with Arseny to the market.

If I get a single line from Uncle Sasha I will telegraph. I

[1] The painter.
[2] From the theatre funds ; money owing to Tchehov is meant.

fancy that he is alive, well and all right, but in continual movement, which prevents him from sleeping or writing letters.

Well, God be with you, little wife, I kiss you once more, I press your little hands and kiss and embrace you a hundred times.

Your A—.

Tell the actress who is playing the maid Dunyasha to read ' The Cherry Orchard ' in the ' Znanie ' edition or in the proofs ; there she will see where she has to powder and so on. She must read it, everything is scratched out and in a muddle in your copies.

417

March 25 (1904. *Yalta*).

Greetings, my joy ! No letter from you to-day, but I am not cross, I am not upset, I know that you are packing to go to Petersburg. There is no news. Orlenev has been here again to-day ; he asked me to write him a three-act play, for five actors, for his foreign tour ; I promised to, but on condition that no one else should play it but Orlenev's company. Leonid Andreyev was here last night ; he grumbled at the Art Theatre, at ' Julius Caesar ' and so on ; his wife, who has grown thinner and older, was here too ! It was rather dull.

To-day is still but cold.

I embrace you, my own, and kiss you, the Lord be with you. Don't be faithless to me and don't forget me.

Your A—.

418

TELEGRAM

March 26 (1904. *Yalta*).

Christ is risen congratulate Nemirovitch Stanislavsky Vishnevsky Katchalov wish all good health kiss you ANTONIO.

419

March 26 (1904. *Yalta*).

Greetings, my little crinoline, my jolly granny. Yesterday and in the night and to-day I have had diarrhoea. I am on the trot the whole time, and what is most mortifying is that it 's all for no apparent reason, as I eat nothing but soup and meat. It must be the effect of the Yalta climate.

What a queer creature you are, darling ! Of course I don't want the house at Gurzuf, I would let any one you like have it, but is it conceivable that a whole family could live there, especially with an invalid child ? [1] They will need provisions every day, they will need furniture, drains, and, above all, they must have a good doctor within reach at every hour of the day and night. And are there any of these conveniences at Gurzuf ? Loulou certainly ought to be living at Yalta, in a good flat, with proper sanitation, with a little garden, with a verandah, with good furniture. She does not want to stay in Yalta, but not (as you write) because she is afraid of infection ; she is afraid, not of infection, but of relations. But that you can't understand, it 's beyond you, and there is no making you see it. But I tell you once more : Loulou ought to live in Yalta, and if not in Yalta, at Sevastopol ; the boy can't be left without a doctor, who may be wanted any minute, do understand that !

Very good, we may do it like this : take the house for the summer, and then in the autumn or winter buy it on the conditions you mention in your letter, *i.e.* that the rent already paid should be deducted from the price. Martynov will, I expect, come and see me, I will talk it over in detail with him.

To-day I heard that you are divorcing me. Is this true ? Who is going to beat you ? . . . Oy, you had better think twice about it !

I am working, but not quite successfully. I am hindered by the war and for the last few days by diarrhoea. I keep fancying that no one is going to read it on account of the war.

[1] O. L. asked him to lend the house for the summer to Loulou and her children.

Well, doggy, I stroke you and pull your tail. Behave yourself, write to your husband as often as you can. I embrace my poppet.

A—.

The bungalow at Gurzuf is empty now, the schoolmaster is not there so far as I know. But there are wood-lice and centipedes living in it.

420

March 29 (1904. *Yalta*).

My dear doggy, I have already sent you my Easter greetings, now I only send you my love and a vast number of kisses. Your brother Kostya and his wife arrived in Yalta yesterday ; at this moment he is downstairs drinking tea. Both are well and in good spirits, they say that their boy feels pretty well. Now it is clear that Loulou is going to Eupatoria for the summer and then will spend the winter in Yalta. By the way, she likes Yalta, very much, in fact. I fancy they won't be badly off in Eupatoria, only they must not keep calling in fresh doctors. To-morrow Kostya and Loulou are going to Sevastopol.

Martynov has called ; he is a lively man but apparently a poor artist. He has been in the habit of staying at Tsaritsyno for fifteen years, but only in the winter ; he says that the house is dry, that there are no fogs, that it seemed healthy and pleasant there.

You write that I am angry with you. What for, my own ? You must be cross with me and not I with you, bless you, darling !

Loulou and Kostya were at ' The Cherry Orchard ' in March. . . . How awful it is ! An act that ought to take 12 minutes at most lasts 40 minutes. There is only one thing I can say. . . . But there, bless the man.

We have had visitors here all day long, even the schoolmaster from Gurzuf is here. I have received the photographs, thank you, my kind darling. If you are having a good time and enjoying yourself in Petersburg, I am very glad and happy ;

but if you are depressed, it 's piggish. Go about, pay no attention to notices if they are unfriendly, and think of the summer.

Sofya Petrovna Sredin tells me that Ekaterina Pavlovna is spitting blood and so on ; in fact, is in consumption.

Mihailovsky was here yesterday, he says he is going to the Far East very soon. He was dressed like a dandy and was very charming. It is real spring here, but still it is cool.

Write to me, my little gnat, I am dreary without you, you know that very well. I kiss you and embrace you warmly.

Your A—.

I have had a long letter from Kazan, from a student ; he entreats me about something or other, swears that ' The Cherry Orchard ' was magnificently produced in Kazan—and thanks me.

421

March 31 (1904. *Yalta*).

My dear poppet, my dog, it is a long while since I have had a letter from you, but I am not depressed by it, for I know that you have no time for letters now. Well, how are you getting on in Petersburg ? How are you feeling ? What is the weather like ? Here in Yalta, thank God, it is fine. I walk about without goloshes, wearing a hat instead of a fur-cap.

I have read in the newspapers that they are meaning to found a bed in the Evangelical Hospital in Moscow in memory of Strauch ; I have sent twenty-five roubles in your name as your debt. You 'll pay it back ?

Alexandr and his family have left Yalta. I told him to see you and to go to the theatre. He has not been going to the theatre for forty years. He knows nothing and reads nothing. Receive him as kindly as possible, darling. And persuade him to go to your theatre. Persuade him as kindly as possible, as only you know how. Your brother and his wife have gone to Sevastopol, you will soon see him. I liked Loulou. . . .

Apparently she did not like Dr. Alexandrov, and apparently she does not believe that Lyova has tuberculosis. She and Kostya cannot rest and are kept awake at night by the thought that Mihailovsky has two wives and that they know them both. 'We could not get to sleep until three o'clock last night,' they told me, 'we kept thinking of those two wives.' So there you are !

I have read a huge number of manuscripts. To-day I read in 'Rus' about the Art Theatre. It is fair. Yesterday I read Burenin's article and concluded from it that 'Novoye Vremya' had resolved to tear you to pieces, and I rejoiced that no one can tear you to pieces, do what they will. You see you artists have done what you set out to do, you can regard both the present and the future almost dispassionately.

To-day, and as a rule on holidays, I go about in your high boots. Darling, when am I to come ? Soon ? Write full details.

To-day I am quite well.

Well, I embrace you and kiss you and embrace you again. You, too, be well and untroubled.

Your A—.

422

April 1 (1904. *Yalta*).

Greetings, my darling. Write when you will be in Moscow, I must know that, as I want to arrive at the same time.

To-day it is glorious weather, but every one is gloomy, thanks to the telegrams.[1] There is nothing new here ; everything is as usual. To-day I had my hair cut and shampooed at the hairdresser's—and thought of you. If there is anything interesting in the newspapers cut it out with a pair of scissors and send it. 'Rus' I get, 'Novoye Vremya' too—and no other Petersburg papers.

I can imagine the state of mind you are all in. Well, my darling, doggie, I embrace you. Sleep well.

Your A—.

---

[1] From the war.

423

April 4 (1904. *Yalta*).

My sweet pony, greetings ! I have had two telegrams from Nemirovitch about your Petersburg successes, and how the audience looks upon you as a first-class actress ; and to-day I read in ' Novoye Vremya ' an abusive article on ' Julius Caesar.' That you are a great and real actress I have known for ages. I appreciate you highly, my darling ; only please, I entreat you, don't catch cold, don't tire yourself, and sleep properly, promise me that you will take care of yourself. You promise ?

We are having wretched weather. Masha is coughing a little, and is worried because she has sent you two letters and you have not answered her. Snap is sick almost every day. Mirolyubov was here yesterday, he tired me out with his general reflections. If you think eight thousand too little for that house, you can give nine or ten, though I honestly think eight thousand is a liberal price considering how old the house is, and how short the lease. I shall soon be coming, we will talk it over and settle the house question one way or another. It appears that five, six or seven years ago Sizov (of the ' Russian News ') was selling me that same house at Tsaritsyno, *i.e.* he offered it to me and spoke very highly of it. I only thought of that the other day.

To-day is Sunday, and I have taken a powder—heroin, and I like it, I feel peaceful.

Why is the ' Znanie,' with Pyatnitsky and Gorky at the head of it, so long in publishing my play ? You know it is a loss to me, they can't play it in the provinces. Find out, darling, somehow, and if you see Pyatnitsky (Nikolayevsky Street, 4) explain to him that I have lost the season, thanks simply to the absence of the play. They promised to bring it out at the end of January and now it is April. Altogether, I have no luck with my plays. I am not joking when I say that.

I think that you have ceased to love me. Have you ? Own

up. I love you as much as ever, and, indeed, I am wondering whether I could not come to you in Petersburg.

I bless my good wife, I embrace her and kiss her. Be well and merry.

Your A—.

424

April 7 (1904. Yalta).

Greetings, my sweet doggie ! How are you getting on ? How is your friend Tchyumina ? Is her husband dancing attendance on you ? I am alive and by way of being well, not counting diarrhoea, which has been going on for a week now, and which will, I fancy, drive me out of Yalta sooner than is expected. Altogether, I have a bother with my inside, there is no making it keep calm.

The Tatarinov girl has just come and invited us to her wedding. Somebody is marrying her. For two days in succession the artists Korovin and Baron Klodt have come and stayed a long time ; the first is talkative and interesting, the second is silent, but one feels that he is an interesting man too. Dr. Borodulin, whom you know, is in trouble, cancer of the alimentary canal. Dr. Sredin, too, is still ill ; his consumption has passed into the second stage, and now he is tormented by nephritis, i.e. inflammation of the kidneys. Dr. Alexin has grown thin and looks older. Dr. Tchehov is in love with his wife and suffering from diarrhoea.

So Kugel praised the play ? We ought to send him half a pound of tea and a pound of sugar—to encourage him in case of need. You might tell Nemirovitch to.

Madame Vishnevsky (the relative of your A. L. Vishnevsky) has so distinguished herself in Moscow that the merchants are subscribing nothing now, though the Red Cross is in no way to blame. I heard of that lady and her husband years ago. Tell Vishnevsky that I fully sympathise with him.

Write to me a little oftener, my sweet darling, don't forget me. Cut articles out of the papers and send them me. Or send me papers without cutting out the articles. Just tie them up and put a two-kopeck stamp on them, do you understand ?

Keep well, my joy, don't be bored, don't be depressed, soon we shall see each other. Do you know Schulz's house, near Bolshevo Station, on the Yaroslavl line ? I am told we could take it for the summer.

I embrace and kiss you.

Your A—.

425

April 8 (1904. *Yalta*).

Well, my darling, greetings again. You write that you have had no letter from me for three days. You are wrong there, as I write to you every day or on rare occasions every second day ; I never make an *entr'acte* of two days.

I have diarrhoea again, to-day I have taken opium and bismuth, and so it will be probably until I am in Moscow.

I have had an invitation to the Tatarinov wedding. I have had two parcels of reviews from Stanislavsky. I have not attempted to read the German notice. I have put it aside until you come. I fancy the German is abusive.

Has my brother Alexandr been to see you ? and are my brothers ever at the theatre ? They ought to have a look at ' Julius Caesar ' anyway. Buy me a fashionable necktie in Petersburg, or even two. Or else I 'll beat you. You ought to be afraid of me, I am a stern man.

If you have any news of Uncle Sasha, do let me know how and where he is. And of Uncle Karl too.

Well, my doggie, I stroke you and pat you on the back. Take care of yourself, don't tire yourself too much, sleep as much as you can, and worry as little as you can.

I hear Snap's low bass bark in the yard. Some one has come Madame Sredin.

I kiss and embrace you, my joy.

Your A—.

426

April 10 (1904.   *Yalta*).

My dear little linnet, you are angry with me and grumbling and I am really not to blame.   I think I did not speak about Tsaritsyno to Masha at all, I know nothing about it ;   I saw Martynov about whom you wrote, but he used to live at Tsaritsyno only in the winter, and judges of the summer by hearsay, and altogether I did not like him for some reason, he struck me as rather a grey figure.   I remember that ten or twelve years ago Sizov of the ' Russian News ' was trying to sell me the same house.   As a matter of fact I assumed that it was chiefly for you to settle this house question and not I.   You see, in such questions I am not good for much.

Why is it that on the posters and in the newspaper advertisements my play is so persistently called a drama ? [1] Nemirovitch and Stanislavsky see in my play something absolutely different from what I have written, and I am ready to bet anything that neither of them has once read my play through attentively.   Forgive me, but I assure you it is so.   I am thinking not only of the scenery of the second act, which is so awful, and not only of N., who has replaced N. N. and does exactly the same and absolutely nothing of what I have written.

It is warm, but cold in the shade, and the evenings are cold.   I walk about lazily, for I am somehow short of breath. Some wretched travelling company is performing ' The Cherry Orchard ' here in Yalta.

I am looking forward with impatience to seeing you, my joy. Without you I don't get on very grandly ; ' the day is over and thank God,' without thoughts, without desires, only with games of patience and pacing up and down the room.   I have not been to the baths for ages, I feel as though it were six years. I read all the newspapers, even the Government Gazette, and am growing dingy from it.

---

[1] ' The Cherry Orchard ' was by Tchehov called a comedy.

Write and tell me until what day you will be in Petersburg,
do me the favour.   Don't forget me, think sometimes of the
man whom you once married.   I kiss my darling.

Your A—.

427

April 11 (1904.   *Yalta*).

My dear practical wife, Masha has already gone to Moscow,
and I shall go as soon as I receive orders from my stern better-
half.   There is no news, everything goes well.   There is a
furious vile wind raging.

Please tell Ekaterina Nikolayevna Nemirovitch that I am
very grateful to her for the kind, warm words which you repeat
to me in your letter, and that I am not at all deserving of
those words.

I am awaiting your arrangements about our tour, about the
house, about our whole life.   I have a longing, an awful longing, to beat you a little, to show you my power ; I long to
walk up and down Petrovka and Tverskaya with you.

There, be well and merry, Christ be with you.   Remember,
remember that I love you, do not be false to me.

Your A—.

You want to wash my head with liquid-tar soap ; good,
wash it.

428

April 13 (1904.   *Yalta*).

My dear old woman, greetings to you from your little old
man, whom you have already forgotten, and whom, as I fancy,
you have chucked for good.   Yesterday I had a letter and a
review from Arabazhin, a nice man.   He asked me to write
him my opinion and to tell him whether he is right in saying that Lopahin is in love with Lyubov Andreyevna.

Madame Z is a greedy lady who eats with the voracity of a
shark and looks like the keeper of a bawdy house ; but she
has her good qualities too ; for instance, she is a capital sailor.
I was once with her on a cutter on a very choppy sea, and she

did not turn a hair. 'The Cherry Orchard' is appearing to-day in Yalta—it is on a stage a yard wide.

Snap is stupidly dignified; he spends the day in the yard, barking in a bass voice, and sleeps in Mother's room; every day he goes with Arseny to the market.

There are only thirty days in April, so you won't be able to come on the 31st.[1] Better come the 1st of May. As soon as I reach Moscow I shall go straight to the baths, then I shall lie down and cover myself with my Bokhara rug.

The wind is still blowing and blowing.

Write and tell me, if you don't forget, what I ought to bring with me from Yalta, how many night-shirts, how many shirts and pants. About the latter you might consult Tchyumina; though I fancy her husband does not wear them, but just walks about without.

Yesterday I heard the news that Tatyana Shtchepkin-Kupernik is married.

Well, my joy, my precious, I kiss you and embrace you many times. To-day I am all right, I feel well. You, too, keep well, pony.

429

April 15 (1904. *Yalta*).

My dear, good darling, yesterday there was no letter from you, to-day there is not one either, and in this Yalta I am lonely as a comet and feel not particularly well. The day before yesterday in the local theatre (without side-scenes and without dressing-rooms) some vile actors, headed by one Daryalova (so called in imitation of the actress Daryal), produced 'The Cherry Orchard,' following the *mise-en-scène* of the Art Theatre, and to-day there are notices and to-morrow there will be notices and the day after to-morrow; the telephone keeps ringing and friends keep sighing, while I, so to speak, a sick man here for the good of my health, am bound to dream of how to escape. You might suggest this as a comic subject, say to Amfiteatrov! However amusing it may

---

[1] O. L. wrote, April 8 : 'Our last performance is on the 29th, so I shall be in Moscow on the morning of the 31st.'

all seem, there's no denying that the provincial actors behave like scoundrels.

The express trains have already begun running, so that I shall arrive in Moscow in the morning, my joy. I shall come as soon as ever it is possible, that is, the 1st of May. I can't stay here—what with diarrhoea and the actors and the public and the telephone and the devil knows what !

What sort of houses are you having now ? Are they full ? I can fancy how tired out you all are. While I sit and keep dreaming of fishing and pondering what I am to do with all the fish I have caught. Though I shall only catch one perch in a whole summer, and he will only be caught owing to a suicidal tendency.

Write to me, darling, write, or I shall scream for help.

I send you a cutting from our 'Crimea Courier,' read it.

Well, God be with you, my joy, live and sleep well, dream and think of your husband. You see, I love you and I love your letters and the way you act on the stage and the way you walk. The only thing I don't love is when you dawdle too long over the washstand.

Your A—.

430

April 17 (1904. *Yalta*).

My dear goldfish, greetings. To-day again no letter from you, but I don't mind, I am not offended and I am not depressed, as soon, very soon, we shall see each other. I have sent the notices to Dresden,[1] but I fancy some of them had been lost. They make a big parcel anyway.

As soon as we are together we will turn our combined energies to settling the house question. Most likely we shall have to fix our choice on the house at Tsaritsyno. It is rather damp, that is true, but on the other hand it is very near Moscow with a very good train service, and in it you would feel at home and not on a visit. We must furnish your room in it as splendidly and comfortably as possible so that you may grow to like it.

[1] O. L. had asked him to send notices of ' The Cherry Orchard ' to her brother Vladimir in Dresden.

Here in Yalta we are having rain and cool weather. Here in Yalta we are having diarrhoea, too, which I cannot stop in any way, neither by drugs nor by diet.

Korovin, the artist, is a passionate fisherman; he has been expounding to me a special method of fishing without bait; the method is English and magnificent, only it needs a good river like the one at Lyubimovka. I am intending to order a boat from Petersburg. But again, all that will not be before my arrival in Moscow.

Your very nice good-natured sow with her three little pigs on her back sends you her love. Snap, for some reason, dashes at Nastya barking when she calls him squint-eyed.

Is Marya Petrovna still ill? If she has come to Petersburg give her my greetings. Give my greetings to all the company, in fact, and to Tchyumina.

How terribly short of breath I am!

Why was there no performance on the 13th of April? Was some one taken ill, or were you all too tired?

I shall go on writing to you for another few days, and then I shall drop it and begin getting ready for the journey. But think of sitting at Sevastopol from two o'clock until half-past eight!

Where am I to sit? At Shaposhnikov's? My dear!

There is nothing new, everything goes on in the old way. I embrace you, my good actress, I embrace you and take you by your little chin.

Your A—.

431

April 18 (1904. *Yalta*).

Dear dog, I shall hardly get to Petersburg, it would be too exhausting, but I shall get to Moscow soon, very soon. In the first place, I want to see you. In the second, there is no possibility of living in Yalta, there are such masses of people of all sorts worrying me. To-day a gentleman came, left a manuscript and a letter asking for money, and promised to come again in the evening; Sofya Petrovna Sredin is just coming

with a very boring gentleman who is to take my photograph.
And so on and so on. By the way, to complete the picture I
am sending you the notice published in to-day's ' Crimean
Courier.' And it is like this every day, and how is one to get
well and not be running to the closet ?

Darling, dear one, child, my own, in Petersburg there is an
exhibition in the Yussupov Garden in Great Sadovy Street,
boats and tents and so on. You might go and look at it ! It
is in the hall of the Society for Saving from Drowning. Perhaps
you will pick out a light, pretty and inexpensive boat. Or
find out where their shop is and go to their shop. The lighter
the boat the better. Ask the price, note down the name and
number of the boat, so that it would be possible to order it
afterwards, and ask whether a boat can be sent as ordinary
goods. The point is that the railway insists on giving a whole
truck to a boat and so its transport runs up to a hundred
roubles.

God be with you, my own. I love you. If Misha goes to
the theatre to see my play, convey to him my most heartfelt
and respectful gratitude for the honour done me. But I doubt
whether he will condescend so far.

I am dreaming so of the summer ! I am so longing to be
alone, to write, to think !

I embrace you, darling.

Your A.

432

April 20 (1904. *Yalta*).

My dear dog, to-day I have had a letter from Sobolyevsky,
the editor of the ' Russian News.' He writes about the house :
' The house is situated in the very best part of Tsaritsyno,
absolutely dry, it is well-built and fitted for living in comfortably all the year round. . . . If you care to instal your-
selves there, there is no doubt that material profit would be
their last consideration in making terms with you.' He writes
further that some years ago a sturgeon weighing nearly 120
pounds was caught in the Tsaritsyno pond.

To-day I will write to Sobolyevsky that you are coming to Moscow on the 1st of May and will see Madame Yezutchevsky on the 2nd or 3rd and in all probability settle with her. And on the 5th we will move in.

Well, I shall send you one or two more letters and then stop. I shall leave Yalta not without satisfaction ; I am dull here, there is no spring, and besides I am ill. Yesterday I had to run out not less than five times, though I ate nothing particular, I keep to my diet—and besides there is my cough. I have not had my teeth stopped yet ; yesterday I drove into town to see Ostrovsky and did not find him at home, he had gone to Alushta. Without my wife I am very dreary, and I am afraid to set up a mistress. Yevtihy Karpov, Suvorin's manager, is in Yalta ; Ilyinskaya [1] was here yesterday and she told me that he is coming to see me. It is raining. I have had a letter from Lazarevsky from Vladivostock. If, as you say, my letters come unpunctually, yours stumble along as though they were drunk. I get two letters at once. Evidently they, *i.e.* your letters, are detained somewhere and read. It is so necessary !

You ask what is life ? That is just the same as asking what is a carrot. A carrot is a carrot, and nothing more is known about it.

There is something new as you say in the ' Grasshopper,' [2] so it may be, but there is no talent for the stage in her at all. By temperament she is a tramp, an idle vagrant, and not an actress.

Keep well, don't be bored, don't be depressed. You will soon see your husband. I embrace you.

Your A.

433

April 22 (1904. *Yalta*).

My darling, wife, I am writing you my last letter, and after that, if need be, I will send telegrams. Yesterday I was unwell, to-day I am, too, but still I am easier to-day ; I am

---

[1] An actress at the Little Theatre.

[2] The nickname in the Tchehov family of Darya Mihailovna Ozarovsky, an actress in the Petersburg Alexandrinsky Theatre.

eating nothing except eggs and soup. It is raining, the weather is vile, cold ; still, in spite of my illness and the rain, I have been to the dentist.

The Twenty-second Siberian Regiment took part in the battle, and of course Uncle Sasha is in that regiment : I cannot get him out of my head. They write that nine officers in command of companies were killed or wounded, and Uncle Sasha was in command of a company. Oh well, God is merciful ; Sasha, your dearest uncle, will be saved. I can fancy how tired out he is and how cross !

Z. was here yesterday, a dramatist of no talent, but of boundlessly grandiose pretensions. These figures are old and stale, and I am bored with them, bored to stupefaction by their insincere cordiality. I shall arrive in Moscow in the morning, the express trains have already begun running. Oh, my rug ! Oh, the veal cutlets ! Doggie, how I am pining for you !

I embrace you and kiss you ; behave yourself, and if you have ceased to love me or have grown cold, just say so, don't mind me.

I have written to you about the house in Tsaritsyno. I have told you already about the letter I have had from Sobolyevsky. Well, Christ be with you, my joy.

Your A.

434

TELEGRAM

April 26 (1904. *Yalta*).

Ticket taken coming Monday stopping teeth health good though stomach queer kiss greeting Uncle Vanya [1] ANTONIO.

Tchehov went to Moscow at the end of April, was at once taken seriously ill, went by the doctors' advice to Germany on June 3, and died at Badenweiler on the night of July 1,[2] 1904.

[1] O. L.'s maternal uncle Ivan, a naval officer.
[2] The dates throughout are in accordance with the Old Style of reckoning, except in the case of one letter from abroad.

The Index

Index

391